A Great Cloud
of Witnesses

A Great Cloud of Witnesses

A Calendar of Commemorations

Church Publishing
NEW YORK

Copyright © 2016 by The Domestic and Foreign Missionary Society
of The Protestant Episcopal Church in the United States of America

Portions of this book may be reproduced by a congregation for its own use. Commercial or large-scale reproduction for sale of any portion of this book or of the book as a whole, without the written permission of Church Publishing Incorporated, is prohibited.

Cover design and typesetting by Linda Brooks

ISBN-13: 978-0-89869-962-3 (binder)
ISBN-13: 978-0-89869-966-1 (pbk.)
ISBN-13: 978-0-89869-963-0 (ebook)

Church Publishing, Incorporated.
19 East 34th Street
New York, New York 10016

www.churchpublishing.org

Contents

Introduction   VII
    On Commemorations and the Book of Common Prayer   VIII
    On the Making of Saints   X
    How to Use These Materials   XIII

Commemorations
    Calendar of Commemorations
    Commemorations

Appendix   A1

Commons of Saints and Propers for Various Occasions   A5
    Commons of Saints   A7
    Various Occasions from the Book of Common Prayer   A37
    New Propers for Various Occasions   A63

Guidelines for Continuing Alteration of the Calendar   A71
    Criteria for Additions to *A Great Cloud of Witnesses*   A73
    Procedures for Local Calendars and Memorials   A75
    Procedures for Churchwide Recognition   A76
    Procedures to Remove Commemorations   A77

Introduction

This volume, *A Great Cloud of Witnesses*, is a further step in the development of liturgical commemorations within the life of The Episcopal Church. These developments fall under three categories. First, this volume presents a wide array of possible commemorations for individuals and congregations to observe. Recognizing that there are many perspectives on the identity and place of exemplary Christians in the life of the Church, this volume proposes that the metaphor of a "family history" is a fitting way to describe who is included. As such, the title of this volume is drawn from the Epistle to the Hebrews, recalling that "we are surrounded by so great a cloud of witnesses" (Hebrews 12:1). The people found in this volume are not all definitively declared to be saints, but are Christians who have inspired other Christians in different times and places.

Second, it represents a refinement of the core Calendar of commemorations for The Episcopal Church, which centers on the feasts of our Lord and other major feasts listed in the Book of Common Prayer (pp. 16–17). The calendar in A Great Cloud of Witnesses does not purport to be a definitive collection of saints, but rather an additional calendar of optional commemorations that represent the breadth of the Christian family story.

Third, materials for weekday celebrations during seasons of the Church are located in a separate volume, Weekday Eucharistic Propers 2015.

On Commemorations and the Book of Common Prayer

The Book of Common Prayer proclaims in the ecumenical creeds and in our prayers its belief in the "communion of the saints." We speak of the saints as "chosen vessels of [God's] grace and the lights of the world in their generations."[1] The "obedience of [God's] saints" offers the Church "an example of righteousness" and gives us "in their eternal joy a glorious pledge of the hope of our calling."[2] The canticle *Te Deum laudamus* (Canticle 21, "You Are God") calls out some specific categories of saints in classical terms, contiguous with both the angels in heaven and the Church on earth, when it speaks of "the glorious company of apostles," "the noble fellowship of prophets," and "the white-robed army of martyrs."[3] Too, our prayers speak of the role of the saints within our baptismal community:

> O God, the King of saints, we praise and glorify your holy Name for all your servants who have finished their course in your faith and fear: for the blessed Virgin Mary; for the holy patriarchs, prophets, apostles, and martyrs; and for all your other righteous servants, known to us and unknown; and we pray that, encouraged by their examples, aided by their prayers, and strengthened by their fellowship, we also may be partakers of the inheritance of the saints in light; through the merits of your Son Jesus Christ our Lord. Amen.[4]

The saints encourage us; they pray for us; they strengthen us.

Despite these affirmations of the saints as constitutive members of our baptismal community, the Prayer Book shows a great reluctance to define the term or to make specific identifications. The Catechism touches on this issue only briefly, identifying the communion of the saints in broad relational terms: "The communion of saints is the whole family of God, the living and the dead, those whom we love and those whom we hurt, bound together in Christ by sacrament, prayer, and praise."[5] In Christian language throughout the ages, "saint" has carried two referents, a general one that applies to the whole Church—which is the meaning invoked here—and a more specific one

---
1 Preface for a Saint (1), BCP, 348 / 380.
2 Preface for a Saint (2), BCP, 348 / 380.
3 BCP, 95 / 53.
4 BCP, 504 / 489.
5 BCP, 862.

that applies to individuals who have been identified as "chosen vessels of [God's] grace and the lights of the world in their generations" from among their fellows.

The Calendar in the Prayer Book contains a number of names. Of these, the term "saint" appears only a handful of times and always in connection to a limited set of people who appear in the New Testament: Mary and Joseph, John the Baptist, the apostles, the evangelists, Paul, and others such as Mary Magdalene, Stephen, James of Jerusalem, and Michael.

The state of additional persons not given the title of "saint" is ambiguous. These are the commemorations permitted within the Days of Optional Observance as described in the general rubrics of the Calendar (BCP, 18). A clear definition of the status of these persons is absent.

This ambiguity is appropriate to the range of theologies around sainthood and holiness within The Episcopal Church. While some Episcopalians actively venerate the saints, others hold positions proceeding from Reformation desires to reform the cults of saints, such as those found in the Thirty-Nine Articles (Article XXII, BCP, 872). In other words, the ambiguity exists for the sake of inclusivity and maintains the Anglican tradition of a comprehensive approach to questions not decisively settled by Scripture and the teaching of the received ecumenical councils.

In 2003, the 74th General Convention of The Episcopal Church directed the Standing Commission on Liturgy and Music to "undertake a revision of *Lesser Feasts and Fasts 2000*, to reflect our increasing awareness of the importance of the ministry of all the people of God and of the cultural diversity of The Episcopal Church, of the wider Anglican Communion, of our ecumenical partners, and of our lively experience of sainthood in local communities," and to focus reflection upon "the significance of that experience of local sainthood in encouraging the living out of baptism."[6] That, in turn, led to study and discussion resulting in *Holy Women, Holy Men*, which continued in a state of trial use through 2015.

The reception of *Holy Women, Holy Men* and additional commemoration requests brought to General Convention since 2009

---

[6] General Convention Resolution 2003–A100.

suggested that the range of sanctoral theologies (that is, theologies of sainthood) within the Church remained as broad as ever, resulting in disagreements concerning who does and does not belong in the Calendar. At the same time, many people have expressed appreciation for the expansion of the Calendar because it has broadened their knowledge of the Christian family story.

In order to maintain a comprehensive stance toward differing theologies of sainthood and to recognize the desire to remember people important to the Church without passing judgment on their sanctoral status or requiring them to fit within a particular mold of saintliness, we have created this new resource entitled *A Great Cloud of Witnesses: A Calendar of Commemorations*. This resource recognizes individuals who have made significant contributions to our understanding of our calling as the Body of Christ within the complexities of the twenty-first-century world without making a statement one way or another on their sanctity. It serves as a family history, identifying those people inside and outside the Episcopal/Anglican tradition who help us proclaim the Gospel in word, deed, and truth.

Holy Women, Holy Men, and *Lesser Feasts and Fasts* before it, also included liturgical material for weekday celebrations during the seasons of the Church year. To streamline our liturgical resources, this material is now located in a separate volume, *Weekday Eucharistic Propers 2015*.

On the Making of Saints

While *A Great Cloud of Witnesses* does not intend to be a calendar that presents a definitive list of saints, there is no doubt that many of the people within it will be recognized as saints. In its call to revise *Lesser Feasts and Fasts*, General Convention emphasized the importance of the local recognition of sanctity. As we look across the Church's broad history, this is, in fact, the predominant level on which sanctity has been identified. Local communities celebrated local heroes. Too, local communities gave special emphasis to those fellow, yet heroic, members of the Body of Christ with whom they shared a special bond—whether through a common occupation, a common circumstance, or through their physical presence in the form of relics.

Saints were declared by parishes and by dioceses. In most places and times, there was no formal set of criteria that had to be met. Instead, the local communities operated on a broad basic principle: that Christ was known more intimately through these individuals, and that the holiness of the person was both evidence of their participation in the greater life of God and an inspiration for those around them to "go and do likewise."

The process of declaring saints was centralized within the Roman Catholic Church with the *Decretals* of Gregory IX in 1234, asserting that canonization could only occur with the authorization of the pope. This was part and parcel of the centralization of authority to the papal office in the high medieval period. Over the following centuries, bureaucratic regulations and a specific legal process were created to ensure a formal process. Only at this point were specific criteria drawn up, including the requirement of two documented miracles. In other words, this curial, top-down, centralized approach to naming saints has only existed in one part of the Church for less than half of its existence. Conversely, some of the most beloved saints within the Roman Catholic Church, such as Benedict of Nursia and Augustine of Hippo, never went through this process!

The Calendar of the first American Book of Common Prayer, authorized in 1789, contained most of the feasts now recognized as Holy Days and no others. In this regard, it follows the example of the earliest Anglican prayer books. The same Calendar appeared—with a few additions like the Transfiguration in 1892—through the 1928 Prayer Book. While some had argued for the inclusion of post-biblical saints in the Calendar of the 1928 Prayer Book, this did not come to pass; however, a Common of Saints was provided, officially permitting the local eucharistic celebration of saints, while still retaining an official Calendar obligating only the universally acknowledged saints of the Apostolic Age. The publication of the supplementary *American Missal* in 1931 by noted church musician and liturgist Winfred Douglas containing an expanded Calendar of saints demonstrates the local desire for such celebrations during this time; the official condemnation of this work by some thirty bishops of the day testify to the differences of opinion regarding the expanded Calendar as well as many other matters.

In the first stages of revision leading to the 1979 Book of Common Prayer, the Standing Liturgical Commission appointed a Calendar committee headed by the Rev. Dr. Massey Shepherd to study the issue of the Calendar once again. The process of additions to the Calendar has been a piece of the broader development of the Book of Common Prayer. Additions to the Calendar typically begin with recommendations from individuals and dioceses, reflective of local commemoration practices, made to General Convention, which then asks the Standing Commission on Liturgy and Music to review the proposals and make a recommendation to the next convention. This process of proposal based on local commemorations and affirmation by General Convention represents the baptismal ecclesiology of the Book of Common Prayer, in which constituent members of the Church contribute to the wider vitality and mission of the Church.

In responding to the diversity of theology of sainthood in The Episcopal Church, it seems best to identify two calendars: a core calendar of commemorations around which there is general consensus and a long tradition of observation, and a broader calendar of commemorations that represents a wider family history that people and congregations will engage. The first, the core Calendar of The Episcopal Church, is defined as those Holy Days listed on pages 16 and 17 within the authorized Book of Common Prayer:

Feasts of our Lord

The Holy Name
The Presentation
The Annunciation
The Visitation

Saint John the Baptist
The Transfiguration
Holy Cross Day

Other Major Feasts

All feasts of Apostles
All feasts of Evangelists
Saint Stephen
The Holy Innocents
Saint Joseph
Saint Mary Magdalene

Saint Mary the Virgin
Saint Michael and All Angels
Saint James of Jerusalem
Independence Day
Thanksgiving Day

The second, *A Great Cloud of Witnesses,* provides a broader calendar, consistent with the call of the 2003 General Convention for a revision of the Calendar of the Church that reflects the lively experience of holiness, especially on the level of the local community. In this way, *A Great Cloud of Witnesses* is a tool for learning about the history of the Church and identifying those who have inspired and challenged us from the time of the New Testament to the present. Some of the individuals within it are recognized as saints in many parts of the Church universal today. Others are not. Some present special challenges—whether from their mode of life, what we now perceive as misunderstandings of the Gospel call, a lack of charity toward others, or other reasons.[7] We intend *A Great Cloud of Witnesses* to serve several purposes. First, it is a catechetical tool to educate the faithful about the breadth of witness to the transforming work of God in Christ Jesus. Second, it is a collection that provides a range of options for commemorations in the form of eucharistic celebrations, prayer offices, or individual devotions.

Following the broad stream of Christian tradition, there are no formal criteria for defining saints. Rather, holiness and faithful witness are celebrated locally by a decision that individuals so honored shine forth Christ to the world. They illuminate different facets of Christian maturity to spur us on to an adult faith in the Risen Christ and the life of the Spirit. As illustrations, they mirror the myriad virtues of Christ in order that, in their examples, we might recognize those same virtues and features of holiness in people closer to our own times and contexts. And, seeing them in those around us, we may be better able to cultivate these virtues and forms of holiness in the life of the Church—through grace—as we strive to imitate Christ as well.

How to Use These Materials

Each entry includes a biographical narrative of the person or people, highlighting the significance of their life and witness. A devotional collect is provided in both Rite I and Rite II language. Tags "for liturgical celebration" identify Commons and Various Occasions related to the life, work, or impact of the occasion. When

---

[7] To name one challenge, the anti-Semitism/anti-Judaism of some pre-modern writers and teachers is a significant stumbling block to celebrating them as saints.

a local community decides to commemorate a person or group, the appropriate propers are selected from the Common of Saints. Alternatively, a Eucharist celebrating a related Various Occasion might include the devotional collect as the conclusion to the Prayers of the People. The Common of Saints from the Book of Common Prayer has been enriched, particularly through the addition of more options for biblical readings, to allow a community to more closely tailor the set of readings to the witness of the person celebrated. The "New Commons for Various Occasions" first appearing in *Holy Women, Holy Men* are also included here.

Commemorations

Calendar of Commemorations

JANUARY

1
2 Vedanayagam Samuel Azariah, First Indian Anglican Bishop, Dornakal, 1945
3 William Passavant, Prophetic Witness, 1894
4 Elizabeth Seton, Founder of the American Sisters of Charity, 1821
5
6
7
8 Harriet Bedell, Deaconess and Missionary, 1969
9 Julia Chester Emery, Missionary, 1922
10 William Laud, Archbishop of Canterbury, 1645
11
12 Aelred, Abbot of Rievaulx, 1167
13 Hilary, Bishop of Poitiers, 367
14
15 (alternative date for Martin Luther King, Jr.; see April 4)
16 Richard Meux Benson, Religious, 1915, and Charles Gore, Bishop of Worcester, of Birmingham, and of Oxford, 1932

17 Antony, Abbot in Egypt, 356
18
19 Wulfstan, Bishop of Worcester, 1095
20 Fabian, Bishop and Martyr of Rome, 250
21 Agnes, Martyr at Rome, 304
22 Vincent, Deacon of Saragossa, and Martyr, 304
23 Phillips Brooks, Bishop of Massachusetts, 1893
24 Ordination of Florence Li Tim-Oi, First Woman Priest in the Anglican Communion, 1944
25
26 Timothy, Titus, and Silas, Companions of Saint Paul
27 Lydia, Dorcas, and Phoebe, Witnesses to the Faith
28 Thomas Aquinas, Priest and Theologian, 1274
29 Andrei Rublev, Monk and Iconographer, 1430
30
31 John Bosco, Priest, 1888
31 Samuel Shoemaker, Priest and Evangelist, 1963

FEBRUARY

1 Brigid (Bride), 523
2
3 The Dorchester Chaplains: Lieutenant George Fox, Lieutenant Alexander D. Goode, Lieutenant Clark V. Poling, and Lieutenant John P. Washington, 1943
4 Anskar, Archbishop of Hamburg, Missionary to Denmark and Sweden, 865
5 Roger Williams, 1683, and Anne Hutchinson, 1643, Prophetic Witnesses
6 The Martyrs of Japan, 1597

7   Cornelius the Centurion
8
9
10
11 Frances Jane (Fanny) Van Alstyne Crosby, Hymnwriter, 1915
12 Charles Freer Andrews, Priest and "Friend of the Poor" in India, 1940
13 Absalom Jones, Priest, 1818
14 Cyril, Monk, and Methodius, Bishop, Missionaries to the Slavs, 869, 885
15 Thomas Bray, Priest and Missionary, 1730
16 Charles Todd Quintard, Bishop of Tennessee, 1898
17 Janani Luwum, Archbishop of Uganda, and Martyr, 1977
18 Martin Luther, Theologian, 1546
19
20 Frederick Douglass, Orator and Advocate for Truth and Justice, 1895
21 John Henry Newman, Priest and Theologian, 1890
22 Eric Liddell, Missionary to China, 1945
23 Polycarp, Bishop and Martyr of Smyrna, 156
24
25 John Roberts, Priest, 1949
26 Emily Malbone Morgan, Prophetic Witness, 1937
27 George Herbert, Priest, 1633
28 Anna Julia Haywood Cooper, 1964, and Elizabeth Evelyn Wright, 1904, Educators
29

FEBRUARY

MARCH

- 1 David, Bishop of Menevia, Wales, c. 544
- 2 Chad, Bishop of Lichfield, 672
- 3 John and Charles Wesley, Priests, 1791, 1788
- 4 Paul Cuffee, Witness to the Faith among the Shinnecock, 1812
- 5
- 6 William W. Mayo, 1911, and Charles Menninger, 1953, and Their Sons, Pioneers in Medicine
- 7 Perpetua, Felicity, and their Companions, Martyrs at Carthage, 202
- 8 Geoffrey Anketell Studdert Kennedy, Priest, 1929
- 9 Gregory, Bishop of Nyssa, c. 394
- 10
- 11
- 12 Gregory the Great, Bishop of Rome, 604
- 13 James Theodore Holly, Bishop of Haiti, and of the Dominican Republic, 1911 (see also November 8)
- 14
- 15
- 16
- 17 Patrick, Bishop and Missionary of Ireland, 461
- 18 Cyril of Jerusalem, Liturgist, Catechist, and Bishop, 386
- 19
- 20 Thomas Ken, Bishop of Bath and Wells, 1711
- 21 Thomas Cranmer, Archbishop of Canterbury and Martyr, 1556
- 22 James De Koven, Priest and Teacher, 1879
- 23 Gregory the Illuminator, Bishop and Missionary of Armenia, c. 332
- 24 Óscar Romero, Archbishop of San Salvador, 1980, and the Martyrs of El Salvador
- 25

26 Richard Allen, First Bishop of the African Methodist Episcopal Church, 1831

27 Charles Henry Brent, Bishop of the Philippines, and of Western New York, 1929

28 James Solomon Russell, Priest, 1935

29 John Keble, Priest, 1866

30 Innocent of Alaska, Bishop, 1879

31 John Donne, Priest, 1631

APRIL

1 Frederick Denison Maurice, Priest, 1872

2 James Lloyd Breck, Priest, 1876

3 Richard, Bishop of Chichester, 1253

4 Martin Luther King, Jr., Civil Rights Leader and Martyr, 1968 (see also Jan. 15)

5 Pandita Mary Ramabai, Prophetic Witness and Evangelist in India, 1922

6 Daniel G. C. Wu, Priest and Missionary among Chinese Americans, 1956

7 Tikhon, Patriarch of Russia, Confessor and Ecumenist, 1925

8 William Augustus Muhlenberg, Priest, 1877 and Anne Ayres, Religious, 1896

9 Dietrich Bonhoeffer, Theologian and Martyr, 1945

10 William Law, Priest, 1761

10 Pierre Teilhard de Chardin, Scientist and Military Chaplain, 1955

11 George Augustus Selwyn, Bishop of New Zealand, and of Lichfield, 1878

12 Adoniram Judson, Missionary to Burma, 1850

13

14 Edward Thomas Demby, 1957, and Henry Beard Delany, 1928, Bishops

APRIL

15 Damien, Priest and Leper, 1889, and Marianne, Religious, 1918, of Molokai
16 Mary (Molly) Brant (Konwatsijayenni), Witness to the Faith among the Mohawks, 1796
17 Emily Cooper, Deaconess, 1909
18
19 Alphege, Archbishop of Canterbury, and Martyr, 1012
20
21 Anselm, Archbishop of Canterbury, 1109
22 John Muir, Naturalist and Writer, 1914, and Hudson Stuck, Priest and Environmentalist, 1920
23 George, Soldier and Martyr, c. 304
23 Toyohiko Kagawa, Prophetic Witness in Japan, 1960
24 Genocide Remembrance
25
26 Robert Hunt, Priest and First Chaplain at Jamestown, 1607
27 Christina Rossetti, Poet, 1894
28
29 Catherine of Siena, 1380
30 Sarah Josepha Buell Hale, Editor and Prophetic Witness, 1879

MAY

1
2 Athanasius, Bishop of Alexandria, 373
3
4 Monnica, Mother of Augustine of Hippo, 387
5
6
7 Harriet Starr Cannon, Religious, 1896

MAY

8 Dame Julian of Norwich, c. 1417
9 Gregory of Nazianzus, Bishop of Constantinople, 389
10 Nicolaus Ludwig von Zinzendorf, Prophetic Witness, 1760
11
12
13 Frances Perkins, Public Servant and Prophetic Witness, 1965
14
15 Junia and Andronicus
16 The Martyrs of the Sudan
17 William Hobart Hare, Bishop of Niobrara, and of South Dakota, 1909
17 Thurgood Marshall, Lawyer and Jurist, 1993
18
19 Dunstan, Archbishop of Canterbury, 988
20 Alcuin, Deacon, and Abbot of Tours, 804
21 John Eliot, Missionary among the Algonquin, 1690
22
23 Nicolaus Copernicus, 1543, and Johannes Kepler, 1630, Astronomers
24 Jackson Kemper, First Missionary Bishop in the United States, 1870
25 Bede, the Venerable, Priest, and Monk of Jarrow, 735
26 Augustine, First Archbishop of Canterbury, 605
27 Bertha and Ethelbert, Queen and King of Kent, 616
28 John Calvin, Theologian, 1564
29
30 Jeanne d'Arc (Joan of Arc), Mystic and Soldier, 1431
31

The First Book of Common Prayer, 1549, is appropriately observed on a weekday following the Day of Pentecost.

MAY

JUNE

1. Justin, Martyr at Rome, c. 167
2. Blandina and Her Companions, the Martyrs of Lyons, 177
3. The Martyrs of Uganda, 1886
4. John XXIII (Angelo Guiseppe Roncalli), Bishop of Rome, 1963
5. Boniface, Archbishop of Mainz, Missionary to Germany, and Martyr, 754
6. Ini Kopuria, Founder of the Melanesian Brotherhood, 1945
7. The Pioneers of the Episcopal Anglican Church of Brazil, 1890
8. Roland Allen, Mission Strategist, 1947
9. Columba, Abbot of Iona, 597
10. Ephrem of Edessa, Syria, Deacon, 373
11.
12. Enmegahbowh, Priest and Missionary, 1902
13. Gilbert Keith Chesterton, Apologist and Writer, 1936
14. Basil the Great, Bishop of Caesarea, 379
15. Evelyn Underhill, 1941
16. George Berkeley, 1753, and Joseph Butler, 1752, Bishops and Theologians
17.
18. Bernard Mizeki, Catechist and Martyr in Mashonaland, 1896
19. Adelaide Teague Case, Teacher, 1948
20.
21.
22. Alban, First Martyr of Britain, c. 304
23.
24.
25. James Weldon Johnson, Poet, 1938

26 Isabel Florence Hapgood, Translator, Ecumenist, and Journalist, 1929
27 Cornelius Hill, Priest and Chief among the Oneida, 1907
28 Irenaeus, Bishop of Lyons, c. 202
29
30

JULY

1 Harriet Beecher Stowe, Writer and Prophetic Witness, 1896
1 Pauli Murray, Priest, 1985
2 Walter Rauschenbusch, 1918, Washington Gladden, 1918, and Jacob Riis, 1914, Prophetic Witnesses
3
4
5
6 John (Jan) Hus, Prophetic Witness and Martyr, 1415
7
8
9
10
11 Benedict of Nursia, Abbot of Monte Cassino, c. 540
12 Nathan Söderblom, Archbishop of Uppsala and Ecumenist, 1931
13 Conrad Weiser, Witness to Peace and Reconciliation, 1760
14 Samson Occom, Witness to the Faith in New England, 1792
15
16 "The Righteous Gentiles"
17 William White, Bishop of Pennsylvania, 1836
18 Bartolomé de las Casas, Friar and Missionary to the Indies, 1566

19 Macrina, Monastic and Teacher, 379
20 Elizabeth Cady Stanton, 1902; Amelia Bloomer, 1894; Sojourner Truth, 1883; and Harriet Ross Tubman, 1913, Liberators and Prophets
21 Albert John Luthuli, Prophetic Witness in South Africa, 1967
22
23 John Cassian, Abbot at Marseilles, 435
24 Thomas à Kempis, Priest, 1471
25
26 Joachim and Anne, Parents of the Blessed Virgin Mary
26 Charles Raymond Barnes, 1938
27 William Reed Huntington, Priest, 1909
28 Johann Sebastian Bach, 1750, George Frederick Handel, 1759, and Henry Purcell, 1695, Composers
29 Mary, Martha, and Lazarus of Bethany
29 First Ordination of Women to the Priesthood in The Episcopal Church, 1974
30 William Wilberforce, 1833, and Anthony Ashley-Cooper, Lord Shaftesbury, 1885, Prophetic Witnesses
31 Ignatius of Loyola, Priest and Monastic, 1556

AUGUST

1 Joseph of Arimathea
2 Samuel Ferguson, Missionary Bishop for West Africa, 1916
3 George Freeman Bragg, Jr., Priest, 1940
3 William Edward Burghardt Du Bois, Sociologist, 1963
4
5 Albrecht Dürer, 1528, Matthias Grünewald, 1529, and Lucas Cranach the Elder, 1553, Artists
6

7   John Mason Neale, Priest, 1866
7   Catherine Winkworth, Poet, 1878
8   Dominic, Priest and Friar, 1221
9   Herman of Alaska, Missionary to the Aleut, 1837
10 Laurence, Deacon, and Martyr at Rome, 258
11 Clare, Abbess at Assisi, 1253
12 Florence Nightingale, Nurse, Social Reformer, 1910
13 Jeremy Taylor, Bishop of Down, Connor, and Dromore, 1667
14 Jonathan Myrick Daniels, Seminarian and Martyr, 1965
15
16
17 Samuel Johnson, 1772, Timothy Cutler, 1765, and Thomas Bradbury Chandler, 1790, Priests
17 The Baptisms of Manteo, and Virginia Dare, 1587
18 William Porcher DuBose, Priest, 1918
18 Artemisia Bowden, 1969
19
20 Bernard, Abbot of Clairvaux, 1153
21
22
23 Martin de Porres, 1639, Rosa de Lima, 1617, and Toribio de Mogrovejo, 1606, Witnesses to the Faith in South America
24
25 Louis, King of France, 1270
26
27 Thomas Gallaudet, 1902, with Henry Winter Syle, 1890
28 Augustine, Bishop of Hippo, and Theologian, 430
28 Moses the Black, Desert Father and Martyr, c. 400

AUGUST

29 John Bunyan, Writer, 1688
30 Charles Chapman Grafton, Bishop of Fond du Lac, and Ecumenist, 1912
31 Aidan, 651, and Cuthbert, 687, Bishops of Lindisfarne

SEPTEMBER

1 David Pendleton Oakerhater, Deacon and Missionary, 1931
2 The Martyrs of New Guinea, 1942
3 Prudence Crandall, Teacher and Prophetic Witness, 1890
4 Paul Jones, 1941
4 Albert Schweitzer, 1965
5 Gregorio Aglipay, Priest and Founder of the Philippine Independent Church, 1940
6
7 Elie Naud, Huguenot Witness to the Faith, 1722
8 Nikolai Grundtvig, Bishop and Hymnwriter, 1872
8 Søren Kierkegaard, Teacher and Philosopher, 1855
9 Constance, Nun, and Her Companions, 1878
10 Alexander Crummell, 1898
11 Harry Thacker Burleigh, Composer, 1949
12 John Henry Hobart, Bishop of New York, 1830
13 John Chrysostom, Bishop of Constantinople, 407
14
15 Cyprian, Bishop and Martyr of Carthage, 258
15 James Chisholm, Priest, 1855
16 Ninian, Bishop in Galloway, c. 430
17 Hildegard, 1179
18 Edward Bouverie Pusey, Priest, 1882

18　Dag Hjalmar Agne Carl Hammarskjöld, 1961
19　Theodore of Tarsus, Archbishop of Canterbury, 690
20　John Coleridge Patteson, Bishop of Melanesia, and his Companions, Martyrs, 1871
21
22　Philander Chase, Bishop of Ohio, and of Illinois, 1852
23　Thecla
24　Anna Ellison Butler Alexander, 1947
25　Sergius, Abbot of Holy Trinity, Moscow, 1392
26　Lancelot Andrewes, Bishop of Winchester, 1626
26　Wilson Carlile, Priest, 1942
27　Vincent de Paul, Religious, and Prophetic Witness, 1660
27　Thomas Traherne, Priest, 1674
28　Richard Rolle, 1349, Walter Hilton, 1396, and Margery Kempe, c. 1440, Mystics
29
30　Jerome, Priest, and Monk of Bethlehem, 420

OCTOBER

1　Remigius, Bishop of Rheims, c. 530
2
3
3　John Raleigh Mott, Evangelist and Ecumenical Pioneer, 1955
4　Francis of Assisi, Friar, 1226
5
6　William Tyndale, 1536, and Miles Coverdale, 1568, Translators of the Bible
7　Henry Melchior Muhlenberg, Lutheran Pastor in North America, 1787

8   William Dwight Porter Bliss, Priest, 1926, and Richard Theodore Ely, Economist, 1943
9   Wilfred Thomason Grenfell, Medical Missionary, 1940
10 Vida Dutton Scudder, Educator and Witness for Peace, 1954
11 Philip, Deacon and Evangelist
12
13
14 Samuel Isaac Joseph Scherechewsky, Bishop of Shanghai, 1906
15 Teresa of Avila, Nun, 1582
16 Hugh Latimer and Nicholas Ridley, Bishops and Martyrs, 1555
17 Ignatius, Bishop of Antioch, and Martyr, c. 115
18
19 Henry Martyn, Priest, and Missionary to India and Persia, 1812
19 William Carey, Missionary to India, 1834
20
21
22
23
24 Hiram Hisanori Kano, 1986
25
26 Alfred the Great, King of the West Saxons, 899
27
28
29 James Hannington, Bishop of Eastern Equatorial Africa, and his Companions, Martyrs, 1885
30 John Wyclif, Priest and Prophetic Witness, 1384
31 Paul Shinji Sasaki, Bishop of Mid-Japan, and of Tokyo, 1946, and Philip Lindel Tsen, Bishop of Honan, China, 1954

OCTOBER

NOVEMBER

1
2 Commemoration of All Faithful Departed
3 Richard Hooker, Priest, 1600
4
5
6 William Temple, Archbishop of Canterbury, 1944
7 Willibrord, Archbishop of Utrecht, Missionary to Frisia, 739
8 (alternative date for James Theodore Holly; see March 13)
9
10 Leo the Great, Bishop of Rome, 461
11 Martin, Bishop of Tours, 397
12 Charles Simeon, Priest, 1836
13
14 Samuel Seabury, First American Bishop, 1796
15 Francis Asbury, 1816, and George Whitefield, 1770, Evangelists
16 Margaret, Queen of Scotland, 1093
17 Hugh, 1200, and Robert Grosseteste, 1253, Bishops of Lincoln
18 Hilda, Abbess of Whitby, 680
19 Elizabeth, Princess of Hungary, 1231
20 Edmund, King of East Anglia, 870
21 William Byrd, 1623, John Merbecke, 1585, and Thomas Tallis, 1585, Musicians
22 Cecilia, Martyr at Rome, c. 230
22 Clive Staples Lewis, Apologist and Spiritual Writer, 1963
23 Clement, Bishop of Rome, c. 100
24
25 James Otis Sargent Huntington, Priest and Monk, 1935

26 Isaac Watts, Hymnwriter, 1748

27

28 Kamehameha and Emma, King and Queen of Hawaii, 1864, 1885

29

30

DECEMBER

1 Nicholas Ferrar, Deacon, 1637

1 Charles de Foucauld, Hermit and Martyr in the Sahara, 1916

2 Channing Moore Williams, Missionary Bishop in China and Japan, 1910

3 Francis Xavier, Missionary to the Far East, 1552

4 John of Damascus, Priest, c. 760

5 Clement of Alexandria, Priest, c. 210

6 Nicholas, Bishop of Myra, c. 342

7 Ambrose, Bishop of Milan, 397

8 Richard Baxter, Pastor and Writer, 1691

9

10 Karl Barth, Pastor and Theologian, 1968

10 Thomas Merton, Contemplative and Writer, 1968

11

12

13 Lucy (Lucia), Martyr at Syracuse, 304

14 Juan de la Cruz (John of the Cross), Mystic, 1591

15 John Horden, Bishop and Missionary in Canada, 1893

15 Robert McDonald, Priest, 1913

16 Ralph Adams Cram, 1942, and Richard Upjohn, 1878, Architects, and John LaFarge, Artist, 1910

17 William Lloyd Garrison, 1879, and Maria Stewart, 1879, Prophetic Witnesses
18
19 Lillian Trasher, Missionary in Egypt, 1961
20
21
22 Henry Budd, Priest, 1875
22 Charlotte Diggs (Lottie) Moon, Missionary in China, 1912
23
24
25
26
27
28
29 Thomas Becket, 1170
30 Frances Joseph Gaudet, Educator and Prison Reformer, 1934
31 Samuel Ajayi Crowther, Bishop in the Niger Territories, 1891

DECEMBER

Commemorations

JANUARY

1
2 Vedanayagam Samuel Azariah, First Indian Anglican Bishop, Dornakal, 1945
3 William Passavant, Prophetic Witness, 1894
4 Elizabeth Seton, Founder of the American Sisters of Charity, 1821
5
6
7
8 Harriet Bedell, Deaconess and Missionary, 1969
9 Julia Chester Emery, Missionary, 1922
10 William Laud, Archbishop of Canterbury, 1645
11
12 Aelred, Abbot of Rievaulx, 1167
13 Hilary, Bishop of Poitiers, 367
14
15 (alternative date for Martin Luther King, Jr.; see April 4)
16 Richard Meux Benson, Religious, 1915, and Charles Gore, Bishop of Worcester, of Birmingham, and of Oxford, 1932
17 Antony, Abbot in Egypt, 356

18

19 Wulfstan, Bishop of Worcester, 1095
20 Fabian, Bishop and Martyr of Rome, 250
21 Agnes, Martyr at Rome, 304
22 Vincent, Deacon of Saragossa, and Martyr, 304
23 Phillips Brooks, Bishop of Massachusetts, 1893
24 Ordination of Florence Li Tim-Oi, First Woman Priest in the Anglican Communion, 1944

25

26 Timothy, Titus, and Silas, Companions of Saint Paul
27 Lydia, Dorcas, and Phoebe, Witnesses to the Faith
28 Thomas Aquinas, Priest and Theologian, 1274
29 Andrei Rublev, Monk and Iconographer, 1430

30

31 John Bosco, Priest, 1888
31 Samuel Shoemaker, Priest and Evangelist, 1963

January 2

Vedanayagam Samuel Azariah
First Indian Anglican Bishop, Dornakal, 1945

Vedanayagam Samuel Azariah was the Anglican Church's first Indian bishop.

His father was a village vicar and his mother spent long hours on her son's religious instruction. After more than a decade working with the Young Men's Christian Association (YMCA), he was ordained a priest in 1909, and in 1912 was ordained bishop of the new Diocese of Dornakal, a populous diocese located in Andhra Pradesh, South India, near Chennai (formerly Madras). Zealous to promote church growth, he was also a strong advocate of ecumenism and church unity among India's numerous Protestant denominations.

Azariah was a mainstream broad church Anglican with a high priority for evangelism, and much of his preaching centered on the resurrection. His ministry cut across class lines and focused heavily on rural Dalits ("untouchable" caste members). The bishop's traditional Anglicanism frustrated many Indian political leaders, who hoped he would be a leading voice for Indian nationalism. Azariah also took sharp issue with Mahatma Gandhi, who was unalterably opposed to Christians trying to convert Indians. Azariah saw conversion as foundational to Christian mission. Gandhi acknowledged that the dominant Hindu religion needed reform, but Azariah saw it as being repressive and grounded in a destructive caste system. He said, "It is by proclamation of the truth that the early Church turned the world upside down . . . It is this that will today redeem Indian society and emancipate it from the thralldom of centuries."

By 1935, the Dornakal diocese had 250 ordained Indian clergy and more than 2,000 village teachers, plus a growing number of medical clinics, cooperative societies, and printing presses. Traveling over the vast diocese by bullock cart or bicycle, and accompanied by his wife and coworker, Anbu, Azariah often built his village sermons around "the four demons – Dirt, Disease, Debt, and Drink." He believed in adapting liturgy to local cultures. Epiphany Cathedral,

Dornakal, which took a quarter of a century to build, exemplifies the bishop's vision of how local cultures can express Christian truths. He saw in the cathedral's mixture of Muslim, Hindu, and Christian designs an architectural expression of the gifts and beauty of other faith traditions finding their fulfillment in Christianity. He believed in adapting liturgy so as to embrace the culture's traditions.

Azariah died in Dornakal in 1945.

I   Loving God, who dost raise from every nation, people, tribe, and tongue witnesses to thy glory: May we who celebrate thy servant Samuel Azariah be strengthened by his witness to thy love without concern for class or caste, that people of all languages and cultures might be drawn into thy loving embrace, Father, Son, and Holy Spirit, now and for ever. Amen.

II Loving God, who raises from every nation, people, tribe, and tongue witnesses to your glory: May we who celebrate your servant Samuel Azariah be strengthened by his witness to your love without concern for class or caste, that people of all languages and cultures might be drawn into your loving embrace, Father, Son, and Holy Spirit, now and for ever. Amen.

For Liturgical Celebration: [Common of a Pastor, A14] [Common of a Missionary, A11] [For the Ministry II, A50] [For the Mission of the Church, A52]

January 3

William Passavant
Prophetic Witness, 1894

William Passavant, a Pennsylvania Lutheran pastor, was born in Zelienople, Pennsylvania, on October 9, 1821. He attended Jefferson College and later Gettysburg Seminary.

Passavant was a parish pastor at heart and served in that capacity for much of his ministry, even while pursuing other duties. Passavant was the founder of numerous hospitals, orphanages, and other charitable organizations, principally in Western Pennsylvania, but the reach of his efforts extended from Boston and New York in the east to Chicago and Milwaukee in the mid-west. Many of these institutions continue to this day.

On a visit to Germany, Passavant came into contact with Theodor Fliedner, the founder of the reconstituted deaconess movement among German Lutherans, and, in 1849, he invited Fliedner to come to Pittsburgh and bring four of his deaconesses to serve in the hospital there. A year later, in 1850, the first American Lutheran deaconesses were set apart by Passavant, and thus began the renewed deaconess movement among American Lutherans.

Passavant was driven by a desire to see the consequences of the gospel worked out in practical ways in the lives of people in need. For Passavant, the Church's commitment to the gospel must not be spiritual only. It must be visible. For him, it was essential that gospel principles were worked out in clear missionary actions. Passavant also knew the importance of education and was the founder of a number of church schools scattered across the mid-west, principal among these being Thiel College, a Lutheran-affiliated college in Greenville, Pennsylvania.

In addition to his charitable, philanthropic, and educational work, and his guidance of the early years of the deaconess movement, Passavant was also a cutting-edge communicator of his time. He founded two church newspapers, *The Missionary* and *The Workman*, both designed to interpret the church's mission, in consonance with the Lutheran confessions, for the purpose of provoking the desire of the faithful toward loving service to those in need without concern for race, color, creed, or national origin. Later generations of Lutheran communicators look to Passavant as one of the trailblazers of the field of religious journalism.

Passavant died on January 3, 1894.

I   Compassionate God, who hast raised up ministers among thy people: May we ever desire, like thy servant William Passavant, to support the work of equipping the saints for service among the sick and the friendless; through Jesus Christ, the divine Physician, who hast prepared for us an eternal home, and who with thee and the Holy Spirit liveth and reigneth, one God, in glory everlasting. Amen.

II   Compassionate God, who raises up ministers among your people: May we ever desire, like your servant William Passavant, to support the work of equipping the saints for service among the sick and the friendless; through Jesus Christ, the divine Physician, who has prepared for us an eternal home, and who with you and the Holy Spirit lives and reigns, one God, in glory everlasting. Amen.

For Liturgical Celebration: [Common of a Pastor, A14] [Common of a Prophetic Witness, A31] [For Social Service, A59]

January 4

Elizabeth Seton
Founder of the American Sisters of Charity, 1821

Elizabeth Ann Seton was born in New York City on August 28, 1774. She was the founder of the Sisters of Charity, the first community of sisters established in the United States.

Elizabeth Seton was reared in The Episcopal Church, her family having been loyalists during the American Revolution. From a young age, she desired to aid the sick and poor. In 1795 she married William Seton, and their family came to include five children. During this time she also founded the Society for the Relief of Poor Widows with Small Children. In 1801, the family business went bankrupt. In 1803, her husband showed the symptoms of tuberculosis, and they set sail for Italy in the hopes that the warm climate would cure his disease. The Italian authorities, fearing yellow fever, quarantined them in a cold stone hospital for the dying. William soon died and left Elizabeth a young widow with five children and few resources. While struggling with these losses, she was befriended by Roman Catholics and, as a result, was drawn to Roman Catholicism.

Returning to New York, she encountered bitter opposition from her Episcopalian family for her new religious leanings. With five children to support, she found herself alone and in financial straits. She turned to Roman Catholic clergy for support and, in 1805, she formally became a member of the Roman Catholic Church.

In 1806, she met Father Louis Dubourg, S.S., who wanted to start a congregation of women religious, patterned after the French Daughters of Charity of St. Vincent de Paul. In 1809 Elizabeth took vows and became "Mother Seton" to a small community of seven women, known as the Sisters of Charity of St. Joseph, dedicated to teaching. The sisters were given land in rural Maryland and, in 1810, they opened St. Joseph's Free School to educate needy girls. The Sisters intertwined social ministry, education, and religious formation in all their varied works. Seton dispatched sisters to operate orphanages in Philadelphia and New York City. Out of the pioneering work of

Elizabeth Seton, five independent communities of the Sisters of Charity now exist, offering ministry and care for the most vulnerable.

Elizabeth Ann Seton remained the Mother of the Sisters of Charity until her death on January 4, 1821.

I   Holy God, who didst bless Elizabeth Seton with thy grace as wife, mother, educator, and founder, that she might spend her life in service to thy people: Help us, by her example, to express our love for thee in love of others; through Jesus Christ our Redeemer, who liveth and reigneth with thee and the Holy Spirit, one God, for ever and ever. Amen.

II   Holy God, you blessed Elizabeth Seton with your grace as wife, mother, educator, and founder, that she might spend her life in service to your people: Help us, by her example, to express our love for you in love of others; through Jesus Christ our Redeemer, who lives and reigns with you and the Holy Spirit, one God, for ever and ever. Amen.

For Liturgical Celebration: [Common of a Monastic or Professed Religious, A20] [For the Unity of the Church, A48] [For Social Service, A59]

January 8

Harriet Bedell
Deaconess and Missionary, 1969

Harriet Bedell was born in Buffalo, New York, on March 19, 1875. Inspired by an Episcopal missionary, she enrolled as a student at the New York Training School for Deaconesses, where she was instructed in religion, missions, teaching, and hygiene. She then became a missionary-teacher among the Cheyenne at the Whirlwind Mission in Oklahoma. In 1916, Bedell was sent to Stevens Village, Alaska, where she was finally set apart as a deaconess in 1922. She also served as a teacher and nurse at St. John's in the Wilderness at Allakaket, just 40 miles south of the Arctic Circle, from which she sometimes traveled by dogsled to remote villages. During her last years in Alaska, Bedell opened a boarding school.

In 1932, hearing about the plight of the Seminoles in Florida, Bedell used her own salary to reopen a mission among the Mikasuki Indians. There, she worked to revive some of their traditional crafts: doll-making, basket-weaving, and intricate patchwork designs. The arts and crafts store that they established to sell their handicrafts improved the economy of the Blades Cross Mission. Though officially forced to retire at age 63, Bedell continued her ministry of health care, education, and economic empowerment until 1960 when Hurricane Donna wiped out her mission.

Active into her eighties, Deaconess Bedell drove an average of 20,000 miles per year during her ministry. She was one of the most popular writers in the national Episcopal mission periodical, *The Spirit of Missions*. Bedell won the respect of indigenous people through her compassion and respect for their way of life and beliefs. While active in ministry among the Cheyenne, she was eventually adopted into the tribe and given the name "Bird Woman." The Diocese of Southwest Florida has long celebrated Harriet Bedell Day on January 8, the anniversary of her death in 1969.

Rite I   Holy God, thou didst choose thy faithful servant Harriet Bedell to exercise the ministry of deaconess and to be a missionary among indigenous people: Fill us with compassion and respect for all people, and empower us for the work of ministry throughout the world; through Jesus Christ our Lord, who liveth and reigneth with thee and the Holy Spirit, one God, for ever and ever. Amen.

Rite II Holy God, you chose your faithful servant Harriett Bedell to exercise the ministry of deaconess and to be a missionary among indigenous peoples: Fill us with compassion and respect for all people, and empower us for the work of ministry throughout the world; through Jesus Christ our Lord, who lives and reigns with you and the Holy Spirit, one God, for ever and ever. Amen.

For Liturgical Celebration: [Common of a Missionary, A11] [Common of a Pastor, A14] [For the Ministry III, A51] [For the Mission of the Church, A52]

January 9

Julia Chester Emery
Missionary, 1922

Julia Chester Emery was born in Dorchester, Massachusetts, on September 24, 1852. In 1876 she succeeded her sister, Mary, as Secretary of the Woman's Auxiliary of the Board of Missions, which had been established by the General Convention in 1871.

During the forty years she served as Secretary, Julia helped the Church to recognize its call to proclaim the gospel both at home and overseas. Her faith, her courage, her spirit of adventure, and her ability to inspire others combined to make her a leader respected and valued by the whole Church.

She visited every diocese and missionary district within the United States, encouraging and expanding the work of the Woman's Auxiliary, and in 1908 she served as a delegate to the Pan-Anglican Congress in London. From there she traveled around the world, visiting missions in remote areas of China, in Japan, Hong Kong, the Philippines, Hawaii, and then all the dioceses on the Pacific Coast before returning to New York. In spite of the fact that travel was not easy, she wrote that she went forth "with hope for enlargement of vision, opening up new occasions for service, acceptance of new tasks."

Through her leadership a network of branches of the Woman's Auxiliary was established which shared a vision of and a commitment to the Church's mission. An emphasis on educational programs, a growing recognition of social issues, development of leadership among women, and the creation of the United Thank Offering are a further part of the legacy Julia left to the Church when she retired in 1916.

In 1921, the year before she died, on January 9, 1922, the following appeared in the *Spirit of Missions*: "In all these enterprises of the Church, no single agency has done so much in the last half-century to further the Church's Mission as the Woman's Auxiliary." Much of that accomplishment was due to the creative spirit of its Secretary for forty of those fifty years, Julia Chester Emery.

Rite I   God of all creation, thou callest us in Christ to make disciples of all nations and to proclaim thy mercy and love: Grant that we, after the example of thy servant Julia Chester Emery, may have vision and courage in proclaiming the Gospel to the ends of the earth; through Jesus Christ, our light and our salvation, who liveth and reigneth with thee and the Holy Spirit, one God, for ever and ever. Amen.

Rite II   God of all creation, you call us in Christ to make disciples of all nations and to proclaim your mercy and love: Grant that we, after the example of your servant Julia Chester Emery, may have vision and courage in proclaiming the Gospel to the ends of the earth; through Jesus Christ, our light and our salvation, who lives and reigns with you and the Holy Spirit, one God, for ever and ever. Amen.

For Liturgical Celebration: [Common of a Missionary, A11] [For the Ministry III, A51] [For the Mission of the Church, A52]

January 10

William Laud
Archbishop of Canterbury, 1645

William Laud, born in 1573, became Archbishop of Canterbury in 1633, having been Charles I's principal ecclesiastical adviser for several years before. He was the most prominent of a new generation of churchmen who disliked many of the ritual practices which had developed during the reign of Elizabeth I, and who were bitterly opposed by the Puritans.

Laud believed the Church of England to be in direct continuity with the medieval Church, and he stressed the unity of Church and State, exalting the role of the king as the supreme governor. He emphasized the priesthood and the sacraments, particularly the Eucharist, and caused consternation by insisting on the reverencing of the altar, returning it to its pre-Reformation position against the east wall of the church, and hedging it about with rails.

As head of the courts of High Commission and Star Chamber, Laud was abhorred for the harsh sentencing of prominent Puritans. His identification with the unpopular policies of King Charles, his support of the war against Scotland in 1640, and his efforts to make the Church independent of Parliament, made him widely disliked. He was impeached for treason by the Long Parliament in 1640, and finally beheaded on January 10, 1645.

Laud's reputation has remained controversial to this day. Honored as a martyr and condemned as an intolerant bigot, he was compassionate in his defense of the rights of the common people against the landowners. He was honest, devout, loyal to the king and to the rights and privileges of the Church of England. He tried to reform and protect the Church in accordance with his sincere convictions. But in many ways he was out of step with the views of the majority of his countrymen, especially about the "Divine Right of Kings."

He made a noble end, praying on the scaffold: "The Lord receive my soul, and have mercy upon me, and bless this kingdom with peace and charity, that there may not be this effusion of Christian blood amongst them."

Rite I   Keep us, O Lord, constant in faith and zealous in witness, that, like thy servant William Laud, we may live in thy fear, die in thy favor, and rest in thy peace; for the sake of Jesus Christ thy Son our Lord, who liveth and reigneth with thee and the Holy Spirit, one God, for ever and ever. Amen.

Rite II   Keep us, O Lord, constant in faith and zealous in witness, that, like your servant William Laud, we may live in your fear, die in your favor, and rest in your peace; for the sake of Jesus Christ your Son our Lord, who lives and reigns with you and the Holy Spirit, one God, for ever and ever. Amen.

For Liturgical Celebration: [Common of a Pastor, A14] [Common of a Martyr, A7] [Of the Holy Cross, A41]

January 12
Aelred, Abbot of Rievaulx
1167

Aelred was born in 1109, of a family which had long been treasurers of the shrine of Cuthbert of Lindisfarne at Durham Cathedral. While still a youth, he was sent for education in upper-class life to the court of King David of Scotland, son of Queen Margaret. The King's stepsons, Simon and Waldef, were his models and intimate friends. After intense disillusion and inner struggle, Aelred went to Yorkshire, where he became a Cistercian monk at the abbey of Rievaulx in 1133.

Aelred soon became a major figure in English church life. Sent to Rome on diocesan affairs of Archbishop William of York, he returned by way of Clairvaux. Here he made a deep impression on Bernard, who encouraged the young monk to write his first work, *Mirror of Charity*, on Christian perfection. In 1143, Aelred led the founding of a new Cistercian house at Revesby. Four years later, he was appointed abbot of Rievaulx. By the time of his death from kidney disease in 1167, the abbey had more than 600 monks, including Aelred's biographer and friend, Walter Daniel. During this period, Aelred wrote his best known work, *Spiritual Friendship*.

Friendship, Aelred teaches, is both a gift from God and a creation of human effort. While love is universal, freely given to all, friendship is a particular love between individuals, of which the example is Jesus and John the Beloved Disciple. As abbot, Aelred allowed his monks to hold hands and give other expressions of friendship. In the spirit of Anselm of Canterbury and Bernard of Clairvaux, Aelred writes:

> There are four qualities which characterize a friend: Loyalty, right intention, discretion, and patience. Right intention seeks for nothing other than God and natural good. Discretion brings understanding of what is done on a friend's behalf, and ability to know when to correct faults. Patience enables one to be justly rebuked, or to bear adversity on another's behalf. Loyalty guards and protects friendship, in good or bitter times.

Aelred died in 1167.

Rite I   Almighty God, who didst endow thy abbot Aelred with the gift of Christian friendship and the wisdom to lead others in the way of holiness: Grant to thy people that same spirit of mutual affection, that, in loving one another, we may know the love of Christ and rejoice in the gift of thy eternal goodness; through the same Jesus Christ our Savior, who liveth and reigneth with thee and the Holy Spirit, one God, now and for ever. Amen.

Rite II   Almighty God, you endowed the abbot Aelred with the gift of Christian friendship and the wisdom to lead others in the way of holiness: Grant to your people that same spirit of mutual affection, that, in loving one another, we may know the love of Christ and rejoice in the gift of your eternal goodness; through the same Jesus Christ our Savior, who lives and reigns with you and the Holy Spirit, one God, now and for ever. Amen.

For Liturgical Celebration: [Common of a Monastic or Professed Religious, A20] [For all Baptized Christians, A42]

January 13

Hilary, Bishop of Poitiers
367

Hilary, Bishop of Poitiers, was a prolific writer on Scripture and doctrine, an orator, and a poet to whom some of the earliest Latin hymns have been attributed. Augustine called him "the illustrious doctor of the Churches." Jerome considered him "the trumpet of the Latins against the Arians."

Hilary was born in Poitiers, in Gaul, about 315, into a pagan family of wealth and power. In his writings, he describes the stages of the spiritual journey that led him to the Christian faith. He was baptized when he was about thirty.

In 350, Hilary was made Bishop of Poitiers. Although he demurred, he was finally persuaded by the people's acclamations. He proved to be a bishop of skill and courage. His orthodoxy was shown when, in 355, the Emperor Constantius ordered all bishops to sign a condemnation of Athanasius, under pain of exile. Hilary wrote to Constantius, pleading for peace and unity. His plea accomplished nothing, and, when he dissociated himself from three Arian bishops in the West, Constantius ordered Julian (later surnamed the Apostate) to exile him to Phrygia. There he remained for three years, without complaining, writing scriptural commentaries and his principal work, *On the Trinity*.

Hilary was then invited by a party of "semi-Arians," who hoped for his support, to a Council at Seleucia in Asia, largely attended by Arians; but with remarkable courage, in the midst of a hostile gathering, Hilary defended the Council of Nicaea and the Trinity, giving no aid to the "semi-Arians." He wrote again to Constantius, offering to debate Saturninus, the Western bishop largely responsible for his exile. The Arians feared the results of such an encounter and persuaded Constantius to return Hilary to Poitiers.

In 360, Hilary was welcomed back to his see with great demonstrations of joy and affection. He continued his battle against Arianism, but he never neglected the needs of his people. Angry in controversy with heretical bishops, he was always a loving and compassionate pastor to his diocese. He died in Poitiers in 367. Among his disciples was Martin, later Bishop of Tours, whom Hilary encouraged in his endeavors to promote the monastic life.

The hymn "Hail this day's joyful return" (*The Hymnal 1982*, #223; #224) is attributed to Hilary.

Rite I   O Lord our God, who didst raise up thy servant Hilary to be a champion of the catholic faith: Keep us steadfast in that true faith which we professed at our baptism, that we may rejoice in having thee for our Father, and may abide in thy Son, in the fellowship of the Holy Spirit; thou who livest and reignest for ever and ever. Amen.

Rite II O Lord our God, you raised up your servant Hilary to be a champion of the catholic faith: Keep us steadfast in that true faith which we professed at our baptism, that we may rejoice in having you for our Father, and may abide in your Son, in the fellowship of the Holy Spirit; who live and reign for ever and ever. Amen.

For Liturgical Celebration: [Common of a Pastor, A14] [Common of a Theologian and Teacher, A17] [Of the Holy Trinity, A37]

January 15

(alternative date for Martin Luther King, Jr. – see April 4)

January 16

Richard Meux Benson, *Religious, 1915,*
and Charles Gore,
Bishop of Worcester, of Birmingham, and of Oxford, 1932

Richard Meux Benson and Charles Gore are remembered for their role in the revival of Anglican monasticism in the nineteenth century.

Richard Meux Benson, the principal founder of the Society of Saint John the Evangelist, was born on July 6, 1824, in London. As a student at Christ Church, Oxford, he came under the influence of Edward Bouverie Pusey, who became his spiritual mentor and lifelong friend.

In 1849 Benson was ordained a priest and became rector of Cowley, a village neighboring Oxford. In 1866, together with two other priests, he founded the Society of Saint John the Evangelist (SSJE), "a small body to realize and intensify the gifts and energies belonging to the whole Church." SSJE became the first permanent religious community for men in the Church of England since the Reformation, styled as a missionary order patterned on St. Vincent de Paul's Company of Mission Priests. Benson wrote the original SSJE Rule and served as Superior until 1890. Under his leadership, other SSJE houses were founded in Boston, Bombay, Cape Town, and elsewhere. In his writing and person, Benson is remembered as someone with an abiding love for God, the quality of which drew others into deeper lives of commitment to God.

Benson died on January 14, 1915, in England.

Charles Gore was born in 1853 in Wimbledon and educated at Oxford. He was ordained in 1876 and served in positions at Cuddesdon College and Pusey House, Oxford, both of which were focused upon theological education and the formation of clergy. While at Pusey House, Gore founded the Community of the Resurrection, a community for men that sought to combine the rich traditions of the religious life with a lively concern for the demands of ministry in the modern world.

Gore, a prolific writer, was a principal leader of liberal Anglo-Catholicism in late nineteenth and early twentieth century Anglicanism. He was concerned to make available to the Church the critical scholarship of the age, particularly with respect to the Bible, as reflected in *Lux Mundi*, the collection of essays he edited in 1889. A second but no less important concern was to prick the conscience of the church and plead for its engagement in the work of social justice for all. Between 1902 and 1919, Gore served successively as bishop of the dioceses of Worcester, Birmingham, and Oxford.

Gore died in London on January 17, 1932.

Rite I   Gracious God, who hast inspired a rich variety of ministries in thy Church: We offer thanks for Richard Meux Benson and Charles Gore, instruments in the revival of Anglican monasticism. Grant that we, following their example, may call for perennial renewal in thy Church through conscious union with Christ, witnessing to the social justice that is a mark of the reign of our Savior Jesus, who is the light of the world; and who liveth and reigneth with thee and the Holy Spirit, one God, for ever and ever. Amen.

Rite II Gracious God, you have inspired a rich variety of ministries in your Church: We give you thanks for Richard Meux Benson and Charles Gore, instruments in the revival of Anglican monasticism. Grant that we, following their example, may call for perennial renewal in your Church through conscious union with Christ, witnessing to the social justice that is a mark of the reign of our Savior Jesus, who is the light of the world; and who lives and reigns with you and the Holy Spirit, one God, for ever and ever. Amen.

For Liturgical Celebration: [Common of a Monastic or Professed Religious, A20] [Common of a Pastor, A14] [Common of a Theologian and Teacher, A17] [Of the Incarnation, A39]

January 17

Antony
Abbot in Egypt, 356

In the third century, many young men turned away from the corrupt and decadent society of the time, and went to live in deserts or on mountains, in solitude, fasting, and prayer. Antony of Egypt was an outstanding example of this movement, but he was not merely a recluse. He was a founder of monasticism, and wrote a rule for anchorites.

Antony's parents were Christians, and he grew up to be quiet, devout, and meditative. When his parents died, he and his younger sister were left to care for a sizable estate. Six months later, in church, he heard the reading about the rich young ruler whom Christ advised to sell all he had and give to the poor. Antony at once gave his land to the villagers and sold most of his goods, giving the proceeds to the poor. Later, after meditating on Christ's bidding, "Do not be anxious about tomorrow," he sold what remained of his possessions, placed his sister in a "house of maidens," and became an anchorite (solitary ascetic).

Athanasius, who knew Antony personally, writes that he spent his days praying, reading, and doing manual labor. For a time, he was tormented by demons in various guises. He resisted, and the demons fled. Moving to the mountains across the Nile from his village, Antony dwelt alone for twenty years. In 305, he left his cave and founded a "monastery," a series of cells inhabited by ascetics living under his rule. Athanasius writes of such colonies: "Their cells, like tents, were filled with singing, fasting, praying, and working, that they might give alms, and having love and peace with one another."

Antony visited Alexandria, first in 321, to encourage those suffering martyrdom under the Emperor Maximinus; later, in 355, to combat the Arians by preaching, conversions, and the working of miracles. Most of his days were spent on the mountain with his disciple Macarius.

He willed a goat-skin tunic and a cloak to Athanasius, who said of him: "He was like a physician given by God to Egypt. For who met him grieving and did not go away rejoicing? Who came full of anger and was not turned to kindness? . . . What monk who had grown slack was not strengthened by coming to him? Who came troubled by doubts and failed to gain peace of mind?"

Antony died in 356.

Rite I O God, by thy Holy Spirit thou didst enable thy servant Antony to withstand the temptations of the world, the flesh, and the devil: Give us grace, with pure hearts and minds, to follow thee, the only God; through Jesus Christ our Lord, who liveth and reigneth with thee and the same Spirit, one God, for ever and ever. Amen.

Rite II O God, by your Holy Spirit you enabled your servant Antony to withstand the temptations of the world, the flesh, and the devil: Give us grace, with pure hearts and minds, to follow you, the only God; through Jesus Christ our Lord, who lives and reigns with you and the Holy Spirit, one God, for ever and ever. Amen.

For Liturgical Celebration: [Common of a Monastic or Professed Religious, A20] [Of the Holy Spirit, A38]

January 19

Wulfstan
Bishop of Worcester, 1095

Wulfstan was one of the few Anglo-Saxon bishops to retain his see after the Norman Conquest of England in 1066. Beloved by all classes of society for his humility, charity, and courage, he was born in Warwickshire about 1008, and educated in the Benedictine abbeys of Evesham and Peterborough. He spent most of his life in the cathedral monastery of Worcester as monk, prior, and then as bishop of the see from 1062 until his death on January 18, 1095. He accepted the episcopate with extreme reluctance, but having resigned himself to it, he administered the diocese with great effectiveness. Since the see of Worcester was claimed by the province of York before its affiliation as a suffragan see of Canterbury in 1070, Wulfstan was consecrated at York. As bishop, he rapidly became famous for his continued monastic asceticism and personal sanctity.

Even though Wulfstan had been sympathetic to King Harold of Wessex, he was among those who submitted to William the Conqueror at Berkhamstead in 1066. He therefore was allowed to retain his see. At first, the Normans tended to disparage him for his lack of learning and his inability to speak French, but he became one of William's most trusted advisers and administrators, and remained loyal in support of William I and William II in their work of reform and orderly government. He assisted in the compilation of the Domesday Book and supported William I against the rebellious barons in 1075. William came to respect a loyalty based on principle and not on self-seeking. Archbishop Lanfranc also recognized the strength of Wulfstan's character, and the two men worked together to end the practice at Bristol of kidnaping Englishmen and selling them as slaves in Ireland.

Because he was the most respected prelate of the Anglo-Saxon Church, Wulfstan's profession of canonical obedience to William the Conqueror's Archbishop of Canterbury, Lanfranc, proved to be a key factor in the transition from Anglo-Saxon to Anglo-Norman

Christianity. William's policy, however, was to appoint his own fellow Normans to the English episcopate, and, by the time of William's death, in 1087, Wulfstan was the only English-born bishop still living.

Rite I Almighty God, whose only-begotten Son led captivity captive and gave gifts to thy people: Multiply among us faithful pastors, who, like thy holy bishop Wulfstan, will give courage to those who are oppressed and held in bondage; and bring us all, we pray, into the true freedom of thy kingdom; through Jesus Christ our Lord, who liveth and reigneth with thee and the Holy Spirit, one God, for ever and ever. Amen.

Rite II Almighty God, your only-begotten Son led captivity captive and gave gifts to your people: Multiply among us faithful pastors, who, like your holy bishop Wulfstan, will give courage to those who are oppressed and held in bondage; and bring us all, we pray, into the true freedom of your kingdom; through Jesus Christ our Lord, who lives and reigns with you and the Holy Spirit, one God, for ever and ever. Amen.

For Liturgical Celebration: [Common of a Pastor, A14] [For the Ministry II, A50] [For the Unity of the Church, A48]

January 20

Fabian
Bishop and Martyr of Rome, 250

In 236, an assembly was held at Rome to elect a pope as successor to Antherus. In the throng was Fabian, a layman from another part of Italy. Suddenly, according to the historian Eusebius, a dove flew over the crowd and lighted on Fabian's head. In spite of the fact that he was both a total stranger and not even a candidate for election, the people unanimously chose Fabian to be pope, shouting, "He is worthy! He is worthy!" Fabian was ordained to the episcopate without opposition.

During his fourteen years as pontiff, Fabian made numerous administrative reforms. He developed the parochial structure of the Church in Rome, and established the custom of venerating martyrs at their shrines in the catacombs. He appointed seven deacons and seven sub-deacons to write the lives of the martyrs, so that their deeds should not be forgotten in times to come.

When Privatus, in Africa, stirred up a new heresy, Fabian vigorously opposed and condemned his actions. He also brought back to Rome, for proper burial, the remains of Pontian, a pope whom the emperor had exiled in 235 to a certain and rapid death in the mines of Sardinia.

The Emperor Decius ordered a general persecution of the Church in 239 and 240, probably the first persecution to be carried out in all parts of the empire. Fabian was one of the earliest of those martyred, setting a courageous example for his followers, many of whom died in great torment.

Cyprian of Carthage, in a letter to Cornelius, Fabian's successor, wrote that Fabian was an incomparable man. "The glory of his death," Cyprian commented, "befitted the purity and holiness of his life."

Fabian's tombstone, the slab which covered his gravesite, still exists. It is in fragments, but the words "Fabian . . . bishop . . . martyr" are still dimly visible.

Rite I   Almighty God, who didst call Fabian to be a faithful pastor and servant of thy people, and to lay down his life in witness to thy Son: Grant that we, strengthened by his example and aided by his prayers, may in times of trial and persecution remain steadfast in faith and endurance, for the sake of him who laid down his life for us all, Jesus Christ our Savior; who liveth and reigneth with thee and the Holy Spirit, one God, for ever and ever. Amen.

Rite II Almighty God, you called Fabian to be a faithful pastor and servant of your people, and to lay down his life in witness to your Son: Grant that we, strengthened by his example and aided by his prayers, may in times of trial and persecution remain steadfast in faith and endurance, for the sake of him who laid down his life for us all, Jesus Christ our Savior; who lives and reigns with you and the Holy Spirit, one God, for ever and ever. Amen.

For Liturgical Celebration: [Common of a Pastor, A14] [Common of a Martyr, A7] [Of the Holy Cross, A41]

January 21

Agnes
Martyr at Rome, 304

As a child of twelve years, Agnes suffered for her faith, in Rome, during the cruel persecution of the Emperor Diocletian. After rejecting blandishments and withstanding threats and tortures by her executioner, she remained firm in refusal to offer worship to the heathen gods, and was burned at the stake—or, according to another early tradition, was beheaded with the sword. The early Fathers of the Church praised her courage and chastity, and remarked upon her name, which means "pure" in Greek and "lamb" in Latin.

Pilgrims still visit Agnes' tomb and the catacomb surrounding it, beneath the basilica of her name on the Via Nomentana in Rome that Pope Honorius I (625–638) built in her honor to replace an older shrine erected by the Emperor Constantine. On her feast day at the basilica, two lambs are blessed, whose wool is woven into a scarf called the pallium, with which the Pope invests archbishops. Pope Gregory the Great sent such a pallium in 601 to Augustine, the first Archbishop of Canterbury. A representation of the pall appears on the coat of arms of Archbishops of Canterbury to this day.

Rite I   Almighty and everlasting God, who dost choose those whom the world deemeth powerless to put the powerful to shame: Grant us so to cherish the memory of thy youthful martyr Agnes, that we may share her pure and steadfast faith in thee; through Jesus Christ our Lord, who liveth and reigneth with thee and the Holy Spirit, one God for ever and ever. Amen.

Rite II Almighty and everlasting God, you choose those whom the world deems powerless to put the powerful to shame: Grant us so to cherish the memory of your youthful martyr Agnes, that we may share her pure and steadfast faith in you; through Jesus Christ our Lord, who lives and reigns with you and the Holy Spirit, one God for ever and ever. Amen.

For Liturgical Celebration: [Common of a Martyr, A7] [Of the Holy Cross, A41]

January 22

Vincent
Deacon of Saragossa, and Martyr, 304

Vincent has been called the protomartyr of Spain. Little is known about the actual events surrounding his life, other than his name, his order of ministry, and the place and time of his martyrdom. He was a native of Huesca, in northeastern Spain, and was ordained deacon by Valerius, Bishop of Saragossa. In the early years of the fourth century, the fervent Christian community in Spain fell victim to a persecution ordered by the Roman emperors Diocletian and Maximian. Dacian, governor of Spain, arrested Valerius and his deacon Vincent, and had them imprisoned at Valencia.

According to one legend, Valerius had a speech impediment, and Vincent was often called upon to preach for him. When the two prisoners were challenged to renounce their faith, amid threats of torture and death, Vincent said to his bishop, "Father, if you order me, I will speak." Valerius is said to have replied, "Son, as I committed you to dispense the word of God, so I now charge you to answer in vindication of the faith which we defend." The young deacon then told the governor that he and his bishop had no intention of betraying the true God. The vehemence and enthusiasm of Vincent's defense showed no caution in his defiance of the judges, and Dacian's fury was increased by this exuberance in Christian witness. Valerius was exiled, but the angry Dacian ordered that Vincent be tortured.

Although the accounts of his martyrdom have been heavily embellished by early Christian poets, Augustine of Hippo writes that Vincent's unshakeable faith enabled him to endure grotesque punishments and, finally, death.

Records of the transfer and present whereabouts of Vincent's relics are of questionable authenticity. We are certain, however, that his cult spread rapidly throughout early Christendom and that he was venerated as a bold and outspoken witness to the truth of the living Christ.

Rite I   Almighty God, whose deacon Vincent, upheld by thee, was not terrified by threats nor overcome by torments: Strengthen us, we beseech thee, to endure all adversity with invincible and steadfast faith; through Jesus Christ our Lord, who liveth and reigneth with thee and the Holy Spirit, one God, for ever and ever. Amen.

Rite II   Almighty God, your deacon Vincent, upheld by you, was not terrified by threats nor overcome by torments: Strengthen us to endure all adversity with invincible and steadfast faith; through Jesus Christ our Lord, who lives and reigns with you and the Holy Spirit, one God, for ever and ever. Amen.

For Liturgical Celebration: [Common of a Martyr, A7] [For Social Service, A59] [Of the Holy Cross, A41]

January 23

Phillips Brooks
Bishop of Massachusetts, 1893

Writing about Phillips Brooks in 1930, William Lawrence, who as a young man had known him, began, "Phillips Brooks was a leader of youth . . . His was the spirit of adventure, in thought, life, and faith." To many who know him only as the author of "O little town of Bethlehem," this part of Brooks' life and influence is little known.

Born in Boston in 1835, Phillips Brooks began his ministry in Philadelphia. His impressive personality and his eloquence immediately attracted attention. After ten years in Philadelphia, he returned to Boston as rector of Trinity Church, which was destroyed in the Boston fire three years later. It is a tribute to Brooks' preaching, character, and leadership that in four years of worshiping in temporary and bare surroundings, the congregation grew and flourished. The new Trinity Church was a daring architectural enterprise for its day, with its altar placed in the center of the chancel, "a symbol of unity; God and man and all God's creation," and was a symbol of Brooks' vision—a fitting setting for the greatest preacher of the century.

This reputation has never been challenged. His sermons have passages that still grasp the reader, though they do not convey the warmth and vitality which so impressed his hearers. James Bryce wrote, "There was no sign of art about his preaching, no touch of self-consciousness. He spoke to his audience as a man might speak to his friend, pouring forth with swift, yet quiet and seldom impassioned earnestness, the thoughts of his singularly pure and lofty spirit."

Brooks died in Boston on January 23, 1893.

Brooks ministered with tenderness, understanding, and warm friendliness. He inspired men to enter the ministry, and taught many of them the art of preaching. He was conservative and orthodox in his theology; but his generosity of heart led him to be regarded as the leader of the liberal circles of the Church.

Rite I   O everlasting God, who didst reveal truth to thy servant Phillips Brooks, and didst so form and mold his mind and heart that he was able to mediate that truth with grace and power: Grant, we pray, that all whom thou dost call to preach the Gospel may steep themselves in thy Word, and conform their lives to thy will; through Jesus Christ our Lord, who liveth and reigneth with thee and the Holy Spirit, one God, for ever and ever. Amen.

Rite II O everlasting God, you revealed truth to your servant Phillips Brooks, and so formed and molded his mind and heart that he was able to mediate that truth with grace and power: Grant, we pray, that all whom you call to preach the Gospel may steep themselves in your Word, and conform their lives to your will; through Jesus Christ our Lord, who lives and reigns with you and the Holy Spirit, one God, for ever and ever. Amen.

For Liturgical Celebration: [Common of a Pastor, A14] [For the Ministry II, A50] [For the Mission of the Church, A52]

January 24

Ordination of Florence Li Tim-Oi
First Woman Priest in the Anglican Communion, 1944

Named by her father "much beloved daughter," Li Tim-Oi was born in Hong Kong in 1907. When she was baptized as a student, she chose the name of Florence in honor of Florence Nightingale. Florence studied at Union Theological College in Guangzhou (Canton). In 1938, upon graduation, she served in a lay capacity, first in Kowloon and then in nearby Macao.

In May 1941 Florence was ordained deaconess. Some months later, Hong Kong fell to Japanese invaders, and priests could not travel to Macao to celebrate the Eucharist. Despite this setback, Florence continued her ministry. Her work came to the attention of Bishop Ronald Hall of Hong Kong, who decided that "God's work would reap better results if she had the proper title" of priest.

On January 25, 1944, the Feast of the Conversion of St. Paul, Bishop Hall ordained her priest, the first woman so ordained in the Anglican Communion.

When World War II came to an end, Florence Li Tim-Oi's ordination was the subject of much controversy. She made the personal decision not to exercise her priesthood until it was acknowledged by the wider Anglican Communion. Undeterred, she continued to minister with great faithfulness, and in 1947 was appointed rector of St. Barnabas Church in Hepu where, on Bishop Hall's instructions, she was still to be called priest.

When the Communists came to power in China in 1949, Florence undertook theological studies in Beijing to further understand the implications of the Three-Self Movement (self-rule, self-support, and self- propagation) which now determined the life of the churches. She then moved to Guangzhou to teach and to serve at the Cathedral of Our Savior. However, for sixteen years, from 1958 onwards, during the Cultural Revolution, all churches were closed. Florence was forced to work first on a farm and then in a factory. Accused of counter-revolutionary activity, she was required to undergo political re-education. Finally, in 1974, she was allowed to retire from her work in the factory.

In 1979 the churches reopened, and Florence resumed her public ministry. Then, two years later, she was allowed to visit family members living in Canada. While there, to her great joy, she was licensed as a priest in the Diocese of Montreal and later in the Diocese of Toronto, where she finally settled, until her death on February 26, 1992.

Rite I Gracious God, we thank thee for calling Florence Li Tim-Oi, much-beloved daughter, to be the first woman to exercise the office of a priest in our Communion: By the grace of thy Spirit, inspire us to follow her example, serving thy people with patience and happiness all our days, and witnessing in every circumstance to our Savior Jesus Christ, who liveth and reigneth with thee and the same Spirit, one God, for ever and ever. Amen.

Rite II Gracious God, we thank you for calling Florence Li Tim-Oi, much-beloved daughter, to be the first woman to exercise the office of a priest in our Communion: By the grace of your Spirit, inspire us to follow her example, serving your people with patience and happiness all our days, and witnessing in every circumstance to our Savior Jesus Christ, who lives and reigns with you and the same Spirit, one God, for ever and ever. Amen.

For Liturgical Celebration: [Common of a Pastor, A14] [For the Ministry I, A49] [For the Mission of the Church, A52]

January 26

Timothy, Titus, and Silas
Companions of Saint Paul

Timothy and Silas are mentioned in The Acts of the Apostles. Timothy's father was Greek and his mother a Jewish believer. Paul chose him as a companion for his mission to Asia Minor but counseled that he be circumcised because the "Jews who were in those places" knew that his father was a Greek (Acts 16:1–3). Timothy undertook missions to the Thessalonians, Corinthians, and the Ephesians. Eusebius counts him as the first bishop of Ephesus.

Silas is mentioned by his Latinized name, Silvanus, in 1 & 2 Thessalonians 1:1. He was a prophet in the Jerusalem church (Acts 15:22–35), but also a Roman citizen (Acts 16:37–8). He went with Paul and Barnabas to deliver the decision of the apostolic council in Jerusalem (Acts 15:1–21) that Gentile believers did not have to observe the law of Moses. Paul chose Silas to accompany him on missions to Asia Minor and Macedonia, where he may have remained after Paul left (Acts 15:41–18:5). Tradition has it that he died there after some years of missionary work.

Titus, a Greek, accompanied Paul to Jerusalem for the apostolic council. Titus was sent on missions to Corinth, from which he gave Paul encouraging reports (2 Corinthians 7:13–15). Paul, who calls him "my true child in the common faith" (Titus 1:14), left him to organize the church in Crete (Titus 1:5), and Eusebius reports that he was the first bishop there.

Titus reportedly became Bishop of Crete, and died at Gortyn, on that island, near the end of the first century. Tradition holds that Silas became Bishop of Corinth, and died in Macedonia, although no date has been recorded.

These three are celebrated on the day after the Feast of the Conversion of St. Paul because of their close connections with him. Though they were all young and inexperienced, they were entrusted with missions and matters that helped form the very life and history of the Church.

Faithfulness, love, and devotion to Christ saw them through situations they could not have imagined.

Rite I   Almighty God, who didst call Timothy, Titus, and Silas to lay a foundation of faith for thy Church: Grant that we also may be living stones built upon the foundation of Jesus Christ our Savior; who with thee and the Holy Spirit liveth and reigneth, one God, now and for ever. Amen.

Rite II Almighty God, who called Timothy, Titus, and Silas to lay a foundation of faith for your Church: Grant that we also may be living stones built upon the foundation of Jesus Christ our Savior; who with you and the Holy Spirit lives and reigns, one God, now and for ever. Amen.

For Liturgical Celebration: [Common of a Pastor, A14] [Common of a Missionary, A11] [For the Ministry II, A50] [For the Mission of the Church, A52]

January 27

Lydia, Dorcas, and Phoebe
Witnesses to the Faith

The commemoration of these three devout women follows directly on the observance of three of Paul's male co-workers in the Lord. It is a reminder that though the first century was a patriarchal time from which we have very few women's voices, the apostles and indeed the whole early church depended on women for sustenance, protection, and support.

Lydia was Paul's first European convert. She was a Gentile woman in Philippi who, like many others, was attracted to Judaism. As what the Jewish community called a "God-fearer" she was undoubtedly accorded respect by the Jewish community, but still would have been marginalized. Paul encountered her on a riverbank where she and a group of women had gathered for Sabbath prayers. Undoubtedly Paul preached to them and Lydia "opened her heart" and, together with the whole household of which she was head, was baptized.

Lydia was a prosperous cloth-merchant and a person of means. She was able to lodge Paul, Timothy, and their companions in her house, which Paul used as a local base of operations (Acts 16:11-40).

Phoebe was the apparent patroness of the Christian community in Cenchreae near Corinth. She is the first person mentioned in the long list of Paul's beloved associates in Chapter 16 of Romans. Paul refers to her as a "sister," as a "deacon," and as a "patroness" or "helper" of many. In other words, Paul includes her as part of his family in Christ and infers that she has housed and provided legal cover for the local church. Paul's use of the word "deacon" should be regarded with caution, since the diaconate as an order had not yet developed in the Church, but it does suggest the kind of ministry out of which the notion of ordained deacons developed. It would not be too much to call her a "proto-deacon."

Dorcas (Tabitha in Aramaic) was a revered disciple in Joppa who devoted herself to "good works and acts of charity." When she fell ill and died, the community sent for Peter, who came and, after prayer, revived her (Acts 9:36-42).

Though we have no record of the words of these three women, the apostolic testimony to their faith and their importance to the mission of the early church speaks for itself.

Rite I Filled with thy Holy Spirit, gracious God, thine earliest disciples served thee with the gifts each had been given: Lydia in business and stewardship, Dorcas in a life of charity, and Phoebe as a deacon who served many. Inspire us today to build up thy Church with our gifts in hospitality, charity, and bold witness to the gospel of Christ; who liveth and reigneth with thee in the unity of the Holy Spirit, one God, now and for ever. Amen.

Rite II Filled with your Holy Spirit, gracious God, your earliest disciples served you with the gifts each had been given: Lydia in business and stewardship, Dorcas in a life of charity, and Phoebe as a deacon who served many. Inspire us today to build up your Church with our gifts in hospitality, charity, and bold witness to the gospel of Christ; who lives and reigns with you in the unity of the Holy Spirit, one God, now and for ever. Amen.

For Liturgical Celebration: [Common of a Missionary, A11] [For all Baptized Christians, A42] [For Social Service, A59] [For the Ministry III, A51]

January 28

Thomas Aquinas
Priest and Theologian, 1274

Thomas Aquinas is the greatest theologian of the high Middle Ages, and, next to Augustine, perhaps the greatest theologian in the history of Western Christianity. Born into a noble Italian family, probably in 1225, he entered the new Dominican Order of Preachers and soon became an outstanding teacher in an age of intellectual ferment.

Perceiving the challenges that the recent rediscovery of Aristotle's works might entail for traditional catholic doctrine, especially in its emphasis upon empirical knowledge derived from reason and sense perception, independent of faith and revelation, Thomas asserted that reason and revelation are in basic harmony. "Grace" (revelation), he said, "is not the denial of nature" (reason), "but the perfection of it." This synthesis Thomas accomplished in his greatest works, the *Summa Theologica* and the *Summa Contra Gentiles*, which even today continue to exercise profound influence on Christian thought and philosophy. He was considered a bold thinker, even a "radical," and certain aspects of his thought were condemned by the ecclesiastical authorities. His canonization on July 18, 1323, vindicated him.

Thomas understood God's disclosure of his Name, in Exodus 3:14, "I Am Who I Am," to mean that God is Being, the Ultimate Reality from which everything else derives its being. The difference between God and the world is that God's essence is to exist, whereas all other beings derive their being from him by the act of creation. Although, for Thomas, God and the world are distinct, there is, nevertheless, an analogy of being between God and the world, since the Creator is reflected in his creation. It is possible, therefore, to have a limited knowledge of God, by analogy from the created world. On this basis, human reason can demonstrate that God exists; that he created the world; and that he contains in himself, as their cause, all the perfections which exist in his creation. The distinctive truths of Christian faith, however, such as the Trinity and the Incarnation, are known only by revelation.

Thomas died in 1274, just under fifty years of age. In 1369, on January 28, his remains were transferred to Toulouse. In addition to his many theological writings, he composed several eucharistic hymns. They include "O saving Victim" (*The Hymnal 1982*, #310; #311) and "Now, my tongue, the mystery telling" (*The Hymnal 1982*, #329; #330; #331).

Rite I Almighty God, who hast enriched thy Church with the singular learning and holiness of thy servant Thomas Aquinas: Enlighten us more and more, we pray, by the disciplined thinking and teaching of Christian scholars, and deepen our devotion by the example of saintly lives; through Jesus Christ our Lord, who liveth and reigneth with thee and the Holy Spirit, one God, for ever and ever. Amen.

Rite II Almighty God, you have enriched your Church with the singular learning and holiness of your servant Thomas Aquinas: Enlighten us more and more, we pray, by the disciplined thinking and teaching of Christian scholars, and deepen our devotion by the example of saintly lives; through Jesus Christ our Lord, who lives and reigns with you and the Holy Spirit, one God, for ever and ever. Amen.

For Liturgical Celebration: [Common of a Theologian and Teacher, A17] [Common of a Monastic or Professed Religious, A20] [Of the Holy Trinity, A37]

January 29

Andrei Rublev
Monk and Iconographer, 1430

Generally acknowledged as Russia's greatest iconographer, Andrei Rublev was born around 1365 near Moscow. While very young, he entered the monastery of The Holy Trinity and, in 1405, with the blessing of his *igumen* (the Orthodox equivalent of abbot), he transferred to the Spaso-Andronikov monastery where he received the tonsure and studied iconography with Theophanes the Greek and the monk Daniel. Among his most revered works are those in the Dormition Cathedral in Vladimir, a city east of Moscow.

The icon ("image" in Greek) is central to Orthodox spirituality. It finds its place in liturgy and in personal devotion. An icon is two-dimensional; despite being an image of someone, it is not a physical portrait. Western art, especially since the Renaissance, has sought to represent figures or events so that the viewer might better imagine them. A Western crucifix seeks to enable us to imagine what Golgotha was like. Icons seek to provide immediate access to the spiritual and the divine unmediated by the human, historical imagination.

Rublev was trained in the spiritual discipline of iconography. Writing an icon involved the ritual of preparing the surface, applying the painted and precious metal background, and then creating the image, first outlining it in red. Throughout, he would repeatedly say the "Jesus Prayer" ("Lord Jesus, Son of God, have mercy on me"). He was creating a window into the Divine which he knew was always before him but which was invisible to the human eye. He knew he was able to create such an image of God because he himself was made in the image of God. His object was to be totally focused on receiving God's love and loving in return.

Rublev is best known for his icon of the Holy Trinity based on the story of the three visitors of Abraham in Genesis 18. He died peacefully in 1430. In 1551, the "Council of the One Hundred Chapters" decreed that all icons in the Russian church were to be drawn from the models provided by ancient Greek icon writers and Rublev.

As Jesus was the icon of God, so each one of us is also. Ascetic practice aims at freeing that image from sinful distraction and claiming it more and more. To venerate an icon is to find some of the ineffable beauty that is God, that is manifest in Christ and the saints, and is also in each one of us.

Rite I Holy God, we bless thee for the gift of thy monk and icon writer Andrei Rublev, who, inspired by the Holy Spirit, provided a window into heaven for generations to come, revealing the majesty and mystery of the holy and blessed Trinity; who liveth and reigneth through ages of ages. Amen.

Rite II Holy God, we bless you for the gift of your monk and icon writer Andrei Rublev, who, inspired by the Holy Spirit, provided a window into heaven for generations to come, revealing the majesty and mystery of the holy and blessed Trinity; who lives and reigns through ages of ages. Amen.

For Liturgical Celebration: [Common of an Arist, Writer, or Composer] [Common of a Monastic or Professed Religious, A20]

January 31

John Bosco
Priest, 1888

John Bosco was born on August 16, 1815, near Turin, Italy. His father died when he was two, leaving his mother to provide marginal subsistence for the family. He showed a remarkably sweet and kind disposition, which put him at odds with many of the boys with whom he grew up. When he was nine, he received a vision: Christ and the Blessed Virgin encouraged him to be kind, obedient, and hard-working and told him that, in doing so, a great future would be shown him. Bosco always counted this as the beginning of his vocation.

Bosco was fascinated by the traveling circuses which visited his region and went about learning to juggle, walk a tightrope, and do magic tricks. He put on local "shows," which drew both children and adults. The "price" of admission to these exhibitions was time spent at the end of the show saying prayers together. With help from some patrons who recognized his intelligence and talent, he attended seminary, and, after ordination, he obtained an appointment as chaplain to a girls boarding school. Because of his teaching ministry, he was accorded the title "Don."

Bosco was not satisfied ministering only to well-to-do young women. In time, every Sunday and feast day the campus filled up with local boys who came for catechism, basic schooling, and supervised play. The raucous energy of the boys scandalized the school and Don Bosco was fired. In 1846 he was able to open an orphanage and put the new work under the patronage of St. Francis de Sales. With the help of an assistant priest and some seminarians he had groomed from among his boys, he formed the Salesian Order. This order, grudgingly admired by secular politicians, was recognized by the Pope and grew to include women religious, lay brothers, and dedicated laity, operating orphanages, vocational schools, and nighttime primary schools for working people.

Don Bosco summed up his theory of education: "Every education teaches a philosophy by suggestion, implication, atmosphere. Every part has a connection with every other part. If it does not combine to convey some general view of life, it is not education at all."

Don Bosco died in Turin on January 31, 1888.

Rite I   Loving God, who dost tenderly care for children and orphans: Fill us with love like that shown forth in the witness of John Bosco, that we may give ourselves completely to thy service and to the salvation of all; through thy Son Jesus Christ, who liveth and reigneth with thee and the Holy Spirit, one God, for ever and ever. Amen.

Rite II Loving God, who tenderly cares for children and orphans: Fill us with love like that shown forth in the witness of John Bosco, that we may give ourselves completely to your service and to the salvation of all; through your Son Jesus Christ, who lives and reigns with you and the Holy Spirit, one God, for ever and ever. Amen.

For Liturgical Celebration: [Common of a Pastor, A14] [For Education, A60]

January 31
Samuel Shoemaker
Priest and Evangelist, 1963

Born in Baltimore on December 27, 1893, Samuel Shoemaker was a highly influential priest of The Episcopal Church and is remembered for his empowerment of the ministry of the laity.

While attending Princeton University, Shoemaker came under the influence of several major evangelical thinkers, among them Robert Speer and John Mott. After college, he spent several years in China and came under the influence of Frank Buchman, founder of the Oxford Group, a group initially oriented toward the personal evangelization of the wealthy and influential. Although he would eventually break from Buchman, aspects of the Oxford Group's approach would influence Shoemaker for the rest of his life.

Training for the priesthood at General Theological Seminary, Shoemaker became an Episcopal priest in 1921. After a brief curacy and further involvement with student ministry at Princeton, Shoemaker was called in 1925 to become the Rector of Calvary Church, New York City, a post he held for sixteen years. During his tenure, Calvary's ministry grew exponentially, largely through Shoemaker's ability to hold in creative tension the power of personal evangelism and giving authentic witness to one's faith while remaining faithful to the liturgical and sacramental traditions of the Church.

Two significant movements—Faith at Work and Alcoholics Anonymous—have their roots in Shoemaker's work at Calvary Church, New York. Faith at Work, founded in 1926, grew out of Shoemaker's passion for personal witness in the workplace. In the 1940's, the movement became increasingly ecumenical and many of the leaders of spiritual renewal in mainstream American evangelicalism have connections to Shoemaker's Faith at Work movement.

Also during Shoemaker's tenure at Calvary, New York, Alcoholics Anonymous was founded. Although Shoemaker did not create A.A., his work provided the foundation, based upon principles he learned earlier from the Oxford Group, for the recognition and flourishing of the movement. Much of the teaching upon which A.A. is built bears the unmistakable influence of Shoemaker, who is generally regarded as the spiritual mentor of the movement.

Later in life, Shoemaker served as Rector of Calvary Church, Pittsburgh. He died on January 31, 1963 in Baltimore.

Rite I   Holy God, we give thanks to thee for the vision of Samuel Shoemaker, who labored for the renewal of all people: Grant, we pray, that we may follow his example to help others find salvation through the knowledge and love of Jesus Christ our Savior; who with thee and the Holy Spirit liveth and reigneth, one God, for ever and ever. Amen.

Rite II   Holy God, we thank you for the vision of Samuel Shoemaker, who labored for the renewal of all people: Grant, we pray, that we may follow his example to help others find salvation through the knowledge and love of Jesus Christ our Savior; who with you and the Holy Spirit lives and reigns, one God, for ever and ever. Amen.

For Liturgical Celebration: [Common of a Pastor, A14] [Common of a Missionary, A11] [For the Ministry I, A49] [For the Mission of the Church, A52]

FEBRUARY

1 Brigid (Bride), 523
2
3 The Dorchester Chaplains: Lieutenant George Fox, Lieutenant Alexander D. Goode, Lieutenant Clark V. Poling, and Lieutenant John P. Washington, 1943
4 Anskar, Archbishop of Hamburg, Missionary to Denmark and Sweden, 865
5 Roger Williams, 1683, and Anne Hutchinson, 1643, Prophetic Witnesses
6 The Martyrs of Japan, 1597
7 Cornelius the Centurion
8
9
10
11 Frances Jane (Fanny) Van Alstyne Crosby, Hymnwriter, 1915
12 Charles Freer Andrews, Priest and "Friend of the Poor" in India, 1940
13 Absalom Jones, Priest, 1818
14 Cyril, Monk, and Methodius, Bishop, Missionaries to the Slavs, 869, 885
15 Thomas Bray, Priest and Missionary, 1730
16 Charles Todd Quintard, Bishop of Tennessee, 1898
17 Janani Luwum, Archbishop of Uganda, and Martyr, 1977
18 Martin Luther, Theologian, 1546
19
20 Frederick Douglass, Orator and Advocate for Truth and Justice, 1895
21 John Henry Newman, Priest and Theologian, 1890
22 Eric Liddell, Missionary to China, 1945

23 Polycarp, Bishop and Martyr of Smyrna, 156
24
25 John Roberts, Priest, 1949
26 Emily Malbone Morgan, Prophetic Witness, 1937
27 George Herbert, Priest, 1633
28 Anna Julia Haywood Cooper, 1964, and Elizabeth Evelyn Wright, 1904, Educators
29

February 1
Brigid (Bride)
523

Born at Fauchart about the middle of the fifth century, Brigid may have met Patrick as a young girl. She was said to be the daughter of Dubhthach, poet laureate of King Loeghaire, and was reared in a Druid household. She decided early in life to dedicate her life to God alone as a Christian. She received a nun's veil from Bishop Macaile of Westmeath.

Gathering around her a group of women, Brigid, in 470, founded a nunnery at Kildare, a place whose name meant "Church of the Oak." Here had flourished the cult of a pagan goddess honored with a sacred fire which she and her successors maintained. To secure the sacraments, Brigid persuaded the anchorite Conlaed to receive episcopal ordination and to bring his community of monks to Kildare, thus establishing the only known Irish double monastery of men and women. Brigid actively participated in policy-making decisions in Church conventions. One story has it that she received episcopal orders, which may reflect only the fact that she exercised the jurisdictional authority that was customarily wielded by medieval abbesses.

Next to Patrick, Brigid is the most beloved of Irish saints. Many stories are told of Brigid's concern for the poor and needy. When a leper woman asked for milk, she was healed also of her infirmity. Two blind men were given their sight. Best known is the tale of Brigid's taming of a wolf at the request of a local chieftain. Her feast day itself, February 1, was long held sacred as Imbolg, the Celtic festival of Spring.

Brigid died about 523 at Kildare, outside whose small cathedral the foundations of her original nunnery, with its fire shrine, are still shown to tourists. Her remains are said to have been re-interred, at the time of the Danish invasions of the ninth century, with those of Patrick, at Downpatrick.

Brigid, also known as Bride, was also very popular in England, Scotland, and Wales (under her Gaelic name Ffraid) where many churches have been dedicated to her. The best known of them is that church which was designed by Christopher Wren on Fleet Street in London.

Rite I   O God, by whose grace thy servant Brigid, kindled with the flame of thy love, became a burning and a shining light in thy Church: Grant that we also may be aflame with the spirit of love and discipline, and walk before thee as children of light; through Jesus Christ our Lord, who liveth and reigneth with thee, in the unity of the Holy Spirit, one God, now and ever. Amen.

Rite II   O God, by whose grace your servant Brigid, kindled with the flame of your love, became a burning and a shining light in your Church: Grant that we also may be aflame with the spirit of love and discipline, and walk before you as children of light; through Jesus Christ our Lord, who lives and reigns with you, in the unity of the Holy Spirit, one God, now and ever. Amen.

For Liturgical Celebration: [Common of a Monastic or Professed Religious, A20] [Of the Holy Spirit, A38] [Of the Incarnation, A39]

February 3

The Dorchester Chaplains:
Lieutenant George Fox, Lieutenant Alexander D. Goode, Lieutenant Clark V. Poling, and Lieutenant John P. Washington, 1943

On January 23, 1943, the USAT Dorchester, a converted cruise ship, set sail with a troop convoy from New York City for Greenland with 902 persons on board. Among them were four U.S. Army chaplains, Lt. George L. Fox (Methodist), Lt. Alexander D. Goode (Jewish), Lt. Clark V. Poling (Dutch Reformed), and Lt. John P. Washington (Roman Catholic).

George Fox had served as a medical corps assistant in World War I, where he was decorated for heroism. Alexander Goode joined the National Guard while he was studying for the rabbinate. Clark Poling's father told him that chaplains had a high mortality rate. He prayed for strength, courage, and understanding, then joined the Army Chaplains Corps. John Washington was a gang leader in Newark, New Jersey, when he was called to the priesthood.

On February 3, one day from their destination, a German U-boat fired torpedoes, striking the boiler room of the Dorchester. Even though everyone was sleeping with their life jackets, many of the soldiers left them behind as they clambered topside to seek escape and safety. Unfortunately, only two of the fourteen lifeboats were successfully lowered into the water, making it necessary for most men to dive into the nineteen degree water.

The four chaplains moved among the men, assisting, calming, and passing out life jackets from the ship's store to those forced to jump into the freezing ocean. Having given up their own life vests to save the lives of the soldiers, the chaplains remained on the aft deck, arms linked in prayer until the ship sank, claiming their lives. Two hundred thirty men were rescued from the icy waters by other ships in the convoy. Many survived because of the selflessness and heroism of the four chaplains. The memory of the self-sacrifice of these chaplains is maintained today within the the United States military chaplains corps.

Chaplains Fox, Goode, Poling, and Washington responded to a high calling to represent God's love among men of war. On the day they died, they personified the words of Jesus found in John 15:13, "Greater love has no one than this, that he lay down his life for his friends."

Rite I Holy God, who didst inspire the Dorchester chaplains to be models of steadfast sacrificial love in a tragic and terrifying time: Help us to follow their example, that their courageous ministry may inspire chaplains, and all who serve, to recognize thy presence in the midst of peril; through Jesus Christ our Savior, who liveth and reigneth with thee and the Holy Spirit, one God, for ever and ever. Amen.

Rite II Holy God, you inspired the Dorchester chaplains to be models of steadfast sacrificial love in a tragic and terrifying time: Help us to follow their example, that their courageous ministry may inspire chaplains and all who serve,to recognize your presence in the midst of peril; through Jesus Christ our Savior, who lives and reigns with you and the Holy Spirit, one God, for ever and ever. Amen.

For Liturgical Celebration: [Common of a Pastor, A14] [Common of a Martyr, A7] [Of the Holy Cross, A41]

February 4

Anskar, Archbishop of Hamburg
Missionary to Denmark and Sweden, 865

Anskar (Latinized as Ansgarius) was one of those valiant Christians of whom it might be said, "These shall plant the seed, but others shall reap the harvest." As Archbishop of Hamburg, he was papal legate for missionary work among the Scandinavians. The immediate result of his devoted and perilous labors was slight: two churches established on the border of Denmark and one priest settled in Sweden. He also participated in the consecration of Gotbert, first bishop in Sweden.

Anskar was born in the Somme region of France in 801, and educated in the outstanding monastic school near Corbie. His teaching skill led him to be chosen to be sent out by Corbie as master of a new monastery school, in Saxon Germany. His strongest call, however, was to be a missionary.

He was stirred, his biographer Rimbert says, by a prolonged vision, in which a voice said, "Go and return to me crowned with martyrdom." When King Harald of Denmark sought missionaries for that country in 826, Anskar was one of those selected. Rimbert notes that Anskar's missionary purpose caused astonishment. Why should he wish to leave his brothers to deal with "unknown and barbarous folk"? Some of the brethren tried to deter him; others mocked him.

Steadfast in his resolve, Anskar established a school and mission in Denmark, working conscientiously but unsuccessfully to convert and evangelize. He was not totally discouraged. Another vision appeared, with a voice saying, "Go and declare the work of God to the nations." Shortly afterward (about 829), he was called to Sweden and eagerly accepted. Meager aid both from the monastery and the emperor frustrated his efforts.

While still a young man, Anskar was consecrated Archbishop of Hamburg in 831, and continued his work among the Scandinavians until 848, when he retired to the See of Bremen and died in 865. The seeds of his efforts were not to bear fruit until over one hundred years later, when Viking devastation, weakness in the Frankish Church, and the lowest ebb of missionary enthusiasm came to an end. The rich harvest of conversion was three generations away. Nevertheless, Anskar is looked upon by Scandinavians as their apostle.

Rite I   Almighty and everlasting God, who sent thy servant Anskar to sow the seeds of faith among the people of Scandinavia: Keep thy Church from discouragement in the day of small things, knowing that when thou hast begun a good work thou shalt bring it to a fruitful conclusion; through Jesus Christ our Lord, who liveth and reigneth with thee and the Holy Spirit, one God, for ever and ever. Amen.

Rite II   Almighty and everlasting God, who sent your servant Anskar to sow the seeds of faith among the people of Scandinavia: Keep your Church from discouragement in the day of small things, knowing that when you have begun a good work you will bring it to a fruitful conclusion; through Jesus Christ our Lord, who lives and reigns with you and the Holy Spirit, one God, for ever and ever. Amen.

For Liturgical Celebration: [Common of a Missionary, A11] [Common of a Pastor, A14] [For the Ministry II, A50] [For the Mission of the Church, A52]

February 5

Roger Williams, 1683, and
Anne Hutchinson, 1643
Prophetic Witnesses

Born in London in 1603, Roger Williams was ordained and served as a priest in the Church of England. Williams found that he could not abide by the rigorous, high-church policies of Archbishop William Laud, and in 1630, he sailed to New England in search of religious liberty.

Upon his arrival in Boston, Williams encountered further obstacles to religious freedom. In particular, Williams objected to the ability of the civil authorities to punish religious offenses, and in his book *The Bloody Tenet of Persecution,* he advocated for a "wall of separation" between civil and religious powers. He believed also in the fundamental right of all people to follow their consciences in matters of religious belief. He left Massachusetts and founded a nearby settlement called Providence, believing God had guided him to this new land. He was eventually granted a charter for the colony of Rhode Island, the new constitution of which granted wide religious latitude and freedom of practice. Williams founded the first Baptist Church in Providence, though he refused to be tied to the tenets of an established church.

Like Roger Williams, Anne Hutchinson (born Anne Marbury at Alford, Lincolnshire, England, in July 1591), also immigrated to Massachusetts in hope of finding religious freedom. She was an outspoken advocate of the rights and equality of women, challenging the dominant views of the Puritan leadership. She held Bible studies in her home for the women of her community, at which she welcomed critical examination of the faith. As a result of her activities, she found herself at odds with not only the religious authorities, but the state civil authorities as well, and, in 1638, she was tried by the General Court of Massachusetts, presided over by Governor John Winthrop, and was branded as a dangerous dissenter and banished from the colony. Anne eventually relocated to what is now the Bronx, New

York, where she and her family were killed, save one daughter, by a group of Siwanoy Indians on August 20, 1643.

Today, both Roger Williams and Anne Hutchinson are remembered as early champions of religious liberty in the United States and as prophets of the individual's freedom of fellowship with the Creator.

Rite I   O God, our light and salvation, who makest all free to worship thee: May we ever strive to be faithful to thy call, following the example of Roger Williams and Anne Hutchinson, that we may faithfully set our hands to the Gospel plow, confident in the truth proclaimed by thy Son Jesus Christ; who with thee and the Holy Spirit liveth and reigneth, one God, for ever and ever. Amen.

Rite II   O God, our light and salvation, who makes all free to worship you: May we ever strive to be faithful to your call, following the example of Roger Williams and Anne Hutchinson, that we may faithfully set our hands to the Gospel plow, confident in the truth proclaimed by your Son Jesus Christ; who with you and the Holy Spirit lives and reigns, one God, for ever and ever. Amen.

For Liturgical Celebration: [Common of a Prophetic Witness, A31] [Common of a Saint, A23]

February 6

The Martyrs of Japan
1597

The introduction of Christianity into Japan in the sixteenth century, first by the Jesuits under Francis Xavier, and then by the Franciscans, has left exciting records of heroism and self-sacrifice in the annals of Christian missionary endeavor. It has been estimated that by the end of that century there were about 300,000 baptized believers in Japan.

Unfortunately, these initial successes were compromised by rivalries among the religious orders; and the interplay of colonial politics, both within Japan and between Japan and the Spanish and Portuguese, aroused suspicion about western intentions of conquest. After a half century of ambiguous support by some of the powerful Tokugawa shoguns, the Christian enterprise suffered cruel persecution and suppression.

The first victims were six Franciscan friars and twenty of their converts who were crucified at Nagasaki, February 5, 1597. In his powerful novel *Silence*, based on the event, Shusaku Endo writes,

> "They were martyred. But what a martyrdom! I had long read about martyrdom in the lives of the saints—how the souls of the martyrs had gone home to Heaven, how they had been filled with glory in Paradise, how the angels had blown trumpets. This was the splendid martyrdom I had often seen in my dreams. But the martyrdom of the Japanese Christians I now describe to you was no such glorious thing. What a miserable and painful business it was! The rain falls unceasingly on the sea. And the sea which killed them surges on uncannily—in silence."

By 1630, what was left of Christianity in Japan was driven underground. Yet it is remarkable that two hundred and fifty years later there were found many men and women, without priests, who had preserved through the generations a vestige of Christian faith.

Rite I   O God our Father, who art the source of strength to all thy saints, and who didst bring the holy martyrs of Japan through the suffering of the cross to the joys of eternal life: Grant that we, encouraged by their example, may hold fast the faith we profess, even to death itself; through Jesus Christ our Lord, who liveth and reigneth with thee and the Holy Spirit, one God, now and for ever. Amen.

Rite II O God our Father, source of strength to all your saints, you brought the holy martyrs of Japan through the suffering of the cross to the joys of eternal life: Grant that we, encouraged by their example, may hold fast the faith we profess, even to death itself; through Jesus Christ our Lord, who lives and reigns with you and the Holy Spirit, one God, now and for ever. Amen.

For Liturgical Celebration: [Common of a Martyr, A7] [Of the Holy Cross, A41] [On the Anniversary of a Disaster, A67]

February 7

Cornelius the Centurion

All that we know about Cornelius is contained in the Acts of the Apostles (chapters 10–11). He was the first Gentile converted to the Christian faith, along with his household. A centurion was commander of a company of one hundred men in the Roman army, responsible for their discipline, both on the field of battle and in camp. A centurion was a Roman citizen, a military career man, well-paid, and generally noted for courage and competence. Some centurions, such as Cornelius, and those whom we know about from the gospel narratives, were men of deep religious piety.

The author of Acts considered Cornelius' conversion very momentous for the future of Christianity. He records that it occurred as the result of divine intervention and revelation, and as a response to the preaching of Peter, the chief apostle. The experience of Cornelius' household was regarded as comparable to a new Pentecost, and it was a primary precedent for the momentous decision of the apostolic council, held in Jerusalem a few years later, to admit Gentiles to full and equal partnership with Jewish converts in the household of faith.

According to tradition, Cornelius was the second Bishop of Caesarea, the metropolitan see of Palestine. Undoubtedly, Cornelius and his household formed the nucleus of the first church in this important city, a church that was gathered by Philip the Evangelist (Acts 8:40 and 21:8).

Rite I O God, by thy Spirit thou didst call Cornelius the Centurion to be the first Christian among the Gentiles: Grant to thy Church, we beseech thee, such a ready will to go where thou dost send and to do what thou dost command that, under thy guidance, it may welcome all who turn to thee in love and faith and proclaim the Gospel to all nations; through Jesus Christ our Lord, who liveth and reigneth with thee and the Holy Spirit, one God, for ever and ever. Amen.

Rite II O God, by your Spirit you called Cornelius the Centurion to be the first Christian among the Gentiles: Grant to your Church such a ready will to go where you send and to do what you command, that, under your guidance, it may welcome all who turn to you in love and faith, and proclaim the Gospel to all nations; through Jesus Christ our Lord, who lives and reigns with you and the Holy Spirit, one God, for ever and ever. Amen.

For Liturgical Celebration: [Common of a Saint, A23] [For the Mission of the Church, A52]

February 11

Frances Jane (Fanny) Van Alstyne Crosby
Hymnwriter, 1915

Fanny Crosby, a lifelong Methodist, was the most prolific writer of hymn texts and gospel songs in the American evangelical tradition of the late nineteenth and early twentieth centuries. She wrote more than eight thousand sacred texts in addition to other poetry.

Frances Jane Crosby was born in Putnam County, New York, on March 24, 1820. Although not born blind, she lost her sight as an infant as a result of complications from a childhood illness. At the age of fifteen, she entered the New York Institute for the Blind, where she would later teach for a number of years. In 1858, she married Alexander van Alstyne, a musician in New York who was also blind.

Crosby's texts were so popular that nearly every well-known composer of gospel music of the period came to her for words to accompany their melodies. In most hymn writing, the words come first and then a composer sets them to music, but for Crosby the words came so quickly and naturally that composers would often take her their tunes and she would immediately begin to shape words that fit the music.

Perhaps the best example of this process led to the creation of Crosby's most well known hymn "Blessed assurance." On a visit to the home of a friend, the composer Phoebe Knapp, a newly composed tune was played for Crosby. After listening to the tune several times, the text began to take shape, and in a very short time one of the world's most popular gospel hymns was born.

The American gospel song is a unique genre of sacred music that combines words expressive of personal faith and witness with tunes that are simple and easily learned. Fanny Crosby's contribution to this genre is unequaled. Dozens of her hymns continue to find a place in the hymnals of Protestant evangelicalism around the world.

Fanny Crosby died on February 12, 1915, in Bridgeport, Connecticut, where she is buried.

Rite I   O God, the blessed assurance of all who trust in thee: We give thanks for thy servant Fanny Crosby, and pray that we, inspired by her words and example, may rejoice to sing ever of thy love, praising our Savior; who liveth and reigneth with thee and the Holy Spirit, one God, now and for ever. Amen.

Rite II   O God, the blessed assurance of all who trust in you: We give you thanks for your servant Fanny Crosby, and pray that we, inspired by her words and example, may rejoice to sing ever of your love, praising our Savior; who lives and reigns with you and the Holy Spirit, one God, now and for ever. Amen.

For Liturgical Celebration: [Common of an Artist, Writer, or Composer, A27] [Common of a Saint, A23]

February 12

Charles Freer Andrews
Priest and "Friend of the Poor" in India, 1940

Affectionately called "Christ's Faithful Apostle" by his friend the Mahatma Gandhi, Charles Freer Andrews dedicated his life's work to relief and justice for the oppressed and poor in India and around the globe.

Born in Birmingham, England, in 1871, he converted to the Church of England while studying at Cambridge and was ordained a priest in 1897. An active member of the Christian Social Union since his college days, Andrews was inspired by the cause of social justice throughout the British Empire, particularly in India. In 1904 he joined the Cambridge Brotherhood in India and began to teach philosophy at St. Stephen's College, Delhi. His Indian students and colleagues, with whom he had grown close, referred to him as Deenabandhu, or "Friend of the Poor."

Andrews openly criticized the racist mistreatment of the Indian people by British officials and, in 1913, he successfully mediated a cotton worker's strike in Madras which had the potential to become violent.

He traveled to South Africa to help the Indians there in their dispute with the Government, and it was then that he met a young lawyer named Mohandas Gandhi. Andrews was impressed with Gandhi's teaching of non-violence and with his knowledge of the Christian faith, and helped him establish an ashram, or Indian hermitage, devoted to the practice of peace. In 1915, Andrews helped convince Gandhi to return to England with him. He also aided Gandhi in his efforts to negotiate matters of Indian autonomy with the British Government.

Andrews' work also took him to Fiji, where he advocated for indentured Indian workers and for the rights of oppressed sugar workers. He eventually returned to England, where he continued to teach about social justice and radical discipleship until his death in 1940.

Rite I Gracious God, who didst call Charles Freer Andrews to show forth thy salvation to the poor: By thy Holy Spirit inspire in us a tender concern, a passionate justice, and an active love for all people, that there may be one Body and one Spirit in Jesus Christ, our Savior; who with thee and the same Spirit liveth and reigneth, one God, now and for ever. Amen.

Rite II Gracious God, you called Charles Freer Andrews to show forth your salvation to the poor: By your Holy Spirit inspire in us a tender concern, a passionate justice, and an active love for all people, that there may be one Body and one Spirit in Jesus Christ, our Savior; who with you and the same Spirit lives and reigns, one God, now and for ever. Amen.

For Liturgical Celebration: [Common of a Pastor, A14] [Common of a Prophetic Witness, A31] [For Social Justice, A58] [For Social Service, A59]

February 13

Absalom Jones
Priest, 1818

Absalom Jones was born on November 6, 1746, a house slave in Delaware. He taught himself to read out of the New Testament, among other books. When sixteen, he was sold to a store owner in Philadelphia. There he attended a night school for blacks, operated by Quakers. At twenty, he married another slave, and purchased her freedom with his earnings.

Jones bought his own freedom in 1784. At St. George's Methodist Episcopal Church, he served as lay minister for its black membership. The active evangelism of Jones and that of his friend, Richard Allen, greatly increased black membership at St. George's. The alarmed vestry decided to segregate blacks into an upstairs gallery, without notifying them. During a Sunday service when ushers attempted to remove them, the blacks indignantly walked out in a body.

In 1787, black Christians organized the Free African Society, the first organized Afro-American society, and Absalom Jones and Richard Allen were elected overseers. Members of the Society paid monthly dues for the benefit of those in need. The Society established communication with similar black groups in other cities. In 1792, the Society began to build a church, which was dedicated on July 17, 1794.

The African Church applied for membership in the Episcopal Diocese of Pennsylvania on the following conditions: 1, that they be received as an organized body; 2, that they have control over their local affairs; 3, that Absalom Jones be licensed as layreader, and, if qualified, be ordained as minister. In October 1794 it was admitted as St. Thomas African Episcopal Church. Bishop White ordained Jones as deacon in 1795 and as priest on September 21, 1802.

Jones was an earnest preacher. He denounced slavery, and warned the oppressors to "clean their hands of slaves." To him, God was the Father, who always acted on "behalf of the oppressed and distressed."

But it was his constant visiting and mild manner that made him beloved by his own flock and by the community. St. Thomas Church, Philadelphia, grew to over 500 members during its first year. Known as "the Black Bishop of The Episcopal Church," Jones was an example of persistent faith in God and in the Church as God's instrument.

Jones died on February 13, 1818, in Philadelphia.

Rite I Set us free, O heavenly Father, from every bond of prejudice and fear; that, honoring the steadfast courage of thy servant Absalom Jones, we may show forth in our lives the reconciling love and true freedom of the children of God, which thou hast given us in thy Son our Savior Jesus Christ; who liveth and reigneth with thee and the Holy Spirit, one God, now and for ever. Amen.

Rite II Set us free, heavenly Father, from every bond of prejudice and fear; that, honoring the steadfast courage of your servant Absalom Jones, we may show forth in our lives the reconciling love and true freedom of the children of God, which you have given us in your Son our Savior Jesus Christ; who lives and reigns with you and the Holy Spirit, one God, now and for ever. Amen.

For Liturgical Celebration: [Common of a Pastor, A14] [Common of a Prophetic Witness, A31] [For Reconciliation and Forgiveness, A68]

February 14

Cyril, Monk,
and Methodius, Bishop
Missionaries to the Slavs, 869, 885

Cyril (born about 828) and Methodius (born about 817), brothers born in Thessalonika, are honored as apostles to the southern Slavs and as the founders of Slavic literary culture. Cyril was a student of philosophy and a deacon, who eventually became a missionary monastic. Methodius was first the governor of a Slavic colony, then turned to the monastic life, and was later elected abbot of a monastery in Constantinople.

In 862, the King of Moravia asked for missionaries who would teach his people in their native language. Since both Cyril and Methodius knew Slavonic, and both were learned men—Cyril was known as "the Philosopher"—the Patriarch chose them to lead the mission.

As part of his task among the Moravians, Cyril invented an alphabet to transcribe the native tongue, probably the "glagolithic," in which Slavo-Roman liturgical books in Russian and Serbian are still written. The so-called "cyrillic" alphabet is thought to have been originated by Cyril's followers.

Pressures by the German clergy, who opposed the brothers' teaching, preaching, and writing in Slavonic, and the lack of a bishop to ordain new priests for their people, caused the two brothers to seek foreign help. They found a warm welcome at Rome from Pope Adrian II, who determined to ordain both men bishops and approved the Slavonic liturgy. Cyril died in 869 at Rome and was buried there. Methodius, now a bishop, returned to Moravia as Metropolitan of Sirmium.

Methodius, still harassed by German bishops, was imprisoned at their behest. Eventually, he was released by Pope John VIII, on the condition that Slavonic, "a barbarous language," be used only for preaching. Later, the enmity of the Moravian prince caused Methodius to be recalled to Rome on charges of heresy. Papal support again allowed him to return to Moravia and to use Slavonic in the liturgy.

Methodius completed a Slavonic translation of the Bible and of Byzantine ecclesiastical law, while continuing his missionary activities. He is believed to have died in 885, probably at his See city, Nitria, in what is now Slovakia. At his funeral, celebrated in Greek, Latin, and Slavonic, "the people came together in huge numbers . . . for Methodius had been all things to all people that he might lead them all to heaven."

Rite I Almighty and everlasting God, who by the power of the Holy Spirit didst move thy servant Cyril and his brother Methodius to bring the light of the Gospel to a hostile and divided people: Overcome, we pray thee, by the love of Christ, all bitterness and contention among us, and make us one united family under the banner of the Prince of Peace; who liveth and reigneth with thee and the same Spirit, one God, now and for ever. Amen.

Rite II Almighty and everlasting God, by the power of the Holy Spirit you moved your servant Cyril and his brother Methodius to bring the light of the Gospel to a hostile and divided people: Overcome all bitterness and strife among us by the love of Christ, and make us one united family under the banner of the Prince of Peace; who lives and reigns with you and the Holy Spirit, one God, now and for ever. Amen.

For Liturgical Celebration: [Common of a Missionary, A11] [Common of a Monastic or Professed Religious, A20] [For the Mission of the Church, A52]

February 15

Thomas Bray
Priest and Missionary, 1730

Thomas Bray was born at Marton, in Shropshire, England, in 1656. After graduating from Oxford and being ordained, he became a country parson in Warwickshire. In 1696 he was invited by the Bishop of London to be responsible for the oversight of Church work in the colony of Maryland. Three years later, as the Bishop's Commissary, he sailed to America for his first, and only, visitation. Though he spent only two and a half months in Maryland, Bray was deeply concerned about the neglected state of the American churches, and the great need for the education of clergymen, lay people, and children. At a general visitation of the clergy at Annapolis, before his return to England, he emphasized the need for the instruction of children, and insisted that no clergyman be given a charge unless he had a good report from the ship in which he crossed the Atlantic, "whether . . . he gave no matter of scandal, and whether he did constantly read prayers twice a day and catechize and preach on Sundays, which, notwithstanding the common excuses, I know can be done by a minister of any zeal for religion." His understanding of, and concern for, Native Americans and blacks were far ahead of his time. He founded thirty-nine lending libraries in America, as well as numerous schools. He raised money for missionary work and influenced young English priests to go to America.

Bray tried hard to have a bishop consecrated for America, but failed. His greatest contributions were the founding of the Society for Promoting Christian Knowledge and the Society for the Propagation of the Gospel, both of which are still effectively in operation after two and a half centuries of work all over the world.

From 1706 to 1730, Bray was the rector of St. Botolph Without, Aldgate, London, where, until his death there on February 15, 1730, at the age of 72, he served with energy and devotion, while continuing his efforts on behalf of black slaves in America, and in the founding of parochial libraries.

When the deplorable condition of English prisons was brought to Bray's attention, he set to work to influence public opinion and to raise funds to alleviate the misery of the inmates. He organized Sunday "Beef and Beer" dinners in prisons, and advanced proposals for prison reform. It was Thomas Bray who first suggested to General Oglethorpe the idea of founding a humanitarian colony for the relief of honest debtors, but he died before the Georgia colony became a reality.

Rite I   O God of compassion, who didst open the heart of thy servant Thomas Bray to the needs of the Church in the New World, and to found societies to relieve them: Make the Church diligent at all times to propagate the Gospel and to promote the spread of Christian knowledge; through Jesus Christ our Lord, who liveth and reigneth with thee and the Holy Spirit, one God, for ever and ever. Amen.

Rite II   O God of compassion, who opened the heart of your servant Thomas Bray to the needs of the Church in the New World, and to found societies to relieve them: Make the Church diligent at all times to propagate the Gospel, and to promote the spread of Christian knowledge; through Jesus Christ our Lord, who lives and reigns with you and the Holy Spirit, one God, for ever and ever. Amen.

For Liturgical Celebration: [Common of a Pastor, A14] [Common of a Missionary, A11] [For the Ministry II, A50] [For the Mission of the Church, A52]

February 16

Charles Todd Quintard
Bishop of Tennessee, 1898

Charles Todd Quintard was the second bishop of the Diocese of Tennessee and the first Vice Chancellor of The University of the South at Sewanee.

Quintard was born in 1824 in Stamford, Connecticut. In 1847 he received the degree of Doctor of Medicine from the Medical College of New York University and worked at New York City's Bellevue Hospital. After a brief episode of practicing medicine in Athens, Georgia, Quintard became the professor of anatomy and physiology at Memphis Medical College and an editor of the Memphis Medical Reporter. In 1848, Quintard married Katherine Isabella Hand, a native of Roswell, Georgia, and together they were the parents of three children.

It was while he was in Memphis that Quintard came to know Bishop James Hervey Otey, the first bishop of Tennessee. Under Otey's personal tutelage, Quintard prepared for holy orders. He was ordained to the diaconate on New Year's Day, 1855, and to the priesthood on the Feast of the Epiphany, 1856. He served as rector of the Church of the Advent, Nashville, until his election as the second bishop of Tennessee in October 1865. He served as bishop until his death in 1898.

During the Civil War, Quintard played dual roles in the Confederate Army as both chaplain and surgeon. Following the war, he was instrumental in bringing together the previously divided factions and extending the reach of The Episcopal Church, particularly among African Americans.

Bishop Quintard was a strong advocate of education at every level and played a major role in the establishment of schools. Perhaps his greatest accomplishment was the rebuilding of The University of the South in Sewanee, Tennessee, after its destruction during the Civil War. He made several successful trips to England to raise the funds to secure the future of the University. From February 1867 to July 1872, Quintard served as the reconstituted University's first Vice Chancellor. Quintard believed that a great Episcopal university was essential, not just to the church in Tennessee and the southeast, but to the whole church, and thus devoted much of his ministry to Sewanee.

Rite I Mighty God, we bless thy Name for the example of thy bishop Charles Todd Quintard, who persevered to reconcile the divisions among the people of his time: Grant, we pray, that thy Church may ever be one, that it may be a refuge for all, for the honor of thy Name; through Jesus Christ, who with thee and the Holy Spirit liveth and reigneth, one God, for ever and ever. Amen.

Rite II Mighty God, we bless your Name for the example of your bishop Charles Todd Quintard, who persevered to reconcile the divisions among the people of his time: Grant, we pray, that your Church may ever be one, that it may be a refuge for all, for the honor of your Name; through Jesus Christ, who with you and the Holy Spirit lives and reigns, one God, for ever and ever. Amen.

For Liturgical Celebration: [Common of a Theologian and Teacher, A17] [For Education, A60]

February 17

Janani Luwum
Archbishop of Uganda, and Martyr, 1977

Janani Luwum was born in 1922 at Acholi in Uganda, near the Sudanese border. After his early years as a teacher and lay reader in Gulu, he was sent to St. Augustine's College, Canterbury. He was ordained priest in 1956 and returned to Uganda to assume responsibility for twenty-four congregations. After several years of service that included work at a local theological college, Luwum returned to England on scholarship for further study at the London College of Divinity.

In 1969, Luwum became Bishop of Northern Uganda, where he was a faithful visitor to his parishes as well as a growing influence at international gatherings of the Anglican Communion. In 1974, he was elected Archbishop of the Church of Uganda, Rwanda, Burundi, and Boga-Zaire.

Luwum's new position brought him into direct contact and eventual confrontation with the Ugandan military dictator, Idi Amin, as the Archbishop sought to protect his people from the brutality of Amin's regime. In August of 1976, Makerere University was sacked by government troops. With Archbishop Luwum as their chair, the Christian leaders of the country drafted a strong memorandum of protest against officially sanctioned rape and murder.

In early February 1977, the Archbishop's residence was searched for arms by government security forces. On February 16, President Amin summoned Luwum to his palace. He went there, accompanied by the other Anglican bishops and by the Roman Catholic cardinal archbishop and a senior leader of the Muslim community. After being accused of complicity in a plot to murder the President, most of the clerics were allowed to leave. However, Archbishop Luwum was ordered to remain behind. As his companions departed, Luwum said, "They are going to kill me. I am not afraid." He was never seen alive again. The following day the government announced that he had been killed in an automobile accident while resisting arrest. Only after some weeks had passed was his bullet-riddled body released to his family for burial.

Early in his confrontation with the Ugandan government, Archbishop Luwum answered one of his critics by saying, "I do not know how long I shall occupy this chair. I live as though there will be no tomorrow . . . While the opportunity is there, I preach the gospel with all my might, and my conscience is clear before God."

Rite I   O God, whose Son the Good Shepherd laid down his life for the sheep: We give thee thanks for thy faithful shepherd, Janani Luwum, who after his Savior's example gave up his life for the people of Uganda. Grant us to be so inspired by his witness that we make no peace with oppression, but live as those who are sealed with the cross of Christ, who died and rose again, and now liveth and reigneth with thee and the Holy Spirit, one God, for ever and ever. Amen.

Rite II   O God, whose Son the Good Shepherd laid down his life for the sheep: We give you thanks for your faithful shepherd, Janani Luwum, who after his Savior's example gave up his life for the people of Uganda. Grant us to be so inspired by his witness that we make no peace with oppression, but live as those who are sealed with the cross of Christ, who died and rose again, and now lives and reigns with you and the Holy Spirit, one God, for ever and ever. Amen.

For Liturgical Celebration: [Common of a Pastor, A14] [Common of a Martyr, A7] [Common of a Prophetic Witness, A31] [Of the Holy Cross, A41]

February 18

Martin Luther
Theologian, 1546

Martin Luther was born November 10, 1483, at Eisleben, in Germany. His intellectual abilities were evident early, and his father planned a career for him in law. Luther's real interest lay elsewhere, however, and in 1505, he entered the local Augustinian monastery. He was ordained a priest on April 3, 1507.

In October 1512, Luther received his doctorate in theology, and shortly afterward he was installed as a professor of biblical studies at the University of Wittenberg. His lectures on the Bible were popular, and within a few years he made the university a center for biblical humanism. As a result of his theological and biblical studies, he called into question the practice of selling indulgences. On the eve of All Saints' Day, October 31, 1517, he posted on the door of the castle church in Wittenberg the notice of an academic debate on indulgences, listing 95 theses for discussion. As the effects of the theses became evident, the Pope called upon the Augustinian order to discipline their member. After a series of meetings, political maneuvers, and attempts at reconciliation, Luther, at a meeting with the papal legate in 1518, refused to recant.

Luther was excommunicated on January 3, 1521. The Emperor Charles V summoned him to the meeting of the Imperial Diet at Worms. There Luther resisted all efforts to make him recant, insisting that he had to be proved in error on the basis of Scripture. The Diet passed an edict calling for the arrest of Luther. Luther's own prince, the Elector Frederick of Saxony, however, had him spirited away and placed for safekeeping in his castle, the Wartburg.

There Luther translated the New Testament into German and began the translation of the Old Testament. He then turned his attention to the organization of worship and education. He introduced congregational singing of hymns, composing many himself, and issued model orders of services. He published his large and small catechisms for instruction in the faith. During the years from 1522 to his death, Luther wrote a prodigious quantity of books, letters, sermons, and tracts. Luther died at Eisleben on February 18, 1546.

Rite I   O God, our refuge and our strength: Thou didst raise up thy servant Martin Luther to reform and renew thy Church in the light of thy word. Defend and purify the Church in our own day and grant that, through faith, we may boldly proclaim the riches of thy grace, which thou hast made known in Jesus Christ our Savior, who with thee and the Holy Spirit, liveth and reigneth, one God, now and for ever. Amen.

Rite II   O God, our refuge and our strength: You raised up your servant Martin Luther to reform and renew your Church in the light of your word. Defend and purify the Church in our own day and grant that, through faith, we may boldly proclaim the riches of your grace, which you have made known in Jesus Christ our Savior, who with you and the Holy Spirit, lives and reigns, one God, now and for ever. Amen.

For Liturgical Celebration: [Common of a Theologian and Teacher, A17] [Of the Holy Trinity, A37]

February 20

Frederick Douglass
Orator and Advocate for Truth and Justice, 1895

Born as a slave in February 1818, Frederick Douglass was separated from his mother at the age of eight and given by his new owner, Thomas Auld, to his brother and sister-in-law, Hugh and Sophia Auld. Sophia attempted to teach Frederick to read, along with her son, but her husband put a stop to this, claiming, "it would forever unfit him to be a slave." Frederick learned to read in secret, earning small amounts of money when he could and paying neighbors to teach him.

In 1838, Frederick Bailey (as he was then known) escaped and changed his name to Frederick Douglass. At the age of 14, he had experienced a conversion to Christ in the African American Episcopal Church, and his recollection of that tradition's spiritual music sustained him in his struggle for freedom: "Those songs still follow me, to deepen my hatred of slavery, and quicken my sympathies for my brethren in bonds."

An outstanding orator, Douglass was sent on speaking tours in the Northern States sponsored by the American Anti-Slavery Society. The more renowned he became, the more he had to worry about recapture. In 1845, he went to England on a speaking tour. His friends in America raised enough money to buy out his master's legal claim to him, so that he could return to the United States in safety. Douglass eventually moved to New York and edited the pro-abolition journal *North Star*, named for the fleeing slave's nighttime guide.

Douglass was highly critical of churches that did not disassociate themselves from slavery. Challenging those churches, he quoted Jesus' denunciation of the Pharisees: "They bind heavy burdens and grievous to be borne, and lay them on men's shoulders; but they themselves will not move them with one of their fingers" (Matthew 23:4).

A strong advocate of racial integration, Douglass disavowed black separatism and wanted to be counted as equal among his white peers.

When he met Abraham Lincoln in the White House, he noted that the President treated him as a kindred spirit without one trace of condescension.

Douglass died in 1895.

Rite I   Almighty God, we bless thy Name for the witness of Frederick Douglass, whose impassioned and reasonable speech moved the hearts of people to a deeper obedience to Christ: Strengthen us also to speak on behalf of those in captivity and tribulation, continuing in the Word of Jesus Christ our Liberator; who with thee and the Holy Spirit dwelleth in glory everlasting. Amen.

Rite II Almighty God, we bless your Name for the witness of Frederick Douglass, whose impassioned and reasonable speech moved the hearts of people to a deeper obedience to Christ: Strengthen us also to speak on behalf of those in captivity and tribulation, continuing in the Word of Jesus Christ our Liberator; who with you and the Holy Spirit dwells in glory everlasting. Amen.

For Liturgical Celebration: [Common of a Prophetic Witness, A31] [Common of a Saint, A23] [For Reconciliation and Forgiveness, A68]

February 21

John Henry Newman
Priest and Theologian, 1890

John Henry Newman was among the founders of the Oxford Movement and a prolific tractarian, having authored two dozen of the *Tracts of the Times*, the series of pamphlets setting forth the tenets of the movement. Most notably, Newman is remembered as the author of Tract 90, in which he sought to reconcile the teaching of Roman Catholicism with the Thirty-Nine Articles of the Church of England.

Newman was born in London in 1801 and was educated at Oxford. While a Fellow and Tutor at Oriel College, his evangelical upbringing gave way to a more catholic understanding of the Christian faith. He was ordained in 1826, and, within two years, became the Vicar of St. Mary's Church, Oxford.

Newman was an avid student of the writings of the early church. Although he could be critical of the teachings of the Roman Church in his day, he was even more troubled by the theological state of the Church of England, particularly when weighed against what he understood to be the standards of the ancient church. His passionate interests in the texts of the early centuries of Christianity led Newman to question the position of Scripture as the unchecked rule and standard of the church's faith. For Newman, Scripture was of critical importance, but it could not stand alone; it had to be held in balance with the writings of the early church and the theological tradition of the church through the ages.

Although the other leaders of the Oxford Movement remained loyal to the Anglican tradition, spending their vocations advocating positions similar to his, Newman found it difficult to withstand the furor of the church's infighting, particularly after the publication of Tract 90. In 1845, he was received into the Roman Catholic Church and soon thereafter went to Rome, where he was ordained to the priesthood. He became a member of the Congregation of the Oratory. Upon his return to England he established a house of the Oratory near Birmingham, where he lived for the rest of his life.

Although his relationship with the Roman Church in England was at times problematic, Pope Leo XIII made him a Cardinal in 1877. He died on August 11, 1890.

Rite I   God of all wisdom, we offer thanks for John Henry Newman, whose eloquence bore witness that thy Church is one, holy, catholic, and apostolic, even amid the changes and cares of this world: Grant that, inspired by his words and example, we may ever follow thy kindly light till we rest in thy bosom, with thy dear Son Jesus Christ and the Holy Spirit; for thou livest and reignest, one God, now and for ever. Amen.

Rite II God of all wisdom, we offer thanks for John Henry Newman, whose eloquence bore witness that your Church is one, holy, catholic, and apostolic, even amid the changes and cares of this world: Grant that, inspired by his words and example, we may ever follow your kindly light till we rest in your bosom, with your dear Son Jesus Christ and the Holy Spirit; for you live and reign, one God, now and for ever. Amen.

For Liturgical Celebration: [Common of a Theologian and Teacher, A17] [Common of a Pastor, A14] [Of the Reign of Christ, A46] [For the Unity of the Church, A48]

February 22

Eric Liddell
Missionary to China, 1945

Eric Henry Liddell was born on January 16, 1902, at Tientsin (now Tianjin), in China, the second son of missionary parents. At the age of six, he was sent with his older brother to Eltham College, Blackheath, London, a boarding school for the children of missionaries. Liddell remained there until he enrolled in Edinburgh University. He excelled in athletics throughout his educational career.

Liddell won a position on the British track and field team for the Paris Olympic games of 1924, winning the gold in the 400 metre, setting a world record, and a bronze in the 200 metre. His best event as a university athlete was the 100 metre, and he was highly favored to win gold in the Olympics, but he elected not to run because the heat was to be held on Sunday, conflicting with his personal commitment keep the sabbath. The award-winning film, *Chariots of Fire*, is the story of Eric Liddell and his participation in Olympiad VIII.

After his graduation from Edinburgh, Liddell returned to North China, near his birthplace, and served as a missionary from 1925-1943. He was ordained in the Church of Scotland in 1932 and in 1934 married Florence Mackenzie, the daughter of Canadian missionaries to China. Together they had three daughters.

Because of ongoing conflict between China and Japan in the 1930's, Liddell and his family endured significant hardships. In 1941, after the Japanese invasion of Pearl Harbor, the British government advised expatriates to leave the country. Florence Liddell took the children and fled to Canada in 1941. Eric and his brother Rob stayed on and continued their work. In 1943, Liddell was interned in the Japanese concentration camp at Weihsein. Although Liddel did have an opportunity to leave the camp as part of an exchange of British and Japanese prisoners, he gave his place to a pregnant woman instead. Having won the respect of his captors, he is remembered by camp survivors for his ministry among them. He died in 1945 shortly before the camp's liberation.

Rite I   God, whose strength bears us up as on mighty wings: We rejoice in remembering thy athlete and missionary, Eric Liddell, to whom thou didst bestow courage and resolution in contest and in captivity; and we pray that we also may run with endurance the race that is set before us and persevere in patient witness, until we wear that crown of victory won for us by Jesus our Savior; who with thee and the Holy Spirit liveth and reigneth, one God, for ever and ever. Amen.

Rite II   God, whose strength bears us up as on mighty wings: We rejoice in remembering your athlete and missionary, Eric Liddell, to whom you gave courage and resolution in contest and in captivity; and we pray that we also may run with endurance the race set before us and persevere in patient witness, until we wear that crown of victory won for us by Jesus our Savior; who with you and the Holy Spirit lives and reigns, one God, for ever and ever. Amen.

For Liturgical Celebration: [Common of a Missionary, A11] [For the Mission of the Church, A52]

February 23

Polycarp
Bishop and Martyr of Smyrna, 156

Polycarp, born AD 69, was one of the leaders of the Church who carried on the tradition of the apostles through the troubled period of Gnostic heresies in the second century. According to Irenaeus, who had known him in his early youth, Polycarp was a pupil of John, "the disciple of the Lord," and had been appointed a bishop by "apostles in Asia."

We possess a letter from Polycarp to the Church in Philippi. It reveals his firm adherence to the faith, and his pastoral concern for fellow Christians in trouble.

An authentic account of the martyrdom of Polycarp on February 23 is also preserved. It probably occurred in the year 156. The account tells of Polycarp's courageous witness in the amphitheater at Smyrna. When the proconsul asked him to curse Christ, Polycarp said, "Eighty-six years I have served him, and he never did me any wrong. How can I blaspheme my King who saved me?" The account reports that the magistrate was reluctant to kill the gentle and harmless old man, but his hand was forced by the mob, who clamored that he be thrown to wild beasts, as was the fate of other Christians on that dreadful day.

Instead, Polycarp was burned at the stake. Before his ordeal, he is reported to have looked up to heaven, and to have prayed: "Lord God Almighty, Father of your beloved and blessed child Jesus Christ, through whom we have received knowledge of you, God of angels and hosts and all creation, and of the whole race of the upright who live in your presence, I bless you that you have thought me worthy of this day and hour, to be numbered among the martyrs and share in the cup of Christ, for resurrection to eternal life, for soul and body in the incorruptibility of the Holy Spirit. Among them may I be accepted before you today, as a rich and acceptable sacrifice just as you, the faithful and true God, have prepared and foreshown and brought about. For this reason and for all things I praise you, I bless you, I glorify you, through the eternal heavenly high priest Jesus Christ, your beloved child, through whom be glory to you, with him and the Holy Spirit, now and for the ages to come. Amen."

Rite I   O God, the maker of heaven and earth, who didst give thy venerable servant, the holy and gentle Polycarp, boldness to confess Jesus Christ as King and Savior and steadfastness to die for his faith: Give us grace, following his example, to share the cup of Christ and to rise to eternal life; through Jesus Christ our Lord, who liveth and reigneth with thee and the Holy Spirit, one God, now and for ever. Amen.

Rite II   O God, the maker of heaven and earth, you gave your venerable servant, the holy and gentle Polycarp, boldness to confess Jesus Christ as King and Savior and steadfastness to die for his faith: Give us grace, following his example, to share the cup of Christ and to rise to eternal life; through Jesus Christ our Lord, who lives and reigns with you and the Holy Spirit, one God, now and for ever. Amen.

For Liturgical Celebration: [Common of a Martyr, A7] [Common of a Pastor, A14] [Of the Holy Cross, A41]

February 25

John Roberts
Priest, 1949

John Roberts was a priest and mission worker among the Shoshone and Arapahoe in Wyoming, where he worked tirelessly from his arrival in 1883 until his death in 1949.

Born March 31, 1853, and educated in Wales, Roberts served briefly in the Bahamas, where he was ordained to the priesthood in 1878, and as chaplain of St. Matthew Cathedral worked among native Bahamians, especially in the leper colonies. Still, as most of his charges were Christian, his ministry there was largely pastoral; he yearned for a bigger challenge, the evangelical task of mission to the unbaptized. Shortly thereafter, on a visit to New York City, he contacted John Spalding, the missionary bishop of Wyoming and Colorado, asking for work among American Indians. Bishop Spalding sent Roberts to serve in Colorado initially, but, by 1883, he had made his way to Wyoming, where he began work among the Shoshone and Arapahoe tribes in the area that is now the Wind River Reservation. Roberts learned the languages of both tribes and made extensive notes on vocabulary that have been invaluable to later generations of scholars.

Roberts shared his work with Laura Brown, a wealthy woman he had met while serving in the Bahamas, where she served as cathedral organist. They married on the day of her arrival in Wyoming, Christmas Day 1884. Together they had six children, five of whom survived the harsh conditions, all of whom learned the tribal languages as well as English.

In 1887, after Roberts had established trusting relationships with the people, the Shoshone chief granted him land on which to build a mission school for girls to complement the nearby government school for boys. In addition to the mission school, Roberts was responsible for starting more than six congregations in Wyoming.

Roberts' zeal for Christian conversions was tempered by a deep respect for indigenous context. He believed it important to preserve the language, customs, and the ancient ways of the native peoples while proclaiming the gospel among them, inviting them to faith, establishing congregations, and serving their needs in the name of Jesus. He died on January 22, 1949.

Rite I   Almighty God, who didst raise up thy servant John Roberts to be a witness among the Shoshone and Arapahoe peoples: May we, inspired by his example and prayers, invite all people to the riches of thy grace; through Jesus Christ our Lord, who liveth and reigneth with thee and the Holy Spirit, one God, now and for ever. Amen.

Rite II Almighty God, who raised up your servant John Roberts to be a witness among the Shoshone and Arapahoe peoples: May we, inspired by his example and prayers, invite all people to the riches of your grace; through Jesus Christ our Lord, who lives and reigns with you and the Holy Spirit, one God, now and for ever. Amen.

For Liturgical Celebration: [Common of a Pastor, A14] [Common of a Missionary, A11] [For the Ministry II, A50] [For the Mission of the Church, A52]

February 26

Emily Malbone Morgan
Prophetic Witness, 1937

Emily Malbone Morgan was born on December 10, 1862, in Hartford, Connecticut. Her family were prominent Hartford citizens, and her Anglican roots ran deep on both sides of her family. With the support of Harriet Hastings, she was the founder of the Society of the Companions of the Holy Cross (SCHC), an order of Episcopal laywomen, in 1884. Rooted in disciplined devotion, SCHC became a strong force for social justice reform during the social gospel era around the turn of the twentieth century.

A primary inspiration for Morgan was her friendship with Adelyn Howard. Howard was homebound and sought Morgan's support for both spiritual companionship and shared intercessory prayer for others. In response, Morgan called together a small group of women that became the Society of the Companions of the Holy Cross.

Morgan had a particular concern for working women who were tired, restless, and had little hope for a vacation. In response, Morgan and her Companions developed summer vacation houses across the northeast, where working women and their daughters could have some time away for physical and spiritual renewal and refreshment.

In 1901, the Society established a permanent home in Byfield, Massachusetts. With the construction of new facilities on the site in 1915, it took the name Adelynrood, which continues to exist as the headquarters and retreat center of the Society.

Morgan never married; she and her sisters in the Society of the Companions of the Holy Cross lived a life of prayer, contemplation, and social justice, particularly for women. She died on February 27, 1937.

Rite I   Gracious God, we give thanks for the life and witness of Emily Malbone Morgan, who gathered women to devote themselves to intercession, social justice, Christian unity, and simple lives: Make us, with her, companions in prayer and in faithful living, dedicated to the Holy Cross of our Savior, Jesus Christ; who with thee and the Holy Spirit liveth and reigneth, one God, for ever and ever. Amen.

Rite II Gracious God, we give thanks for the life and witness of Emily Malbone Morgan, who gathered women to devote themselves to intercession, social justice, Christian unity, and simple lives: Make us, with her, companions in prayer and in faithful living, dedicated to the Holy Cross of our Savior, Jesus Christ; who with you and the Holy Spirit lives and reigns, one God, for ever and ever. Amen.

For Liturgical Celebration: [Common of a Saint, A23] [Common of a Prophetic Witness, A31] [For Rogation Days II, A56] [For Labor Day, A62]

February 27

George Herbert
Priest, 1633

George Herbert is famous for his poems and his prose work, *A Priest to the Temple: or The Country Parson*. He is portrayed by his biographer Izaak Walton as a model of the saintly parish priest. Herbert described his poems as "a picture of the many spiritual conflicts that have passed betwixt God and my soul, before I could submit mine to the will of Jesus my Master; in whose service I have found perfect freedom."

Herbert was born at Montgomery, Wales, on April 3, 1593, a cousin of the Earl of Pembroke. Through his official position as Public Orator of Cambridge, he was brought into contact with the Court of King James I and Prince (later King) Charles. Whatever hopes he may have had as a courtier were dimmed, however, because of his associations with persons who were out of favor with King Charles I—principally John Williams, Bishop of Lincoln.

Herbert had begun studying divinity in his early twenties, and, in 1626, he took Holy Orders. In 1630, King Charles provided him with a living as rector of the parishes of Fugglestone and Bemerton.

His collection of poems, *The Temple*, was given to his friend, Nicholas Ferrar, and published posthumously. Two of his poems are well known hymns: "Teach me, my God and King," (*The Hymnal 1982*, #592) and "Let all the world in every corner sing" (*The Hymnal 1982*, #402; #403). Their grace, strength, and metaphysical imagery influenced later poets, including Henry Vaughan and Samuel Taylor Coleridge.

Lines from his poem on prayer have moved many readers:

> Prayer, the Church's banquet, Angel's age,
> God's breath in man returning to his birth,
> The soul in paraphrase, the heart in pilgrimage,
> The Christian plummet sounding heav'n and earth.

Herbert was unselfish in his devotion and service to others. Izaak Walton writes that many of the parishioners "let their plow rest when Mr. Herbert's saints-bell rung to prayers, that they might also offer their devotion to God with him." His words, "Nothing is little in God's service," have reminded Christians again and again that everything in daily life, small or great, may be a means of serving and worshiping God.

Herbert died on March 1, 1633.

Rite I Almighty God, who didst call thy servant George Herbert from the pursuit of worldly honors to be a pastor of souls and a poet: Give us grace, we pray, joyfully to dedicate all our powers to thy service; through Jesus Christ our Lord, who liveth and reigneth with thee and the Holy Spirit, one God, for ever and ever. Amen.

Rite II Almighty God, you called your servant George Herbert from the pursuit of worldly honors to be a pastor of souls and a poet: Give us grace, we pray, joyfully to dedicate all our powers to your service; through Jesus Christ our Lord, who lives and reigns with you and the Holy Spirit, one God, for ever and ever. Amen.

For Liturgical Celebration: [Common of an Artist, Writer, or Composer, A27] [Common of a Theologian and Teacher, A17]

February 28

Anna Julia Haywood Cooper, *1964,*
and Elizabeth Evelyn Wright, *1904*
Educators

Anna Julia Haywood Cooper was born on August 10, 1858, in Raleigh, North Carolina, to an enslaved woman and a white man, presumably her mother's master. She attended St. Augustine Normal School and Collegiate Institute, founded by The Episcopal Church to educate African American teachers and clergy. There she became an Episcopalian and married George Cooper, one of her instructors, who was the second African American ordained to the Episcopal priesthood in North Carolina. She was an active member of St. Luke's in Washington, D.C., while Alexander Crummell served as its rector.

Cooper emphasized the importance of equal education for African Americans. An advocate for African American women, Cooper assisted in organizing the Colored Women's League and the first Colored Settlement House in Washington, D.C. In 1892, her book *A View from the South* was published, in which she challenged The Episcopal Church to offer more direct support for the African American members of its church in their quest for advancement and improvement in a segregated society.

At the age of 65, on April 3, 1925, Cooper became the fourth African American woman to complete a doctorate, granted by the Sorbonne in Paris. From 1930-1942, she served as President of Freylinghuysen University in Washington, D.C. She died on February 27, 1964, at the age of 105.

Elizabeth Evelyn Wright was born in Talbotton, Georgia, in 1872. Her father was an African American and her mother of Cherokee descent.

With the encouragement of her teachers, she enrolled at Tuskegee Institute in Alabama. She worked for the school during the day and attended night classes, but Olivia Washington, wife of the head of Tuskegee, Booker T. Washington, noted her promise and strength of character. Mrs. Washington made it possible for her to attend day classes.

Wright interrupted her studies and went to Hampton County, South Carolina, to establish a school for rural black children. Arsonists thwarted her efforts, and she returned to Tuskegee to finish her degree, graduating in 1894. She returned to Hampton County to re-start her school, but, once again, her efforts were turned back. Together with two colleagues, Jessie Dorsey and Hattie Davidson, she ventured to friendlier territory near Denmark, South Carolina, in 1897. There she started the Denmark Industrial Institute, modeled after Tuskegee. It continues today as Voorhees College, affiliated with The Episcopal Church.

Wright died on December 14, 1906, in Battle Creek, Michigan.

Rite I   Eternal God, who didst inspire Anna Julia Haywood Cooper and Elizabeth Evelyn Wright with the love of learning and the joy of teaching: Help us also to gather and use the resources of our communities for the education of all thy children; through Jesus Christ our Savior, who liveth and reigneth with thee and the Holy Spirit, one God, for ever and ever. Amen.

Rite II   Eternal God, you inspired Anna Julia Haywood Cooper and Elizabeth Evelyn Wright with the love of learning and the joy of teaching: Help us also to gather and use the resources of our communities for the education of all your children; through Jesus Christ our Savior, who lives and reigns with you and the Holy Spirit, one God, for ever and ever. Amen.

For Liturgical Celebration: [Common of a Saint, A23] [For Education, A60]

MARCH

1 David, Bishop of Menevia, Wales, c. 544
2 Chad, Bishop of Lichfield, 672
3 John and Charles Wesley, Priests, 1791, 1788
4 Paul Cuffee, Witness to the Faith among the Shinnecock, 1812
5
6 William W. Mayo, 1911, and Charles Menninger, 1953, and Their Sons, Pioneers in Medicine
7 Perpetua, Felicity, and their Companions, Martyrs at Carthage, 202
8 Geoffrey Anketell Studdert Kennedy, Priest, 1929
9 Gregory, Bishop of Nyssa, c. 394
10
11
12 Gregory the Great, Bishop of Rome, 604
13 James Theodore Holly, Bishop of Haiti, and of the Dominican Republic, 1911 (see also November 8)
14
15
16
17 Patrick, Bishop and Missionary of Ireland, 461
18 Cyril of Jerusalem, Liturgist, Catechist, and Bishop, 386
19
20 Thomas Ken, Bishop of Bath and Wells, 1711
21 Thomas Cranmer, Archbishop of Canterbury and Martyr, 1556
22 James De Koven, Priest and Teacher, 1879
23 Gregory the Illuminator, Bishop and Missionary of Armenia, c. 332

24 Óscar Romero, Archbishop of San Salvador, 1980, and the Martyrs of El Salvador

25

26 Richard Allen, First Bishop of the African Methodist Episcopal Church, 1831

27 Charles Henry Brent, Bishop of the Philippines, and of Western New York, 1929

28 James Solomon Russell, Priest, 1935

29 John Keble, Priest, 1866

30 Innocent of Alaska, Bishop, 1879

31 John Donne, Priest, 1631

March 1

David
Bishop of Menevia, Wales, c. 544

Despite the overwhelming victory of the pagan Angles, Saxons, and Jutes in the fifth century, one part of Britain continued in the ways of Christianity—Wales, the land west of the Wye River. In this last stronghold of the old Britons, the faith sprung from the legendary staff planted by Joseph of Arimathea at Glastonbury continued to flourish.

To the family of one Sanctus in Menevia there was born, about the year 500, a son named David ("the beloved"). Little is known of his early life, but, while fairly young, he founded a monastery near Menevia and became its abbot. He was later elected bishop. His strongest desire was to study and meditate in the quiet of his monastery, but he was virtually dragged to an assembly of bishops called to combat the heresy of Pelagianism. Once there, David proved to be so eloquent and learned that Archbishop Dubricius chose him as his own successor as Primate of Wales. In time, David founded eleven other monasteries in Wales and made a pilgrimage to Jerusalem.

He is said to have been strict in the governing of his own monastery at Menevia, yet loving in his treatment and correction of wrongdoers. One of his nicknames, "the Waterman," may indicate that he allowed the monks in his care to drink only water at meals instead of the customary wine or mead.

A scholar, a competent administrator, and a man of moderation, David filled the offices he held with distinction. He became a leader and guardian of the Christian faith in Wales. Eventually, he moved the center of episcopal government to Menevia, which is still an episcopal city, now called Ty-Dewi (House of David).

Some facts of his life can be historically established. Among them is that, toward the end of his life, around the year 539, he had several Irish saints as his pupils at the monastery. In legend—and many legends surround his life—David is clearly the foremost saint of Wales.

He is revered and loved to this day as patron of Wales, foremost Christian priest, and courageous leader.

Rite I Almighty God, who didst call thy servant David to be a faithful and wise steward of thy mysteries for the people of Wales: Mercifully grant that, following his purity of life and zeal for the Gospel of Christ, we may, with him, receive our heavenly reward; through Jesus Christ our Lord, who liveth and reigneth with thee and the Holy Spirit, one God, for ever and ever. Amen.

Rite II Almighty God, you called your servant David to be a faithful and wise steward of your mysteries for the people of Wales: Mercifully grant that, following his purity of life and zeal for the Gospel of Christ, we may, with him, receive our heavenly reward; through Jesus Christ our Lord, who lives and reigns with you and the Holy Spirit, one God, for ever and ever. Amen.

For Liturgical Celebration: [Common of a Pastor, A14] [Common of a Missionary, A11] [For the Ministry II, A50] [For the Mission of the Church, A52]

March 2

Chad
Bishop of Lichfield, 672

Chad was born in Northern England around 634, one of four brothers dedicated to service in the Church. Chad was trained by Aidan of Lindisfarne as a follower of the Celtic tradition in ritual. His elder brother Cedd, a godly and upright man, had built a monastery at Lastingham, where he governed as abbot. At his death, Cedd left the abbacy to Chad. According to the Venerable Bede, Chad was "a holy man, modest in his ways, learned in the Scriptures, and zealous in carrying out their teaching."

Impressed by Chad's qualities, the king appointed him Bishop of York. Chad was ordained by "bishops of the British race who had not been canonically ordained," Bede tells us. Chad was, Bede also notes, "a man who kept the Church in truth and purity, humility, and temperance." Following apostolic example, he traveled about his diocese on foot.

The new Archbishop of Canterbury, Theodore, arrived in England four years after Chad's ordination as bishop. Theodore made it clear that Chad's ordination had been irregular, that is, not according to Roman custom; and Chad most humbly offered to resign from office. "Indeed, I never believed myself worthy of it," he said.

Theodore, impressed by such humility, reordained him, and appointed him Bishop of Mercia and Northumbria. Chad continued his custom of traveling on foot until Theodore ordered him to ride, at least on longer journeys. When Chad hesitated, the Archbishop is said to have lifted him bodily onto the horse, "determined to compel him to ride when the need arose."

Chad administered his new diocese with devout concern. He built a monastery, and established monastic rule at Barrow. In his see city of Lichfield, where he had an official dwelling, he preferred to read and meditate in a small house he had built nearby.

Two and one-half years after his reordination, plague broke out, killing many residents of the diocese including Chad himself, whose death Bede describes thus: "He joyfully beheld . . . the day of the Lord, whose coming he had always anxiously awaited. He was mindful to his end of all that the Lord did." He died on March 2, 672, and was buried at the Cathedral Church of St. Peter in Lichfield.

Rite I   Lord Jesus Christ, who didst take the form of a servant to serve thy brothers and sisters: Strengthen us with the prayers and example of thy servant Chad, who became the least of all to minister to all; through the Father and the Holy Spirit, with whom thou livest and reignest, one God, now and for ever. Amen.

Rite II Lord Jesus Christ, who took the form of a servant to serve your brothers and sisters: Strengthen us with the prayers and example of your servant Chad, who became the least of all to minister to all; through the Father and the Holy Spirit, with whom you live and reign, one God, now and for ever. Amen.

For Liturgical Celebration: [Common of a Pastor, A14] [Of the Incarnation, A39] [For the Ministry II, A50]

March 3

John and Charles Wesley
Priests, 1791, 1788

John was the fifteenth, and Charles the eighteenth, child of Samuel Wesley, Rector of Epworth, Lincolnshire, and his wife, Susannah. John was born June 17, 1703, and Charles, December 18, 1707. Of the nineteen Wesley siblings, only ten lived to maturity. Under their mother's tutelage, all of the Wesley children were schooled each day in six-hour sessions, always begun and concluded with the singing of Psalms.

Their theological writings and sermons are still widely appreciated, but it is through their hymns—especially those of Charles, who wrote over six thousand of them—that their religious experience, and their Christian faith and life, continue to affect the hearts of many.

Both Wesleys were educated at Christ Church, Oxford, John later being elected a fellow of Lincoln College, where they gathered a few friends to join a "Holy Club" in strict adherence to the worship and discipline of the Prayer Book, and were thus given the name "Methodists." John was ordained in 1728 and Charles in 1735. Both were profoundly attached to the doctrine and worship of the Church of England, and deeply moved by and critical of the church's neglect of the poor, and remained so, despite abusive opposition to their cause and methods.

The two brothers went together to Georgia in 1735, John as a missionary of the Society for the Propagation of the Gospel, and Charles as secretary to James Oglethorpe, the Governor.

Shortly after their return to England, they each experienced an inner conversion. On May 21, 1738—Pentecost—Charles "felt the Spirit of God striving with his spirit 'till by degrees He chased away the darkness of . . . unbelief." Three days later, at a meeting on May 24 in Aldersgate Street in London with a group of Moravians, during a reading of Luther's *Preface to the Epistle to the Romans,* John recorded, "I felt my heart strangely warmed. I felt I did trust in Christ,

Christ alone, for salvation; and an assurance was given me that he had taken away my sins, even mine, and saved me from the law of sin and death." So the revival was born.

The formal separation of the Methodists from the Church of England occurred after the deaths of the two brothers in London —Charles on March 29, 1788, and John on March 2, 1791—but John's uncanonical ordinations of "elders" for America (bitterly opposed by Charles) doubtless set the basis for it.

Rite I   Lord God, who didst inspire thy servants John and Charles Wesley with burning zeal for the sanctification of souls and didst endow them with eloquence in speech and song: Kindle in thy Church, we beseech thee, such fervor, that those whose faith has cooled may be warmed, and those who have not known thy Christ may turn to him and be saved; who liveth and reigneth with thee and the Holy Spirit, one God, now and for ever. Amen.

Rite II   Lord God, you inspired your servants John and Charles Wesley with burning zeal for the sanctification of souls and endowed them with eloquence in speech and song: Kindle in your Church, we entreat you, such fervor, that those whose faith has cooled may be warmed, and those who have not known Christ may turn to him and be saved; who lives and reigns with you and the Holy Spirit, one God, now and for ever. Amen.

For Liturgical Celebration: [Common of a Missionary, A11] [Common of a Pastor, A14] [Common of a Theologian and Teacher, A17] [For the Ministry I, A49] [For the Mission of the Church, A52]

March 4
Paul Cuffee
Witness to the Faith among the Shinnecock, 1812

Born a member of the Shinnecock Tribe on March 4, 1757, Paul Cuffee was converted to Christianity in his early twenties. He was ordained in the Presbyterian Church and became a famous preacher and missionary to the native communities around the present-day Mastic Beach, at Hampton Bays, and at Montauk, all on Long Island, New York. Known as "Priest Paul," Cuffee was instrumental in working for the survival of native tribes. He demonstrated particular gifts in bringing together a strong witness to the Christian faith in dialogue with those who held traditional native beliefs.

Paul Cuffee strengthened the permanent presence of Native Americans in the area by establishing prayer meeting grounds in several locations. These became safe havens for diplomatic talks and places where native people could practice spiritually. He was a faithful advocate for his people and their way of life. Among the fruits of his efforts was the development of many allies of European descent, thus helping to ensure that Native Americans on Long Island could retain what little land they had left. Part of Cuffee's legacy can still be seen in the ceremonial "June Meeting" for the Shinnecock tribe that includes a Christian worship service, a tradition that continues to this day. Paul Cuffee is remembered for being a "most eloquent speaker" and is mentioned in *Uncle Tom's Cabin*, the influential anti-slavery novel by Harriet Beecher Stowe.

Priest Paul is buried on a tiny plot of land at Canoe Place in Hampton Bays, his historic gravesite diminished by development on the Long Island Railroad. His descendants continue mission work in the area that is a direct result of Priest Paul's efforts. His gravestone reads, "Erected by the New York Missionary Society, in memory of the Rev. Paul Cuffee, an Indian of the Shinnecock tribe, who was employed by the Society for the last thirteen years of his life, on the eastern part of Long Island, where he labored with fidelity and success. Humble, pious and indefatigable in testifying the gospel of the grace of God, he finished his course with joy on the 7th of March, 1812, aged 55 years and 3 days."

Rite I Almighty God, who dost empower evangelists and preachers: Help us to proclaim thy Word with power, like thy servant Paul Cuffee, that more might come to a deeper life in thee; in the Name of thy Son Jesus Christ, who with thee and the Holy Spirit liveth and reigneth, one God, for ever and ever. Amen.

Rite II Almighty God, who empowers evangelists and preachers: Help us to proclaim your Word with power, like your servant Paul Cuffee, that more might come to a deeper life in you; in the Name of your Son Jesus Christ, who with you and the Holy Spirit lives and reigns, one God, for ever and ever. Amen.

For Liturgical Celebration: [Common of a Missionary, A11] [Common of a Pastor, A14] [For Reconciliation and Forgiveness, A68] [For the Mission of the Church, A52]

March 6

William W. Mayo, 1911, and
Charles F. Menninger, 1953,
and Their Sons, Pioneers in Medicine

William W. Mayo, with his two sons, William J. Mayo and Charles H. Mayo, built St. Mary's, the first general hospital in Minnesota. When a devastating tornado struck Rochester, Minnesota, in August 1883, the Mayos joined with the Sisters of St. Francis to respond to the disaster. This partnership between the Episcopalian Mayos and the Roman Catholic Sisters raised a few eyebrows, but became well known for a new type of patient care that emphasized the whole person, spiritually as well as physically.

Building on a vision of doctors working as a team with other medical professionals, not as solo diagnosticians, the Mayos aggressively opened their doors to other doctors and medical researchers. St. Mary's Hospital and what would become The Mayo Clinic became a model for integrating person-centered medical care with the best in cutting-edge scientific and medical research. The Mayo Clinics continue today as outstanding centers for patient care and medical research.

Charles F. Menninger, together with his sons, Karl and William, were pioneers in establishing a new kind of psychiatric treatment facility in Topeka, Kansas, founded in 1925. They played a major role in transforming the care of the mentally ill in ways that were not only more medically effective, but were also more humane. Among the notable accomplishments of the Menninger Clinic has been its advocacy for better treatment and a more informed public policy in support of the needs of the mentally ill.

In 1973, Dr. Karl Menninger wrote the influential book, *Whatever Became of Sin?* The work looks at sin—personal, corporate, and systemic—and insists that recognizing sin, within us and among us, is a key component in personal and relational health. He believed strongly that naming sin and dealing with its consequences contributes positively to good health in persons and in communities. The book was a standard textbook in theological seminaries for a generation or more.

The work of the Mayos and Menningers was transformative because of their commitment to treating the whole person—physically, emotionally, and spiritually.

Rite I   Divine Physician, your Name is blessed for the work and witness of the Mayos and the Menningers, and the revolutionary developments that they brought to the practice of medicine. As Jesus went about healing the sick as a sign of the reign of God come near, bless and guide all those inspired to the work of healing by thy Holy Spirit, that they may follow his example for the sake of thy kingdom and the health of thy people; through the same Jesus Christ, who with thee and the Holy Spirit liveth and reigneth, one God, now and for ever. Amen.

Rite II Divine Physician, we bless your Name for the work and witness of the Mayos and the Menningers, and the revolutionary developments that they brought to the practice of medicine. As Jesus went about healing the sick as a sign of the reign of God come near, bless and guide all those inspired to the work of healing by your Holy Spirit, that they may follow his example for the sake of your kingdom and the health of your people; through the same Jesus Christ, who with you and the Holy Spirit lives and reigns, one God, now and for ever. Amen.

For Liturgical Celebration: [Common of a Saint, A23] [For Vocation in Daily Work, A61] [For the Ministry III, A51] [For the Sick, A57] [For Social Service, A59]

March 7

Perpetua, Felicity and their Companions
Martyrs at Carthage, 202

Vibia Perpetua, born in 181, was a young widow, mother of an infant, and owner of several slaves, including Felicitas and Revocatus. With two other young Carthaginians, Secundulus and Saturninus, they were catechumens preparing for baptism.

Early in the third century, Emperor Septimius Severus decreed that all persons should sacrifice to the divinity of the emperor. There was no way that a Christian, confessing faith in the one Lord Jesus Christ, could do this. Perpetua and her companions were arrested and held in prison under miserable conditions.

In a document attributed to Perpetua, we learn of visions she had in prison. One was of a ladder to heaven, which she climbed to reach a large garden; another was of her brother who had died when young of a dreadful disease, but was now well and drinking the water of life; the last was of herself as a warrior battling the Devil and defeating him to win entrance to the gate of life. "And I awoke, understanding that I should fight, not with beasts, but with the Devil . . . So much about me up to the day before the games; let him who will write of what happened then."

At the public hearing before the Proconsul, she refused even the entreaties of her aged father, saying, "I am a Christian."

On March 7, 203, Perpetua and her companions, encouraging one another to bear bravely whatever pain they might suffer, were sent to the arena to be mangled by a leopard, a boar, a bear, and a savage cow. Perpetua and Felicitas, tossed by the cow, were bruised and disheveled, but Perpetua, "lost in spirit and ecstasy," hardly knew that anything had happened. To her companions she cried, "Stand fast in the faith and love one another. And do not let what we suffer be a stumbling block to you."

Eventually, all were put to death by a stroke of a sword through the throat. The soldier who struck Perpetua was inept. His first blow merely pierced her throat between the bones. She shrieked with pain, then aided the man to guide the sword properly. The report of her death concludes, "Perhaps so great a woman, feared by the unclean spirit, could not have been killed unless she so willed it."

Rite I   O God, the King of Saints, who didst strengthen thy servants Perpetua, Felicity, and their companions to make a good confession and encourage one another in the time of trial: Grant that we who cherish their blessed memory may be encouraged by their prayers to share their pure and steadfast faith and win with them the palm of victory; through Jesus Christ our Lord, who liveth and reigneth with thee and the Holy Spirit, one God, for ever and ever. Amen.

Rite II   O God, the King of Saints, who strengthened your servants Perpetua, Felicity, and their companions to make a good confession and encourage one another in the time of trial: Grant that we who cherish their blessed memory may be encouraged by their prayers to share their pure and steadfast faith and win with them the palm of victory; through Jesus Christ our Lord, who lives and reigns with you and the Holy Spirit, one God, for ever and ever. Amen.

For Liturgical Celebration: [Common of a Martyr, A7] [Of the Holy Cross, A41]

March 8

Geoffrey Anketell Studdert Kennedy
Priest, 1929

G. A. Studdert Kennedy was born in Leeds, England, in 1883, one of nine children. His father, William Studdert Kennedy, was vicar in Leeds. Studdert Kennedy earned a degree in classics and divinity in 1904 at Trinity College, Dublin. After his ordination, he served parishes in Rugby and Worcester.

At the outbreak of the First World War, Studdert Kennedy volunteered as a chaplain to soldiers on the Western Front. Along with the spiritual comfort he gave to the wounded and dying, he was famous for handing out Woodbine cigarettes to the soldiers, who called him "Woodbine Willie."

He received the Military Cross in 1917 for conspicuous gallantry and devotion to duty during the attack on Messines Ridge on the Somme. He had volunteered for a number of tasks carried out under heavy fire, including bringing in three wounded men from the battlefield. One story re-told by the BBC "tells of him crawling out to a working party putting up wire in front of their trench. A nervous soldier challenged him, asking who he was, and he said 'The Church.' When the soldier asked what the Church was doing out there, he replied 'Its job.'"

Studdert Kennedy's religious poetry is represented in the lyric of the hymn, "Not here for high and holy things" (*The Hymnal 1982*, #9). His verse, some based on his experience as war-time military chaplain, was published in the volumes *Rough Rhymes of a Padre* (1918) and *More Rough Rhymes* (1919). He also published a collection of sermons entitled *I Believe: Sermons on the Apostles' Creed* (1928). His later poems and prose works express the Christian socialism and pacifism he adopted during his war years. He eventually worked for the Industrial Christian Fellowship. On one of his speaking tours on their behalf, he became ill, and he died in Liverpool on March 8, 1929.

Studdert Kennedy remains a powerful influence on the pacifist cause and anti-capitalist critiques, and his many writings have inspired figures such as the former Archbishop of Capetown, South Africa, Desmond Tutu, and the German Reformed theologian, Jürgen Moltmann.

Rite I Glorious God, we give thanks for high and holy things as well as the common things of earth: Awaken us to recognize thy presence in each other and in all creation, so that we, like Geoffrey Studdert Kennedy, may love and magnify thee as the holy, undivided Trinity; who liveth and reigneth one God, for ever and ever. Amen.

Rite II Glorious God, we give thanks for high and holy things as well as the common things of earth. Awaken us to recognize your presence in each other and in all creation, so that we, like Geoffrey Studdert Kennedy, may love and magnify you as the holy, undivided Trinity; who lives and reigns, one God, for ever and ever. Amen.

For Liturgical Celebration: [Common of a Pastor, A14] [For Peace, A55]

March 9

Gregory, Bishop of Nyssa
c. 394

Gregory was a man enchanted with Christ and dazzled by the meaning of his Passion. He was born in Caesarea in Cappadocia (Turkey) about 334, the younger brother of Basil the Great, and, in his youth, was but a reluctant Christian.

When he was twenty, the transfer of the relics of the Forty Martyrs of Sebaste to the family chapel at Annesi quickened Gregory's faith, and he became a practicing Christian and a lector. He abandoned this ministry, however, to become a rhetorician like his father.

His brother Basil, in his struggle against the Emperor Valens, compelled Gregory to become Bishop of Nyssa, a town ten miles from Caesarea. Knowing himself to be unfit for the charge, Gregory described his ordination as the most miserable day of his life. He lacked the important episcopal skills of tact and understanding, and had no sense of the value of money. Falsely accused of embezzling Church funds, Gregory went into hiding for two years, not returning to his diocese until Valens died.

Although he resented his brother's dominance, Gregory was shocked by Basil's death in 379. Several months later, he received another shock: his beloved sister Macrina was dying. Gregory hastened to Annesi and conversed with her for two days about death, and the soul, and the meaning of the resurrection. Choking with asthma, Macrina died in her brother's arms.

The two deaths, while stunning Gregory, also freed him to develop as a deeper and richer philosopher and theologian. He reveals his delight in the created order in his treatise, *On the Making of Man*. He exposes the depth of his contemplative and mystical nature in his *Life of Moses* and again in his *Commentary on the Song of Songs*. His *Great Catechism* is still considered second only to Origen's treatise, *On First Principles*.

In 381, Gregory attended the Second Ecumenical Council at Constantinople, where he was honored as the "pillar of the Church." In the fight for the Nicene faith, he was one of the three great Eastern theologians, with Basil the Great and Gregory of Nazianzus, known as the Cappadocian Fathers.

Gregory died on March 9, probably in Nyssa, in about the year 394.

Rite I Almighty God, who hast revealed to thy Church thine eternal Being of glorious majesty and perfect love as one God in Trinity of Persons: Give us grace that, like thy bishop Gregory of Nyssa, we may continue steadfast in the confession of this faith, and constant in our worship of thee, Father, Son, and Holy Spirit; who livest and reignest now and for ever. Amen.

Rite II Almighty God, you have revealed to your Church your eternal Being of glorious majesty and perfect love as one God in Trinity of Persons: Give us grace that, like your bishop Gregory of Nyssa, we may continue steadfast in the confession of this faith, and constant in our worship of you, Father, Son, and Holy Spirit; for you live and reign for ever and ever. Amen.

For Liturgical Celebration: [Common of a Theologian and Teacher, A17] [Common of a Pastor, A14] [Of the Holy Trinity, A37] [For the Ministry II, A50]

March 12

Gregory the Great
Bishop of Rome, 604

Only two Popes, Leo I and Gregory I, have been given the popular title of "the Great." Both served in the difficult times of the barbarian invasions of Italy. Gregory also knew the horrors of "plague, pestilence, and famine." He was born of a patrician family about 540, and became Prefect of Rome in 573. Shortly thereafter he retired to a monastic life in a community which he founded in his ancestral home on the Coelian Hill. Pope Pelagius II made him Ambassador to Constantinople in 579, where he learned much about the larger affairs of the Church. Not long after his return home, Pope Pelagius died of the plague, and in 590, Gregory was elected as his successor.

Gregory's pontificate was one of strenuous activity. He organized the defense of Rome against the attacks of the Lombards and fed its populace from papal granaries in Sicily. In this, as in other matters, he administered "the patrimony of St. Peter" with energy and efficiency. His ordering of the Church's liturgy and chant has molded the spirituality of the Western Church until the present day. Though unoriginal in theology, his writings provided succeeding generations with basic texts, especially the *Pastoral Care*, a classic on the work of the ministry.

In the midst of all his cares and duties, Gregory prepared and fostered the evangelizing mission to the Anglo-Saxons under Augustine and other monks from his own monastery. The Venerable Bede justly called Gregory "The Apostle of the English."

Gregory died on March 12, 604, and was buried in St. Peter's Basilica. His life was a true witness to the title he assumed for his office: "Servant of the servants of God."

Rite I   Almighty and merciful God, who didst raise up Gregory of Rome to be a servant of the servants of God, and didst inspire him to send missionaries to preach the Gospel to the English people: Preserve in thy Church the catholic and apostolic faith they taught, that thy people, being fruitful in every good work, may receive the crown of glory that never fades away; through Jesus Christ our Lord, who liveth and reigneth with thee and the Holy Spirit, one God, for ever and ever. Amen.

Rite II   Almighty and merciful God, you raised up Gregory of Rome to be a servant of the servants of God, and inspired him to send missionaries to preach the Gospel to the English people: Preserve in your Church the catholic and apostolic faith they taught, that your people, being fruitful in every good work, may receive the crown of glory that never fades away; through Jesus Christ our Lord, who lives and reigns with you and the Holy Spirit, one God, for ever and ever. Amen.

For Liturgical Celebration: [Common of a Theologian and Teacher, A17] [Common of a Pastor, A14] [Of the Reign of Christ, A46] [For the Ministry II, A50]

March 13

James Theodore Holly
Bishop of Haiti, and of the Dominican Republic, 1911

James Theodore Augustus Holly was born a free African American in Washington, D.C., on October 3, 1829. Baptized and confirmed in the Roman Catholic Church, he later became an Episcopalian. Holly was ordained deacon at St. Matthew's Church in Detroit on June 17, 1855, and ordained a priest by the bishop of Connecticut on January 2, 1856. He was appointed rector of St. Luke's, New Haven. In the same year he founded the Protestant Episcopal Society for Promoting the Extension of the Church among Colored People, an antecedent of the Union of Black Episcopalians. He became a friend of Frederick Douglass, and the two men worked together on many programs.

In 1861, Holly resigned as rector of St. Luke's to lead a group of African Americans settling in Haiti. Although his wife, his mother, and two of his children died during the first year, along with other settlers, Holly stayed on with two small sons, proclaiming that just "as the last surviving apostle of Jesus was in tribulation … on the forlorn isle of Patmos, so, by His Divine Providence, [Christ] had brought this tribulation upon me for a similar end in this isle in the Caribbean Sea." He welcomed the opportunity to speak of God's love to a people who needed to hear it.

Through an agreement between the House of Bishops of The Episcopal Church and the Orthodox Apostolic Church of Haiti, Holly was consecrated a missionary bishop to build the church in Haiti on November 8, 1874, making him the first African American to be raised to the office of bishop in The Episcopal Church. In 1878, Bishop Holly attended the Lambeth Conference, the first African American to do so, and he preached at Westminster Abbey on St. James' Day of that year. In the course of his ministry, he doubled the size of his diocese, and established medical clinics where none had been before.

Bishop Holly served the Diocese of Haiti until his death in Haiti on March 13, 1911. He had charge of the Diocese of the Dominican Republic as well, from 1897 until he died. He is buried on the grounds of St. Vincent's School for Handicapped Children in Port-au-Prince.

Rite I Most gracious God, we give thanks that thy servant James Theodore Holly labored to build a Church in which all might be free: Grant that, inspired by his testimony, we may overcome our prejudice and honor those whom thou dost call from every family, language, people, and nation; through Jesus Christ our Lord, who liveth and reigneth with thee and the Holy Spirit, one God, now and for ever. Amen.

Rite II Most gracious God, we thank you that your servant James Theodore Holly labored to build a Church in which all might be free: Grant that, inspired by his testimony, we may overcome our prejudice and honor those whom you call from every family, language, people, and nation; through Jesus Christ our Lord, who lives and reigns with you and the Holy Spirit, one God, now and for ever. Amen.

For Liturgical Celebration: [Common of a Pastor, A14] [Common of a Prophetic Witness, A31] [For the Ministry II, A50] [For Reconciliation and Forgiveness, A68]

March 17

Patrick
Bishop and Missionary of Ireland, 461

Patrick was born into a Christian family somewhere on the northwest coast of Britain in about 390. His grandfather had been a Christian priest and his father, Calpornius, a deacon. Calpornius was an important official in the late Roman imperial government of Britain. It was not unusual in this post-Constantinian period for such state officials to be in holy orders. When Patrick was about sixteen, he was captured by a band of Irish slave-raiders. He was carried off to Ireland and forced to serve as a shepherd. When he was about twenty-one, he escaped and returned to Britain, where he was educated as a Christian. He tells us that he took holy orders as both presbyter and bishop, although no particular see is known as his at this time. A vision then called him to return to Ireland. This he did about the year 431.

Tradition holds that Patrick landed not far from the place of his earlier captivity, near what is now known as Downpatrick (a "down" or "dun" is a fortified hill, the stronghold of a local Irish king). He then began a remarkable process of missionary conversion throughout the country that continued until his death, probably in 461. He made his appeal to the local kings and through them to their tribes. Christianizing the old pagan religion as he went, Patrick erected Christian churches over sites already regarded as sacred, had crosses carved on old druidic pillars, and put sacred wells and springs under the protection of Christian saints.

Many legends of Patrick's Irish missionary travels possess substrata of truth, especially those telling of his conversion of the three major Irish High Kings. At Armagh, he is said to have established his principal church. To this day, Armagh is regarded as the primatial see of all Ireland.

Two works are attributed to Patrick: an autobiographical *Confession*, in which he tells us, among other things, that he was criticized by his contemporaries for lack of learning, and a *Letter to Coroticus*, a British chieftain. The *Lorica* or *St. Patrick's Breastplate* ("I bind unto myself today") is probably not his, but it expresses his faith and zeal.

Rite I   Almighty God, who in thy providence didst choose thy servant Patrick to be the apostle of the Irish people, to bring those who were wandering in darkness and error to the true light and knowledge of thee: Grant us so to walk in that light that we may come at last to the light of everlasting life; through Jesus Christ our Lord, who liveth and reigneth with thee and the Holy Spirit, one God, for ever and ever. Amen.

Rite II Almighty God, in your providence you chose your servant Patrick to be the apostle of the Irish people, to bring those who were wandering in darkness and error to the true light and knowledge of you: Grant us so to walk in that light that we may come at last to the light of everlasting life; through Jesus Christ our Lord, who lives and reigns with you and the Holy Spirit, one God, for ever and ever. Amen.

For Liturgical Celebration: [Common of a Missionary, A11] [Common of a Pastor, A14] [For the Ministry II, A50] [For the Mission of the Church, A52]

March 18

Cyril of Jerusalem
Liturgist, Catechist, and Bishop, 386

Born in Jerusalem about 315, Cyril became bishop of that city probably in 349. In the course of political and ecclesiastical disputes, he was banished and restored three times. Cyril is the one we have most to thank for the development of catechetical instruction and liturgical observances during Lent and Holy Week. His *Catechetical Lectures on the Christian Faith*, given before Easter to candidates for baptism, were probably written by him sometime between 348 and 350.

The work consists of an introductory lecture, or *Procatechesis*, and eighteen *Catecheses* based upon the articles of the creed of the Church at Jerusalem. All these lectures (the earliest catechetical materials surviving today) may have been used many times over by Cyril and his successors, and considerably revised in the process. They were probably part of the pre-baptismal instruction that Egeria, a pilgrim nun from western Europe, witnessed at Jerusalem in the fourth century and described with great enthusiasm in the account of her pilgrimage. Many of the faithful would also attend these instructions.

Cyril's five *Mystagogical Catecheses on the Sacraments*, intended for the newly baptized after Easter, are now thought to have been composed, or at least revised, by John, Cyril's successor as Bishop of Jerusalem from 386 to 417.

It is likely that it was Cyril who instituted the observances of Palm Sunday and Holy Week during the latter years of his episcopate in Jerusalem. In doing so, he was taking practical steps to organize devotions for countless pilgrims and local inhabitants around the sacred sites. In time, as pilgrims returned to their homes from Palestine, these services were to influence the development of Holy Week observances throughout the entire Church. Cyril attended the Second Ecumenical Council at Constantinople, in 381, and died at Jerusalem on March 18, 386.

Cyril's thought has greatly enriched the observance of Holy Week in the 1979 Book of Common Prayer.

Rite I Strengthen, O God, thy Church in the sacraments of thy grace, that we, in union with the teaching and prayers of thy servant Cyril of Jerusalem, may enter more fully into thy Paschal mystery; through Jesus Christ our Lord, who liveth and reigneth with thee and the Holy Spirit, one God, now and for ever. Amen.

Rite II Strengthen, O God, your Church in the sacraments of your grace, that we, in union with the teaching and prayers of your servant Cyril of Jerusalem, may enter more fully into your Paschal mystery; through Jesus Christ our Lord, who lives and reigns with you and the Holy Spirit, one God, now and for ever. Amen.

For Liturgical Celebration: [Common of a Theologian and Teacher, A17] [Common of a Pastor, A14] [Of the Holy Eucharist, A40] [On the Anniversary of the Dedication of a Church, A47]

March 20

Thomas Ken
Bishop of Bath and Wells, 1711

Thomas Ken was born at Berkhampsted, Hertfordshire, England, in July, in 1637. Throughout his life he was both rewarded and punished for his integrity. His close relationship with the royal family began when he became chaplain to Princess Mary of Orange at The Hague. Ken was appalled at the Prince of Orange's treatment of his wife, and rebuked him publicly.

In 1683, Ken returned to England and became chaplain to Charles II. His integrity stirred him to rebuke Charles for lax behavior. When Ken was notified that the King's mistress, the actress Nell Gwynne, was to be lodged at his house, he refused, saying, "a woman of ill-repute ought not to be endured in the house of a clergyman, and especially the King's chaplain." The King took no offense, but in the next year made Ken the Bishop of Bath and Wells, declaring that none should have the position except "the little … fellow that refused his lodging to poor Nelly."

In 1688, when Charles' successor, James II, tried to undermine the authority of the Church of England and restore Roman Catholicsm, Ken was one of seven bishops who refused to read the King's Declaration of Indulgence, which offered toleration to Protestant non-conformists and to Roman Catholics. The seven bishops were sent to the Tower, but were acquitted in the courts, and became popular heroes. After the Revolution of 1688, however, Ken's conscience did not permit him to swear allegiance to William of Orange, who became King William III. As a Non-Juror, Ken was deprived of his see.

Ken's conscience would not let him rest and his disagreement with others of the "Non-Juring" party over various matters troubled him for the rest of his life. He deplored the Non-Juror schism, and after the accession of Queen Anne in 1702, he made his peace with the Church of England, encouraging his fellow Non-Jurors to return to their parish churches in 1710. Ken announced his intention to do the same, but died on March 19, 1711, before doing so.

A man of deep piety, Ken was the author of several religious works, which were immensely popular in the eighteenth century. He is best known as a writer of hymns, particularly the well-known evening hymn, "All praise to thee, my God, this night" (*The Hymnal 1982*, #43), which concludes with his doxology, "Praise God from whom all blessings flow." One of the most compelling products of his piety and his pen is the prayer, "Our God, amidst the deplorable division of your church, let us never widen its breaches, but give us universal charity to all who are called by your name. Deliver us from the sins and errors, the schisms and heresies of the age. Give us grace daily to pray for the peace of your church, and earnestly to seek it and to excite all we can to praise and love you; through Jesus Christ, our one Savior and Redeemer."

Rite I Almighty God, who didst give thy servant Thomas Ken grace and courage to bear witness to the truth before rulers and kings: Give us strength also that, following his example, we may constantly defend what is right, boldly reprove what is evil, and patiently suffer for the truth's sake; through Jesus Christ our Lord, who liveth and reigneth with thee and the Holy Spirit, one God, for ever and ever. Amen.

Rite II Almighty God, you gave your servant Thomas Ken grace and courage to bear witness to the truth before rulers and kings: Give us strength also that, following his example, we may constantly defend what is right, boldly reprove what is evil, and patiently suffer for the truth's sake; through Jesus Christ our Lord, who lives and reigns with you and the Holy Spirit, one God, for ever and ever. Amen.

For Liturgical Celebration: [Common of an Artist, Writer, or Composer, A27] [Common of a Pastor, A14] [For the Ministry II, A50]

March 21

Thomas Cranmer
Archbishop of Canterbury and Martyr, 1556

Thomas Cranmer was born at Aslockton in Nottinghamshire, England, on July 2, 1489. At fourteen, he entered Jesus College, Cambridge, where by 1514 he had obtained his BA and MA degrees and a Fellowship. In 1526, he became a Doctor of Divinity, a lecturer in his college, and examiner in the University. During his years at Cambridge, he diligently studied the Bible and the new doctrines emanating from the continental Reformation.

A chance meeting with King Henry VIII at Waltham Abbey in 1529 led to Cranmer's involvement in the "King's Affair" – the annulment of Henry's marriage to Catherine of Aragon. Cranmer prepared the King's defense and presented it to the universities in England and Germany, and to Rome.

While in Germany, Cranmer associated with the Lutheran reformers, especially with Andreas Osiander, whose daughter he married. When Archbishop Warham died, the King obtained papal confirmation of Cranmer's appointment to the See of Canterbury, and he was consecrated on March 30, 1533. Among his earliest acts was to declare the King's marriage null and void. He then validated the King's marriage to Anne Boleyn. Her child, the future Queen Elizabeth I, was Cranmer's godchild.

During the reign of Edward VI, Cranmer had a free hand in reforming the worship, doctrine, and practice of the Church. Thomas Cranmer was principally responsible for the first Book of Common Prayer of 1549, and for the second Book, in 1552. But at Edward's death he unfortunately subscribed to the dying King's will that the succession should go to Lady Jane Grey. For this, and also for his reforming work, he was arrested, deprived of his office and authority, and condemned by Queen Mary I, daughter of Henry VIII by Catherine, and a staunch Roman Catholic. He was burned at the stake on March 21, 1556.

Cranmer wrote two recantations during his imprisonment, but in the end he denied his recantations, and died heroically, saying, "Forasmuch as my hand offended in writing contrary to my heart, there my hand shall first be punished; for if I may come to the fire, it shall first be burned."

Rite I Merciful God, who through the work of Thomas Cranmer didst renew the worship of thy Church by restoring the language of the people, and through whose death didst reveal thy power in human weakness: Grant that by thy grace we may always worship thee in spirit and in truth; through Jesus Christ, our only Mediator and Advocate, who liveth and reigneth with thee and the Holy Spirit, one God, for ever and ever. Amen.

Rite II Merciful God, through the work of Thomas Cranmer you renewed the worship of your Church by restoring the language of the people, and through his death you revealed your power in human weakness: Grant that by your grace we may always worship you in spirit and in truth; through Jesus Christ, our only Mediator and Advocate, who lives and reigns with you and the Holy Spirit, one God, for ever and ever. Amen.

For Liturgical Celebration: [Common of a Martyr, A7] [Common of an Artist, Writer, or Composer, A27] [Common of a Pastor, A14] [Of the Holy Cross, A41]

March 22

James De Koven
Priest and Teacher, 1879

James De Koven was born in Middletown, Connecticut, on September 19, 1831, ordained by Bishop Kemper in 1855, and appointed professor of ecclesiastical history at Nashotah House. In addition, he administered a preparatory school and assisted at the Church of St. John Chrysostom in Delafield, Wisconsin.

Nashotah House was associated, from the time of its foundation, with many of the principles of the Oxford Movement, above all in its emphasis on the sacramental life of the Church and the expression of devotion to the Eucharist—including such practices as bowing to the altar, at the name of Jesus, and before receiving Communion. In 1859, De Koven became Warden of Racine College at Racine, Wisconsin.

De Koven came to national attention at the General Conventions of 1871 and 1874, when the controversy over "ritualism" was at its height. In 1871, he asserted that the use of candles on the altar, incense, and genuflections were lawful, because they symbolized "the real, spiritual presence of Christ" which The Episcopal Church upheld, along with the Orthodox and the Lutherans. To the General Convention of 1874, De Koven expressed the religious conviction that underlay his churchmanship: "You may take away from us, if you will, every external ceremony; you may take away altars, and super-altars, lights and incense and vestments; . . . and we will submit to you. But, gentlemen . . . to adore Christ's Person in his Sacrament—that is the inalienable privilege of every Christian and Catholic heart. How we do it, the way we do it, the ceremonies with which we do it, are utterly, utterly, indifferent. The thing itself is what we plead for."

Because of his advocacy of the "ritualist" cause, consents were not given to his consecration as Bishop of Wisconsin in 1874, and of Illinois in 1875.

Despite calls to serve at prominent parishes in New York City, Boston, Cincinnati, and Philadelphia, he remained in his post at Racine College, where his students admired him as "a model of great learning, gracious manners, personal holiness, and extraordinary compassion." He died there on March 19, 1879, and is buried on the grounds.

———⁂———

Rite I   Almighty and everlasting God, who led thy servant James De Koven to honor thy presence at the altar, and constantly to point to thy Christ: Grant that all ministers and stewards of thy mysteries may impart to thy faithful people the knowledge of thy presence and the truth of thy grace; through the same Jesus Christ our Lord, who liveth and reigneth with thee and the Holy Spirit, one God, for ever and ever. Amen.

Rite II   Almighty and everlasting God, who led your servant James De Koven to honor your presence at the altar, and constantly to point to your Christ: Grant that all ministers and stewards of your mysteries may impart to your faithful people the knowledge of your presence and the truth of your grace; through the same Jesus Christ our Lord, who lives and reigns with you and the Holy Spirit, one God, for ever and ever. Amen.

For Liturgical Celebration: [Common of a Pastor, A14] [Common of a Theologian and Teacher, A17] [Of the Holy Trinity, A37]

March 23

Gregory the Illuminator
Bishop and Missionary of Armenia, c. 332

Armenia was the first nation-state to become officially Christian, and this set a precedent for the legalization of Christianity by the Emperor Constantine. As a buffer state between the more powerful empires of Rome and Persia, Armenia endured many shifts of policy, as first one and then the other empire took it "under protection."

The accounts of Gregory, known as the Illuminator (or Enlightener) and as "Apostle of the Armenians," are a mixture of legend and fact. He was born about 257. After his father assassinated the Persian King Chosroes I, the infant boy was rescued and taken to Caesarea in Cappadocia, where he was brought up as a Christian. He married a woman named Mary, who bore him two sons. About 280, he returned to Armenia, after experiencing various fortunes of honor and imprisonment, succeeded in converting King Tiridates to his faith. With the help of the King the country was Christianized, and paganism was rooted out. About 300, Gregory was ordained a bishop at Caesarea. He established his cathedral at Valarshapat, with his center of work nearby at Echmiadzin, now in Armenia, and still the spiritual center of Armenian Christianity.

There is no record that Gregory attended the First Ecumenical Council at Nicaea in 325, but a tradition records that he sent in his stead his younger son Aristages, whom he ordained as his successor. His last years were spent in solitude, and he died about 332.

Rite I   Almighty God, who willest to be glorified in all thy saints, and didst raise up thy servant Gregory the Illuminator to be a light in the world, and to preach the Gospel to the people of Armenia: Shine, we pray thee, in our hearts, that we also in our generation may show forth thy praise, who hast called us out of darkness into thy marvelous light; through Jesus Christ our Lord, who liveth and reigneth with thee and the Holy Spirit, one God, now and for ever. Amen.

Rite II   Almighty God, whose will it is to be glorified in all your saints, and who raised up your servant Gregory the Illuminator to be a light in the world, and to preach the Gospel to the people of Armenia: Shine, we pray, in our hearts, that we also in our generation may show forth your praise, who called us out of darkness into your marvelous light; through Jesus Christ our Lord, who lives and reigns with you and the Holy Spirit, one God, now and for ever. Amen.

For Liturgical Celebration: [Common of a Missionary, A11] [Common of a Pastor, A14] [For the Ministry II, A50] [For the Mission of the Church, A52]

March 24

Óscar Romero, *Archbishop of San Salvador, 1980* *and the* Martyrs of El Salvador

Óscar Arnulfo Romero y Galdémez was born on August 15, 1917, in San Salvador. At the age of twelve, he was apprenticed to a carpenter, but was later able to attend seminary. His family's economic circumstances forced him to withdraw to work in a gold mine. Ultimately he entered another seminary and was eventually sent to the Gregorian University in Rome to study theology. After his ordination to the priesthood, he returned to his native land, where he worked among the poor, served as an administrator for the Church, and started an Alcoholics Anonymous group in San Miguel.

When he was appointed a bishop, radicals distrusted his conservative sympathies. However, after his appointment as Archbishop of San Salvador in 1977, a progressive Jesuit friend of his, Rutilio Grande, was assassinated, and Romero began protesting the government's injustice to the poor and its policies of torture. He met with Pope John Paul II in 1980 and complained that the leaders of El Salvador engaged in terror and assassinations. He also pleaded with the American government to stop military aid to his country, but this request was ignored.

Romero was shot to death while celebrating Mass at a small hospital chapel near his cathedral on March 24, 1980. The previous day, he preached a sermon calling on soldiers to disobey orders that violated human rights. He had said, "A bishop will die, but the Church of God which is the people will never perish." The Roman Catholic Church declared him "a servant of God," and he is honored as a martyr by many Christian denominations worldwide.

Almost nine months after Romero's assassination, four women—two Maryknoll Sisters, an Ursuline Sister, and a lay missioner—were also killed in the course of their duties by the El Salvadoran army. Six Jesuit priests, their housekeeper, and her daughter were similarly murdered in November of 1989. A statue of Romero stands at the door of Westminster Abbey in London as part of a commemoration of twentieth-century martyrs.

Rite I Almighty God, who didst call thy servant Óscar Romero to be a voice for the voiceless poor, and to give his life as a seed of freedom and a sign of hope: Grant that, inspired by his sacrifice and the example of the martyrs of El Salvador, we may without fear or favor witness to thy Word who abides, thy Word who is Life, even Jesus Christ our Lord, to whom, with thee and the Holy Spirit, be praise and glory now and for ever. Amen.

Rite II Almighty God, you called your servant Óscar Romero to be a voice for the voiceless poor, and to give his life as a seed of freedom and a sign of hope: Grant that, inspired by his sacrifice and the example of the martyrs of El Salvador, we may without fear or favor witness to your Word who abides, your Word who is Life, even Jesus Christ our Lord, to whom, with you and the Holy Spirit, be praise and glory now and for ever. Amen.

For Liturgical Celebration: [Common of a Martyr, A7] [Common of a Prophetic Witness, A31] [Common of a Pastor, A14] [Of the Holy Cross, A41]

March 26

Richard Allen
First Bishop of the African Methodist Episcopal Church, 1831

Richard Allen was born into slavery in 1760 in Germantown, Pennsylvania. Allen, his parents, and his siblings were eventually sold to owner Stokely Sturgis, whose plantation was in Delaware. The Methodists were already active in Delaware, and Sturgis allowed Allen to attend church. At the age of 17, Richard underwent a classic conversion experience: "I cried to the Lord both day and night," Allen said. "All of a sudden my dungeon shook, my chains flew off, and, glory to God, I cried."

Allen brought members of the Methodist Church into his master's home, where Sturgis heard a sermon by the great Methodist preacher Freeborn Garrettson. Sturgis was himself converted, and he allowed Allen to hire himself out and purchase his freedom; five years later, Richard Allen was a free man.

In 1786, Allen became a preacher at St. George's Methodist Church, but he was restricted to preaching at early morning services. Eventually, as black membership increased, the vestry decided to build a segregated section for black worshippers. Allen, along with his friend Absalom Jones, resented the segregation of his fellow black Christians and, in 1787, Allen and Jones led black worshippers out of St. George's in protest.

While Jones and many of those associated with him joined The Episcopal Church, Allen chose to continue in his Methodist tradition. He had been cooperating with Bishop Francis Asbury to spread Methodism among African Americans, and, in 1794, he founded Bethel Church in Philadelphia. When the newly formed African Methodist Episcopal Church declared its independence, Allen became its first Bishop.

Throughout his life, Richard Allen remained an advocate of freedom for all people, even operating a station on the Underground Railroad for escaped slaves. His ardent belief in the brotherhood of all who belonged to Christ is best expressed in one of the many hymns he wrote:

> Why do they then appear so mean
> And why so much despised?
> Because of their rich robes unseen
> The world is not appriz'd.

Allen died in 1831.

Rite I Loving God, who hast made us all thy children by adoption in Jesus Christ: May we, following the example of thy servant Richard Allen, proclaim liberty to all who are enslaved and captive in this world; through Jesus Christ, Savior of all, who with thee and the Holy Spirit liveth and reigneth, one God, for ever and ever. Amen.

Rite II Loving God, who makes us all your children by adoption in Jesus Christ: May we, following the example of your servant Richard Allen, proclaim liberty to all who are enslaved and captive in this world; through Jesus Christ, Savior of all, who with you and the Holy Spirit lives and reigns, one God, for ever and ever. Amen.

For Liturgical Celebration: [Common of a Pastor, A14] [Common of a Prophetic Witness, A31] [For Reconciliation and Forgiveness, A68]

March 27

Charles Henry Brent
Bishop of the Philippines and of Western New York, 1929

Charles Henry Brent was born at New Castle, Ontario, Canada, on April 9, 1862, and was educated at Trinity College, University of Toronto. Ordained priest in 1887 in Canada, he came to the United States in his first call as an assistant at St. Paul's Cathedral in Buffalo, New York. In 1888 he became associate rector at St. John the Evangelist in Boston, Massachusetts, with responsibility for St Augustine's, an African American congregation. He was serving at St. Stephen's, Boston, when, in 1901, he was elected by the House of Bishops as Missionary Bishop of the Philippines.

In the Philippines, he began a crusade against the opium traffic, a campaign he later expanded to the continent of Asia. He became President of the Opium Conference in Shanghai in 1909, and represented the United States on the League of Nations Narcotics Committee. He also established cordial relations with the Philippine Independent Church, which led, ultimately, to intercommunion with that Church.

Bishop Brent served as Senior Chaplain of the American Expeditionary Forces in World War I. When General Pershing was given the command in 1917, he asked Brent to organize the chaplaincy for the force and then persuaded him to stay on to run the organization he had created, a first for the US Army in terms of scale and centralization, the precedent for the creation of the post of Chief of Chaplains in 1920. In 1918, he accepted election as Bishop of Western New York, having declined three previous elections in order to remain at his post in the Philippines.

Brent was the outstanding figure of The Episcopal Church on the world scene for two decades. The central focus of his life and ministry was the cause of Christian unity. After attending the World Missionary Conference in Edinburgh in 1910, he led The Episcopal Church in the movement that culminated in the first World Conference on Faith and Order, which was held in Lausanne, Switzerland, in 1927, and over which he presided. He died in 1929 and is buried in the main cemetery in Lausanne in the section reserved for "honored foreigners"; his tomb is still often visited and adorned with commemorative plaques brought by delegations from the Philippines.

James Thayer Addison, the historian, described Brent as "a saint of disciplined mental vigor, one whom soldiers were proud to salute and whom children were happy to play with, who could dominate a parliament and minister to an invalid, a priest and bishop who gloried in the heritage of his Church, yet who stood among all Christian brothers as one who served . . . He was everywhere an ambassador of Christ."

Brent was also a man of prayer. One of his prayers for the mission of the Church has been included in the Book of Common Prayer: "Lord Jesus Christ, you stretched out your arms of love on the hard wood of the cross that everyone might come within the reach of your saving embrace: So clothe us with your Spirit that we, reaching forth our hands in love, may bring those who do not know you to the knowledge and love of you; for the honor of your Name."

Rite I   Heavenly Father, whose Son prayed that we all might be one: Deliver us from arrogance and prejudice, and give us wisdom and forbearance, that, following thy servant Charles Henry Brent, we may be united in one family with all who confess the Name of thy Son Jesus Christ; who liveth and reigneth with thee and the Holy Spirit, one God, now and for ever. Amen.

Rite II   Heavenly Father, whose Son prayed that we all might be one: Deliver us from arrogance and prejudice, and give us wisdom and forbearance, that, following your servant Charles Henry Brent, we may be united in one family with all who confess the Name of your Son Jesus Christ; who lives and reigns with you and the Holy Spirit, one God, now and for ever. Amen.

For Liturgical Celebration: [Common of a Missionary, A11] [Common of a Pastor, A14] [For the Unity of the Church, A48] [For the Mission of the Church, A52]

March 28

James Solomon Russell
Priest, 1935

James Solomon Russell was born into slavery on December 20, 1857, near Palmer Springs, Virginia. He became known as the father of St. Paul's College (one of the three historically Black Episcopal Colleges) and was the founder of numerous congregations, a missionary, and a writer.

He was the first student of St. Stephen's Normal and Theological Institute (which later became the Bishop Payne Divinity School) in Petersburg, Virginia. In 1888, one year after his ordination as a priest in The Episcopal Church, Russell and his wife Virginia opened St. Paul's Normal School in Lawrenceville, Virginia. Russell's vision for the school was to provide both a literary and an industrial education. Religion was a mandatory subject, and students attended chapel twice daily. Russell served as the school's principal and chaplain until his retirement in 1929.

For 52 years of ordained ministry in the Diocese of Southern Virginia, he worked tirelessly to encourage black candidates to enter Holy Orders so that they could care for the growing numbers of black Episcopalians. In 1893, Russell was named the first Archdeacon for Colored Work. Southern Virginia had the largest population of African American Episcopalians in the United States, thanks in large measure to Russell's evangelistic efforts. In 1927, Russell was the first African American elected bishop in The Episcopal Church. However, he declined election as Suffragan Bishop for Colored Work in the Dioceses of Arkansas and North Carolina, and he was glad that his action helped defeat the idea of subordinate racial bishops.

Russell's ministry continued until his death on March 28, 1935. His autobiography, *Adventure in Faith*, was published the following year.

Rite I   O God, the font of resurrected life, we bless thee for the courageous witness of thy deacon, James Solomon Russell, whose mosaic ministry overcame all adversities; draw us into the wilderness and speak tenderly to us there so that we might love and worship thee as he did, assured in our legacy of saving grace through Jesus Christ, who liveth and reigneth with thee and the Holy Spirit, for ever and ever. Amen.

Rite II   God, font of resurrected life, we bless you for the courageous witness of your deacon, James Solomon Russell, whose mosaic ministry vaulted over adversity; allure us into the wilderness and speak tenderly to us there so that we might love and worship you as he did, sure of our legacy of saving grace through Jesus Christ, who lives and reigns with you and the Holy Spirit, always and ever. Amen.

For Liturgical Celebration: [Common of a Pastor, A14] [Common of a Prophetic Witness, A31] [For Education, A60]

March 29

John Keble
Priest, 1866

John Keble, born on April 23, 1792, received his early education in his father's vicarage. At fourteen, he won a scholarship to Oxford and graduated in 1811 with highest honors. He served the University in several capacities, including ten years as Professor of Poetry. After ordination in 1816, he had a series of rural curacies, and finally settled in 1836 into a thirty-year pastorate at the village of Hursley, near Winchester.

Among his cycle of poems entitled *The Christian Year* (1827), which he wrote to restore among Anglicans a deep feeling for the Church Year, remains a familiar hymn (*The Hymnal 1982*, #10):

> New ev'ry morning is the love
> Our wakening and uprising prove:
> Through sleep and darkness safely brought,
> Restored to life and power and thought.

The work went through ninety-five editions, but this was not the fame he sought: his consuming desire was to be a faithful pastor, who finds his fulfillment in daily services, confirmation classes, visits to village schools, and a voluminous correspondence with those seeking spiritual counsel.

England was going through a turbulent change from a rural to an industrial and urban society. England and Ireland were incorporated in 1801 and the (Protestant) Church of Ireland became part of the Church of England. Up until 1833, Ireland had twenty-two Anglican bishops and archbishops for a population of about 800,000 persons, a ratio considerably smaller than that of the English dioceses. The "Irish Church Measure" of 1833 would have reduced the number of Anglican bishops and archbishops by ten, amalgamating episcopal oversight to a proportion equal in both countries and saving money needed at the parish level. Keble vigorously attacked this Parliamentary action as a "National Apostasy" undermining the independence of the Church in a sermon by that title, now referred to as his Assize Sermon of 1833.

His Assize Sermon of 1833 was the spark that ignited the Oxford Movement. Those drawn to the Movement began to publish a series of "Tracts for the Times" (hence the popular name "Tractarians")—which sought to recall the Church to its ancient sacramental heritage. John Henry Newman was the intellectual leader of the Movement, Edward Bouverie Pusey was the prophet of its devotional life, and John Keble was its pastoral inspiration.

Though bitterly attacked, his loyalty to his Church was unwavering. Within three years of his death at Bournemouth, in Hampshire, on March 29, 1866, at age 74, a college bearing his name was established at Oxford "to give an education in strict fidelity to the Church of England." For Keble, this would have meant dedication to learning in order "to live more nearly as we pray."

Rite I   Grant, O God, that in all time of our testing we may know thy presence and obey thy will; that, following the example of thy servant John Keble, we may accomplish with integrity and courage that which thou givest us to do and endure that which thou givest us to bear; through Jesus Christ our Lord, who liveth and reigneth with thee and the Holy Spirit, one God, for ever and ever. Amen.

Rite II Grant, O God, that in all time of our testing we may know your presence and obey your will; that, following the example of your servant John Keble, we may accomplish with integrity and courage what you give us to do and endure what you give us to bear; through Jesus Christ our Lord, who lives and reigns with you and the Holy Spirit, one God, for ever and ever. Amen.

For Liturgical Celebration: [Common of a Pastor, A14] [Common of a Theologian and Teacher, A17] [Common of an Artist, Writer, or Composer, A27] [Of the Holy Trinity, A37]

March 30

Innocent of Alaska
Bishop, 1879

Innocent, whose secular name was John Veniaminov, was born in on August 26, 1797, in the village of Anginskoye, Verkholensk District, in the Irkutsk province of Russia.

Following only two years of service as a parish priest, John Veniaminov volunteered for the mission to the Aleutian islands. In May of 1823, John, his wife, his infant son, and his brother Stefan set forth on their long and arduous journey, which took more than a year.

He immediately began the work of evangelism and conversion that would last nearly fifty years and would lead to his being called "The Apostle of North America." He taught the islanders to be carpenters, blacksmiths, and bricklayers, and, with their help, he built a church for the local people.

John Veniaminov's parish included not only the island of Unalaska, but also the Fox Islands and Pribilof Islands, whose inhabitants had been converted to Christianity before his arrival. He became familiar with the language and dialects of the people he served, traveling the icy waters between the islands in a canoe. He devised a Cyrillic alphabet for the Aleut language, and translated the Gospel of Matthew and many of the most used hymns and prayers into Aleut.

In 1829, he traveled to Nushagak where he preached the gospel to the peoples of the Bering seacoast. In 1834, he was transferred to Sitka Island and began his mission work with the Tlingit people. He won the confidence of the Tlingit chiefs by introducing smallpox vaccine to them in 1836 and saving many lives when a smallpox epidemic reached the New Archangel/Sitka area. Despite their faithful adherence to their own customs and traditions, he learned their language and converted many of them to Christ.

On the death of his wife, he became a monk in 1840 and took the name 'Innocent.' Later that year, he was consecrated Bishop of Kamchatka, the Kuril Islands, and the Aleutian Islands. He continued making long missionary journeys during his tenure as bishop, and contemporaries record "that the natives loved their teacher and illuminator like a real father, since he was indeed both benefactor and father, teacher and patron to his spiritual children that he had saved for Christ." After elevation to archbishop in 1850, on November 19, 1867, Innocent was appointed as Metropolitan of Moscow, the leader of the Russian Orthodox Church.

He died March 31, 1879, in Moscow.

Rite I Holy Immortal One, who didst bless thy people by calling Innocent from leading thy Church in Russia to be an apostle and light to the people of Alaska and to proclaim the dispensation and grace of God: Guide our steps, that as he didst labor humbly in danger and hardship, we may witness to the Gospel of Christ wherever we are led, and serve thee as gladly in privation as in power; through Jesus Christ our Lord, who liveth and reigneth with thee and the Holy Spirit, one God, to the ages of ages. Amen.

Rite II Holy Immortal One, you blessed your people by calling Innocent from leading your Church in Russia to be an apostle and light to the people of Alaska and to proclaim the dispensation and grace of God: Guide our steps, that as he labored humbly in danger and hardship, we may witness to the Gospel of Christ wherever we are led, and serve you as gladly in privation as in power; through Jesus Christ our Lord, who lives and reigns with you and the Holy Spirit, one God, to the ages of ages. Amen.

For Liturgical Celebration: [Common of a Missionary, A11] [Common of a Pastor, A14] [For the Ministry II, A50] [For the Mission of the Church, A52]

March 31

John Donne
Priest, 1631

"Any man's death diminishes me, because I am involved in mankind. And therefore never send to know for whom the bell tolls: It tolls for thee."

These words are familiar to many; their author, John Donne, though less well known, is one of the greatest of English poets. In his own time, he was the best-known preacher in the Church of England. He came to that eminence by a tortuous path. Born into a wealthy and pious Roman Catholic family on January 21, 1572, in London, he was educated at both Oxford and Cambridge, and studied law at Lincoln's Inn. Some time later he conformed to the Established Church and embarked upon a promising political career of service to the State. The revelation of his secret marriage in 1601 to the niece of his employer, the Lord Keeper of the Great Seal, brought his public career to an end. In 1615, he was persuaded by King James I and others to receive ordination.

Following several brief parish pastorates, Donne rose rapidly in popularity as Dean of St. Paul's Cathedral, London, from 1621 until his death. He drew great throngs to the Cathedral and to Paul's Cross, a nearby open-air pulpit. His sermons reflect the wide learning of the scholar, the passionate intensity of the poet, and the profound devotion of one struggling in his own life to relate the freedom and demands of the gospel to the concerns of a common humanity, on every level and in all its complexities.

The hymn "Wilt thou forgive that sin where I begun" (*The Hymnal 1982*, #140) is one of his poetic legacies. In another of his poems, he wrote:

> We thinke that Paradise and Calvarie,
> Christs Crosse, and Adams tree, stood in one place;
> Looke, Lord, and finde both Adams met in me;
> As the first Adams sweat surrounds my face

May the last Adams blood my soule embrace.
So, in his purple wrapp'd receive mee Lord,
By these his thornes give me his other Crowne;
And as to others soules I preach'd thy word,
Be this my Text, my Sermon to my owne.
Therefore that he may raise the Lord throws down.

John Donne died in London on March 31, 1631.

Rite I   Almighty God, the root and fountain of all being: Open our eyes to see, with thy servant John Donne, that whatsover hath any being is a mirror in which we may behold thee; through Jesus Christ our Lord, who liveth and reigneth with thee and the Holy Spirit, one God, for ever and ever. Amen.

Rite II   Almighty God, the root and fountain of all being: Open our eyes to see, with your servant John Donne, that whatever has any being is a mirror in which we may behold you; through Jesus Christ our Lord, who lives and reigns with you and the Holy Spirit, one God, for ever and ever. Amen.

For Liturgical Celebration: [Common of an Artist, Writer, or Composer, A27] [Common of a Pastor, A14]

APRIL

1 Frederick Denison Maurice, Priest, 1872
2 James Lloyd Breck, Priest, 1876
3 Richard, Bishop of Chichester, 1253
4 Martin Luther King, Jr., Civil Rights Leader and Martyr, 1968 (see also Jan. 15)
5 Pandita Mary Ramabai, Prophetic Witness and Evangelist in India, 1922
6 Daniel G. C. Wu, Priest and Missionary among Chinese Americans, 1956
7 Tikhon, Patriarch of Russia, Confessor and Ecumenist, 1925
8 William Augustus Muhlenberg, Priest, 1877 and Anne Ayres, Religious, 1896
9 Dietrich Bonhoeffer, Theologian and Martyr, 1945
10 William Law, Priest, 1761
10 Pierre Teilhard de Chardin, Scientist and Military Chaplain, 1955
11 George Augustus Selwyn, Bishop of New Zealand, and of Lichfield, 1878
12 Adoniram Judson, Missionary to Burma, 1850
13
14 Edward Thomas Demby, 1957, and Henry Beard Delany, 1928, Bishops
15 Damien, Priest and Leper, 1889, and Marianne, Religious, 1918, of Molokai
16 Mary (Molly) Brant (Konwatsijayenni), Witness to the Faith among the Mohawks, 1796
17 Emily Cooper, Deaconess, 1909
18
19 Alphege, Archbishop of Canterbury, and Martyr, 1012
20

21   Anselm, Archbishop of Canterbury, 1109

22   John Muir, Naturalist and Writer, 1914, and Hudson Stuck, Priest and Environmentalist, 1920

23   George, Soldier and Martyr, c. 304

23   Toyohiko Kagawa, Prophetic Witness in Japan, 1960

24   Genocide Remembrance

25

26   Robert Hunt, Priest and First Chaplain at Jamestown, 1607

27   Christina Rossetti, Poet, 1894

28

29   Catherine of Siena, 1380

30   Sarah Josepha Buell Hale, Editor and Prophetic Witness, 1879

April 1

Frederick Denison Maurice
Priest, 1872

In the same year that Karl Marx declared religion to be the "opiate of the people," Frederick Denison Maurice wrote, "We have been dosing our people with religion when what they want is not this but the living God." Like Marx, Maurice wanted to solve the questions of our complex society; unlike Marx, he called for a radical, but non-violent, reform, by the renewal of "faith in a God who has redeemed mankind, in whom I may vindicate my rights as a man." Maurice was a founder of the Christian Socialist Movement, which, he wrote, "will commit us at once to the conflict we must engage in sooner or later with the unsocial Christians and unchristian Socialists."

Maurice was born in 1805 into the family of a Unitarian minister whose life was marked by intense religious controversy. Maurice studied civil law at Cambridge, but refused the degree in 1827, because, as a Dissenter, he could not subscribe to the Thirty-nine Articles of Religion. After several personal crises, however, he became an Anglican and was ordained in 1834. Soon afterwards he was appointed Professor of English Literature and History at King's College, London, and, in 1846, to the chair of Theology.

In his book, *The Kingdom of Christ*, published in 1838, Maurice investigates the causes and cures of Christian divisions. The book has become a source of Anglican ecumenism. Maurice was dismissed from his professorships because of his leadership in the Christian Socialist Movement, and because of the supposed unorthodoxy of his *Theological Essays* (1853).

Maurice saw worship as the meeting point of time and eternity, and as the fountain of energies for the Church's mission. He wrote, "I do not think we are to praise the liturgy but to use it. When we do not want it for our life, we may begin to talk of it as a beautiful composition."

After the death of the Christian Socialist Movement in 1854, Maurice founded the Working Men's College, and resumed teaching at Queen's College, London. Maurice awakened Anglicanism to the need for concern with the problems of society. In later years, he was honored even by former opponents. He was rector of two parishes, and was professor of Moral Theology at Cambridge from 1866 until his death.

Rite I   Almighty God, who hast restored our human nature to heavenly glory through the perfect obedience of our Savior Jesus Christ: Keep alive in thy Church, we beseech thee, a passion for justice and truth; that, like thy servant Frederick Denison Maurice, we may work and pray for the triumph of the kingdom of thy Christ; who liveth and reigneth with thee and the Holy Spirit, one God, now and for ever. Amen.

Rite II   Almighty God, you restored our human nature to heavenly glory through the perfect obedience of our Savior Jesus Christ: Keep alive in your Church, we pray, a passion for justice and truth; that, like your servant Frederick Denison Maurice, we may work and pray for the triumph of the kingdom of your Christ; who lives and reigns with you and the Holy Spirit, one God, now and for ever. Amen.

For Liturgical Celebration: [Common of a Theologian and Teacher, A17] [Common of a Prophetic Witness, A31] [Common of a Pastor, A14] [Of the Incarnation, A39] [For Rogation Days II, A56]

April 2
James Lloyd Breck
Priest, 1876

James Lloyd Breck was one of the most important missionaries of The Episcopal Church in the nineteenth century. He was called "The Apostle of the Wilderness."

Breck was born in Philadelphia in 1818, and like many important churchmen of his time, was greatly influenced by the pastoral devotion, liturgical concern, and sacramental emphasis of William Augustus Muhlenberg. Breck attended Muhlenberg's school in Flushing, New York, before entering the University of Pennsylvania. Muhlenberg inspired him, when he was sixteen years old, to dedicate himself to a missionary life. The dedication was crystallized when Breck, with three other classmates from the General Theological Seminary, founded a religious community at Nashotah, Wisconsin, which in 1844 was on the frontier.

Nashotah became a center of liturgical observance, of pastoral care, and of education. Isolated families were visited, mission stations established, and, probably for the first time since the Revolution, Episcopal missionaries were the first to reach the settlers.

Though Nashotah House flourished, and became one of the seminaries of The Episcopal Church, the "religious house" ideal did not. Breck moved on to St. Paul, Minnesota, where he began the work of The Episcopal Church. At Gull Lake, he organized St. Columba's Mission for the Chippewa. It laid the foundation for work among the Native Americans by their own native priests, although the mission itself did not survive.

In 1855, Breck married, and in 1858 settled in Faribault, Minnesota, where his mission was associated with one of the first cathedrals established in The Episcopal Church in the United States. He also founded Seabury Divinity School, which later merged with Western Theological Seminary, to become Seabury-Western. In 1867, Breck went on to California, inspired principally by the opportunity of founding a new theological school. His schools at Benicia, California, did not survive, but the five parishes which he founded did, and the Church in California was strengthened immensely through his work. He died of exhaustion, at the age of 57, in 1876.

―⁂―

Rite I Teach thy Church, O Lord, we beseech thee, to value and support pioneering and courageous missionaries, whom thou callest, as thou didst call thy servant James Lloyd Breck, to preach, and teach, and plant thy Church on new frontiers; through Jesus Christ our Lord, who liveth and reigneth with thee and the Holy Spirit, one God, for ever and ever. Amen.

Rite II Teach your Church, O Lord, we pray, to value and support pioneering and courageous missionaries, whom you call, as you called your servant James Lloyd Breck, to preach, and teach, and plant your Church on new frontiers; through Jesus Christ our Lord, who lives and reigns with you and the Holy Spirit, one God, for ever and ever. Amen.

For Liturgical Celebration: [Common of a Missionary, A11] [Common of a Pastor, A14] [For the Ministry II, A50] [For the Mission of the Church, A52] [For Education, A60]

April 3

Richard
Bishop of Chichester, 1253

Born in Burford, Worcestershire, around 1197, Richard and his older brother Robert were quite young when their parents died, leaving a rich estate with a guardian to manage it. The guardian allowed the estate to dwindle, and Richard worked long hours to restore it.

Pressure was put on Richard to marry, but he, who from earliest years had preferred books to almost anything else, turned the estate over to his brother and went to Oxford. Often hungry, cold, and not always sure of his next day's keep, Richard managed to succeed in his studies under such teachers as Robert Grosseteste.

He continued to study law at Paris and Bologna, earned a doctorate, and returned to Oxford to become University Chancellor. Shortly afterward, the Archbishop of Canterbury, Edmund Rich, appointed him to be his own chancellor. The friendship between the primate and his young assistant was close: Richard also became his biographer. Conflict with King Henry III eventually forced Archbishop Rich into exile in France, where Richard nursed him in his final illness. After the Archbishop's death, Richard moved to the Dominican house at Orleans for further study and teaching. He was ordained priest in 1243.

He then returned to England, and was elected Bishop of Chichester in 1244. King Henry opposed the election, confiscated all the revenues of the diocese, and even locked Richard out of the episcopal dwelling. Richard was given lodging by a priest, Simon of Tarring. During these years he functioned as a missionary bishop, traveling about the diocese on foot, visiting fishermen and farmers, holding synods with great difficulty, and endeavoring to establish order. Threatened by the Pope, Henry finally acknowledged Richard as Bishop in 1246.

For eight years, he served his diocese as preacher, confessor, teacher, and counselor. While campaigning in 1253, for a new crusade against the Saracens, he contracted a fatal fever. Nine years after his death, he was canonized. His best remembered words are:

> Dear Lord, of thee three things I pray:
> To see thee more clearly,
> Love thee more dearly,
> Follow thee more nearly.

Rite I   We thank thee, Lord God, for all the benefits thou hast given us in thy Son Jesus Christ, our most merciful Redeemer, Friend, and Brother, and for all the pains and insults he has borne for us; and we pray that, following the example of thy saintly bishop Richard of Chichester, we may see Christ more clearly, love him more dearly, and follow him more nearly; who liveth and reigneth with thee and the Holy Spirit, one God, now and for ever. Amen.

Rite II   We thank you, Lord God, for all the benefits you have given us in your Son Jesus Christ, our most merciful Redeemer, Friend, and Brother, and for all the pains and insults he has borne for us; and we pray that, following the example of your saintly bishop Richard of Chichester, we may see Christ more clearly, love him more dearly, and follow him more nearly; who lives and reigns with you and the Holy Spirit, one God, now and for ever. Amen.

For Liturgical Celebration: [Common of a Pastor, A14] [For the Ministry II, A50] [Of the Holy Spirit, A38]

April 4

Martin Luther King, Jr.
Civil Rights Leader and Martyr, 1968

Martin Luther King, Jr. was born on January 15, 1929, in Atlanta. As the son and grandson of Baptist preachers, he was steeped in the Black Church tradition. Following graduation from Morehouse College (Atlanta, Georgia) in 1948, King entered Crozer Theological Seminary (Chester, Pennsylvania), having been ordained the previous year into the ministry of the National Baptist Church. He graduated from Crozer in 1951 and received his doctorate in theology from Boston University in 1955.

In 1954, King became pastor of a church in Montgomery, Alabama. There, Black indignation at inhumane treatment on segregated buses culminated in December, 1955, in the arrest of Rosa Parks for refusing to give up her seat to a white man. King was catapulted into national prominence as the leader of the Montgomery bus boycott. He became increasingly the articulate prophet, who could not only rally the Black masses, but could also move the consciences of Whites.

King founded the Southern Christian Leadership Conference to spearhead non-violent mass demonstrations against racism. Many confrontations followed, most notably in Birmingham and Selma, Alabama, and in Chicago. King's campaigns were instrumental to the passage of the Civil Rights Acts of 1964, 1965, and 1968. King then turned his attention to economic empowerment of the poor and opposition to the Vietnam War, contending that racism, poverty, and militarism were interrelated. He was awarded the Nobel Peace Prize in 1964 for his commitment to non-violent social change.

King lived in constant danger: his home was dynamited, he was almost fatally stabbed, and he was harassed by death threats. He was even jailed 30 times; but through it all he was sustained by his deep faith. In 1957, he received, late at night, a vicious telephone threat. Alone in his kitchen he wept and prayed. He relates that he heard the Lord speaking to him and saying, "Martin Luther, stand up for righteousness, stand up for justice," and promising never to leave him alone—"No, never alone." King refers to his vision as his "Mountain-top Experience."

After preaching at Washington Cathedral on March 31, 1968, King went to Memphis in support of sanitation workers in their struggle for better wages. There, he proclaimed that he had been "to the mountain-top" and had seen "the Promised Land," and that he knew that one day he and his people would be "free at last." On the following day, April 4, he was cut down by an assassin's bullet.

Rite I   Almighty God, who by the hand of Moses thy servant didst lead thy people out of slavery, and didst make them free at last: Grant that thy Church, following the example of thy prophet Martin Luther King, may resist oppression in the name of thy love, and may strive to secure for all thy children the blessed liberty of the Gospel of Jesus Christ; who liveth and reigneth with thee and the Holy Spirit, one God, now and for ever. Amen.

Rite II Almighty God, by the hand of Moses your servant you led your people out of slavery, and made them free at last: Grant that your Church, following the example of your prophet Martin Luther King, may resist oppression in the name of your love, and may strive to secure for all your children the blessed liberty of the Gospel of Jesus Christ; who lives and reigns with you and the Holy Spirit, one God, now and for ever. Amen.

For Liturgical Celebration: [Common of a Martyr, A7] [Common of a Prophetic Witness, A31] [Common of a Pastor, A14] [Of the Holy Cross, A41] [For Reconciliation and Forgiveness, A68]

April 5

Pandita Mary Ramabai
Prophetic Witness and Evangelist in India, 1922

Pandita Ramabai was born on April 26, 1858, in Gangamoola, India. She faced most of the obstacles a woman could encounter in the India of her lifetime. She was denied access to formal education and was ostracized from society as first an orphan and then a widow. She experienced first-hand the effects of India's rigid caste system that placed discriminatory walls between social and racial groups. Yet she fought back, first as a Hindu, then as a Christian.

Her father was a scholar who taught her both the Sanskrit language and the Vedas, the source of classical Hindu beliefs. An 1876 famine killed most of her family and a few years later a cholera epidemic killed her husband of nineteen months. Acutely aware of the difficulties facing Indian women, Ramabai was increasingly drawn to social work and in 1883 traveled to England where she spent time with the Community of Saint Mary the Virgin, an Anglican religious community near Oxford. She was baptized in 1883 and worked actively in London with a community of nuns who ministered to former prostitutes. She also attended the Cheltenham Ladies College, an institution that favored women's suffrage and instructing young women in the same subjects taught in schools for young men.

Ramabai returned to India in 1889 and founded the Mukti Mission, a home for abandoned widows and orphans of the Brahmin high priestly caste in Bombay (now known as Mumbai). When India was again struck by famine in 1896, she extended the mission's outreach to include women and orphans of all castes, and gradually added a clinic and vocational training courses.

Fluent in several languages, Ramabai translated the Bible into Marathi, a West Indian language. Indians who encountered her gave her the title "Pandita," meaning "the learned one." Ramabai, like Mother Teresa later, worked tirelessly among India's poor, depending on the generosity of others to fund her activities. Her evangelical enthusiasm never waned. "What a blessing this burden does not fall on me. But Christ bears it on his shoulders," she wrote, and "no one but He could transform and uplift the downtrodden womanhood of India and of every land." Pandita Ramabai died on April 5, 1922, at the age of 64.

Rite I   Everliving God, who didst call the women at the tomb to witness to the resurrection of thy Son: We offer thanks for the courageous and independent spirit of thy servant Pandita Ramabai, the mother of modern India; and we pray that we, like her, may embrace thy gift of new life, caring for the poor, braving resentment to uphold the dignity of women, and offering the riches of our culture to our Savior Jesus Christ; who liveth and reigneth with thee in the unity of the Holy Spirit, one God, now and for ever. Amen.

Rite II Everliving God, you called the women at the tomb to witness to the resurrection of your Son: We thank you for the courageous and independent spirit of your servant Pandita Ramabai, the mother of modern India; and we pray that we, like her, may embrace your gift of new life, caring for the poor, braving resentment to uphold the dignity of women, and offering the riches of our culture to our Savior Jesus Christ; who lives and reigns with you in the unity of the Holy Spirit, one God, now and for ever. Amen.

For Liturgical Celebration: [Common of a Prophetic Witness, A31] [Common of a Missionary, A11] [Common of a Saint, A23] [For all Baptized Christians, A42] [For the Mission of the Church, A52]

April 6

Daniel G. C. Wu
Priest and Missionary among Chinese Americans, 1956

Church work among Chinese Americans in the San Francisco Bay Area dates back to the middle of the nineteenth century, but flourished under the leadership of Daniel Gee Ching Wu.

Born on October 19, 1883, in China, Wu traveled to Hawaii for work. There Deaconess Emma Drant asked Gee Ching Wu to teach her Chinese in exchange for lessons in English. At the time, Wu was not a Christian, but during their time together, Drant's Christian convictions inspired his conversion. Wu was baptized, taking the name Daniel. Drant left for San Francisco, where she began mission work among the Chinese and, in 1905, called together a worshiping community to be called True Sunshine Episcopal Mission. After the 1906 earthquake, many residents of San Francisco, including many Chinese, fled across the bay to Oakland, and a second Chinese mission took root there. Needing help, Drant called upon Daniel Wu to come from Hawaii and support her missionary efforts.

From the time of his arrival in 1907, Wu managed the work of the two missions while studying for ordination at the Church Divinity School of the Pacific. He was ordained in 1912 and became the Vicar of True Sunshine Episcopal Mission in San Francisco and Our Savior Episcopal Mission in Oakland, both of which were already thriving congregations.

Daniel Wu devoted his ministry to work among Chinese immigrants. He frequently worked the docks and ports of entry, made contact with those newly arrived, and assisted in whatever way possible to ease their transition to their new home. To keep them connected to their heritage, Wu and the people of his congregations offered classes in Chinese to the children and instruction in English to the adults. They offered a variety of programs that helped newcomers to adjust to their new country without losing the culture and heritage of their homeland.

For thirty-six years, Daniel Wu and his people opened their hearts and their churches to generations of Chinese Americans and played a singularly important role in establishing the ministry of The Episcopal Church among those of Asian descent.

Rite I   Loving God, we give thanks for Daniel Wu and his work among the Chinese immigrants whose lives he touched in his day: By the power of thy Holy Spirit give to thy Church compassion and respect for all people, wherever they reside, that, inspired by thy love, every community might be filled with thy wisdom and call forth leaders to guide thy flock in faithfulness to the Eternal Word, Jesus Christ; who with thee and the Holy Spirit liveth and reigneth, one God, now and for ever. Amen.

Rite II   Loving God, we give thanks for Daniel Wu and his work among the Chinese immigrants whose lives he touched in his day: By the power of your Holy Spirit give to your Church compassion and respect for all people, wherever they reside, that, inspired by your love, every community might be filled with your wisdom and call forth leaders to guide your flock in faithfulness to the Eternal Word, Jesus Christ; who with you and the Holy Spirit lives and reigns, one God, now and for ever. Amen.

For Liturgical Celebration: [Common of a Missionary, A11] [Common of a Pastor, A14] [For the Ministry I, A49] [For the Mission of the Church, A52]

April 7

Tikhon, Patriarch of Russia
Confessor and Ecumenist, 1925

Vasily Ivanovich Belavin (Tikhon's given name) was born January 19, 1865. He grew up in a rural area among peasants in a village where his father was a priest of the Russian Orthodox Church. Even as a child, he loved religion, and by age thirteen began his seminary training, where his classmates nicknamed him "Patriarch." At 23, he graduated as a layman and began to teach moral theology. Three years later, he became a monk and was given the name Tikhon.

By 1897, he was consecrated Bishop of Lublin, and in 1898 became Archbishop of the Aleutians and Alaska, the leader of Russian Orthodoxy in North America. Tikhon was held in such esteem that the United States made him an honorary citizen. While in this country, he established many new cathedrals and churches, and participated in ecumenical events with other denominations, in particular The Episcopal Church. In 1900, at the consecration of Bishop Reginald Weller as coadjutor of the Diocese of Fond du Lac, the diocesan, Bishop Grafton, invited Tikhon to sit on his own throne. The Archbishop would have participated in the laying-on-of-hands if the Episcopal House of Bishops had not forbidden it. Tikhon later established warm relations with the Diocese of California.

In 1907, Tikhon returned to Russia and a decade later was elected Patriarch of Moscow. The outbreak of the Russian Revolution threw the Church into disarray. When a severe famine caused many peasants to starve in 1921, the Patriarch ordered the sale of many church treasures to purchase food for the hungry. Soon the government began seizing church property for itself, and many believers were killed in defense of their faith. The Communists tried to wrest control of the Church from Tikhon, while he, in turn, attempted to shelter his people. To this end, he discouraged the clergy from making political statements that might antagonize the government. He prayed, "May God teach every one of us to strive for His truth, and for the good of the Holy Church, rather than something for our sake." Imprisoned by the Soviets for more than a year, he was criticized both by the

Communist Party and by those Orthodox bishops who believed he had compromised too much with the government. On April 7, 1925, he died, worn out by his struggles. In 1989, the Council of Bishops of the Russian Orthodox Church glorified Patriarch Tikhon, numbering him among the saints of the Church.

Rite I   Holy God, holy and mighty, who hast called us together into one communion and fellowship: Open our eyes, we pray thee, as thou didst open the eyes of thy servant Tikhon, that we may see the faithfulness of others as we strive to be steadfast in the faith delivered to us, that the world may see and know thee; through Jesus Christ our Lord, to whom, with thee and the Holy Spirit, be glory and praise unto ages of ages. Amen.

Rite II Holy God, holy and mighty, you call us together into one communion and fellowship: Open our eyes, we pray, as you opened the eyes of your servant Tikhon, that we may see the faithfulness of others as we strive to be steadfast in the faith delivered to us, that the world may see and know you; through Jesus Christ our Lord, to whom, with you and the Holy Spirit, be glory and praise unto ages of ages. Amen.

For Liturgical Celebration: [Common of a Pastor, A14] [For the Unity of the Church, A48]

April 8

William Augustus Muhlenberg, Priest, 1877, and Anne Ayres, Religious, 1896

William Augustus Muhlenberg was born in Philadelphia in 1796, into a prominent German Lutheran family, and was drawn to The Episcopal Church by its use of English. He deliberately chose to remain unmarried to free himself for a variety of ministries. He was deeply involved in the Sunday School movement, and was concerned that the Church should minister to all social groups. Aware of the limitations of the hymnody of his time, he wrote hymns and compiled hymnals, thus widening the range of music in Episcopal churches.

The use of music, flowers, and color, and the emphasis on the church year in worship, became a potent influence. In 1846, he founded the Church of the Holy Communion in New York City. Again, he was bold and innovative: free pews for everyone, a parish school, a parish unemployment fund, and trips to the country for poor city children. His conception of beauty in worship, vivid and symbolic, had at its heart the Holy Communion itself, celebrated every Sunday. Many of his principles are set forth in the Muhlenberg Memorial to General Convention in 1853.

Anne Ayres was born in London, England, in 1816, and immigrated to New York in 1836. She began work as a tutor for the children of wealthy New Yorkers, but soon came under the influence of Muhlenberg. She took religious vows on November 1, 1845, and was the founder and First Sister of the Sisterhood of the Holy Communion, the first Anglican religious order for women in North America. The House of the Bishops of The Episcopal Church formally recognized the Sisterhood in 1852.

The companionship in ministry between Muhlenberg and Ayres led to the founding of St. Luke's Hospital in the City of New York, where Ayres and her sisters looked after most of the patient care and nursing. They also cooperated in establishing St. Johnland on the north shore of Long Island, an attempt to transplant families into an intentional

Christian community far from the urban squalor of late nineteenth century New York City.

Muhlenberg and Ayres died in 1877 and 1896, respectively.

Rite I   God of justice and truth, let not thy Church close its eyes to the plight of the poor and neglected, the homeless and destitute, the old and the sick, the lonely and those who have none to care for them. Give us that vision and compassion with which thou didst so richly endow William Augustus Muhlenberg and Anne Ayres, that we may labor tirelessly to heal those who are broken in body or spirit, and to turn their sorrow into joy; through Jesus Christ, who liveth and reigneth with thee and the Holy Spirit, one God, for ever and ever. Amen.

Rite II God of justice and truth, do not let your Church close its eyes to the plight of the poor and neglected, the homeless and destitute, the old and the sick, the lonely and those who have none to care for them. Give us that vision and compassion with which you so richly endowed William Augustus Muhlenberg and Anne Ayres, that we may labor tirelessly to heal those who are broken in body or spirit, and to turn their sorrow into joy; through Jesus Christ, who lives and reigns with you and the Holy Spirit, one God, for ever and ever. Amen.

For Liturgical Celebration: [Common of a Pastor, A14] [For Social Service, A59]

April 9

Dietrich Bonhoeffer
Theologian and Martyr, 1945

Dietrich Bonhoeffer was born at Breslau, Germany (now Wroclaw, Poland) on February 4, 1906. He studied at the universities of Berlin and Tübingen. His doctoral thesis was published in 1930 as *Communio Sanctorum*.

From the first days of the Nazi accession to power in 1933, Bonhoeffer was involved in protests against the regime. From 1933 to 1935 he was the pastor of two small congregations in London, but nonetheless was a leading spokesman for the Confessing Church, the center of Protestant resistance to the Nazis. In 1935, Bonhoeffer was appointed to organize and head a new seminary for the Confessing Church at Finkenwald. He described the community in *Life Together* and later wrote *The Cost of Discipleship*.

Bonhoeffer became increasingly involved in the political struggle after 1939, when he was introduced to the group seeking Hitler's overthrow. Bonhoeffer considered refuge in the United States, but he returned to Germany where he was able to continue his resistance. In May 1942, he flew to Sweden to meet Bishop Bell of the Church of England and convey through him to the British government proposals for a negotiated peace. The offer was rejected by the Allies who insisted upon unconditional surrender.

Bonhoeffer was arrested April 5, 1943, and imprisoned in Berlin. After an attempt on Hitler's life failed on July 20, 1944, documents were discovered linking Bonhoeffer to the conspiracy. He was taken to Buchenwald concentration camp, then to Schoenberg Prison. On Sunday, April 8, 1945, just as he concluded a service in a school building in Schoenberg, two men came in with the chilling summons, "Prisoner Bonhoeffer . . . come with us." He said to another prisoner, "This is the end. For me, the beginning of life." Bonhoeffer was hanged the next day, April 9, at Flossenburg Prison.

There is in Bonhoeffer's life a remarkable unity of faith, prayer, writing, and action. The pacifist theologian came to accept the guilt of plotting the death of Hitler, because he was convinced that not to do so would be a greater evil. Discipleship was to be had only at great cost.

Rite I   Almighty God, the beyond in the midst of our life, thou gavest grace to thy servant Dietrich Bonhoeffer to know and to teach the truth as it is in Jesus Christ, and to bear the cost of following him: Grant that we, strengthened by his teaching and example, may live under thy Word in all its forms and richness, and embrace its call to faithfulness with an undivided heart; through Jesus Christ our Savior, who liveth and reigneth with thee and the Holy Spirit, one God, for ever and ever. Amen.

Rite II Almighty God, the beyond in the midst of our life, you gave grace to your servant Dietrich Bonhoeffer to know and to teach the truth as it is in Jesus Christ, and to bear the cost of following him: Grant that we, strengthened by his teaching and example, may live under your Word in all its forms and richness, and embrace its call to faithfulness with an undivided heart; through Jesus Christ our Savior, who lives and reigns with you and the Holy Spirit, one God, for ever and ever. Amen.

For Liturgical Celebration: [Common of a Martyr, A7] [Common of a Theologian and Teacher, A17] [Common of a Prophetic Witness, A31] [Of the Holy Cross, A41] [Of the Reign of Christ, A46]

April 10

William Law
Priest, 1761

"If we are to follow Christ, it must be in our common way of spending every day. If we are to live unto God at any time or in any place, we are to live unto him in all times and in all places. If we are to use anything as the gift of God, we are to use everything as his gift." So wrote William Law in 1728 in *A Serious Call to a Devout and Holy Life*.

This quiet schoolmaster of Putney, England, could hardly be considered a revolutionary, yet his book had near-revolutionary repercussions. His challenge to take Christian living very seriously received more enthusiastic response than he could ever have imagined, especially in the lives of Henry Venn, George Whitefield, and John Wesley, all of whom he strongly influenced. More than any other man, William Law laid the foundation for the religious revival of the eighteenth century, the Evangelical Movement in England, and the Great Awakening in America.

Law came to typify the devout parson in the eyes of many. His life was characterized by simplicity, devotion, and works of charity. Because he was a Non-Juror, who refused to swear allegiance to the House of Hanover, he was deprived of the usual means of making a living as a clergyman in the Church of England. He therefore worked as a tutor to the father of Edward Gibbon, the historian, from 1727 to 1737. He organized schools and homes for the poor. He stoutly defended the Sacraments and Scriptures against attacks of the Deists. He spoke out eloquently against the warfare of his day. His richly inspired sermons and writings have gained him a permanent place in Christian literature.

Law died at Kings Cliffe on April 9, 1761.

Rite I O God, by whose grace thy servant William Law, kindled with the flame of thy love, became a burning and shining light in thy Church: Grant that we, also, may be aflame with the spirit of love and discipline and walk before thee as children of light; through Jesus Christ our Lord, who liveth and reigneth with thee, in the unity of the Holy Spirit, one God, now and for ever. Amen.

Rite II O God, by whose grace your servant William Law, kindled with the flame of your love, became a burning and shining light in your Church: Grant that we, also, may be aflame with the spirit of love and discipline and walk before you as children of light; through Jesus Christ our Lord, who lives and reigns with you, in the unity of the Holy Spirit, one God, now and for ever. Amen.

For Liturgical Celebration: [Common of a Theologian and Teacher, A17] [Common of a Pastor, A14] [For all Baptized Christians, A42] [For Vocation in Daily Work, A61]

April 10
Pierre Teilhard de Chardin
Scientist and Military Chaplain, 1955

Pierre Teilhard de Chardin was a ground-breaking paleontologist and Christian mystic whose vision encompassed the evolution of all matter toward a final goal in which material and spiritual shall coincide and God shall be all in all.

Teilhard was born in 1881. In 1899, he entered the Jesuit novitiate, moving to England in 1902, when French law nationalized the properties of religious orders. After taking a degree in literature in 1902, he went to Egypt to teach chemistry in the Jesuit College in Cairo. There he fell in love with the east. Teilhard moved back to England in 1908 and began to synthesize his already vast knowledge of evolution, philosophy, and theology. He was ordained priest in 1911.

Teilhard did research at the Natural History Museum in Paris, leading to the Sorbonne (University of Paris), where he completed his doctorate in paleontology. He went to China where, with other researchers, he made public the famous "Peking Man" hominid in 1926. Teilhard developed a vision of creation which held that evolution was the process by which matter inexorably arranges itself toward greater complexity until recognizable consciousness emerges. For Teilhard, this described a continuing process of human evolution that moves toward a new level of consciousness in which the universe will come to perfect unity and find itself one with God. God, then, is the highest point of pure consciousness, always "pulling" the evolutionary process towards its promised destiny, which he called the "Omega Point."

Teilhard struggled with the Roman Church that was suspicious of his seemingly radical and heterodox writings. He was forbidden to teach and had to defend himself against charges of heresy. Teilhard remained loyal. After his death, many came to recognize his vision as a deeply Christian one that sought to reconcile the biblical vision of God's final triumph over sin and disunity with the undeniable discoveries of evolutionary science.

Shortly before he died, he prayed: "O God, if in my life I have not been wrong, allow me to die on Easter Sunday." He died on April 10, 1955: Easter Sunday.

Rite I   Eternal God, the whole cosmos sings of thy glory, from the dividing of a single cell to the vast expanse of interstellar space: We offer thanks for thy theologian and scientist Pierre Teilhard de Chardin, who didst perceive the divine in the evolving creation. Enable us to become faithful stewards of thy divine works and heirs of thy everlasting kingdom; through Jesus Christ, the firstborn of all creation, who with thee and the Holy Spirit liveth and reigneth, one God, for ever and ever. Amen.

Rite II   Eternal God, the whole cosmos sings of your glory, from the dividing of a single cell to the vast expanse of interstellar space: We bless you for your theologian and scientist Pierre Teilhard de Chardin, who perceived the divine in the evolving creation. Enable us to become faithful stewards of your divine works and heirs of your eternal kingdom; through Jesus Christ, the firstborn of all creation, who with you and the Holy Spirit lives and reigns, one God, for ever and ever. Amen.

For Liturgical Celebration: [Common of a Theologian and Teacher, A17] [Common of a Scientist or Environmentalist, A35] [Common of a Pastor, A14] [For the Goodness of God's Creation, A65]

April 11

George Augustus Selwyn
Bishop of New Zealand, and of Lichfield, 1878

George Augustus Selwyn was born on April 5, 1809, at Hampstead, London. He was educated at Eton, and in 1831 graduated from St. John's College, Cambridge, of which he became a Fellow.

Ordained in 1833, Selwyn served as a curate at Windsor until his selection as first Bishop of New Zealand in 1841. On the voyage to his new field, he mastered the Maori language and was able to preach in it upon his arrival. In the tragic ten-year war between the English and the Maoris, Selwyn was able to minister to both sides and to keep the affection and admiration of both natives and colonists. He began missionary work in the Pacific Islands in 1847.

In addition to learning the Maori language and customs, Selwyn became an accomplished navigator, cartographer, and sailor in order to spread the gospel through the Pacific Islands. Reportedly, a sailor once noted, "To see the Bishop handle a boat was almost enough to make a man a Christian."

Selwyn's first general synod in 1859 laid down a constitution, influenced by that of The Episcopal Church, which was important for all English colonial churches.

After the first Lambeth Conference in 1867, Selwyn was reluctantly persuaded to accept the See of Lichfield in England. He died on April 11, 1878, and his grave in the cathedral close has been a place of pilgrimage for the Maoris to whom he first brought the light of the gospel.

Bishop Selwyn twice visited The Episcopal Church in America and was the preacher at the 1874 General Convention.

Rite I Almighty and everlasting God, we thank thee for thy servant George Augustus Selwyn, whom thou didst call to preach the Gospel to the people of New Zealand and Melanesia and to lay a firm foundation for the growth of thy Church in many nations. Raise up in this and every land evangelists and heralds of thy kingdom, that thy Church may proclaim the unsearchable riches of our Savior Jesus Christ; who liveth and reigneth with thee and the Holy Spirit, one God, now and for ever. Amen.

Rite II Almighty and everlasting God, we thank you for your servant George Augustus Selwyn, whom you called to preach the Gospel to the people of New Zealand and Melanesia and to lay a firm foundation for the growth of your Church in many nations. Raise up in this and every land evangelists and heralds of your kingdom, that your Church may proclaim the unsearchable riches of our Savior Jesus Christ; who lives and reigns with you and the Holy Spirit, one God, now and for ever. Amen.

For Liturgical Celebration: [Common of a Missionary, A11] [Common of a Pastor, A14] [For the Ministry II, A50] [For the Mission of the Church, A52]

April 12

Adoniram Judson
Missionary to Burma, 1850

Adoniram Judson is remembered as the first American missionary to devote his life and work to proclaiming the gospel in a distant land. He served as an American Baptist missionary to Burma, presently Myanmar, for nearly forty years.

Born into a devout Congregationalist family in Massachusetts, Judson demonstrated an unusual intellectual ability from an early age. A voracious reader and excellent student, he graduated first in his class at the College of Rhode Island, now Brown University, and further studied at Andover Theological School. Early on, he was drawn toward preparing for missionary work. Judson discovered a particular gift for languages that served him well throughout his missionary endeavors.

In 1811, the American Board of Commissioners for Foreign Missions appointed Judson a missionary to the East. Early in 1812, he married his beloved Ann, and together they set sail, stopping first in India before proceeding to Burma. Upon arrival in 1813, they immersed themselves in three years of intensive study of the Burmese language.

Burma was a difficult context for mission work. It was some years before the first convert to Christianity and, by the early 1820's, only a modest handful of people—about a dozen—claimed the Christian faith. It was during this time that Judson began his monumental work of translating the Bible into Burmese and creating a Burmese grammar book that remains a standard reference work.

During the first war between Britain and Burma in the mid-1820's, Judson was imprisoned and tortured, and his wife, Ann, though not imprisoned, suffered the indignities of being a Christian woman living under a decidedly anti-Christian regime.

It was only after the war and Judson's imprisonment that the evangelical witness among the Burmese began to take hold. Judson's desire to call forth a hundred converts soon bore fruit in more than a hundred congregations and thousands of converts. On Judson's shoulders a new generation of missionaries and local pastors led unbelievers to the gospel in record numbers and Burma became a stronghold of Christian witness in the East.

Judson died on April 12, 1850, on the coast of the Bay of Bengal.

Rite I Eternal God, we offer thanks for the ministry of Adoniram Judson, who out of love for thee and thy people translated the Scriptures into Burmese. Move us, inspired by his example, to support the presentation of thy Good News in every language, for the glory of Jesus Christ; who with thee and the Holy Spirit liveth and reigneth, one God, for ever and ever. Amen.

Rite II Eternal God, we thank you for the ministry of Adoniram Judson, who out of love for you and your people translated the Scriptures into Burmese. Move us, inspired by his example, to support the presentation of your Good News in every language, for the glory of Jesus Christ; who with you and the Holy Spirit lives and reigns, one God, for ever and ever. Amen.

For Liturgical Celebration: [Common of a Missionary, A11] [Common of a Pastor, A14] [For the Mission of the Church, A52]

April 14

Edward Thomas Demby, *1957,*
and Henry Beard Delany, *1928*
Bishops

Edward Thomas Demby and Henry Beard Delany, two of the first African American bishops in The Episcopal Church, were instrumental in the struggle of minorities to take their place in the highest positions of leadership in a church often hostile to their presence.

Born in Wilmington, Delaware, on February 13, 1869, Edward Demby attended Howard University and became an Episcopalian while serving as the Dean of Students at Paul Quinn College in Texas. Bishop John Spalding recognized Demby's gifts for ministry and sent him to work in the Diocese of Tennessee. Ordained a deacon in 1898 and a priest the next year, he served parishes in Illinois, Missouri, and Florida. In 1907, he returned to Tennessee as rector of Emmanuel Church in Memphis. He was also appointed as an Archdeacon for Colored Work, with responsibilities for the segregated "colored convocations" in the South.

While serving as Archdeacon, Demby was elected in 1918 as Bishop Suffragan for Colored Work in the Diocese of Arkansas and the Province of the Southwest. A major contributor to the westward expansion of The Episcopal Church, Demby drew African Americans into the church through his work with black hospitals, schools, and orphanages. Despite the difficulties he encountered among the white leadership in the South, Demby worked his whole life toward the full recognition of African Americans in The Episcopal Church and was instrumental in securing that African Americans held positions of leadership for national church offices concerning ministry to African Americans. He died on October 14, 1957, in Cleveland, Ohio.

Henry Beard Delany was ordained to the episcopate the same year as Edward Demby. Born a slave in St. Mary's, Georgia, on February 5, 1858, he was educated at St. Augustine's College in Raleigh, North Carolina. Ordained a deacon in 1889 and a priest three years later,

Delany served as vice principal of St. Augustine's. In 1908, Delany was appointed as an Archdeacon for Colored Work, working in the Diocese of North Carolina. He was called to be Bishop Suffragan for Colored Work in the Diocese of North Carolina, but his ministry extended into the Dioceses of East and Western North Carolina, South Carolina, and Upper South Carolina.

Delany was a strong advocate for the integration of African American Episcopalians into the wider Church despite the Jim Crow laws of the day and the efforts of many leaders of the white majority in the church who viewed the presence of men like Demby and Delany as threats to their power and authority. He died on April 14, 1928, at St. Augustine's College.

Rite I Loving God, we offer thanks for the ministries of Edward Thomas Demby and Henry Beard Delany, bishops of thy Church who, though limited by segregation, served faithfully to thy honor and glory. Assist us, we pray, to break through the limitations of our own time, that we may minister in obedience to Jesus Christ; who with thee and the Holy Spirit liveth and reigneth, one God, now and for ever. Amen.

Rite II Loving God, we thank you for the ministries of Edward Thomas Demby and Henry Beard Delany, bishops of your Church who, though limited by segregation, served faithfully to your honor and glory. Assist us, we pray, to break through the limitations of our own time, that we may minister in obedience to Jesus Christ; who with you and the Holy Spirit lives and reigns, one God, now and for ever. Amen.

For Liturgical Celebration: [Common of a Pastor, A14] [Common of a Prophetic Witness, A31] [For the Ministry II, A50] [For Reconciliation and Forgiveness, A68]

April 15

Damien, *Priest and Leper, 1889,*
and Marianne, *Religious, 1918*
of Molokai

Fr. Damien was born Joseph de Veuster in 1840 in Belgium, the son of a farmer. At the age of 18, he joined the Congregation of the Sacred Hearts of Jesus and Mary. He made his first vows in 1859 and took the name Damien, after the ancient physician and martyr. When his older brother became ill and was unable to join the mission endeavor in Hawaii, Damien volunteered to take his place.

As Father Damien began his ministry in Hawaii, leprosy was spreading rapidly throughout the Islands. In 1863, King Kamehameha V ordered those with leprosy to be sent to Kalaupapa, an isolated peninsula on the northern coast of Molokai. There, on the side of the peninsula known as Kalawao, those afflicted by the disease were left with no aid.

Damien was among the first priests to arrive in Kalawao, and he remained there for the rest of his life, building houses, an orphanage, a church, and a hospital. He ate with those he served, worshipped with them, and invited them into his home. He eventually contracted leprosy, later known as Hansen's disease, and died in 1889.

Like Father Damien, Marianne Cope aspired to the religious vocation at an early age. She entered the Sisters of St. Francis in Syracuse, New York, in 1862, and in 1870, she began work as a nurse administrator at St. Joseph's Hospital in Syracuse, where she was criticized for accepting alcoholics and other undesirable patients.

In 1883, she received a letter from a priest in Hawaii asking for help managing the hospitals and ministry to leprosy patients. She arrived in Honolulu in 1883 and immediately took over supervision of the Kaka'ako Branch Hospital, which served as a receiving center for leprosy patients from all over the islands. She also opened a care center for the healthy children of leprosy victims.

In 1884, she met Father Damien, and in 1886, she alone ministered to him when his illness made him unwelcome among church and government leaders. She continued her work with hospitals and sufferers of Hansen's disease until her death in 1918.

Rite I   God of compassion, who binds up the wounds of thy children: Help us, following the example of thy servants Damien and Marianne, to be bold and loving in service to all who are shunned for the diseases they suffer, that thy grace may be poured forth upon all; through Jesus Christ, who with thee and the Holy Spirit liveth and reigneth, one God, for ever and ever. Amen.

Rite II God of compassion, who binds up the wounds of your children: Help us, following the example of your servants Damien and Marianne, to be bold and loving in service to all who are shunned for the diseases they suffer, that your grace may be poured forth upon all; through Jesus Christ, who with you and the Holy Spirit lives and reigns, one God, for ever and ever. Amen.

For Liturgical Celebration: [Common of a Pastor, A14] [Common of a Monastic or Professed Religious, A20] [For the Sick, A57] [For Social Service, A59]

April 16

Mary (Molly) Brant (Konwatsijayenni)
Witness to the Faith among the Mohawks, 1796

Mary, or Molly Brant, known among the Mohawks as Konwatsijayenni, was an important presence among the Iroquois Confederacy during the time of the American Revolution. Baptized and raised as an Anglican due to the British presence in her tribal area, she spoke and wrote in English, and she sought to keep the Mohawks, as well as the other tribes of the Iroquois Nation, loyal to the British government during the Revolution.

Born to Peter Tehonwaghkwangeraghkwa and his wife Margaret, she moved west to Ohio with her family and lived there until her father's death. She and her brother Joseph took the name of their stepfather, Brant Kanagaradunkwa, who married their mother in 1753. Her stepfather was a friend of Sir William Johnson, the British Superintendent for North Indian Affairs. Mary met Sir William in 1759, and though they could not legally marry, she became his common law wife, and together they had nine children. She exerted influence among both the British and the Mohawks, and her voice was often sought among tribal councils and in treaty efforts.

Following her husband's death, the Oneidas and the Americans, in retaliation for her loyalty to the British and to the Anglican Church, destroyed her home. She and her children fled and were protected by the principal chief of the Five Nations, whose leaders respected her word and council.

In 1783, she moved to Kingston, Ontario, where the British Government rewarded her for her loyalty. A lifelong Anglican, she helped found St. George's Anglican Church in Kingston. At her death her tribesmen as well as the British with whom she had worked mourned her.

Rite I   O Maker of all creation, who didst endue Molly Brant with the gifts of justice and loyalty and didst make her a wise and prudent mother in the household of the Mohawk Nation: Grant us grace, following her example, to nurture the household of faith with care and compassion; through Jesus Christ our Lord, who liveth and reigneth with thee and the Holy Spirit, one God, in glory everlasting. Amen.

Rite II O Maker of all creation, who endued Molly Brant with the gifts of justice and loyalty and made her a wise and prudent mother in the household of the Mohawk Nation: Grant us grace, following her example, to nurture the household of faith with care and compassion; through Jesus Christ our Lord, who lives and reigns with you and the Holy Spirit, one God, in glory everlasting. Amen.

For Liturgical Celebration: [Common of a Missionary, A11] [Common of a Saint, A23] [For all Baptized Christians, A42] [For the Mission of the Church, A52]

APRIL 16

April 17

Emily Cooper
Deaconess, 1909

Emily Cooper was admitted to the office of deaconess in June 1873, in a service at St. Mary's Episcopal Church, Brooklyn, New York. A widow at age 44, she had gone to Brooklyn from her home in Louisville, Kentucky, for two years of training.

Soon after her commissioning, the Bishop of Kentucky, Benjamin Bosworth Smith, called Cooper to serve in her home diocese. In 1880, she was named director of the new Home of the Innocents, a Louisville home for neglected, unwanted, sick, and abused children. Founded by the Episcopal Diocese of Kentucky, the home initially served as many as fifty children at a time.

Cooper found that many children brought to the home were abandoned there, unnamed. She gave each of these children Christian names and over the years assisted at the baptisms of 244 children. Many of the children arrived at the home already too sick to be saved, and their parents, if known, were too destitute to provide for their burials. Over 200 of the children who died during Cooper's decades of service were buried in unmarked graves in two large plots in Louisville's Cave Hill Cemetery.

In 2005, the Home rediscovered the graves, and over the next four years, they identified the deceased children. Statues placed at the grave sites now bear the names of the children and commemorate Cooper's ministry.

Rite I God of the holy innocents, we thank thee for the motherly witness of thy deaconess Emily Cooper, who, in naming and baptizing, did not forget the children: Draw our hearts and minds to the plight of little ones, remembering always the teaching of thy Son that, in receiving a little child in his name, we receive Christ himself, who liveth and reigneth with thee and the Spirit, as one, caring for ever and ever. Amen.

Rite II God of the holy innocents, we thank you for the motherly witness of your deaconess Emily Cooper, who, in naming and baptizing, did not forget the children: Draw our hearts and minds also to the plight of little ones, always remembering your Son's teaching that in receiving a little child in his name, we receive Christ himself, who lives and reigns with you and the Spirit, as one, caring for ever and ever. Amen.

For Liturgical Celebration: [Common of a Saint, A23] [For all Baptized Christians, A42] [For Social Service, A59]

April 19

Alphege
Archbishop of Canterbury, and Martyr, 1012

Born in 954, Alphege (or Aelfheah) gave his witness in the troubled time of the second wave of Scandinavian invasion and settlement in England. After serving as a monk at Deerhurst, and then as Abbot of Bath, he became, in 984, through Archbishop Dunstan's influence, Bishop of Winchester. He was instrumental in bringing the Norse King Olaf Tryggvason, only recently baptized, to King Aethelred in 994 to make his peace and to be confirmed at Andover.

Transferred to Canterbury in 1005, Alphege was captured by the Danes in 1011. He refused to allow a personal ransom to be collected from his already over-burdened people. Seven months later he was brutally murdered, despite the Viking commander Thorkell's effort to save him by offering all his possessions except his ship for the Archbishop's life.

The Anglo-Saxon Chronicle relates that the Danes were "much stirred against the Bishop, because he would not promise them any fee, and forbade that any man should give anything for him. They were also much drunken . . . and took the Bishop, and led him to their hustings, on the eve of the Saturday after Easter . . . and then they shamefully killed him. They overwhelmed him with bones and horns of oxen; and one of them smote him with an axe-iron on the head; so that he sunk downwards with the blow. And his holy blood fell on the earth, whilst his sacred soul was sent to the realm of God."

Rite I   Lord Jesus Christ, who didst willingly walk the way of the cross: Strengthen thy Church through the example and prayers of thy servant Alphege to hold fast the path of discipleship; for with the Father and the Holy Spirit thou livest and reignest, one God, for ever and ever. Amen.

Rite II Lord Jesus Christ, who willingly walked the way of the cross: Strengthen your Church through the example and prayers of your servant Alphege to hold fast the path of discipleship; for with the Father and Holy Spirit you live and reign, one God, for ever and ever. Amen.

For Liturgical Celebration: [Common of a Martyr, A7] [Common of a Pastor, A14] [Of the Holy Cross, A41] [For the Ministry II, A50]

April 21

Anselm
Archbishop of Canterbury, 1109

Anselm was born in Italy about 1033 and took monastic vows in 1060 at the Abbey of Bec in Normandy. He succeeded his teacher Lanfranc as Prior of Bec in 1063, and as Archbishop of Canterbury in 1093. His episcopate was stormy, in continual conflict with the crown over the rights and freedom of the Church. His greatest talent lay in theology and spiritual direction.

As a pioneer in the scholastic method, Anselm remains the great exponent of the so-called "ontological argument" for the existence of God: God is "that than which nothing greater can be thought." Even the fool, who (in Psalm 14) says in his heart "There is no God," must have an idea of God in his mind, the concept of an unconditional being (*ontos*) than which nothing greater can be conceived; otherwise he would not be able to speak of "God" at all. And so this something, "God," must exist outside the mind as well; because, if he did not, he would not in fact be that than which nothing greater can be thought. Since the greatest thing that can be thought must have existence as one of its properties, Anselm asserts, "God" can be said to exist in reality as well as in the intellect, but is not dependent upon the material world for verification. To some, this "ontological argument" has seemed mere deductive rationalism; to others it has the merit of showing that faith in God need not be contrary to human reason.

Anselm is also the most famous exponent of the "satisfaction theory" of the atonement. Anselm explains the work of Christ in terms of the feudal society of his day. If a vassal breaks his bond, he has to atone for this to his lord; likewise, sin violates a person's bond with God, the supreme Lord, and atonement or satisfaction must be made. Of ourselves, we are unable to make such atonement, because God is perfect and we are not. Therefore, God himself has saved us, becoming perfect man in Christ, so that a perfect life could be offered in satisfaction for sin.

Undergirding Anselm's theology is a profound piety. His spirituality is best summarized in the phrase, "faith seeking understanding." He writes, "I do not seek to understand that I may believe, but I believe in order that I may understand. For this, too, I believe, that unless I first believe, I shall not understand."

Rite I   Almighty God, who didst raise up thy servant Anselm to teach the Church of his day to understand its faith in thine eternal Being, perfect justice, and saving mercy: Provide thy Church in every age with devout and learned scholars and teachers, that we may be able to give a reason for the hope that is in us; through Jesus Christ our Lord, who liveth and reigneth with thee and the Holy Spirit, one God, for ever and ever. Amen.

Rite II   Almighty God, you raised up your servant Anselm to teach the Church of his day to understand its faith in your eternal Being, perfect justice, and saving mercy: Provide your Church in every age with devout and learned scholars and teachers, that we may be able to give a reason for the hope that is in us; through Jesus Christ our Lord, who lives and reigns with you and the Holy Spirit, one God, for ever and ever. Amen.

For Liturgical Celebration: [Common of a Theologian and Teacher, A17] [Common of a Pastor, A14] [Of the Incarnation, A39] [For the Ministry II, A50]

April 22

John Muir, *Naturalist and Writer, 1914, and*
Hudson Stuck, *Priest and Environmentalist, 1920*

Born in Scotland in 1838, John Muir immigrated to the United States in 1849, settling in Wisconsin. Muir sought the spiritual freedom of the natural world. As a college student, Muir studied botany, of which he later said, "This fine lesson charmed me and sent me flying to the woods and meadows with wild enthusiasm."

In 1868, Muir arrived in Yosemite Valley, California, which he called "the grandest of all the special temples of nature." During a hiking trip through the Sierras, Muir developed theories about the development and ecosystem of the areas. Some years later, Muir took up the cause of preservation, eventually co-founding the Sierra Club, an association of environmental preservationists.

Muir, an ardent believer in the national parks as "places of rest, inspiration, and prayers," adamantly opposed the free exploitation of natural resources for commercial use. This position put him at odds with conservationists who saw natural forests as sources of timber and who wanted to conserve them for that reason.

Muir was influential in convincing President Theodore Roosevelt that federal management and control were necessary to insure the preservation of the national forests. Today, he is revered as an inspiration for preservationists and his life's work stands as a powerful testament to the majesty and beauty of God's creation.

Hudson Stuck was an Episcopal priest and explorer. Born in England in 1863, he came to the United States in 1885. He graduated from The University of the South in 1892. From 1894 to 1904, Stuck was Dean of the Episcopal Cathedral in Dallas, Texas. In 1905 he moved to Fort Yukon, Alaska, where he spent the rest of his life, serving as archdeacon of the Diocese of Alaska.

With a group of fellow explorers, Stuck was the first to completely ascend Denali (Mt. McKinley). He later wrote of the experience as a "privileged communion" to be received in awe and wonder. Upon reaching the pinnacle of Denali, Stuck led the climbers in prayer and thanksgiving.

Archdeacon Stuck died in 1920.

Rite I   Blessed Creator of the earth and all that inhabits it: We offer thanks for thy prophets John Muir and Hudson Stuck, who rejoiced in thy beauty made known in the natural world; and we pray that, inspired by their love of thy creation, we may be wise and faithful stewards of the world thou hast created, that generations to come may also lie down to rest among the pines and rise refreshed for their work; in the Name of the one through whom all things art made new, Jesus Christ our Savior, who with thee and the Holy Spirit liveth and reigneth, one God, now and for ever. Amen.

Rite II   Blessed Creator of the earth and all that inhabits it: We thank you for your prophets John Muir and Hudson Stuck, who rejoiced in your beauty made known in the natural world; and we pray that, inspired by their love of your creation, we may be wise and faithful stewards of the world you have created, that generations to come may also lie down to rest among the pines and rise refreshed for their work; in the Name of the one through whom you make all things new, Jesus Christ our Savior, who with you and the Holy Spirit lives and reigns, one God, now and for ever. Amen.

For Liturgical Celebration: [Common of a Prophetic Witness, A31] [Common of a Scientist or Environmentalist, A35] [For the Care of God's Creation, A63] [For the Goodness of God's Creation, A65]

April 23

George
Soldier and Martyr, c. 304

George is the patron saint of England by declaration of King Edward II in 1347. He is remembered as a martyr, having given his life in witness to the gospel during the persecution of the Church in the early fourth century. Very few details of his life have survived, and his story is replete with legend. By the middle of the fifth century, he was commemorated in local calendars, and historical records of the period testify to his existence.

George was a soldier by vocation, serving as an officer in the Roman army. It is said that he "gave his goods to the poor and openly confessed Christianity before the court."

George's initial notoriety may well have resulted from his faithfulness and witness to Christ during the Diocletian persecutions, 303-304, a particularly destructive period through which the Church suffered.

Much of the legend of George dates back only to the eighth century, and more of it developed in the centuries that followed. The infamous story of George slaying the dragon, probably developed from Greek mythology, is not associated with him until the twelfth century. The inclusion of George's story in the thirteenth century manuscript, The Golden Legend, accounts for his growing popularity in the Middle Ages.

In the twelfth century George was recognized as the patron saint of soldiers and he was called upon in support of those who would fight in the Crusades. The shield under which his soldiers fought became a symbol of national pride for the English and in time was adapted into the national flag. Interestingly, the "St. George's Shield"—white shield emblazoned with a red cross—is the basis of The Episcopal Church flag and seal.

Rite I   Lord Jesus Christ, whose cross didst seal thy servant George: Grant that we, strengthened by his example and prayers, may triumph to the end over all evils, to the glory of thy Name; for with the Father and Holy Spirit thou livest and reignest, one God, for ever and ever. Amen.

Rite II Lord Jesus Christ, whose cross did seal your servant George: Grant that we, strengthened by his example and prayers, may triumph to the end over all evils, to the glory of your Name; for with the Father and Holy Spirit you live and reign, one God, for ever and ever. Amen.

For Liturgical Celebration: [Common of a Martyr, A7] [Of the Holy Cross, A41]

April 23

Toyohiko Kagawa
Prophetic Witness in Japan, 1960

Toyohiko Kagawa, born on July 10, 1888, in Kobe, Japan, was a Japanese evangelist, advocate of social change, and pacifist.

Kagawa was the son of a wealthy Kobe Buddhist business entrepreneur-politician and his concubine, both of whom died when Kagawa was four years old. The youth was raised by Presbyterian missionaries and had a conversion experience at age fifteen. "O God, make me like Christ" he prayed repeatedly.

Kagawa studied at theological seminaries in Japan and at Princeton University and Princeton Theological Seminary, but was increasingly drawn to an evangelism of social reform, seeking to apply Christ's teachings directly to Japan's poor in a theologically uncomplicated way. He lived for much of the 1910 – 1924 period in a six-foot-square windowless shed in Kobe's slums. A skilled organizer, he helped found trade unions and credit unions among dock workers, factory laborers, and subsistence farmers. Trade unions were forbidden at the time, and Kagawa was twice imprisoned. He was also a pacifist and organized the National Anti-War League in 1928. Kagawa was arrested in 1940 for publicly apologizing to the people of China for Japan's invasion of that country. An advocate for universal male suffrage (granted in 1925), he later became a voice for women's right to vote as well.

A prolific author, his autobiographical novel *Crossing the Death Line* (1920) became a best seller, and many of his other novels and writings in a Christian Socialist vein were translated into English. He used the revenues from his substantial book sales to fund his extensive slum work. Although Kagawa was under police surveillance much of his life, the Japanese government called on him to organize the rebuilding of Tokyo after a 1923 earthquake and again at the end of World War II to serve as head of the country's social welfare programs.

Although some knew him best as a social reformer and pacifist, Kagawa saw himself first of all an evangelist. "Christ alone can make all things new," he said, "The spirit of Christ must be the soul of all real social reconstruction."

Kagawa died on April 23, 1960 in Tokyo.

———⚬⚬⚬———

Rite I We bless thy Name, O God, for the witness of Toyohiko Kagawa, reformer and teacher, who was persecuted for his pacifist principles and went on to lead a movement for democracy in Japan; and we pray that thou wouldst strengthen and protect all who suffer for their fidelity to Jesus Christ; who with thee and the Holy Spirit liveth and reigneth, one God, for ever and ever. Amen.

Rite II We bless your Name, O God, for the witness of Toyohiko Kagawa, reformer and teacher, who was persecuted for his pacifist principles and went on to lead a movement for democracy in Japan; and we pray that you would strengthen and protect all who suffer for their fidelity to Jesus Christ; who with you and the Holy Spirit lives and reigns, one God, for ever and ever. Amen.

For Liturgical Celebration: [Common of a Prophetic Witness, A31] [For Peace, A55] [For Social Justice, A58]

April 24

Genocide Remembrance

This day is set aside in the calendar of the church to hold in remembrance those who have died and those whose lives have been severely damaged as a result of acts of genocide: the systematic and intentional destruction of a people by death, by the imposition of severe mental or physical abuse, by the forced displacement of children, or by other atrocities designed to destroy the lives and human dignity of large groups of people.

This day is chosen for the commemoration because the international community recognizes April 24 as a day of remembrance for the Armenian Genocide, the systematic annihilation of the Armenian people during and just after World War I. On April 24, 1915, more than 250 Armenian notables—civic and political leaders, teachers, writers, and members of the clergy—were rounded up, imprisoned, tortured, and killed. Before the cessation of conflict, it is estimated that as many as one-and-a-half million Armenians perished, many as the result of forced marches, deliberate starvation, and heinous massacres.

President Theodore Roosevelt declared the Armenian Genocide to be the greatest crime of World War I. The close relationships between Anglicans and Episcopalians and our sisters and brothers in the Armenian Church make the remembrance of this day a particular sign of our fellowship in the body of Christ.

Tragically, human history is littered with such atrocities, and the Armenian Genocide was far from the last such mass extermination of people in the twentieth century. One need only mention Croatia, Nazi Germany, Zanzibar, Guatemala, Bangladesh, Burundi, Equatorial Guinea, East Timor, Cambodia, Afghanistan, Kurdish Iraq, and Tibet, and this is by no means a comprehensive list. The unflinching resolve of people of faith, in prayer and in action, is critical if the travesty of human genocide is to be curbed and eventually stopped.

Rite I   Almighty God, our Refuge and our Rock, whose loving care knoweth no bounds and embraceth all the peoples of the earth: Defend and protect those who fall victim to the forces of evil, and, as we remember this day those who endured depredation and death because of who they were, not because of what they had done or failed to do, give us the courage to stand against hatred and oppression and to seek the dignity and well-being of all for the sake of our Savior Jesus Christ, in whom thou hast reconciled the world to thyself; and who liveth and reigneth with thee and the Holy Spirit, one God, now and for ever. Amen.

Rite II   Almighty God, our Refuge and our Rock, your loving care knows no bounds and embraces all the peoples of the earth: Defend and protect those who fall victim to the forces of evil, and, as we remember this day those who endured depredation and death because of who they were, not because of what they had done or failed to do, give us the courage to stand against hatred and oppression and to seek the dignity and well-being of all for the sake of our Savior Jesus Christ, in whom you have reconciled the world to yourself; and who lives and reigns with you and the Holy Spirit, one God, now and for ever. Amen.

For Liturgical Celebration: [Common of a Martyr, A7] [Of the Holy Cross, A41] [On the Anniversary of a Disaster, A67] [For Reconciliation and Forgiveness, A68]

April 26

Robert Hunt
Priest and First Chaplain at Jamestown, 1607

Robert Hunt was born in England around 1568. He was a parish priest in Reculver, Kent, beginning in 1594, and in 1604 became vicar of Heathfield Parish in the Diocese of Chichester.

In 1607, Hunt accompanied Captain John Smith and the Jamestown colonists, serving as their priest and chaplain. The first celebration of the Anglican rite of Holy Eucharist recorded in North America took place on May 24, 1607, and Hunt is believed to have presided. Captain Smith's diary notes another celebration of the Holy Eucharist on June 21, 1607, and Hunt is more clearly indicated as the presiding priest.

In Captain Smith's journal, the following tribute to Robert Hunt and his ministry may be found: "He was an honest, religious and courageous divine. He preferred the service of God in so good a voyage to every thought of ease at home. He endured every privation, yet none ever heard him repine. During his life, our factions were oft healed and our great extremities so comforted that they seemed easy in comparison with what we endured after his memorable death. We all received from him the Holy Communion as a pledge of reconciliation, for we all loved him for his exceeding goodness."

Hunt died sometime prior to April 10, 1608. A memorial has been erected by the National Park Service in Historic Jamestown.

Rite I   Almighty God, we bless thy Name for the life and witness of Robert Hunt, first chaplain to the Jamestown colony, who sought to unite thy people in thy love amid great hardship: Help us, like him, to work for reconciliation wherever we may be placed; through Jesus Christ thy Son, who with thee and the Holy Spirit liveth and reigneth, one God, for ever and ever. Amen.

Rite II Almighty God, we bless your Name for the life and witness of Robert Hunt, first chaplain to the Jamestown colony, who sought to unite your people in your love amid great hardship: Help us, like him, to work for reconciliation wherever we may be placed; through Jesus Christ your Son, who with you and the Holy Spirit lives and reigns, one God, for ever and ever. Amen.

For Liturgical Celebration: [Common of a Pastor, A14] [Of the Holy Eucharist, A40]

April 27

Christina Rossetti
Poet, 1894

Christina Rossetti, among the more important poets of the nineteenth century, was born in 1830 to a professor and his devout, evangelical wife. Her eldest sister, Maria, entered an Anglican convent, and her poet-painter brother, Dante, was a leading figure in the Pre-Raphaelite movement of the nineteenth century. She suffered from poor health most of her life, being diagnosed variously with tuberculosis or angina and led a retiring, somewhat cloistered life. In spite of this she produced an enormous quantity of verse and was in lively and ongoing conversation with members of Dante's "Pre-Raphaelite Brotherhood." She died of cancer in 1894.

Mid-nineteenth century England, during the Industrial Revolution and the establishment of the British Empire, experienced enormous political and cultural change and social displacement. The old, agrarian society was being swept away by the movement to cities and the creation of a new middle class. Many people, even those who had greatly benefitted from these changes, were revolted by the ugliness and misery that attended urban slums and abandoned rural areas alike. One response was a nostalgic attempt to recover England's mythic and legendary past. This produced a rather romantic interest in the medieval. "Gothic," originally a derogatory term meaning rude or barbaric, became both a term of approval and a style of architecture and decoration that swept the country.

The Tractarian or Oxford Movement shared these concerns and protested against modernity by seeking a recovery of much of the doctrine and sacramental practice of the medieval church. Tractarian emphasis on the sacramental taught that the ordinary things of nature: water, oil, bread, and wine were the means of God's grace and indeed God's presence. They also taught that a life of personal holiness dedicated to the service of others is the road to union with Christ.

Unlike some of the Pre-Raphaelites with whom she was in relationship, Rossetti embraced Christian faith and practice. Over five hundred of her poems were devotional. They were related to the liturgy, to the feasts and fasts of the liturgical year, and to biblical "dialogues" with Christ.

Rite I   O God, whom heaven cannot hold, who didst inspire Christina Rossetti to express the mystery of the Incarnation through her poems: Help us to follow her example in giving our hearts to Christ, who is love; and who is alive and reignest with thee and the Holy Spirit, one God, in glory everlasting. Amen.

Rite II   O God, whom heaven cannot hold, you inspired Christina Rossetti to express the mystery of the Incarnation through her poems: Help us to follow her example in giving our hearts to Christ, who is love; and who is alive and reigns with you and the Holy Spirit, one God, in glory everlasting. Amen.

For Liturgical Celebration: [Common of an Artist, Writer, or Composer, A27] [Common of a Saint, A23]

APRIL 27

April 29

Catherine of Siena
1380

Catherine Benincasa was the youngest of twenty-five children of a wealthy dyer of Siena. At six years of age, she had a remarkable vision that probably decided her life's vocation. Walking home from a visit, she stopped on the road and gazed upward, oblivious to everything around her. "I beheld our Lord seated in glory with St. Peter, St. Paul, and St. John." She went on to say, later, that the Savior smiled on her and blessed her.

From then on, Catherine spent most of her time in prayer and meditation, despite her mother's attempts to force her to be like other girls. To settle matters, Catherine cut off her hair, her chief beauty. The family harassed her continually; but in the end, convinced that she was deaf to all opposition, her father let her do as she would: close herself away in a darkened room, fast, and sleep on boards. Eventually, she was accepted as a Dominican postulant.

Catherine had numerous visions, and was also tried most severely by loathsome temptations and degrading images. Frequently, she felt totally abandoned by the Lord. At last, in 1366, the Savior appeared with Mary and the Heavenly Host, and espoused her to himself, so ending her years of lonely prayer and struggle. She became a nurse, as Dominicans regularly did, caring for patients with leprosy and cancer, whom other nurses disliked to treat.

Opinion in Siena was sharply divided about whether she was a saint or a fanatic, but when the Bishop of Capua was appointed her confessor, he helped her to win full support from the Dominican Mother House. Catherine was a courageous worker in time of severe plague; she visited prisoners condemned to death; she constantly was called upon to arbitrate feuds and to prepare troubled sinners for confession.

During the great schism of the papacy, with rival popes in Rome and Avignon, Catherine wrote tirelessly to princes, kings, and popes, urging them to restore the unity of the Church. She even went to Rome to press further for the cause.

Besides her many letters to all manner of people, Catherine wrote a *Dialogue*, a mystical work dictated in ecstasy. Exhausted and paralyzed, she died at the age of thirty-three.

Rite I   Everlasting God, who didst so kindle the flame of holy love in the heart of blessed Catherine of Siena, as she meditated on the passion of thy Son our Savior, that she devoted her life to the poor and the sick, and to the peace and unity of the Church: Grant that we also may share in the mystery of Christ's death, and rejoice in the revelation of his glory; who liveth and reigneth with thee and the Holy Spirit, one God, now and for ever. Amen.

Rite II   Everlasting God, you so kindled the flame of holy love in the heart of blessed Catherine of Siena, as she meditated on the passion of your Son our Savior, that she devoted her life to the poor and the sick, and to the peace and unity of the Church: Grant that we also may share in the mystery of Christ's death, and rejoice in the revelation of his glory; who lives and reigns with you and the Holy Spirit, one God, now and for ever. Amen.

For Liturgical Celebration: [Common of a Theologian and Teacher, A17] [Common of a Monastic or Professed Religious, A20] [Of the Holy Trinity, A37] [Common of a Prophetic Witness, A31]

April 30

Sarah Josepha Buell Hale
Editor and Prophetic Witness, 1879

Sarah Josepha Buell was born in New Hampshire in 1788 to Captain Gordon Buell and Martha Buell, both of whom were advocates for equal education for both sexes. In 1813, she married David Hale, a promising lawyer who shared her intellectual interests. In 1822, David died four days before the birth of their fifth child.

Sarah Buell Hale wore black for the rest of her life and, to support her family, she turned to her considerable literary skills. In a year, a volume of poetry appeared, followed by a successful novel, *Northwood: A Tale of New England*, which was among the first American novels by women and one of the first dealing with slavery. The success generated by *Northwood* enabled her to edit the popular *Ladies' Magazine*, which she hoped would aid in educating women, as she wrote, "not that they may usurp the situation, or encroach upon the prerogatives of man; but that each individual may lend her aid to the intellectual and moral character of those within her sphere."

In 1830, she published a book of verses for children aimed at the Sunday school market; it included the now-famous "Mary Had a Little Lamb," originally called "Mary's Lamb." Following the examples of her parents, she labored consistently for women's education and helped found Vassar College. Her publications, including the influential *Godey's Lady's Book*, promoted concern for women's health, property rights, and opportunities for public recognition. Hale's influence was widespread, particularly for middle class women, in matters of child-rearing, morality, literature, and dress. Although the editor of Godey's instructed her to avoid party politics in the publication, she dedicated much energy to causes which could unite North and South across party lines. She worked diligently to preserve Bunker Hill and George Washington's plantation home, Mount Vernon, as American monuments. She is perhaps most famous for the nationalization of the Thanksgiving holiday, toward which she worked many years and which finally received presidential sanction under Abraham Lincoln.

Her work, in both the women's and national spheres, was exemplary for its conciliatory nature, its concern for the unity of the nation, and for her desire to honor the work and influence of women in society.

Rite I Gracious God, we bless thy Name for the vision and witness of Sarah Hale, whose advocacy for the ministry of women helped to support the deaconess movement. Make us grateful for thy many blessings, that we may come closer to Christ in our own families; through Jesus Christ our Savior, who liveth and reigneth with thee and the Holy Spirit, one God, for ever and ever. Amen.

Rite II Gracious God, we bless your Name for the vision and witness of Sarah Hale, whose advocacy for the ministry of women helped to support the deaconess movement. Make us grateful for your many blessings, that we may come closer to Christ in our own families; through Jesus Christ our Savior, who lives and reigns with you and the Holy Spirit, one God, for ever and ever. Amen.

For Liturgical Celebration: [Common of a Prophetic Witness, A31] [Common of an Artist, Writer, or Composer, A27] [For Vocation in Daily Work, A61]

MAY

1
2 Athanasius, Bishop of Alexandria, 373
3
4 Monnica, Mother of Augustine of Hippo, 387
5
6
7 Harriet Starr Cannon, Religious, 1896
8 Dame Julian of Norwich, c. 1417
9 Gregory of Nazianzus, Bishop of Constantinople, 389
10 Nicolaus Ludwig von Zinzendorf, Prophetic Witness, 1760
11
12
13 Frances Perkins, Public Servant and Prophetic Witness, 1965
14
15 Junia and Andronicus
16 The Martyrs of the Sudan
17 William Hobart Hare, Bishop of Niobrara, and of South Dakota, 1909
17 Thurgood Marshall, Lawyer and Jurist, 1993
18
19 Dunstan, Archbishop of Canterbury, 988
20 Alcuin, Deacon, and Abbot of Tours, 804
21 John Eliot, Missionary among the Algonquin, 1690
22
23 Nicolaus Copernicus, 1543, and Johannes Kepler, 1630, Astronomers
24 Jackson Kemper, First Missionary Bishop in the United States, 1870

25 Bede, the Venerable, Priest, and Monk of Jarrow, 735
26 Augustine, First Archbishop of Canterbury, 605
27 Bertha and Ethelbert, Queen and King of Kent, 616
28 John Calvin, Theologian, 1564
29
30 Jeanne d'Arc (Joan of Arc), Mystic and Soldier, 1431
31

The First Book of Common Prayer, 1549, is appropriately observed on a weekday following the Day of Pentecost.

May 2

Athanasius
Bishop of Alexandria, 373

Rarely in the history of the Church has the course of its development been more significantly determined by one person than it was by Athanasius in the fourth century. Gregory of Nazianzus called him "the pillar of the Church," and Basil the Great said he was "the God-given physician of her wounds."

Athanasius was born about 295 in Alexandria and was ordained deacon in 319. He quickly attracted attention by his opposition to the presbyter Arius, whose denial of the full divinity of the Second Person of the Trinity was gaining widespread acceptance. Alexander, the Bishop of Alexandria, took Athanasius as his secretary and adviser to the first Ecumenical Council, at Nicaea in 325, which dealt with the Arian conflict. Athanasius was successful in winning approval for the phrase in the Nicene Creed which has ever since been recognized as expressing unequivocally the full godhead of the Son: "of one Being with the Father" (*homoousios*).

When Alexander died in 328, Athanasius became bishop. He fearlessly defended the Nicene Christology against emperors, magistrates, bishops, and theologians. Five times he was sent into exile. He often seemed to stand alone for the orthodox faith. "*Athanasius contra mundum* (against the world)" became a by-word. Yet, by the time of his last exile, his popularity among the citizens of Alexandria was so great that the Emperor had to recall him to avoid insurrection in the city.

Athanasius wrote voluminously: biblical interpretation, theological exposition, sermons, and letters. His treatise, *On the Incarnation of the Word of God*, is a still widely read classic.

In it, he writes, "The Savior of us all, the Word of God, in his great love took to himself a body and moved as Man among men, meeting their senses, so to speak, half way. He became himself an object for the senses, so that those who were seeking God in sensible things might apprehend the Father through the works which he, the Word of God, did in the body. Human and human-minded as men were, therefore, to whichever side they looked in the sensible world, they found themselves taught the truth."

Athanasius died in Alexandria in 373.

Rite I   O Lord, who didst establish thy servant Athanasius, through wisdom, in thy truth: Grant that we, perceiving the humanity and divinity of thy Son Jesus Christ, may follow in his footsteps and ascend the way to eternal life; who liveth and reigneth with thee and the Holy Spirit, one God, now and for ever. Amen.

Rite II   O Lord, who established your servant Athanasius, through wisdom, in your truth: Grant that we, perceiving the humanity and divinity of your Son Jesus Christ, may follow in his footsteps and ascend the way to eternal life; who lives and reigns with you and the Holy Spirit, one God, now and for ever. Amen.

For Liturgical Celebration: [Common of a Theologian and Teacher, A17] [Common of a Pastor, A14] [Of the Incarnation, A39] [For the Ministry II, A50]

May 4

Monnica
Mother of Augustine of Hippo, 387

Monnica's life story is enshrined in the spiritual autobiography of her eldest son, in *The Confessions* of Saint Augustine. Born in North Africa about 331, of Berber parents, Monnica was married to a Latinized provincial of Tagaste named Patricius, whom she won to the Christian faith before his death. In her earlier years she was not without worldly ambitions and tastes. She grew in Christian maturity and spiritual insight through an ever-deepening life of prayer.

Her ambition for her gifted son was transformed into a passionate desire for his conversion to Christ. After his baptism in Milan in 387, by Bishop Ambrose, Augustine and his mother, together with a younger brother, planned to return home to Africa. While awaiting ship at Ostia, the port of Rome, Monnica fell ill.

Augustine writes, "One day during her illness she had a fainting spell and lost consciousness for a short time. We hurried to her bedside, but she soon regained consciousness and looked up at my brother and me as we stood beside her. With a puzzled look, she asked, 'Where was I?' Then, watching us closely as we stood there speechless with grief, she said, 'You will bury your mother here.' "

Augustine's brother expressed sorrow, for her sake, that she would die so far from her own country. She said to the two brothers, "It does not matter where you bury my body. Do not let that worry you. All I ask of you is that, wherever you may be, you should remember me at the altar of the Lord." To the question, whether she was not afraid at the thought of leaving her body in an alien land, she replied, "Nothing is far from God, and I need have no fear that he will not know where to find me, when he comes to raise me to life at the end of the world."

Recent excavations at Ostia have uncovered her original tomb. Her mortal remains, however, were transferred in 1430 to the Church of St. Augustine in Rome.

Rite I O Lord, who through spiritual discipline didst strengthen thy servant Monnica to persevere in offering her love and prayers and tears for the conversion of her husband and of Augustine their son: Deepen our devotion, we pray, and use us in accordance with thy will to bring others, even our own kindred, to acknowledge Jesus Christ as Savior and Lord; who with thee and the Holy Spirit liveth and reigneth, one God, for ever and ever. Amen.

Rite II O Lord, through spiritual discipline you strengthened your servant Monnica to persevere in offering her love and prayers and tears for the conversion of her husband and of Augustine their son: Deepen our devotion, we pray, and use us in accordance with your will to bring others, even our own kindred, to acknowledge Jesus Christ as Savior and Lord; who with you and the Holy Spirit lives and reigns, one God, for ever and ever. Amen.

For Liturgical Celebration: [Common of a Saint, A23] [For all Baptized Christians, A42] [For the Ministry III, A51]

May 7

Harriet Starr Cannon
Religious, 1896

Harriet Starr Cannon founded the Community of St. Mary, the first religious order for women formally recognized in The Episcopal Church.

Cannon was born in Charleston, South Carolina, in 1823 and was orphaned in 1824, when her parents died of yellow fever. She grew up with her only surviving sibling in Bridgeport, Connecticut, in the home of relatives. In 1851, Cannon entered the Sisters of the Holy Communion, an order founded by William Augustus Muhlenberg, Rector of the Church of the Holy Communion in New York City. The Sisters were heavily involved in the operation of clinics and care facilities that would become St. Luke's Hospital in the City of New York. During her years with the Sisters of the Holy Communion, Cannon served as a nurse.

Over time, Harriet Cannon yearned for a more traditional monastic form of religious life. When agreement could not be reached with the Sisters of the Holy Communion, Cannon and a small group of her sisters moved to form a new order. On the Feast of the Presentation, February 2, 1865, Horatio Potter, Bishop of the Diocese of New York, received from Harriet Cannon and her sisters the traditional vows of poverty, chastity, and obedience, at St. Michael's Church in Manhattan. The sisters began life together as the Community of St. Mary, and Harriet Cannon became the Order's first Superior.

The apostolate of The Community of St. Mary began with nursing and the care of women who had endured difficult circumstances. After time, however, Mother Cannon and her Sisters became increasingly committed to providing free schools for the education of young women in addition to their medical work. The Community continued to grow and developed schools for girls, hospitals, and orphanages in New York, Tennessee, and Wisconsin. Mother Cannon died April 5, 1896, at Peekskill, New York.

The Community of St. Mary played a critical role in response to the yellow fever epidemic in Memphis in the 1870's. Sister Constance and her companions are remembered on September 9.

Rite I Gracious God, who didst call Harriet Starr Cannon and her companions to revive the religious life in The Episcopal Church and to dedicate their lives to thee: Grant that we, after their example, may ever surrender ourselves to the revelation of thy holy will; through our Savior Jesus Christ, who liveth and reigneth with thee and the Holy Spirit, one God, for ever and ever. Amen.

Rite II Gracious God, you called Harriet Starr Cannon and her companions to revive the religious life in The Episcopal Church and to dedicate their lives to you: Grant that we, after their example, may ever surrender ourselves to the revelation of your holy will; through our Savior Jesus Christ, who lives and reigns with you and the Holy Spirit, one God, for ever and ever. Amen.

For Liturgical Celebration: [Common of a Monastic or Professed Religious, A20] [Of the Holy Spirit, A38]

May 8

Dame Julian of Norwich
c. 1417

Of Dame Julian's early life we know little, only the probable date of her birth (1342). Her own writings in the *Revelations of Divine Love* are concerned only with her visions, or "showings," that she experienced when she was thirty years old.

She had been gravely ill and was given the last rites; suddenly, on the seventh day, all pain left her, and she had fifteen visions of the Passion. These brought her great peace and joy. "From that time I desired oftentimes to learn what was our Lord's meaning," she wrote, "and fifteen years after I was answered in ghostly understanding: 'Wouldst thou learn the Lord's meaning in this thing? Learn it well. Love was his meaning. Who showed it thee? Love. What showed he thee? Love. Wherefore showed it he? For Love. Hold thee therein and thou shalt learn and know more in the same.' Thus it was I learned that Love was our Lord's meaning."

Julian had long desired three gifts from God: "the mind of his passion, bodily sickness in youth, and three wounds—of contrition, of compassion, of will-full longing toward God." Her illness brought her the first two wounds, which then passed from her mind. The third, "will-full longing" (divinely inspired longing), never left her.

She became a recluse, an anchoress, at Norwich soon after her recovery from illness, living in a small dwelling attached to the Church of St. Julian. Even in her lifetime, she was famed as a mystic and spiritual counselor and was frequently visited by clergymen and lay persons, including the famous mystic Margery Kempe. Kempe says of Julian: "This anchoress was expert in knowledge of our Lord and could give good counsel. I spent much time with her talking of the love of our Lord Jesus Christ."

The Lady Julian's book is a tender and beautiful exposition of God's eternal and all-embracing love, showing how his charity toward the human race is exhibited in the Passion. Again and again she referred to Christ as "our courteous Lord." Many have found strength in the words the Lord had given her: "I can make all things well; I will make all things well; I shall make all things well; and thou canst see for thyself that all manner of things shall be well."

Rite I   Lord God, who in thy compassion didst grant to the Lady Julian many revelations of thy nurturing and sustaining love: Move our hearts, like hers, to seek thee above all things, for in giving us thyself thou givest us all; through Jesus Christ our Lord, who liveth and reigneth with thee and the Holy Spirit, one God, for ever and ever. Amen.

Rite II Lord God, in your compassion you granted to the Lady Julian many revelations of your nurturing and sustaining love: Move our hearts, like hers, to seek you above all things, for in giving us yourself you give us all; through Jesus Christ our Lord, who lives and reigns with you and the Holy Spirit, one God, for ever and ever. Amen.

For Liturgical Celebration: [Common of a Theologian and Teacher, A17] [Common of a Monastic or Professed Religious, A20] [Of the Incarnation, A39]

May 9

Gregory of Nazianzus
Bishop of Constantinople, 389

Gregory of Nazianzus, one of the Cappadocian Fathers, loved God, the art of letters, and the human race—in that order. He was born about 330 in Nazianzus in Cappadocia (now Turkey), the son of a local bishop. He studied rhetoric in Athens with his friend Basil of Caesarea, and Julian, later to be the apostate emperor.

Gregory, together with Basil, compiled an anthology of Origen's works, *The Philokalia*. Two years later, he returned to his home, a town then rent by heresies and schism. His defense of his father's orthodoxy in the face of a violent mob brought peace to the town and prominence to Gregory.

In 361, against his will, Gregory was ordained presbyter, and settled down to live an austere, priestly life. He was not to have peace for long. Basil, in his fight against the Arian Emperor Valens, compelled Gregory to become Bishop of Sasima. According to Gregory, it was "a detestable little place without water or grass or any mark of civilization." He felt, he said, like "a bone flung to the dogs." His friendship with Basil suffered a severe break.

Deaths in his family, and that of his estranged friend Basil, brought Gregory himself to the point of death. He withdrew for healing.

In 379, Gregory moved to Constantinople, a new man and no longer in despair. He appeared as one afire with the love of God. His fame as a theologian rests on five sermons he delivered during this period on the doctrine of the Trinity. They are marked by clarity, strength, and a charming gaiety.

The next year, the new Emperor Theodosius entered Constantinople and expelled its Arian bishop and clergy. Then, on a rainy day, the crowds in the Great Church of Hagia Sophia acclaimed Gregory bishop, after a ray of sunlight suddenly shone on him.

Power and position meant nothing to Gregory. After the Ecumenical Council of 381, he retired to Nazianzus, where he died in 389. Among the Fathers of the Church, he alone is known as "The Divine," "The Theologian."

Rite I Almighty God, who hast revealed to thy Church thine eternal Being of glorious majesty and perfect love as one God in Trinity of persons: Give us grace that, like thy bishop Gregory of Nazianzus, we may continue steadfast in the confession of this faith, and constant in our worship of thee, Father, Son, and Holy Spirit; who livest and reignest for ever and ever. Amen.

Rite II Almighty God, you have revealed to your Church your eternal Being of glorious majesty and perfect love as one God in Trinity of Persons: Give us grace that, like your bishop Gregory of Nazianzus, we may continue steadfast in the confession of this faith, and constant in our worship of you, Father, Son, and Holy Spirit; for you live and reign for ever and ever. Amen.

For Liturgical Celebration: [Common of a Theologian and Teacher, A17] [Common of a Pastor, A14] [Of the Holy Trinity, A37] [For the Ministry II, A50]

May 10

Nicolaus Ludwig von Zinzendorf
Prophetic Witness, 1760

Nicolaus von Zinzendorf was a Count of the Holy Roman Empire who always had more interest in religious matters than in affairs of court. Following studies at the pietist center of Halle, he developed his own "theology of the heart," which placed great emphasis on a close personal relationship with the suffering Savior. This "heart religion" was not just inner emotion, however, but was to result in a life totally devoted to the Savior. "All of life becomes a liturgy," said Zinzendorf, and even the most mundane task can be an act of worship.

Always a champion of the underdog, he granted asylum to Bohemian Protestant exiles. Following a unifying experience on August 13, 1727, in their settlement of Herrnhut on his estate, the old church of the *Unitas Fratrum* (Bohemian Brethren) was reborn and developed a rich liturgical and devotional life. This Moravian Church, as it came to be called, launched pioneer mission work, first in the Caribbean and then around the world. Zinzendorf himself became a bishop, and devoted his personal fortune to furthering the work of the church.

He was an early advocate of ecumenism, and, in America, he attempted to bring Protestant denominations together in the "Pennsylvania Synods." He was not a systematic theologian, but produced numerous theological writings, widely read in Germany. In addition to these, he was a prolific hymn writer, and many of his hymn texts remain in use today in the Moravian Church and beyond. His view of the church is summed up in his stanza:

> Christian hearts, in love united,
> seek alone in Jesus rest;
> has he not your love excited?
> Then let love inspire each breast.
> Members on our Head depending,
> lights reflecting him, our Sun,
> brethren—his commands attending,
> we in him, our Lord, are one.
> (*Moravian Book of Worship* 1995, 673)

Rite I God of new life in Christ: We remember the bold witness of thy servant Nicolaus von Zinzendorf, through whom thy Spirit moved to draw many to faith and conversion of life. We pray that we, like him, may rejoice to sing thy praise; through Jesus Christ our Lord, who liveth and reigneth with thee and the Holy Spirit, one God, now and for ever. Amen.

Rite II God of new life in Christ: We remember the bold witness of your servant Nicolaus von Zinzendorf, through whom your Spirit moved to draw many to faith and conversion of life. We pray that we, like him, may rejoice to sing your praise; through Jesus Christ our Lord, who lives and reigns with you and the Holy Spirit, one God, now and for ever. Amen.

For Liturgical Celebration: [Common of a Prophetic Witness, A31] [Common of an Artist, Writer, or Composer, A27] [For Vocation in Daily Work, A61]

May 13

Frances Perkins
Public Servant and Prophetic Witness, 1965

Frances Perkins was the first woman to serve a President of the United States as a member of the Cabinet.

Born in Boston on April 10, 1880, and educated at Mount Holyoke College and Columbia University, Perkins was passionate about the social problems occasioned by the continuing effects of industrialization and urbanization.

As a young adult, she discovered The Episcopal Church and was confirmed at the Church of the Holy Spirit in Lake Forest, Illinois, on June 11, 1905, and she remained a faithful and active Episcopalian for the remainder of her life.

After moving to New York, she became an advocate for industrial safety and persistent voice for the reform of what she believed were unjust labor laws. This work got the attention of two of New York's governors, Al Smith and Franklin D. Roosevelt, in whose state administrations she took part.

President Roosevelt appointed her to a Cabinet post as Secretary of Labor, a position she would hold for twelve years. As Secretary of Labor, Perkins would have a major role in shaping the New Deal legislation signed into law by President Roosevelt, most notably the establishment of the Social Security program.

During her years of public service, Frances Perkins depended upon her faith, her life of prayer, and the guidance of her church for the support she needed to assist the United States and its leadership to face the enormous problems of the time. During her time as Secretary of Labor, she would take time away from her duties on a monthly basis and make a retreat with the All Saints Sisters of the Poor in nearby Catonsville, Maryland. She spoke publicly of how the Incarnation informed her conviction that humans ought to work with God to create a just Christian social order.

Following her public service, she became a professor of industrial and labor relations at Cornell University. She remained active in teaching, social justice advocacy, and in the mission of The Episcopal Church. She was an eloquent example of lay ministry, writing that "the special vocation of the laity is to conduct and carry on the worldly and secular affairs of modern society . . . in order that all men may be maintained in health and decency." She died in New York City on May 14, 1965.

Rite I Loving God, we bless thy Name for Frances Perkins, who in faithfulness to her baptism sought to build a society in which all may live in health and decency: Help us, following her example and in union with her prayers, to contend tirelessly for justice and for the protection of all, that we may be faithful followers of Jesus Christ; who with thee and the Holy Spirit liveth and reigneth, one God, for ever and ever. Amen.

Rite II Loving God, we bless your Name for Frances Perkins, who in faithfulness to her baptism sought to build a society in which all may live in health and decency: Help us, following her example and in union with her prayers, to contend tirelessly for justice and for the protection of all, that we may be faithful followers of Jesus Christ; who with you and the Holy Spirit lives and reigns, one God, for ever and ever. Amen.

For Liturgical Celebration: [Common of a Prophetic Witness, A31] [Common of a Saint, A23] [For all Baptized Christians, A42] [For Vocation in Daily Work, A61]

May 15

Junia and Andronicus

At the end of his letter to the Romans, the apostle Paul identifies Junia and Andronicus as "prominent among the apostles." They had been in prison with him and had come to know Christ before he did.

In Eastern Orthodox tradition, these apostles are remembered for the converts they won in their extensive travels to preach the gospel, and they are honored as martyrs for Christ. Their feast day has been celebrated in Eastern churches since the early seventh century.

In the late fourth century, John Chrysostom wrote about them, praising Junia as a woman and an apostle. St. Joseph the Hymnographer, writing in the ninth century, lauded them in a liturgical hymn:

> With piety we will honor the bright stars and holy
> Apostles Junia and the God-inspired Andronicus.
> The blessed Paul proclaims you both as truly distinguished
> Among the Apostles, and blessed in the Church.

Rite I Almighty God, whose Son, the risen Christ, sent forth thine apostles Andronicus and Junia to proclaim the gospel and extend thy reign: Send us forth in thy Holy Spirit, that women and men may minister as one in faithful witness to the gospel of Jesus Christ; who liveth and reigneth with thee and the Holy Spirit in perfect unity, one God, now and for ever. Amen

Rite II Almighty God, whose Son, the risen Christ, sent forth your apostles Andronicus and Junia to proclaim the gospel and extend your reign: send us forth in your Holy Spirit, that women and men may minister as one in faithful witness to the gospel of Jesus Christ; who lives and reigns with you and the Holy Spirit in perfect unity, one God, now and for ever. Amen.

For Liturgical Celebration: [Common of a Pastor, A14] [For the Ministry II, A50] [For the Unity of the Church, A48]

May 16

The Martyrs of the Sudan

"The blood of the martyrs is the seed of the Church," the third-century North African teacher Tertullian once wrote. And in no place is that observation more apt than in the region of the Sudan. Once Africa's largest country, it has been torn by violence since independence from Egyptian and British rule in 1956. The 2011 division of the region into two countries, the Republic of Sudan and South Sudan, has not resolved its conflicts.

British policy in the late nineteenth century was to arbitrarily divide the vast country between a Muslim North and a multiethnic South, limiting Christian missionary activity largely to the latter, an artificial division that created enduring problems. Since independence, on January 1, 1956, a series of civilian governments and military dictatorships ruled, leading to decades of civil war. During the 1980s Sudan's internal armed conflict assumed an increasingly religious character, fueled by a northern-dominated Islamic government imposing authoritarian political control, Islam as the state religion, a penal code based on Sharia law, and restrictions on free speech and free assembly.

On May 16, 1983, a small number of Episcopal and Roman Catholic clerical and lay leaders declared they "would not abandon God as they knew him." Possibly over two million persons, most of them Christians, were then killed in a two-decade civil war, until a Comprehensive Peace Treaty was signed in January 2005. During those years, up to four million southern Christians were internally displaced, and another million forced into exile in Africa and elsewhere. Yet despite the total destruction of churches, schools, and other institutions, Sudanese Christianity, which includes four million members of The Episcopal Church of the Sudan, has both solidified as a faith community and gradually expanded at home and among refugees, providing steadfast hope in an often-desperate setting.

This hymn, written by Sudanese children in exile in Ethiopia, reflects both the tragedy and depth of faith of Sudan's Christians:

> Look upon us, O Creator who has made us.
> God of all peoples, we are yearning for our land.
> Hear the prayer of our souls in the wilderness.
> Hear the prayer of our bones in the wilderness.
> Hear our prayer as we call out to you.

Rite I O God, steadfast in the midst of persecution, by whose providence the blood of the martyrs is the seed of the Church: As the martyrs of the Sudan refused to abandon Christ even in the face of torture and death, and so by their sacrifice brought forth a plenteous harvest, may we, too, be steadfast in our faith in Jesus Christ; who with thee and the Holy Spirit liveth and reigneth, one God, for ever and ever. Amen.

Rite II O God, steadfast in the midst of persecution, by your providence the blood of the martyrs is the seed of the Church: As the martyrs of the Sudan refused to abandon Christ even in the face of torture and death, and so by their sacrifice brought forth a plentiful harvest, may we, too, be steadfast in our faith in Jesus Christ; who with you and the Holy Spirit lives and reigns, one God, for ever and ever. Amen.

For Liturgical Celebration: [Common of a Martyr, A7] [Of the Holy Cross, A41] [On the Anniversary of a Disaster, A67]

May 17

William Hobart Hare
Bishop of Niobrara and of South Dakota, 1909

William Hobart Hare was born on May 17, 1838, in Princeton, New Jersey, the grandson of Bishop John Henry Hobart. Although he studied at the University of Pennsylvania, he never received a degree and prepared for ordination without attending seminary. He was ordained to the diaconate in 1859 and to the priesthood in 1862. He served St. Luke's and St. Paul's, Chestnut Hill, both in Philadelphia.

He moved to Minnesota in 1863 with the hope that a different climate would improve his wife's failing health. It was there that he first came into contact with Native Americans, an encounter that would change his life and shape his vocation. Hare returned to Philadelphia in 1867 to become the Rector of the Church of the Ascension, but his personal interest in the church's ministry among Native Americans never waned.

In 1871, the House of Bishops of The Episcopal Church created the Missionary District of Niobrara encompassing much of the Dakotas. A year later, the House of Bishops elected Hare to become the Bishop of Niobrara, and he was ordained to the episcopate on January 9, 1873.

Bishop Hare, often referred to as "The Apostle to the Sioux," devoted himself to work among the Native Americans in the vast expanse of the Niobrara Territory. Well ahead of his time in his approach to mission work, Hare believed it was important to honor as much of the tradition and culture of the people as possible. His desire was not to destroy the fabric of Sioux culture, but to bring the gospel into the midst of it so that the people could also come to know Jesus. Instead of suppressing the customs of the people, he saw them as vessels that could communicate God's grace.

In 1883, the House of Bishops divided the Missionary District of Niobrara into the districts of North and South Dakota. Bishop Hare from that point took responsibility for what would become the Diocese of South Dakota. He worked vigorously to ensure that the Native Americans in his area of care had access to education and healthcare. By his initiative, the number of native catechists and clergy grew greatly. By the end of his life, over half of the Native Americans in South Dakota were Episcopalians, with Hare having confirmed over 7,000 of them. The Niobrara deanery became a site of gathering for Episcopalian Native Americans across the Great Plains that continues to this day. Hare died on October 23, 1909.

Rite I Holy God, who didst call thy servant William Hobart Hare to proclaim the means of grace and the hope of glory to the peoples of the Great Plains: We give thanks to thee for the devotion of those who received the Good News gladly, and for the faithfulness of the generations who have succeeded them. Strengthen us with thy Holy Spirit, that we may walk in their footsteps and lead many to faith in Jesus Christ; who liveth and reigneth with thee and the Holy Spirit, one God, now and for ever. Amen.

Rite II Holy God, you called your servant William Hobart Hare to proclaim the means of grace and the hope of glory to the peoples of the Great Plains: We give you thanks for the devotion of those who received the Good News gladly, and for the faithfulness of the generations who have succeeded them. Strengthen us with your Holy Spirit, that we may walk in their footsteps and lead many to faith in Jesus Christ; who lives and reigns with you and the Holy Spirit, one God, now and for ever. Amen.

For Liturgical Celebration: [Common of a Missionary, A11] [Common of a Pastor, A14] [For the Ministry II, A50] [For the Mission of the Church, A52]

May 17

Thurgood Marshall
Lawyer and Jurist, 1993

Thurgood Marshall was a distinguished American jurist and the first African American to become an Associate Justice of the United States Supreme Court.

Marshall was born on July 2, 1908, in Baltimore, Maryland. He attended Frederick Douglass High School in Baltimore and Lincoln University in Pennsylvania. Pushed toward other professions, Marshall was determined to be an attorney. He was denied admission to the University of Maryland Law School, due to its segregationist admissions policy. He enrolled and graduated magna cum laude from the Law School of Howard University in Washington.

Marshall began the practice of law in Baltimore in 1933 and began representing the local chapter of the NAACP in 1934, eventually becoming the legal counsel for the national organization, working in New York City. He won his first major civil rights decision in 1936, Murray v. Pearson, which forced the University of Maryland to open its doors to blacks.

At the age of 32, Marshall successfully argued his first case before the United States Supreme Court and went on to win 29 of the 32 cases he argued before the court. As a lawyer, his crowning achievement was arguing successfully for the plaintiffs in Brown v. Board of Education of Topeka, in 1954. The Supreme Court ruled that the "separate but equal" doctrine was unconstitutional and ordered the desegregation of public schools across the nation.

President Lyndon Johnson appointed Marshall as the 96th Associate Justice of the United States Supreme Court in 1967, a position he held for 24 years. Marshall compiled a long and impressive record of decisions on civil rights, not only for African Americans, but also for women, Native Americans, and the incarcerated; he was a strong advocate for individual freedoms and human rights. He adamantly believed that capital punishment was unconstitutional and should be abolished.

As a child, Marshall attended St. Katherine's, one of Baltimore's historic African American parishes. While living in New York, he was the senior warden of St. Philip's Church in Harlem and served as a deputy to General Convention in 1964. During his years in Washington, Marshall and his family were members of St. Augustine's Episcopal Church, where he was affectionately known as "the Judge." He is remembered as "a wise and godly man who knew his place and role in history and obeyed God's call to follow justice wherever it led." Thurgood Marshall died on January 24, 1993.

Rite I   Eternal and ever-gracious God, who didst bless thy servant Thurgood Marshall with exceptional grace and courage to discern and speak the truth: Grant that, following his example, we may know thee and recognize that we are all thy children, brothers and sisters of Jesus Christ, who teacheth us to love one another; and who liveth and reigneth with thee and the Holy Spirit, one God, for ever and ever. Amen.

Rite II   Eternal and ever-gracious God, you blessed your servant Thurgood Marshall with exceptional grace and courage to discern and speak the truth: Grant that, following his example, we may know you and recognize that we are all your children, brothers and sisters of Jesus Christ, who teaches us to love one another; and who lives and reigns with you and the Holy Spirit, one God, for ever and ever. Amen.

For Liturgical Celebration: [Common of a Prophetic Witness, A31] [For Social Justice, A58] [For Vocation in Daily Work, A61]

May 19

Dunstan, Archbishop of Canterbury
988

In the ninth century, under King Alfred the Great, England had achieved considerable military, political, cultural, and even some ecclesiastical recovery from the Viking invasions. It was not until the following century that there was a revival of monasticism. In that, the leading figure was Dunstan.

Dunstan was born about 909 into a family with royal connections. He became a monk and, in 943, was made Abbot of Glastonbury. During a year-long political exile in Flanders, he encountered the vigorous currents of the Benedictine monastic revival. King Edgar recalled Dunstan to England in 957, appointed him Bishop of Worcester, then of London; and, in 960, named him Archbishop of Canterbury. Together with his former pupils, Bishops Aethelwold of Winchester and Oswald of Worcester (later of York), Dunstan was a leader of the English Church. All three have been described as "contemplatives in action"—bringing the fruits of their monastic prayer life to the immediate concerns of Church and State. They sought better education and discipline among the clergy, the end of landed family interest in the Church, the restoration of former monasteries and the establishment of new ones, a revival of monastic life for women, and a more elaborate and carefully ordered liturgical worship.

This reform movement was set forth in the "Monastic Agreement," a common code for English monasteries drawn up by Aethelwold about 970, primarily under the inspiration of Dunstan. It called for continual intercession for the royal house, and emphasized the close tie between the monasteries and the crown. This close alliance of Church and State, sacramentalized in the anointing of the King, was expressed liturgically in the earliest English coronation ceremony of which a full text survives, compiled for King Edgar by Dunstan and his associates.

The long-term effects of this tenth-century reform resulted in the retention of two peculiarly English institutions: the "monastic cathedral," and the Celtic pattern of "monk-bishops."

Dunstan is reputed to have been an expert craftsman. His name is especially associated with the working of metals and the casting of bells, and he was regarded as the patron saint of those crafts.

He died at Canterbury in 988.

Rite I   Direct thy Church, O Lord, into the beauty of holiness, that, following the good example of thy servant Dunstan, we may honor thy Son Jesus Christ with our lips and in our lives; to the glory of his Name, who liveth and reigneth with thee and the Holy Spirit, one God, now and for ever. Amen.

Rite II Direct your Church, O Lord, into the beauty of holiness, that, following the good example of your servant Dunstan, we may honor your Son Jesus Christ with our lips and in our lives; to the glory of his Name, who lives and reigns with you and the Holy Spirit, one God, now and for ever. Amen.

For Liturgical Celebration: [Common of a Pastor, A14] [Common of an Artist, Writer, or Composer, A27] [Common of a Monastic or Professed Religious, A20] [For the Ministry II, A50] [Common of a Prophetic Witness, A31]

May 20

Alcuin
Deacon, and Abbot of Tours, 804

Alcuin was born about 730 near York, into a noble family related to Willibrord, the first missionary to the Netherlands. He was educated at the cathedral school in York under Archbishop Egbert, a pupil of Bede. He thus inherited the best traditions of learning and zeal of the early English Church. After ordination as a deacon in 770, he became head of the York school. Following a meeting in 781 with the Emperor Charlemagne in Pavia (Italy), he was persuaded to become the Emperor's "prime minister," with special responsibility for the revival of education and learning in the Frankish dominions.

Alcuin was named Abbot of Tours in 796, where he died on May 19, 804, and was buried in the church of St. Martin.

Alcuin was a man of vast learning, personal charm, and integrity of character. In his direction of Charlemagne's Palace School at Aachen, he was chiefly responsible for the preservation of the classical heritage of western civilization. Schools were revived in cathedrals and monasteries, and manuscripts of both pagan and Christian writings of antiquity were collated and copied.

Under the authority of Charlemagne, the liturgy was reformed, and service books gathered from Rome were edited and adapted. To this work we owe the preservation of many of the Collects that have come down to us, including the Collect for Purity at the beginning of the Holy Eucharist.

Rite I   Almighty God, who didst raise up thy servant Alcuin as a beacon of learning: Shine, we pray, in our hearts, that in our generation we may show forth thy praise, for thou didst call us out of darkness into thy marvelous light; through Jesus Christ our Lord, who liveth and reigneth with thee and the Holy Spirit, one God, now and for ever. Amen.

Rite II   Almighty God, who raised up your servant Alcuin as a beacon of learning: Shine, we pray, in our hearts, that in our generation we may show forth your praise, who called us out of darkness into your marvelous light; through Jesus Christ our Lord, who lives and reigns with you and the Holy Spirit, one God, now and for ever. Amen.

For Liturgical Celebration: [Common of a Monastic or Professed Religious, A20] [Common of a Theologian and Teacher, A17] [Of the Holy Trinity, A37]

May 21

John Eliot
Missionary among the Algonquin, 1690

John Eliot, known as "The Apostle to the Indians," was born in 1604 at Widford in Hertfordshire, England. Educated at Cambridge, Eliot's nonconformist beliefs brought him into conflict with the tenets of the established church, and he departed for New England in 1631. Eliot arrived in Boston later that year and became the pastor of a church in nearby Roxbury.

During his tenure as pastor in Roxbury he became concerned with the welfare of the native populations and he learned the Algonquin language. After two years of study he began preaching to them in their own language. Like Roger Williams before him, Eliot had learned the native language and preached to the local tribes, but unlike Williams, Eliot devoted his entire life's work to preaching the gospel to the native people.

In 1649, by act of Parliament, a Corporation for the Promoting and Propagating of the Gospel among the Indians of New England was set up, and, with the financial backing of the English government, Eliot built a native settlement at Natick. The native people were provided with food, clothing, homes, and education, and in 1660 the first Indian church in New England was founded.

During this time, Eliot began his monumental translation of the English Bible into the Algonquin language. Starting with the Ten Commandments and the Lord's Prayer, he was able to complete translations of the Book of Genesis and the Gospel of Matthew with the financial support of the Corporation for the Propagating of the Gospel. In 1661, his Algonquin New Testament was published, a copy of which was sent to King Charles II, and finally, in 1663, his complete translation of the Bible was published. Eliot would revise his translation several times, after most copies had been destroyed in the Indian Wars of 1670, along with many of the Indian settlements he established.

Eliot wrote a number of other books before his death, including a grammar of the Algonquin language. His work was vital to the studies of many linguists after him who were interested in Native American languages.

Rite I Almighty God, by the proclamation of thy Word all nations are drawn to thee: Make us desire, like John Eliot, to share thy Good News with those whom we encounter, so that all people may come to a saving knowledge of thee; through Jesus Christ our Savior, who with thee and the Holy Spirit liveth and reigneth, one God, for ever and ever. Amen.

Rite II Almighty God, by the proclamation of your Word all nations are drawn to you: Make us desire, like John Eliot, to share your Good News with those whom we encounter, so that all people may come to a saving knowledge of you; through Jesus Christ our Savior, who with you and the Holy Spirit lives and reigns, one God, for ever and ever. Amen.

For Liturgical Celebration: [Common of a Missionary, A11] [Common of a Pastor, A14] [For the Ministry I, A49] [For the Mission of the Church, A52]

May 23

Nicolaus Copernicus, *1543,*
and Johannes Kepler, *1630*
Astronomers

Born in 1473, Nicolaus Copernicus first studied law and medicine before serving as a cleric under the direction of his uncle, the Bishop of Warmia (in northeastern Poland). Copernicus first set forth his heliocentric theory of astronomy in a small work called the *Commentariolus*, which was not published until 1878. His argument that the sun, rather than the earth, was the center of the universe around which the planets rotated was developed fully in his 1543 opus *De Revolutionibus Orbium Caelestium*.

The initial ecclesiastical reaction to his revolutionary theory was somewhat muted, but when his thought was further developed by Galileo, the religious debate was intensified, and *De revolutionibus* was placed on the index of banned books. Copernicus had originally dedicated his work to the Pope, and he saw no conflict between his theory and the authority of Scripture.

Among those chiefly responsible for the solidifying of Copernicus' theories was the German astronomer Johannes Kepler. Born nearly a century after Copernicus, Kepler was first educated at Tübingen, where he received instruction in Copernican theory. His first major work on Copernican astronomy was the *Mysterium Cosmographicum*, in which he believed he had demonstrated God's geometric plan for the universe. Kepler saw in the relation between the sun and the rotating planets the image of God himself, and like Copernicus, he saw no conflict between his astronomical views and the account of God in the Scriptures. Kepler is chiefly known for his discovery of the laws of planetary motion, set forth variously in his later works.

Though their works were each controversial in their own way, Copernicus and Kepler laid the groundwork for modern astronomy. Kepler's work was even influential on Isaac Newton's theory of universal gravitation.

Both men, through their life's work, testified to the extraordinary presence of God in creation and maintained, in the face of both religious and scientific controversy, that science can lead us more deeply into an understanding of the workings of the Creator.

Rite I As the heavens declare thy glory, O God, and the firmament showeth thy handiwork, we bless thy Name for the gifts of knowledge and insight thou didst bestow upon Nicolaus Copernicus and Johannes Kepler; and we pray that thou wouldst continue to advance our understanding of thy cosmos, for our good and for thy glory; through Jesus Christ, the firstborn of all creation, who with thee and the Holy Spirit liveth and reigneth, one God, for ever and ever. Amen.

Rite II As the heavens declare your glory, O God, and the firmament shows your handiwork, we bless your Name for the gifts of knowledge and insight you bestowed upon Nicolaus Copernicus and Johannes Kepler; and we pray that you would continue to advance our understanding of your cosmos, for our good and for your glory; through Jesus Christ, the firstborn of all creation, who with you and the Holy Spirit lives and reigns, one God, for ever and ever. Amen.

For Liturgical Celebration: [Common of a Scientist or Environmentalist, A35] [For Space Exploration, A70]

May 24

Jackson Kemper
First Missionary Bishop in the United States, 1870

When the General Convention of 1835 made all the members of The Episcopal Church members also of the Domestic and Foreign Missionary Society, it provided at the same time for missionary bishops to serve in the wilderness and in foreign countries. Jackson Kemper was the first such bishop. Although he was assigned to Missouri and Indiana, he laid foundations also in Iowa, Wisconsin, Minnesota, Nebraska, and Kansas, and made extensive missionary tours in the South and Southwest.

Kemper was born in Pleasant Valley, New York, on December 24, 1789. He graduated from Columbia College in 1809 and was ordained deacon in 1811 and priest in 1814.

He served Bishop White as Assistant at Christ Church, Philadelphia. At his urging, Bishop White made his first and only visitation in western Pennsylvania. In 1835, Kemper was ordained bishop, and immediately set out on his travels.

Because Episcopal clergymen, mostly from well-to-do Eastern homes, found it hard to adjust to the harsh life of the frontier—scorching heat, drenching rains, and winter blizzards—Kemper established Kemper College in St. Louis, Missouri, the first of many similar attempts to train clergymen, and in more recent times lay persons as well, for specialized tasks in the Church. The College failed in 1845 from the usual malady of such projects in the church—inadequate funding. Nashotah House, in Wisconsin, which he founded in 1842, with the help of James Lloyd Breck and his companions, was more successful. So was Racine College, founded in 1852. Both these institutions reflected Kemper's devotion to beauty in ritual and worship.

Kemper pleaded for more attention to the Native Americans and encouraged the translation of services into native languages. He described a service among the Oneida which was marked by "courtesy, reverence, worship—and obedience to that Great Spirit in whose hands are the issues of life."

From 1859 until his death, Kemper was diocesan Bishop of Wisconsin. He is more justly honored by his unofficial title, "The Bishop of the Whole Northwest."

Rite I   Lord God, in whose providence Jackson Kemper was chosen first missionary bishop in this land, and by his arduous labor and travel congregations were established in scattered settlements of the West: Grant that the Church may always be faithful to its mission, and have the vision, courage, and perseverance to make known to all people the Good News of Jesus Christ; who with thee and the Holy Spirit liveth and reigneth, one God, for ever and ever. Amen.

Rite II Lord God, in your providence Jackson Kemper was chosen first missionary bishop in this land, and by his arduous labor and travel congregations were established in scattered settlements of the West: Grant that the Church may always be faithful to its mission, and have the vision, courage, and perseverance to make known to all people the Good News of Jesus Christ; who with you and the Holy Spirit lives and reigns, one God, for ever and ever. Amen.

For Liturgical Celebration: [Common of a Missionary, A11] [Common of a Pastor, A14] [For the Ministry II, A50] [For the Mission of the Church, A52] [For Education, A60]

May 25

Bede, the Venerable
Priest and Monk of Jarrow, 735

At the age of seven, Bede's parents brought him to the nearby monastery at Jarrow (near Durham in northeast England) for his education. There, as he later wrote, "spending all the remaining time of my life . . . I wholly applied myself to the study of Scripture, and amidst the observance of regular discipline, and the daily care of singing in the church, I always took delight in learning, teaching, and writing."

Bede was ordained deacon at nineteen, and presbyter at thirty. He died on the eve of the Ascension in 735 while dictating a vernacular translation of the Gospel According to John. About 1020, his body was removed to Durham and placed in the Galilee, the Lady Chapel at the west end of the Cathedral nave.

Bede was the greatest scholar of his time in the Western Church. He wrote commentaries on the Scriptures based on patristic interpretations. His treatise on chronology was standard for a long time. He also wrote on orthography, poetic meter, and especially on history. His most famous work, the *Ecclesiastical History of England*, written in Latin, remains the primary source for the period 597 to 731, when Anglo-Saxon culture developed and Christianity triumphed. In this work, Bede was clearly ahead of his time. He consulted many documents, carefully evaluated their reliability, and cited his sources. His interpretations were balanced and judicious. He also wrote *The Lives of the Holy Abbots of Wearmouth and Jarrow*, and a notable biography of Cuthbert, both in prose and verse.

His character shines through his work—an exemplary monk, an ardent Christian, devoted scholar, and a man of pure and winsome manners. He received the unusual title of Venerable more than a century after his death. According to one legend, the monk writing the inscription for his tomb was at a loss for a word to fill out the couplet:

Hac sunt in fossa
Bedae—blank—*ossa*

(This grave contains
the—*blank*—Bede's remains)

That night an angel filled in the blank: *Venerabilis*.

———

Rite I   Almighty God, who hast enriched thy Church with the learning and holiness of thy servant Bede: Grant us to find in Scripture and disciplined prayer the image of thy Son our Savior Jesus Christ, and to fashion our lives according to his likeness, to the glory of thy great Name and the benefit of thy holy Church; through the same Jesus Christ our Lord. Amen.

Rite II   Almighty God, who has enriched your Church with the learning and holiness of your servant Bede: Grant us to find in Scripture and disciplined prayer the image of your Son our Savior Jesus Christ, and to fashion our lives according to his likeness, to the glory of your great Name and the benefit of your holy Church; through the same Jesus Christ our Lord. Amen.

For Liturgical Celebration: [Common of a Monastic or Professed Religious, A20] [Common of a Theologian and Teacher, A17] [Of the Holy Trinity, A37] [Of the Reign of Christ, A46]

May 26

Augustine
First Archbishop of Canterbury, 605

Although Christianity had existed in Britain before the invasions of Angles and Saxons in the fifth century, Pope Gregory the Great decided in 596 to send a mission to the pagan Anglo-Saxons. He selected, from his own monastery on the Coelian hill in Rome, a group of monks, led by their prior, Augustine. They arrived in Kent in 597, carrying a silver cross and an image of Jesus Christ painted on a board, which thus became, so far as we know, "Canterbury's first icon." King Ethelbert tolerated their presence and allowed them the use of an old church built on the east side of Canterbury, dating from the Roman occupation of Britain. Here, says the Venerable Bede, they assembled "to sing the psalms, to pray, to say Mass, to preach, and to baptize." This church of St. Martin is the earliest place of Christian worship in England still in use.

Probably in 601, Ethelbert was converted, thus becoming the first Christian king in England. About the same time, Augustine was ordained bishop somewhere in France and named "Archbishop of the English Nation." Thus, the see of Canterbury and its Cathedral Church of Christ owe their establishment to Augustine's mission, as does the nearby Abbey of SS. Peter and Paul, later re-named for Augustine. The "chair of St. Augustine" in Canterbury Cathedral, however, dates from the thirteenth century.

Some correspondence between Augustine and Gregory survives. One of the Pope's most famous counsels to the first Archbishop of Canterbury has to do with diversity in the young English Church. Gregory writes, "If you have found customs, whether in the Roman, Gallican, or any other Churches that may be more acceptable to God, I wish you to make a careful selection of them, and teach the Church of the English, which is still young in the faith, whatever you can profitably learn from the various Churches. For things should not be loved for the sake of places, but places for the sake of good things."

This counsel bears on the search for Christian "unity in diversity" of the ecumenical movement of today.

Augustine died on May 26, probably in 605.

Rite I O Lord our God, who by thy Son Jesus Christ didst call thine apostles and send them forth to preach the Gospel to the nations: We bless thy holy Name for thy servant Augustine, first Archbishop of Canterbury, whose labors in propagating thy Church among the English people we commemorate today; and we pray that all whom thou dost call and send may do thy will, and bide thy time, and see thy glory; through Jesus Christ our Lord, who liveth and reigneth with thee and the Holy Spirit, one God, for ever and ever. Amen.

Rite II O Lord our God, by your Son Jesus Christ you called your apostles and sent them forth to preach the Gospel to the nations: We bless your holy Name for your servant Augustine, first Archbishop of Canterbury, whose labors in propagating your Church among the English people we commemorate today; and we pray that all whom you call and send may do your will, and bide your time, and see your glory; through Jesus Christ our Lord, who lives and reigns with you and the Holy Spirit, one God, for ever and ever. Amen.

For Liturgical Celebration: [Common of a Missionary, A11] [Common of a Pastor, A14] [Common of a Monastic or Professed Religious, A20] [For the Ministry II, A50] [For the Mission of the Church, A52]

May 27

Bertha and Ethelbert
Queen and King of Kent, 616

Christianity had been known in Britain among the Celts since the third century, but in the fifth century, the southeast was invaded by pagan Anglo-Saxons who drove the Celts north and west into Scotland, Ireland, and Wales. Ethelbert succeeded his father as Saxon king of Kent in 560. He was, according to the Venerable Bede, a fair ruler and the first English king to promulgate a code of law. Brisk cross-channel trade with France exposed Ethelbert to Roman customs and luxuries. His admiration for the Frankish ways led him to marry a French Christian princess, Bertha. Although not a Christian himself, Ethelbert promised Bertha's father that she could practice her faith. Good to his word, he welcomed her chaplain and granted him an old Christian mausoleum to convert into the Church of St. Martin, which still stands today.

In 597, the Roman mission to England under Augustine arrived. When he first heard the gospel, Ethelbert was cautious and unconvinced. However, his fair-mindedness and hospitality were evident in his welcome to Augustine: "The words and promises you bring are fair enough, but because they are new to us and doubtful, I cannot accept them and forsake those beliefs which I and the whole English race have held so long. But as you have come on a long pilgrimage and are anxious, I perceive, to share with us things which you believe are true and good, we do not wish to do you harm; on the contrary, we receive you hospitably and provide what is necessary for your support; nor do we forbid you to win all you can to your faith and religion by your preaching."

The following Pentecost, Ethelbert was baptized, becoming the first Christian king in England. Though he helped the missionaries and founded cathedrals and churches throughout southeastern England, including Canterbury Cathedral, he never coerced his people, or even his children, into conversion. Bertha's kind and charitable nature and Ethelbert's respect for law and the dignity of individual conscience represent, to this day, some of the best of the English Christian spirit.

Rite I God of Creation, who didst mold humanity from the fertile earth: Grant that we, following the good examples of Queen Bertha and King Ethelbert, may gladly receive and fruitfully nurture the seed of the Gospel to the bounty of thy kingdom; through Jesus Christ our Lord, who with thee and the Holy Spirit liveth and reigneth, one God, now and for ever. Amen.

Rite II God of Creation, who molded humanity from the fertile earth: Grant that we, following the good examples of Queen Bertha and King Ethelbert, may gladly receive and fruitfully nurture the seed of the Gospel to the bounty of your kingdom; through Jesus Christ our Lord, who with you and the Holy Spirit lives and reigns, one God, now and for ever. Amen.

For Liturgical Celebration: [Common of a Missionary, A11] [Common of a Saint, A23] [For all Baptized Christians, A42] [For the Mission of the Church, A52]

May 28

John Calvin
Theologian, 1564

John Calvin was the premier theologian and leader of the Reformed wing of the Protestant Reformation.

Calvin was born in France in 1509 and reared in a devout Roman Catholic family. He excelled at his studies and, by the age of 19, he had earned a master's degree. His father wanted him to study law, which he did for a time, but Calvin's own passions were theology, languages, rhetoric and the literary sciences. Around 1534, he underwent a major conversion experience, left the Roman Church, and devoted the rest of his life to the evangelical cause of the Protestant Reformation.

Calvin's greatest work is *The Institutes of the Christian Religion*, first published in 1536, but repeatedly updated and revised until its final edition in 1559. Unlike Luther and Zwingli, whose theological writings were "situational" in the sense of addressing particular conflicts, Calvin's *Institutes* were a more systematic treatment of the whole of Reformed evangelical theology. By taking up his reforming agenda fifteen years after Luther and Zwingli, Calvin was able to write in a more reflective and considered mode, beyond the crossfire and immediacy of the early years of the Reformation. Standard themes in Reformed theology—the sovereignty of God, election and predestination, the true nature of the Christian life, and the proper understanding of the authority of Scripture—even now bear strong Calvinist qualities. The *Institutes* continue to be an accessible window into the Reformed theology of the sixteenth century.

Calvin was also interested in theological principles controlling the civil state by imposing moral discipline on the people. His efforts in Geneva to establish such a theocratic moral code enjoyed periods of modest success but were met with resistance as well. Positively, Calvin's theocratic principles of public life led to the creation of hospitals, care for the poor, orphans, widows and the infirm, provisions for better sanitation, and the creation of new industries to employ the people. Calvin's Geneva was also a safe haven for John Knox and other Protestants of the Reformed tradition during times of unrest and exile.

Calvin died in Geneva on May 27, 1564.

Rite I Sovereign and holy God, who didst bring John Calvin from a study of legal systems to understand the godliness of thy divine laws as revealed in Scripture: Fill us with a like zeal to teach and preach thy Word, that the whole world may come to know thy Son Jesus Christ, the true Word and Wisdom; who with thee and the Holy Spirit liveth and reigneth, ever one God, in glory everlasting. Amen.

Rite II Sovereign and holy God, you brought John Calvin from a study of legal systems to understand the godliness of your divine laws as revealed in Scripture: Fill us with a like zeal to teach and preach your Word, that the whole world may come to know your Son Jesus Christ, the true Word and Wisdom; who with you and the Holy Spirit lives and reigns, ever one God, in glory everlasting. Amen.

For Liturgical Celebration: [Common of a Theologian and Teacher, A17] [Common of a Pastor, A14] [Of the Holy Trinity, A37]

May 30

Jeanne d'Arc (Joan of Arc)
Mystic and Soldier, 1431

Jeanne d'Arc, or Joan of Arc, was born the daughter of peasant stock in France in 1412. Called the "Maid of Orleans," she was a religious child, and at a young age she began to experience spiritual visions, which she described as voices emerging from a powerful flash of light. She believed that Saint Michael and Saint Catherine, among other saints, called her to save France from the civil war between the Houses of Orleans and Burgundy. At first, her visions were looked upon skeptically, but she eventually convinced King Charles VII, the not yet consecrated King of France, of the genuineness of her visions.

In consultation with several of his theologians, Charles decided to allow Joan to lead an expedition to Orleans. According to legend, she wore a suit of white armor and carried a banner bearing the symbol of the Trinity and the words "Jesus, Maria." Charles' troops were inspired and won the battle for their city. She convinced Charles to proceed to Reims for his coronation, and she stood at his side throughout the ceremony.

Joan was eventually taken prisoner by Burgundian troops and sold to the English. In 1431, she returned to France, appeared before the Bishop of Beauvais, and was tried at Rouen on charges of witchcraft and heresy. Her visions were declared "false and diabolical" and she was forced to recant. Later that year, however, she was tried and condemned as a relapsed heretic and burnt to death at Rouen. In 1456, following an appeal of her trial, Pope Callistus III declared her to have been falsely accused. She was canonized by Pope Benedict XV in 1920.

Although her efforts were unsuccessful in ending civil war in France, she inspired later generations with her faith, her heroism, and her commitment to God and to her King. She is today one of the patron saints of France.

Rite I Holy God, whose power is made perfect in weakness: we honor thy calling of Jeanne d'Arc, who, though young, rose up in valor to bear thy standard for her country, and endured with grace and fortitude both victory and defeat; and we pray that we, like Jeanne, may bear witness to the truth that is in us to friends and enemies alike, and, encouraged by the companionship of thy saints, give ourselves bravely to the struggle for justice in our time; through Christ our Savior, who with thee and the Holy Spirit liveth and reigneth, one God, now and for ever. Amen.

Rite II Holy God, whose power is made perfect in weakness: we honor you for the calling of Jeanne d'Arc, who, though young, rose up in valor to bear your standard for her country, and endured with grace and fortitude both victory and defeat; and we pray that we, like Jeanne, may bear witness to the truth that is in us to friends and enemies alike, and, encouraged by the companionship of your saints, give ourselves bravely to the struggle for justice in our time; through Christ our Savior, who with you and the Holy Spirit lives and reigns, one God, now and for ever. Amen.

For Liturgical Celebration: [Common of a Martyr, A7] [Of the Holy Cross, A41] [For Social Justice, A58]

The First Book of Common Prayer
1549

The first Book of Common Prayer came into use on the Day of Pentecost, June 9, 1549, in the second year of the reign of King Edward VI. From it have descended all subsequent editions and revisions of the Book in the Churches of the Anglican Communion.

Though prepared by a commission of learned bishops and priests, the format, substance, and style of the Prayer Book were primarily the work of Thomas Cranmer, Archbishop of Canterbury, 1533–1556. The principal sources employed in its compilation were the medieval Latin service books of the Use of Sarum (Salisbury), with enrichments from the Greek liturgies, certain ancient Gallican rites, the vernacular German forms prepared by Luther, and a revised Latin liturgy of the reforming Archbishop Hermann of Cologne. The Psalter and other biblical passages were drawn from the English "Great Bible" authorized by King Henry VIII in 1539, and the Litany was taken from the English form issued as early as 1544.

The originality of the Prayer Book, apart from the felicitous translations and paraphrases of the old Latin forms, lay in its simplification of the complicated liturgical usages of the medieval Church, so that it was suitable for use by the laity as well as by the clergy. The Book thus became both a manual of common worship for Anglicans and a primary resource for their personal spirituality.

Rite I   Almighty and everliving God, whose servant Thomas Cranmer, with others, did restore the language of the people in the prayers of thy Church: Make us always thankful for this heritage; and help us so to pray in the Spirit and with the understanding, that we may worthily magnify thy holy Name; through Jesus Christ our Lord, who liveth and reigneth with thee and the Holy Spirit, one God, for ever and ever. Amen.

Rite II Almighty and everliving God, whose servant Thomas Cranmer, with others, restored the language of the people in the prayers of your Church: Make us always thankful for this heritage; and help us so to pray in the Spirit and with the understanding, that we may worthily magnify your holy Name; through Jesus Christ our Lord, who lives and reigns with you and the Holy Spirit, one God, for ever and ever. Amen.

For Liturgical Celebration: [Of the Holy Trinity, A37] [Of the Holy Spirit, A38]

JUNE

1 Justin, Martyr at Rome, c. 167
2 Blandina and Her Companions, the Martyrs of Lyons, 177
3 The Martyrs of Uganda, 1886
4 John XXIII (Angelo Guiseppe Roncalli), Bishop of Rome, 1963
5 Boniface, Archbishop of Mainz, Missionary to Germany, and Martyr, 754
6 Ini Kopuria, Founder of the Melanesian Brotherhood, 1945
7 The Pioneers of the Episcopal Anglican Church of Brazil, 1890
8 Roland Allen, Mission Strategist, 1947
9 Columba, Abbot of Iona, 597
10 Ephrem of Edessa, Syria, Deacon, 373
11
12 Enmegahbowh, Priest and Missionary, 1902
13 Gilbert Keith Chesterton, Apologist and Writer, 1936
14 Basil the Great, Bishop of Caesarea, 379
15 Evelyn Underhill, 1941
16 George Berkeley, 1753, and Joseph Butler, 1752, Bishops and Theologians
17
18 Bernard Mizeki, Catechist and Martyr in Mashonaland, 1896
19 Adelaide Teague Case, Teacher, 1948
20
21
22 Alban, First Martyr of Britain, c. 304
23
24
25 James Weldon Johnson, Poet, 1938

26 Isabel Florence Hapgood, Translator, Ecumenist, and Journalist, 1929
27 Cornelius Hill, Priest and Chief among the Oneida, 1907
28 Irenaeus, Bishop of Lyons, c. 202
29
30

June 1

Justin, Martyr at Rome
c. 167

Toward the middle of the second century, there came into the young Christian community a seeker for the truth, whose wide interests, noble spirit, and able mind, greatly enriched it.

Justin was born into a Greek-speaking pagan family about the year 110 in Samaria, near Shechem. He was educated in Greek philosophy. Like Augustine after him, he was left restless by all this knowledge. During a walk along the beach at Ephesus, he fell in with a stranger, who told him about Christ. "Straightway a flame was kindled in my soul," he writes, "and a love of the prophets and those who are friends of Christ possessed me." He became a Christian as a result of this encounter, and thereafter regarded Christianity as the only "safe and profitable philosophy."

About 150, Justin moved to Rome. As philosophers did in those days, he started a school—in this case, a school of Christian philosophy—and accepted students. He also wrote. Three of his works are known to us: a dialogue in Platonic style with a Jew named Trypho, and two "apologies." (An apology in this sense, of course, is not an excuse, but a spirited defense.) Justin's *First* and *Second Apologies* defend Christianity against the Greek charge of irrationality and the Roman charge of disloyalty to the empire. These two works provide us with important insights into developing theological ideas and liturgical practices of early Christianity. In the *Dialogue with Trypho*, Justin defends the Church against the Jewish charge of distorting the Old Testament. He interprets the Old Testament as the foreshadowing of the New.

While teaching in Rome, he engaged in a public debate with a philosopher of the Cynic school named Crescens, accusing him of ignorance and immorality. Angered, Crescens preferred legal charges against him. Justin and six of his students were arrested and brought before the prefect Rusticus. As the custom was, Rusticus gave them an opportunity to renounce their faith. All steadfastly refused to do so. Justin and his companions were put to death about the year 167.

Rite I   O God, who hast given thy Church wisdom and revealed deep and secret things: Grant that we, like thy servant Justin and in union with his prayers, may find thy truth an abiding refuge all the days of our lives; through Jesus Christ, who with the Holy Spirit liveth and reigneth with thee, one God, in glory everlasting. Amen.

Rite II O God, who has given your Church wisdom and revealed deep and secret things: Grant that we, like your servant Justin and in union with his prayers, may find your truth an abiding refuge all the days of our lives; through Jesus Christ, who with the Holy Spirit lives and reigns with you, one God, in glory everlasting. Amen.

For Liturgical Celebration: [Common of a Martyr, A7] [Common of a Theologian and Teacher, A17] [Common of a Prophetic Witness, A31] [Of the Holy Cross, A41] [Of the Reign of Christ, A46]

June 2

Blandina *and Her* Companions
the Martyrs of Lyons, 177

In the second century, after a brief respite, Christians in many parts of the Roman empire were once again subjected to persecution. At Lyons and Vienne, in Gaul, there were missionary centers which had drawn many Christians from Asia and Greece. They were living a devout life under the guidance of Pothinus, elderly Bishop of Lyons, when persecution began in 177.

At first, the Christians were socially excluded from Roman homes, the public baths, and the market place; insults, stones, and blows were rained on them by pagan mobs, and Christian homes were vandalized. Soon after, the imperial officials forced Christians to come to the market place for harsh questioning, followed by imprisonment.

Some slaves from Christian households were tortured to extract public accusations that Christians practiced cannibalism, incest, and other perversions. These false accusations roused the mob to such a pitch of wrath that any leniency toward the imprisoned Christians was impossible. Even friendly pagans now turned against them.

The fury of the mob fell most heavily on Sanctus, a deacon; Attalus; Maturus, a recent convert; and Blandina, a slave. According to Eusebius, Blandina was so filled with power to withstand torments that her torturers gave up. "I am a Christian," she said, "and nothing vile is done among us." Sanctus was tormented with red-hot irons. The aged Pothinus, badly beaten, died soon after. Finally, the governor decided to set aside several days for a public spectacle in the amphitheater.

Eusebius depicts Blandina in particular as standing in the person of Christ: "Blandina was suspended on a stake, and exposed to be devoured by the wild beasts who should attack her. And because she appeared as if hanging on a cross, and because of her earnest prayers, she inspired the combatants with great zeal. For they looked on her in her conflict, and beheld with their outward eyes, in the form of their sister, him who was crucified for them, that he might persuade those who believe in him, that every one who suffers for the glory of Christ has fellowship always with the living God."

On the final day of the spectacle, writes Eusebius, "Blandina, last of all, like a noble mother who had encouraged her children and sent them ahead victorious to the King, hastened to join them." Beaten, torn, burned with irons, she was wrapped in a net and tossed about by a wild bull. The spectators were amazed at her endurance.

Eusebius concludes: "They offered up to the Father a single wreath, but it was woven of diverse colors and flowers of all kinds. It was fitting that the noble athletes should endure a varied conflict, and win a great victory, that they might be entitled in the end to receive the crown supreme of life everlasting."

Rite I   Grant, O Lord, that we who keep the feast of the holy martyrs Blandina and her companions may be rooted and grounded in love of thee, and may endure the sufferings of this life for the glory that shall be revealed in us; through Jesus Christ our Lord, who liveth and reigneth with thee and the Holy Spirit, one God, now and for ever. Amen.

Rite II   Grant, O Lord, that we who keep the feast of the holy martyrs Blandina and her companions may be rooted and grounded in love of you, and may endure the sufferings of this life for the glory that shall be revealed in us; through Jesus Christ our Lord, who lives and reigns with you and the Holy Spirit, one God, now and for ever. Amen.

For Liturgical Celebration: [Common of a Martyr, A7] [Of the Holy Cross, A41] [On the Anniversary of a Disaster, A67]

JUNE 2

June 3

The Martyrs of Uganda
1886

On June 3, 1886, thirty-two young men, pages of the court of King Mwanga of Buganda, were burned to death at Namugongo for their refusal to renounce Christianity. In the following months many other Christians throughout the country died by fire or spear for their faith.

These martyrdoms totally changed the dynamic of Christian growth in Uganda. Introduced by a handful of Anglican and Roman Catholic missionaries after 1877, the Christian faith had been preached only to the immediate members of the court, by order of King Mutesa. His successor, Mwanga, became increasingly angry as he realized that the first converts put loyalty to Christ above the traditional loyalty to the king.

Martyrdoms began in 1885 (including Bishop Hannington and his Companions: see October 29th). Mwanga first forbade anyone to go near a Christian mission on pain of death, but finding himself unable to cool the ardor of the converts, resolved to wipe out Christianity.

The Namugongo martyrdoms produced a result entirely opposite to Mwanga's intentions. The example of these martyrs, who walked to their death singing hymns and praying for their enemies, so inspired many of the bystanders that they began to seek instruction from the remaining Christians. Within a few years the original handful of converts had multiplied many times and spread far beyond the court. The martyrs had left the indelible impression that Christianity was truly African, not simply a white man's religion. Most of the missionary work was carried out by Africans rather than by white missionaries, and Christianity spread steadily.

Renewed persecution of Christians by a Muslim military dictatorship in the 1970s proved the vitality of the example of the Namugongo martyrs. Among the thousands of new martyrs, both Anglican and Roman Catholic, was Janani Luwum, Archbishop of the (Anglican) Church of Uganda (see February 17th), whose courageous ministry and death inspired not only his countrymen but also Christians throughout the world.

Rite I   O God, by whose providence the blood of the martyrs is the seed of the Church: Grant that we who remember before thee the blessed martyrs of Uganda, may, like them, be steadfast in our faith in Jesus Christ, to whom they gave obedience, even to death, and by their sacrifice brought forth a plentiful harvest; through Jesus Christ our Lord, who liveth and reigneth with thee and the Holy Spirit, one God, for ever and ever. Amen.

Rite II O God, by your providence the blood of the martyrs is the seed of the Church: Grant that we who remember before you the blessed martyrs of Uganda, may, like them, be steadfast in our faith in Jesus Christ, to whom they gave obedience, even to death, and by their sacrifice brought forth a plentiful harvest; through Jesus Christ our Lord, who lives and reigns with you and the Holy Spirit, one God, for ever and ever. Amen.

For Liturgical Celebration: [Common of a Martyr, A7] [Of the Holy Cross, A41] [On the Anniversary of a Disaster]

June 4

John XXIII (Angelo Guiseppe Roncalli)
Bishop of Rome, 1963

Born in Northern Italy in 1881, Angelo Giuseppe Roncalli was trained in Roman Catholic schools from an early age. After service in the military, Roncalli was ordained a priest in 1904. His passion for social justice for working people and for the poor was formed early and remained an important commitment of his ministry.

Roncalli often received complicated assignments. He was made an archbishop in 1925 and sent as the papal envoy to Bulgaria, where he was responsible for reducing the tensions between Eastern Rite and Latin Rite Catholics during a difficult period.

Some years later, he was the papal representative to Greece and Turkey when anti-religious sentiments were running high. His leadership in Turkey anticipated on a local scale some of the developments of later decades on a universal scale: putting the liturgy and the official documents of the church in the language of the people, and opening conversations with the Eastern Orthodox and those of other faiths. While papal nuncio in Turkey, Roncalli actively aided Jews fleeing Nazi persecution and encouraged priests under him to do the same. Near the end of the Second World War, he was made the papal nuncio to Paris with the task of trying to heal the divisions caused by the war. In 1953, at the age of 72, he was made a cardinal and appointed patriarch of Venice, the first time he had ever been the bishop ordinary of a diocese.

In 1958, Cardinal Roncalli was elected Pope and took the name John XXIII. After the long pontificate of Pius XII, it was widely assumed that John XXIII would be a brief "placeholder" pope of minor consequence. During the first year of his pontificate, he called the Second Vatican Council for the purpose of renewing and revitalizing the church. The work of the Council transformed the church of the twentieth century, not only for Roman Catholics, but for all Christians. With its emphasis on liturgical renewal, ecumenism, world peace, and social justice, the legacy of the Council continues to inspire the mission of the Church among Christians of all traditions.

John XXIII died on June 3, 1963.

Rite I Lord of all truth and peace, who didst raise up thy bishop John to be servant of the servants of God and bestowed on him wisdom to call for the work of renewing your Church: Grant that, following his example, we may reach out to other Christians to clasp them with the love of your Son, and labor throughout the nations of the world to kindle a desire for justice and peace; through Jesus Christ, who is alive and reigneth with thee and the Holy Spirit, one God, now and for ever. Amen.

Rite II Lord of all truth and peace, you raised up your bishop John to be servant of the servants of God and gave him wisdom to call for the work of renewing your Church: Grant that, following his example, we may reach out to other Christians to clasp them with the love of your Son, and labor throughout the nations of the world to kindle a desire for justice and peace; through Jesus Christ, who is alive and reigns with you and the Holy Spirit, one God, now and for ever. Amen.

For Liturgical Celebration: [Common of a Pastor, A14] [For the Unity of the Church, A48]

June 5

Boniface, Archbishop of Mainz
Missionary to Germany, and Martyr, 754

Boniface is justly called one of the "Makers of Europe." He was born at Crediton in Devonshire, England, about 675, and received the English name of Winfred. He was educated at Exeter, and later at Nursling, near Winchester, where he was professed a monk and ordained to the presbyterate.

Inspired by the examples of Willibrord and others, Winfred decided to become a missionary, and made his first journey to Frisia (Netherlands) in 716—a venture with little success. In 719 he started out again; but this time he first went to Rome to seek papal approval. Pope Gregory the Second commissioned him to work in Germany, and gave him the name of Boniface.

For the rest of his days, Boniface devoted himself to reforming, planting, and organizing churches, monasteries, and dioceses in Hesse, Thuringia, and Bavaria. Many helpers and supplies came to him from friends in England. In 722 the Pope ordained him a bishop, ten years later made him an archbishop, and in 743 gave him a fixed see at Mainz.

The Frankish rulers also supported his work. At their invitation, he presided over reforming councils of the Frankish Church; and in 752, with the consent of Pope Zacharias, he anointed Pepin (Pippin) as King of the Franks. Thus, the way was prepared for Charlemagne, son of Pepin, and the revival of a unified Christian dominion in western Europe.

In 753 Boniface resigned his see, to spend his last years again as a missionary in Frisia. On June 5, 754, while awaiting a group of converts for confirmation, he and his companions were murdered by a band of pagans, near Dokkum. His body was buried at Fulda, a monastery he had founded in 744, near Mainz.

Rite I   Almighty God, who didst call thy faithful servant Boniface to be a witness and a martyr in Germany, and by his labor and suffering didst raise up a people for thy own possession: Pour out thy Holy Spirit upon thy Church in every land, that by the service and sacrifice of many thy holy Name may be glorified and thy kingdom enlarged; through Jesus Christ our Lord, who liveth and reigneth with thee and the same Spirit, one God, for ever and ever. Amen.

Rite II Almighty God, you called your faithful servant Boniface to be a witness and a martyr in Germany, and by his labor and suffering you raised up a people for your own possession: Pour out your Holy Spirit upon your Church in every land, that by the service and sacrifice of many your holy Name may be glorified and your kingdom enlarged; through Jesus Christ our Lord, who lives and reigns with you and the Holy Spirit, one God, for ever and ever. Amen.

For Liturgical Celebration: [Common of a Martyr, A7] [Common of a Missionary, A11] [Common of a Pastor, A14] [Of the Holy Cross, A41] [For the Ministry II, A50] [For the Mission of the Church, A52]

June 6

Ini Kopuria
Founder of the Melanesian Brotherhood, 1945

Ini Kopuria, the first Elder Brother of the Melanesian Brotherhood, was born soon after the start of the twentieth century on the island of Guadalcanal in the Solomons.

Ini attended St. Barnabas School on Norfolk Island, an institution started by Bishop J. C. Patteson with the purpose of training young men to teach their own people. Ini's daily contact with the Anglican Christians at St. Barnabas led to his own developed sense of religious calling. One story about his time there relates his strict adherence to a rule of silence during Lent, and on one Ash Wednesday, when confronted by a teacher who questioned this practice, Ini replied by letter, refusing to break his vow. It was then that many around him began to notice his calling to a religious vocation.

Although it was expected that upon leaving school, Ini would return to Guadalcanal to teach his own people, he surprised everyone by becoming a police officer in the Native Armed Constabulary. Though initially unhappy with his role in the police, he earned the respect and admiration of his superiors with his dedication and wisdom. In 1927, after he had left the police force, he was asked by the Commissioner to return to the police and go to the island of Mala to quiet local unrest. Ini is said to have remarked, "It would be bad if I were to go there with a rifle; I may want to return one day with the gospel."

It was during his recovery from an injury in 1924 that Ini came to the realization that only in service to Christ would his life find meaning and fulfillment. Under the direction of his Bishop, John Steward, he took his vows as the first Elder of the Melanesian Brotherhood, an Anglican order devoted to the spread of the gospel among the non-Christian areas of Melanesia. The Order, characterized by its vows of simplicity, in this day continues its work of peacemaking and includes not only Melanesians, but also Polynesians, Filipinos, and Europeans. Ini died on June 6, 1945.

Rite I   Loving God, we bless thy Name for the witness of Ini Kopuria, founder of the Melanesian Brotherhood: Open our eyes that we, with these Anglican brothers, may establish peace and hope in service to others; for the sake of Jesus Christ, who with thee and the Holy Spirit liveth and reigneth, one God, for ever and ever. Amen.

Rite II Loving God, we bless your Name for the witness of Ini Kopuria, founder of the Melanesian Brotherhood: Open our eyes that we, with these Anglican brothers, may establish peace and hope in service to others; for the sake of Jesus Christ, who with you and the Holy Spirit lives and reigns, one God, for ever and ever. Amen.

For Liturgical Celebration: [Common of a Monastic or Professed Religious, A20] [Of the Incarnation, A39] [For the Ministry III, A51]

June 7

The Pioneers of the Episcopal Anglican Church of Brazil
1890

The presence of Anglicans in Brazil is first recorded in the early nineteenth century and took the form of chaplaincies for English expatriates. It was not, however, until 1890 when missionary efforts among the Brazilian people began under the care of two Episcopal Church missionaries, Lucien Lee Kinsolving and James Watson Morris. They held the first service on Trinity Sunday 1890 in Porto Alegre. Within a year, three additional missionaries—William Cabell Brown, John Gaw Meem, and Mary Packard—arrived and joined the work. These five missionaries are the pioneers and considered the founders of the Episcopal Anglican Church of Brazil.

In 1899, Kinsolving was made missionary bishop for the work in Brazil by the House of Bishops of The Episcopal Church, and in 1907 the missionary district of Brazil was established by The General Convention. The number of parishes and institutions continued to increase. The bishops were raised up from among Episcopal Church missionaries who were serving in the missionary district. Fifty years after the work first began, in 1940, the first native Brazilian was elected to the episcopate, Athalício Theodoro Pithan.

By 1950, the work had increased to the point that the missionary district was too large and it was divided into three dioceses. This set the stage for the continued development of the Church in Brazil, which eventually led to the formation of the Episcopal Anglican Church of Brazil as an autonomous Province of the Anglican Communion in 1965. Complete financial independence from The Episcopal Church was completed by 1982, although the two churches continue to have strong bonds of affection and united mission efforts through companion diocese relationships and coordination at the church-wide level.

Rite I   O God, who didst send thy Son to preach peace to those who are far off and to those who are near: We bless thee for those who joined together to establish the Episcopal Anglican Church of Brazil; and we pray that we, like them, may be ready to preach Christ crucified and risen, and to encourage and support those who pioneer new missions in him; who liveth and reigneth with thee and the Holy Spirit, one God, now and for ever. Amen.

Rite II   O God, who sent your Son to preach peace to those who are far off and to those who are near: We bless you for those who joined together to establish the Episcopal Anglican Church of Brazil; and we pray that we, like them, may be ready to preach Christ crucified and risen, and to encourage and support those who pioneer new missions in him; who lives and reigns with you and the Holy Spirit, one God, now and for ever. Amen.

For Liturgical Celebration: [Common of a Missionary, A11] [For the Mission of the Church, A52]

June 8

Roland Allen
Mission Strategist, 1947

Roland Allen was an English missionary, supported by the Society for the Propagation of the Gospel in Foreign Parts (SPG) who served briefly in North China and for many years in East Africa. Allen believed that the mission work of the western churches was paternalistic and deeply rooted in colonialist values that were incompatible with the gospel.

Allen was born in Bristol, England, on December 29, 1868; his father was an Anglican priest. He attended St. John's College at Oxford and was ordained to the priesthood in 1893. His first assignment with SPG was to North China where he served for seven years before returning to England because of poor health. He served briefly as a parish priest before turning to research and writing on mission work and missionary methods. This work led him to East Africa, particularly to Kenya, where he lived for much of the rest of his life.

Allen's most famous work, *Missionary Methods: St. Paul's or Ours*, was published in 1912. Allen argued that St. Paul's vision was to build a community, and raise up leaders so that the sacraments could be administered. The community could be left alone to do its work of converting others to Jesus under the guidance of the Holy Spirit. Allen continued to refine his methods in later writings emphasizing the need for indigenous leadership as opposed to bishops and other leaders coming from foreign territories. In many situations, Allen favored clergy who were "tentmakers"—engaged in secular employment while serving their congregations—after the example of St. Paul.

Allen possessed a gregarious temperament combined with absolute confidence in his ideas. He raised people's ire no matter where he went, but he was also praised for the clarity of his convictions, his passion for the gospel, and his desire to see every local faith community thrive under its own leadership.

Even though Allen's ideas were often viewed with derision or, at least, suspicion, in his own day, he was the catalyst for the reform of mission strategy throughout the world. He died on June 9, 1947, in Nairobi, Kenya.

Rite I   Almighty God, by whose Spirit the Scriptures were opened to thy servant Roland Allen, so that he might lead many to know, live, and proclaim the Gospel of Jesus Christ: Give us grace to follow his example, that the variety of those to whom we reach out in love may receive thy saving Word and witness in their own languages and cultures to thy glorious Name; through Jesus Christ, thy Word made flesh, who liveth and reigneth with thee and the Holy Spirit, one God, now and for ever. Amen.

Rite II   Almighty God, by your Spirit you opened the Scriptures to your servant Roland Allen, so that he might lead many to know, live, and proclaim the Gospel of Jesus Christ: Give us grace to follow his example, that the variety of those to whom we reach out in love may receive your saving Word and witness in their own languages and cultures to your glorious Name; through Jesus Christ, your Word made flesh, who lives and reigns with you and the Holy Spirit, one God, now and for ever. Amen.

For Liturgical Celebration: [Common of a Missionary, A11] [Common of a Pastor, A14] [For the Mission of the Church, A52]

June 9

Columba, Abbot of Iona
597

Many legends have gathered about Columba, but there are also some historical data concerning his many works in the writings of Bede and Adamnan. According to one story, Patrick of Ireland foretold Columba's birth in a prophecy:

> He will be a saint and will be devout,
> He will be an abbot, the king of royal graces,
> He will be lasting and for ever good;
> The eternal kingdom be mine by his protection.

Columba was born in Ireland in 521, and early in life showed scholarly and clerical ability. He entered the monastic life, and almost immediately set forth on missionary travels. Even before ordination to the presbyterate in 551, he had founded monasteries at Derry and Durrow.

Twelve years after his ordination, Columba and a dozen companions set out for northern Britain, where the Picts were still generally ignorant of Christianity. Columba was kindly received, allowed to preach, convert, and baptize. He was also given possession of the island of Iona, where, according to legend, his tiny boat had washed ashore. Here he founded the celebrated monastery which became the center for the conversion of the Picts. From Iona, also, his disciples went out to found other monasteries, which, in turn, became centers of missionary activity.

Columba made long journeys through the Highlands, as far as Aberdeen. He often returned to Ireland to attend synods, and thus established Iona as a link between Irish and Pictish Christians. For thirty years, he evangelized, studied, wrote, and governed his monastery at Iona. He supervised his monks in their work in the fields and workrooms, in their daily worship and Sunday Eucharist, and in their study and teaching. He died peacefully in 597 while working on a copy of the Psalter. He had put down his pen, rested a few hours, and at Matins was found dead before the Altar, a smile on his face. He is quoted by his biographer Adamnan as having said, "This day is called in the sacred Scriptures a day of rest, and truly to me it will be such, for it is the last of my life and I shall enter into rest after the fatigues of my labors."

Rite I O God, who by the preaching of thy blessed servant Columba didst cause the light of the Gospel to shine in Scotland: Grant, we beseech thee that, having his life and labors in remembrance, we may show our thankfulness to thee by following the example of his zeal and patience; through Jesus Christ our Lord, who liveth and reigneth with thee and the Holy Spirit, one God, for ever and ever. Amen.

Rite II O God, by the preaching of your blessed servant Columba you caused the light of the Gospel to shine in Scotland: Grant, we pray, that, having his life and labors in remembrance, we may show our thankfulness to you by following the example of his zeal and patience; through Jesus Christ our Lord, who lives and reigns with you and the Holy Spirit, one God, for ever and ever. Amen.

For Liturgical Celebration: [Common of a Monastic or Professed Religious, A20] [Common of a Missionary, A11] [Of the Incarnation, A39] [For the Mission of the Church, A52]

June 10

Ephrem of Edessa, Syria
Deacon, 373

Ephrem of Edessa was a teacher, poet, orator, and defender of the faith—a voice of Aramaic Christianity, speaking the language Jesus spoke, using the imagery Jesus used. Edessa, a Syrian city, was a center for the spread of Christianity in the East long before the conversion of the western Roman empire.

The Syrians called Ephrem "The Harp of the Holy Spirit," and his hymns still enrich the liturgies of the Syrian Church. Ephrem was one whose writings were influential in the development of Church doctrine. Jerome writes: "I have read in Greek a volume of his on the Holy Spirit; though it was only a translation, I recognized therein the sublime genius of the man."

Ephrem was born at Nisibis in Mesopotamia. At eighteen, he was baptized by James, Bishop of Nisibis. It is believed that Ephrem accompanied James to the famous Council of Nicaea in 325. He lived at Nisibis until 363, when the Persians captured the city and drove out the Christians.

Ephrem retired to a cave in the hills above the city of Edessa. There he wrote most of his spiritual works. He lived on barley bread and dried herbs, sometimes varied by greens. He drank only water. His clothing was a mass of patches. But he was not a recluse, and frequently went to Edessa to preach. Discovering that hymns could be of great value in support of the true faith, he opposed Gnostic hymns with his own, sung by a choir of women. An example is "From God Christ's deity came forth" (*The Hymnal 1982*, #443).

During a famine in 372–373, he distributed food and money to the poor and organized a sort of ambulance service for the sick. He died of exhaustion, brought on by his long hours of relief work.

Of his writings, there remain 72 hymns, commentaries on the Old and New Testaments, and numerous homilies. In his commentary on the Passion, he wrote: "No one has seen or shall see the things which you have seen. The Lord himself has become the altar, priest, and bread, and the chalice of salvation. He alone suffices for all, yet none suffices for him. He is Altar and Lamb, victim and sacrifice, priest as well as food."

Rite I   Pour out on us, O Lord, that same Spirit by which thy deacon Ephrem rejoiced to proclaim in sacred song the mysteries of faith; and so gladden our hearts that we, like him, may be devoted to thee alone; through Jesus Christ our Lord, who liveth and reigneth with thee and the Holy Spirit, one God, now and for ever. Amen.

Rite II Pour out on us, O Lord, that same Spirit by which your deacon Ephrem rejoiced to proclaim in sacred song the mysteries of faith; and so gladden our hearts that we, like him, may be devoted to you alone; through Jesus Christ our Lord, who lives and reigns with you and the Holy Spirit, one God, now and for ever. Amen.

For Liturgical Celebration: [Common of an Artist, Writer, or Composer, A27] [Common of a Thelogian and Teacher, 649]

June 12

Enmegahbowh
Priest and Missionary, 1902

John Johnson Enmegahbowh, an Odawa (Ottawa) Indian from Canada, born in 1807, was raised in the Midewiwin traditional healing way of his grandfather and the Christian religion of his mother. He came into the United States as a Methodist missionary in 1832. At one point Enmegahbowh attempted to abandon missionary work and return to Canada, but the boat was turned back by storms on Lake Superior, providing him a vision: "Here Mr. Jonah came before me and said, 'Ah, my friend Enmegahbowh, I know you. You are a fugitive. You have sinned and disobeyed God. Instead of going to the city of Nineveh, where God sent you to spread his word to the people, you started to go, and then turned aside. You are now on your way to the city of Tarshish . . . '"

Enmegahbowh invited James Lloyd Breck to Gull Lake, where together they founded St. Columba's Mission in 1852. The mission was later moved to White Earth, where Enmegahbowh served until his death in 1902. Unwelcome for a time among some Ojibway groups because he warned the community at Fort Ripley about the 1862 uprising, Enmegahbowh was consistent as a man of peace, inspiring the Waubanaquot (Chief White Cloud) mission, which obtained a lasting peace between the Ojibway and the Dakota peoples.

Enmegahbowh ("The One who Stands Before his People") is the first recognized Native American priest in The Episcopal Church. He was ordained deacon by Bishop Kemper in 1859 and priest by Bishop Whipple in the cathedral at Faribault in 1867. Enmegahbowh helped train many others to serve as deacons throughout northern Minnesota. The powerful tradition of Ojibway hymn singing is a living testimony to their ministry. His understanding of Native tradition enabled him to enculturate Christianity in the language and traditions of the Ojibway. He tirelessly traveled throughout Minnesota and beyond, actively participating in the development of mission strategy and policy for The Episcopal Church.

Enmegahbowh died at the White Earth Indian Reservation in northern Minnesota on June 12, 1902.

Rite I   Almighty God, thou didst lead thy pilgrim people of old with fire and cloud: Grant that the ministers of thy Church, following the example of blessed Enmegahbowh, may stand before thy holy people, leading them with fiery zeal and gentle humility. This we ask through Jesus, the Christ, who liveth and reigneth with thee in the unity of the Holy Spirit, one God, now and for ever. Amen.

Rite II Almighty God, you led your pilgrim people of old with fire and cloud: Grant that the ministers of your Church, following the example of blessed Enmegahbowh, may stand before your holy people, leading them with fiery zeal and gentle humility. This we ask through Jesus, the Christ, who lives and reigns with you in the unity of the Holy Spirit, one God, now and for ever. Amen.

For Liturgical Celebration: [Common of a Missionary, A11] [Common of a Pastor, A14] [For the Ministry II, A50] [For the Mission of the Church, A52] [For Reconciliation and Forgiveness, A68]

June 13

Gilbert Keith Chesterton
Apologist and Writer, 1936

Born on May 29, 1874, Gilbert Keith Chesterton was one of the intellectual giants of his day, and was known for his writing that spanned fields as diverse as literary criticism, fiction and fantasy, satire, and Christian apologetics. Chesterton often blended elements of such genres together, as indicated in his famous novel *The Man Who Was Thursday*, which combines a mystery plot with Christian imagery and symbolism. His work in the field of literary criticism was immensely influential in his day, and his book-length study of Charles Dickens can be credited with bringing that author's work back to the forefront of scholarly study.

As a young man, Chesterton had been fascinated with spiritualism and the occult, but his faith grew stronger over the years, as he devoted himself to the defense of what he called "orthodoxy," which was for him, among other things, an acknowledgement of the mystery and paradox of Christian faith in an age of increasing skepticism. His spiritual journey toward the ancient faith of the Church culminated in his conversion to the Roman Catholic Church in 1922.

In works such as *Orthodoxy* and *The Everlasting Man*, Chesterton defended Christian faith with a unique blend of wit and religious fervor, while simultaneously satirizing the prevailing viewpoints of the day that often sought to dismiss faith as irrational and unnecessary. The latter work was particularly important to C.S. Lewis, who called it "the best apologetic work I know." Today, Chesterton is still known and loved for his sharp wit, his intellectual tenacity, and his refusal to resolve the ambiguities of Christian faith in favor of facile and passing conceptions of truth. His work has influenced intellectual figures as diverse as Ernest Hemingway and Dorothy L. Sayers, and he is a figure beloved of Protestants and Catholics alike.

Chesterton died at Beaconsfield in England on June 14, 1936.

Rite I   O God of earth and altar, who didst give G. K. Chesterton a ready tongue and pen and inspired him to use them in thy service: Mercifully grant that we may be inspired to witness cheerfully to the hope that is in us; through Jesus Christ our Savior, who liveth and reigneth with thee and the Holy Spirit, one God, for ever and ever. Amen.

Rite II   O God of earth and altar, you gave G. K. Chesterton a ready tongue and pen and inspired him to use them in your service: Mercifully grant that we may be inspired to witness cheerfully to the hope that is in us; through Jesus Christ our Savior, who lives and reigns with you and the Holy Spirit, one God, for ever and ever. Amen.

For Liturgical Celebration: [Common of an Artist, Writer, or Composer, A27]

June 14

Basil the Great
Bishop of Caesarea, 379

Basil was born about 329, in Caesarea of Cappadocia, into a Christian family of wealth and distinction. Educated in classical Hellenism, Basil might have continued in academic life, had it not been for the death of a beloved younger brother and the faith of his sister, Macrina. He was baptized at the age of twenty-eight, and ordained a deacon soon after.

Macrina had founded the first monastic order for women at Annesi. Fired by her example, Basil made a journey to study the life of anchorites in Egypt and elsewhere. In 358 he returned to Cappadocia and founded the first monastery for men at Ibora. Assisted by Gregory Nazianzus, he compiled *The Longer* and *Shorter Rules*, which transformed the solitary anchorites into a disciplined community of prayer and work. The *Rules* became the foundation for all Eastern monastic discipline. The monasteries also provided schools to train leaders for Church and State.

Basil was ordained presbyter in 364. In the conflict between the Arians (supported by an Arian Emperor) and orthodox Christians, Basil became convinced that he should be made Bishop of Caesarea. By a narrow margin, he was elected Bishop of Caesarea, Metropolitan of Cappadocia, and Exarch of Pontus. He was relentless in his efforts to restore the faith and discipline of the clergy, and in defense of the Nicene faith. When the Emperor Valens sought to undercut Basil's power by dividing the See of Cappadocia, Basil forced his brother Gregory to become Bishop of Nyssa.

In his treatise, *On the Holy Spirit*, Basil maintained that both the language of Scripture and the faith of the Church require that the same honor, glory, and worship is to be paid to the Spirit as to the Father and the Son. It was entirely proper, he asserted, to adore God in liturgical prayer, not only with the traditional words, "Glory to the Father through the Son in the Holy Spirit;" but also with the formula, "Glory to the Father with the Son together with the Holy Spirit."

Basil was also concerned about the poor and, when he died, he willed to Caesarea a complete new town, built on his estate, with housing, a hospital and staff, a church for the poor, and a hospice for travelers.

He died at the age of fifty, in 379, just two years before the Second Ecumenical Council, which affirmed the Nicene faith.

Rite I   Almighty God, who hast revealed to thy Church thine eternal Being of glorious majesty and perfect love as one God in Trinity of Persons: Give us grace that, like thy bishop Basil of Caesarea, we may continue steadfast in the confession of this faith and constant in our worship of thee, Father, Son, and Holy Spirit; who livest and reignest for ever and ever. Amen.

Rite II Almighty God, you have revealed to your Church your eternal Being of glorious majesty and perfect love as one God in Trinity of Persons; Give us grace that, like your bishop Basil of Caesarea, we may continue steadfast in the confession of this faith and constant in our worship of you, Father, Son and Holy Spirit; for you live and reign for ever and ever. Amen.

For Liturgical Celebration: [Common of a Theologian and Teacher, A17] [Common of a Pastor, A14] [Common of a Monastic or Professed Religious, A20] [Of the Holy Trinity, A37] [For the Ministry II, A50]

June 15
Evelyn Underhill
1941

The only child of a prominent barrister and his wife, Evelyn Underhill was born in Wolverhampton, England, on December 6, 1875, and grew up in London. She was educated there and in a girls' school in Folkestone, where she was confirmed in the Church of England. She had little other formal religious training, but her spiritual curiosity was naturally lively, and she read widely, developing quite early a deep appreciation for mysticism. At sixteen, she began a life-long devotion to writing.

Evelyn had few childhood companions, but one of them, Hubert Stuart Moore, she eventually married. Other friends, made later, included such famous persons as Laurence Housman, Maurice Hewlett, and Sarah Bernhardt. Closest of all were Ethel Ross Barker, a devout Roman Catholic, and Baron Friedrich von Hügel, with whom she formed a strong spiritual bond. He became her director in matters mystical.

In the 1890's, Evelyn began annual visits to the continent of Europe, and especially to Italy. There she became influenced by the paintings of the Italian masters and by the Roman Catholic Church. She spent nearly fifteen years wrestling painfully with the idea of converting to Roman Catholicism, but decided in the end that it was not for her.

In 1921, Evelyn Underhill became reconciled to her Anglican roots, while remaining what she called a "Catholic Christian." She continued with her life of reading, writing, meditation, and prayer. She had already published her first great spiritual work, *Mysticism*. This was followed by many other books, culminating in her most widely read and studied book, *Worship* (1937).

Evelyn Underhill's most valuable contribution to spiritual literature must surely be her conviction that the mystical life is not only open to a saintly few, but to anyone who cares to nurture it and weave it into everyday experience, and also (at the time, a startling idea) that modern psychological theories and discoveries, far from hindering or negating spirituality, can actually enhance and transform it.

Evelyn Underhill's writings proved appealing to many, resulting in a large international circle of friends and disciples, making her much in demand as a lecturer and retreat director. She died, at age 65, in London on June 15, 1941.

Rite I   O God, Origin, Sustainer, and End of all creatures: Grant that thy Church, taught by thy servant Evelyn Underhill, guarded evermore by thy power, and guided by thy Spirit into the light of truth, may continually offer to thee all glory and thanksgiving, and attain with thy saints to the blessed hope of everlasting life, which thou hast promised us by our Savior Jesus Christ; who with thee and the same Spirit liveth and reigneth, one God, now and for ever. Amen.

Rite II O God, Origin, Sustainer, and End of all creatures: Grant that your Church, taught by your servant Evelyn Underhill, guarded evermore by your power, and guided by your Spirit into the light of truth, may continually offer to you all glory and thanksgiving, and attain with your saints to the blessed hope of everlasting life, which you have promised us by our Savior Jesus Christ; who with you and the Holy Spirit lives and reigns, one God, now and for ever. Amen.

For Liturgical Celebration: [Common of a Theologian and Teacher, A17] [Of the Holy Spirit, A38] [Of the Incarnation, A39] [For all Baptized Christians, A42]

June 16

George Berkeley, *1753,*
and Joseph Butler, *1752*
Bishops and Theologians

George Berkeley was born in Ireland in 1684, educated at Trinity College, Dublin, and ordained to the priesthood in 1721. As Dean of Derry, beginning in 1724, he developed an interest in the churches in colonial America as well as concern for the conversion of Native Americans to the Christian faith.

He sailed for America, reaching Newport, Rhode Island, in January, 1729, settling on a plantation nearby, Whitehall, while awaiting the resources to start a college in Bermuda. When his plans failed, he gave Whitehall and his personal library to Yale College and returned to Ireland, where he became Bishop of Cloyne in 1734. Berkeley College at Yale, Berkeley Divinity School, and the City of Berkeley, California, are named for him.

Berkeley was a major philosopher of his time, and among his achievements was the theory of immaterialism—individuals can only directly know objects by the perception of them—an idea that would influence Hume, Kant, and Schopenhauer.

Joseph Butler, once called "the greatest of all the thinkers of the English Church," was born in Berkshire in 1692, into a Presbyterian family. His early education was in dissenting academies, but in his early twenties he became an Anglican. He entered Oxford in 1715 and was ordained in 1718.

Butler distinguished himself as a preacher while serving Rolls Chapel, Chancery Lane, London, and then went on to serve several parishes before being appointed Bishop of Bristol in 1738. He declined the primacy of Canterbury, but accepted translation to Durham in 1750. He died on June 16, 1752, in Bath, and his body was entombed in Bristol Cathedral.

Butler's importance rests chiefly on his acute apology for orthodox Christianity against the Deistic thought prevalent in England in his time, *The Analogy of Religion, Natural and Revealed, to the Constitution and Course of Nature*, 1736. He maintained the "reasonable probability" of Christianity, with action upon that probability as a basis for faith. Butler's was a rational exposition of the faith grounded in deep personal piety, a worthy counterpoint to the enthusiasm of the Wesleyan revival of the same period.

Rite I   O God, by thy Holy Spirit thou givest to some the word of wisdom, to others the word of knowledge, and to others the word of faith: We praise thy Name for the gifts of grace manifested in thy servants George Berkeley and Joseph Butler, and we pray that thy Church may never be destitute of such gifts; through Jesus Christ our Lord, who with thee and the Holy Spirit liveth and reigneth, one God, for ever and ever. Amen.

Rite II   O God, by your Holy Spirit you give to some the word of wisdom, to others the word of knowledge, and to others the word of faith: We praise your Name for the gifts of grace manifested in your servants George Berkeley and Joseph Butler, and we pray that your Church may never be destitute of such gifts; through Jesus Christ our Lord, who with you and the Holy Spirit lives and reigns, one God, for ever and ever. Amen.

For Liturgical Celebration: [Common of a Theologian and Teacher, A17] [Common of a Pastor, A14] [For the Ministry II, A50] [For Education, A60]

June 18

Bernard Mizeki
Catechist and Martyr in Mashonaland, 1896

Bernard Mizeki was born about the year 1861 in Portuguese East Africa (Mozambique). In his early teens, he escaped from his native land and arrived in Cape Town, South Africa, where he was befriended and converted by Anglican missionaries. He was baptized on March 9, 1886.

In 1891, Bernard Mizeki volunteered as a catechist for the pioneer mission in Mashonaland (a region in what is now northern Zimbabwe) and was stationed at Nhowe. On June 18, 1896, during an uprising of the native people against the Europeans and their African friends, Bernard was marked out especially. Though warned to flee, he would not desert his converts at the mission station. He was stabbed to death, but his body was never found, and the exact site of his burial is unknown.

A shrine near Bernard's place of martyrdom attracts many pilgrims today, and the Anglican Churches of Central and of Southern Africa honor him as their primary native martyr and witness.

Rite I   Almighty and everlasting God, who kindled the flame of thy love in the heart of thy holy martyr Bernard Mizeki: Grant to us, thy humble servants, a like faith and power of love, that we, who rejoice in his triumph, may profit by his example; through Jesus Christ our Lord, who liveth and reigneth with thee and the Holy Spirit, one God, for ever and ever. Amen.

Rite II Almighty and everlasting God, who kindled the flame of your love in the heart of your holy martyr Bernard Mizeki: Grant to us, your humble servants, a like faith and power of love, that we, who rejoice in his triumph, may profit by his example; through Jesus Christ our Lord, who lives and reigns with you and the Holy Spirit, one God, for ever and ever. Amen.

For Liturgical Celebration: [Common of a Martyr, A7] [Common of a Missionary, A11] [Of the Holy Cross, A41] [For the Ministry III, A51] [For the Mission of the Church, A52]

June 19

Adelaide Teague Case
Teacher, 1948

Adelaide Teague Case was born in St. Louis, Missouri, on January 10, 1887, but her family soon moved to New York City. She received her undergraduate education at Bryn Mawr and her graduate degrees from Columbia University. By the time she had completed her doctorate, a position had been created for her on the faculty of the Teachers' College at Columbia, where she rose to the status of full professor and head of the department of religious education. She is remembered for advocating a child-centered rather than teacher-centered approach to education.

In 1941, when her professional accomplishments were at their height, the Episcopal Theological School in Cambridge, Massachusetts, was able to convince her to leave her distinguished and comfortable position at Columbia, and she was appointed Professor of Christian Education. Although other women had taught occasional courses in the seminaries of the church, Case was the first to take her place as a full-time faculty member at the rank of Professor.

Case identified with the liberal Catholic tradition in Anglicanism. This is reflected in her first book, *Liberal Christianity and Religious Education*, in which she emphasized teaching children to engage in reasonable inquiry into their faith. Case was also active in the Religious Education Association, the Episcopal Pacifist Fellowship, and the Woman's Auxillary of The Episcopal Church. From 1946 to 1948, she served on the National Council of The Episcopal Church. Case was a proponent of women's ordination and a frequent preacher in the chapel at ETS. She continued to teach at ETS until her death on June 19, 1948, in Boston.

Students and faculty colleagues remember her contagious faith in Christ, her deep sense of humanity, and her seemingly boundless compassion. Although she carried herself with style and grace, Case had struggled with health problems her entire life, but those who knew her testify to the fact that in spite of those challenges she was spirited, energetic, and fully devoted to her work. It was often said of her that she was a true believer in Christ, and that one saw Christ living in and through her.

Case believed that the point of practicing the Christian faith was to make a difference in the world. As an advocate for peace, she believed that Christianity had a special vocation to call people into transformed, reconciled relationships for the sake of the wholeness of the human family. She is said to have discovered these things not in theology or educational theory, but in a life of common prayer and faithful eucharistic practice.

Rite I   Everliving God, who didst raise up thy servant Adelaide Case, whose compassion and commitment to peace inspired generations of students: Grant that we, following her example, may serve thee in our vocations, laboring for thy reign of peace, through the companionship of Jesus Christ, thy Saving Word; who with thee and the Holy Spirit liveth and reigneth, one God, now and for ever. Amen.

Rite II Everliving God, who raised up your servant Adelaide Case, whose compassion and commitment to peace inspired generations of students: Grant that we, following her example, may serve you in our vocations, laboring for your reign of peace, through the companionship of Jesus Christ, your Saving Word; who with you and the Holy Spirit lives and reigns, one God, now and for ever. Amen.

For Liturgical Celebration: [Common of a Theologian and Teacher, A17] [Common of a Saint, A23] [For all Baptized Christians, A42] [For Education, A60]

June 22

Alban, First Martyr of Britain
c. 304

Alban is the earliest Christian in Britain who is known by name and, according to tradition, the first British martyr. He was a soldier in the Roman army, stationed at Verulamium, a city about twenty miles northeast of London, now called St. Alban's. He gave shelter to a Christian priest who was fleeing from persecution and was converted by him. When officers came to Alban's house, he dressed himself in the garments of the priest and gave himself up. Alban was tortured and martyred in place of the priest, on the hilltop where the Cathedral of St. Alban's now stands. The traditional date of his martyrdom is 303 or 304, but recent studies suggest that the year was actually 209, during the persecution under the Emperor Septimius Severus.

The site of Alban's martyrdom soon became a shrine. King Offa of Mercia established a monastery there about the year 793, and, in the high Middle Ages, St. Alban's ranked as the premier abbey in England. The great Norman abbey church, begun in 1077, now serves as the cathedral of the diocese of St. Alban's, established in 1877. It is the second longest church in England (Winchester Cathedral is the longest, by six feet), and it is built on higher ground than any other English cathedral. In a chapel east of the choir and high altar, there are remains of the fourteenth century marble shrine of St. Alban.

The Venerable Bede gives this account of Alban's trial: "When Alban was brought in, the judge happened to be standing before an altar, offering sacrifice to devils . . . 'What is your family and race?' demanded the judge. 'How does my family concern you?' replied Alban; 'If you wish to know the truth about my religion, know that I am a Christian and am ready to do a Christian's duty.' 'I demand to know your name,' insisted the judge. 'Tell me at once.' 'My parents named me Alban,' he answered, 'and I worship and adore the living and true God, who created all things.' "

Rite I   Almighty God, by whose grace and power thy holy martyr Alban triumphed over suffering and was faithful even to death: Grant us, who now remember him in thanksgiving, to be so faithful in our witness to thee in this world that we may receive with him the crown of life; through Jesus Christ our Lord, who liveth and reigneth with thee and the Holy Spirit, one God, for ever and ever. Amen.

Rite II   Almighty God, by whose grace and power your holy martyr Alban triumphed over suffering and was faithful even to death: Grant us, who now remember him in thanksgiving, to be so faithful in our witness to you in this world that we may receive with him the crown of life; through Jesus Christ our Lord, who lives and reigns with you and the Holy Spirit, one God, for ever and ever. Amen.

For Liturgical Celebration: [Common of a Martyr, A7] [Of the Holy Cross, A41]

June 25

James Weldon Johnson
Poet, 1938

James Weldon Johnson was born on June 17, 1871, in Jacksonville, Florida. His parents stimulated his academic interests, and he was encouraged to study literature and music. Johnson enrolled at Atlanta University with the expressed intention that the education he received there would be used to further the interests of African Americans. He never reneged on that commitment. In the summer after his freshman year, Johnson taught the children of former slaves. Of that experience he wrote, "In all of my experience there has been no period so brief that has meant so much in my education for life as the three months I spent in the backwoods of Georgia." After graduation, he became the principal of the largest high school in Jacksonville, during which time he was paid half of what his white counterparts were paid, even though the school excelled under his leadership.

In 1900, he collaborated with his brother, Rosamond, a composer, to create "Lift Ev'ry Voice and Sing." Written in celebration of President Lincoln's birthday, the song, still popular today, has become known as the "African American National Anthem." Due to the success of their collaboration, Johnson moved to New York in 1901 to join his brother, and together they attained success as lyricist and composer for Broadway.

In 1906, Johnson was invited to work for the diplomatic corps and became U.S. Consul to Venezuela and later Nicaragua. During his Nicaraguan tenure, Johnson was a voice of reason and reconciliation in a time of civil unrest and turmoil. His ability to bring together people of differing viewpoints toward a common vision served Johnson well in the 1920's, when he became an organizer for the National Association for the Advancement of Colored People (NAACP).

Johnson was a prolific poet and anthologist. He edited *The Book of American Negro Poetry* (1922), a major contribution to the history of African American literature. His book of poetry, *God's Trombones* (1927), seven biblical stories rendered into verse, was influenced by his impressions of the rural South.

James Weldon Johnson died on June 26, 1938.

Rite I Eternal God, who gave thy servant James Weldon Johnson a heart and voice to praise thy Name in verse: As he gave us powerful words to glorify thee, may we also speak with joy and boldness to banish hatred from thy creation; in the Name of Jesus Christ, who with thee and the Holy Spirit liveth and reigneth, one God, for ever and ever. Amen.

Rite II Eternal God, who gave your servant James Weldon Johnson a heart and voice to praise your Name in verse: As he gave us powerful words to glorify you, may we also speak with joy and boldness to banish hatred from your creation; in the Name of Jesus Christ, who with you and the Holy Spirit lives and reigns, one God, for ever and ever. Amen.

For Liturgical Celebration: [Common of an Artist, Writer, or Composer, A27]

June 26

Isabel Florence Hapgood
Translator, Ecumenist, and Journalist, 1929

Isabel Hapgood, a lifelong and faithful Episcopalian, was a force behind ecumenical relations between Episcopalians and Russian Orthodoxy in the United States around the turn of the twentieth century. Born in Massachusetts on November 21, 1851, of a wealthy family, Hapgood was educated in private schools. She was a superior student with a particular talent for the study of languages. In addition to the standard fare of the time—Latin and French—she also mastered most of the Romance and Germanic languages of Europe and most notably Russian, Polish, and Church Slavonic. She possessed the particular gift of being able to translate the subtleties of Russian into equally subtle English. Her translations made the works of Dostoyevsky, Tolstoy, Gorky, and Chekov, among others, available to English readers. She was also a prolific journalist, writing regularly for *The Nation* and *The New York Evening Post*, and was a contributor to *The New York Times*, *Harper's Weekly*, *The Century*, and *The Atlantic Monthly*.

Between 1887-1889, Hapgood traveled extensively through Russia. That visit cemented a lifelong love of Russia, its language and culture, and particularly the Russian Orthodox Church. She would make return visits to Russia almost every year for the rest of her life.

Her love of Russian Orthodoxy and its great Divine Liturgy led her to seek the permission of the hierarchy to translate the rites into English. Hapgood's already established reputation as a sensitive translator certainly contributed, but in the meantime she had developed close relationships with Russian clergy and musicians at all levels of the hierarchy. The work, *Service Book of the Holy-Orthodox Catholic Church*, took eleven years to complete. It received support of the Russian Orthodox bishops in North America, particularly Archbishop Tikhon, who was later to give Hapgood's work a second blessing when he became Patriarch of Moscow.

Isabel Florence Hapgood is faithfully recalled among the Russian Orthodox in North America for her contribution to their common life, her desire for closer relations between Russian Orthodox and Episcopalians, and for her making the liturgical treasures of their tradition available to the English-speaking world.

She died on June 26, 1928.

Rite I   Loving God, we give thanks to thee for the work and witness of Isabel Florence Hapgood: Guide us as we persevere in the reconciliation of all people, that all may be one in Christ; who with thee and the Holy Spirit liveth and reigneth, one God, unto the ages of ages. Amen.

Rite II Loving God, we thank you for the work and witness of Isabel Florence Hapgood: Guide us as we persevere in the reconciliation of all people, that all may be one in Christ; who with you and the Holy Spirit lives and reigns, one God, unto the ages of ages. Amen.

For Liturgical Celebration: [Common of an Artist, Writer, or Composer, A27] [Common of a Saint, A23] [For the Unity of the Church, A48]

June 27

Cornelius Hill
Priest and Chief among the Oneida, 1907

Born in 1834, Cornelius Hill was the first great Oneida chief to be born in Wisconsin, after the United States government had forced the Oneida peoples west from New York State.

As a young man, Hill spent several years at Nashotah House, where the Episcopal priests educated him and formed him in the faith, worship, and tradition of the Church. Hill was greatly respected among his people for his intelligence, courage, and ability to lead, and by his teenage years, he had already been made an Oneida chief, named Onan-gwat-go, or "Big Medicine."

Hill's great mentor was the Reverend Edward A. Goodnough, a missionary and teacher who had worked among the Oneidas from 1853-1890. Hill defended Goodnough when the latter resisted land allotment among the chief families as the solution to their poverty and conflicts. Like Goodnough, Hill was a staunch opponent of allotment, and he opposed Chief Daniel Bread, his elder chief, who saw allotment as an inevitable reality. Upon Bread's death, Hill took on a great role in the tribal politics of his people. In 1874, he drafted a petition to the legislature of the State of New York calling on them to respect Oneida claims under state treaties, particularly fishing rights, which had been revoked and which led to economic hardship for Oneidas remaining in the area.

When land allotment became a legal reality under the Dawes General Act of 1893, Hill turned to the Church, and, in 1895, he was ordained an Episcopal deacon. In 1903 he became the first Oneida to be ordained a priest. At the ordination, he repeated his vows in the Oneida language.

Hill saw Christian faith as a way to help his people grapple with the profound and rapid changes which faced them, and the authority of his ordination enhanced his ability to be a bridge between Oneida and white culture. He is, to this day, revered by his people, and many shrines to him exist in the state of Wisconsin.

Rite I   Everliving Lord of the universe, who didst raise up thy priest Cornelius Hill to shepherd and defend his people against attempts to scatter them in the wilderness: Help us, like him, to be dedicated to truth and honor, that we may come to that blessed state thou hast prepared for us; through Jesus Christ, who with thee and the Holy Spirit liveth and reigneth, one God, in glory everlasting. Amen.

Rite II Everliving Lord of the universe, who raised up your priest Cornelius Hill to shepherd and defend his people against attempts to scatter them in the wilderness: Help us, like him, to be dedicated to truth and honor, that we may come to that blessed state you have prepared for us; through Jesus Christ, who with you and the Holy Spirit lives and reigns, one God, in glory everlasting. Amen.

For Liturgical Celebration: [Common of a Pastor, A14] [For the Ministry I, A49] [For Reconciliation and Forgiveness, A68]

June 28

Irenaeus, Bishop of Lyons
c. 202

If theology is "thinking about faith" and arranging those thoughts in some systematic order, then Irenaeus has been rightly recognized by Catholics and Protestants alike as the first great systematic theologian.

There is considerable doubt about the year of Irenaeus' birth; estimates vary from 97 to 160. It is certain that he learned the Christian faith in Ephesus at the feet of the venerable Polycarp, who in turn had known John the Evangelist. Some years before 177, probably while Irenaeus was still in his teens, he carried the tradition of Christianity to Lyons in southern France.

His name means "the peaceable one"—and suitably so. The year 177 brought hardship to the mission in Gaul. Persecution broke out, and a mounting tide of heresy threatened to engulf the Church. Irenaeus, by now a presbyter, was sent to Rome to mediate the dispute regarding Montanism, which the Bishop of Rome, Eleutherus, seemed to embrace. While Irenaeus was on this mission, the aged Bishop of Lyons, Pothinus, died in prison during a local persecution. When Irenaeus returned to Lyons, he was elected bishop to succeed Pothinus.

Irenaeus' enduring fame rests mainly on a large treatise, entitled *The Refutation and Overthrow of Gnosis, Falsely So-Called*, usually shortened to *Against Heresies*. In it, Irenaeus describes the major Gnostic systems, thoroughly, clearly, and often with biting humor. It is one of our chief sources of knowledge about Gnosticism. He also makes a case for Christianity which has become a classic, resting heavily on Scripture and on the continuity between the teaching of the Apostles and the teaching of bishops, generation after generation, especially in the great see cities. Against the Gnostics, who despised the flesh and exalted the spirit, he stressed two doctrines: that of the creation as good, and that of the resurrection of the body.

A late and uncertain tradition claims that he suffered martyrdom, about 202.

Rite I   Almighty God, who didst uphold thy servant Irenaeus with strength to maintain the truth against every blast of vain doctrine: Keep us, we pray, steadfast in thy true religion, that in constancy and peace we may walk in the way that leads to eternal life; through Jesus Christ our Lord, who liveth and reigneth with thee and the Holy Spirit, one God, now and for ever. Amen.

Rite II   Almighty God, you upheld your servant Irenaeus with strength to maintain the truth against every blast of vain doctrine: Keep us, we pray, steadfast in your true religion, that in constancy and peace we may walk in the way that leads to eternal life; through Jesus Christ our Lord, who lives and reigns with you and the Holy Spirit, one God, now and for ever. Amen.

For Liturgical Celebration: [Common of a Theologian and Teacher, A17] [Common of a Pastor, A14] [For the Ministry II, A50]

JULY

1   Harriet Beecher Stowe, Writer and Prophetic Witness, 1896
1   Pauli Murray, Priest, 1985
2   Walter Rauschenbusch, 1918, Washington Gladden, 1918, and Jacob Riis, 1914, Prophetic Witnesses
3
4
5
6   John (Jan) Hus, Prophetic Witness and Martyr, 1415
7
8
9
10
11   Benedict of Nursia, Abbot of Monte Cassino, c. 540
12   Nathan Söderblom, Archbishop of Uppsala and Ecumenist, 1931
13   Conrad Weiser, Witness to Peace and Reconciliation, 1760
14   Samson Occom, Witness to the Faith in New England, 1792
15
16   "The Righteous Gentiles"
17   William White, Bishop of Pennsylvania, 1836
18   Bartolomé de las Casas, Friar and Missionary to the Indies, 1566
19   Macrina, Monastic and Teacher, 379
20   Elizabeth Cady Stanton, 1902; Amelia Bloomer, 1894; Sojourner Truth, 1883; and Harriet Ross Tubman, 1913, Liberators and Prophets
21   Albert John Luthuli, Prophetic Witness in South Africa, 1967
22
23   John Cassian, Abbot at Marseilles, 435
24   Thomas à Kempis, Priest, 1471

25

26 Joachim and Anne, Parents of the Blessed Virgin Mary
26 Charles Raymond Barnes, 1938
27 William Reed Huntington, Priest, 1909
28 Johann Sebastian Bach, 1750, George Frederick Handel, 1759, and Henry Purcell, 1695, Composers
29 Mary, Martha, and Lazarus of Bethany
29 First Ordination of Women to the Priesthood in The Episcopal Church, 1974
30 William Wilberforce, 1833, and Anthony Ashley-Cooper, Lord Shaftesbury, 1885, Prophetic Witnesses
31 Ignatius of Loyola, Priest and Monastic, 1556

July 1

Harriet Beecher Stowe
Writer and Prophetic Witness, 1896

Harriet Beecher Stowe was born on June 14, 1811, and from an early age was influenced by the humanitarian efforts of her famous parents. Her father, Lyman Beecher, was known for his zealous preaching and involvement with the temperance movement, while her mother, Roxana Foote Beecher, ran a school for girls and publicly advocated for the intellectual development of women. Her sister Catharine led the women's opposition against the Jackson administration's Indian Removal Bill.

Harriet Beecher Stowe was an outspoken critic of slavery, an institution that she believed to be fundamentally incompatible with the theology of her Calvinist upbringing. An author of many works, she is justly famous for her novel *Uncle Tom's Cabin* (1852), a sermon-like work that chronicled the life of a slave family in the south. In particular, it recounted the tragic consequences of slavery on families, consequences that were for Stowe to be counted as one of the worst evils of slavery. *Uncle Tom's Cabin* was the bestselling book of the nineteenth century, and was influential in both America and Britain.

Stowe's book inspired anti-slavery movements in the North and provoked widespread anger in the South. Her work intensified the sectional conflicts that would eventually lead to the Civil War. Abraham Lincoln, upon meeting Harriet Beecher Stowe, was alleged to have said, "So this is the little lady who started this great war!"

Stowe's book, together with her public anti-slavery work, was largely responsible for bringing the evils of slavery to light not only in America, but in Britain, Europe, even Russia. Tolstoy greatly esteemed her work and her moral courage, heaping lavish praise on her. She was renowned then, as now, for her boldness and willingness to expose the harsh realities of slavery to the public eye.

She died in Hartford, Connecticut on July 1, 1896.

Rite I   Gracious God, we offer thanks for the witness of Harriett Beecher Stowe, whose fiction inspired thousands with compassion for the shame and sufferings of enslaved peoples, and who enriched her writings with the cadences of the Book of Common Prayer. Help us, like her, to strive for thy justice, that our eyes may see the glory of thy Son, Jesus Christ, when he comes to reign with thee and the Holy Spirit in reconciliation and peace, one God, now and always. Amen.

Rite II   Gracious God, we thank you for the witness of Harriett Beecher Stowe, whose fiction inspired thousands with compassion for the shame and sufferings of enslaved peoples, and who enriched her writings with the cadences of the Book of Common Prayer. Help us, like her, to strive for your justice, that our eyes may see the glory of your Son, Jesus Christ, when he comes to reign with you and the Holy Spirit in reconciliation and peace, one God, now and always. Amen.

For Liturgical Celebration: [Common of a Prophetic Witness, A31] [Common of an Artist, Writer, or Composer, A27]

July 1
Pauli Murray
Priest, 1985

Pauli Murray was an early and committed civil rights activist and the first African American woman priest ordained in The Episcopal Church.

Born in Baltimore in 1910, Murray was raised in Durham, North Carolina, and graduated from Hunter College in 1933. After seeking admission to graduate school at the University of North Carolina in 1938, she was denied entry due to her race. She went on to graduate from Howard University Law School in 1944. While a student at Howard, she participated in sit-in demonstrations that challenged racial segregation in drugstores and cafeterias in Washington, DC. Denied admission to Harvard University for an advanced law degree because of her gender, Murray received her Master of Laws degree from the University of California, Berkeley, in 1945.

In 1948 the Women's Division of Christian Service of the Methodist Church hired Murray to compile information about segregation laws in the South. Her research led to a 1951 book, *States' Laws on Race and Color*, that became a foundational document for Thurgood Marshall in his work on the decisive Brown v. Board of Education Supreme Court decision in 1954.

Committed to dismantling barriers of race, Murray saw the civil rights and women's movements as intertwined and believed that black women had a vested interest in the women's movement. Perceiving a call to ordained ministry, Murray began her studies at General Theological Seminary in 1973. She was ordained deacon in June 1976, and, on January 8, 1977, she was ordained priest at Washington National Cathedral. She served at Church of the Atonement in Washington, D.C., from 1979 to 1981 and at Holy Nativity Church in Baltimore until her death in 1985.

Murray's books include the family memoir *Proud Shoes: Story of an American Family* (1956) and the personal memoir *Song in a Weary Throat: An American Pilgrimage* (1987).

Rite I Liberating God, we thank thee most heartily for the steadfast courage of thy servant Pauli Murray, who didst fight long and well: Unshackle us from the bonds of prejudice and fear, so that we may show forth thy reconciling love and true freedom, which thou didst reveal through thy Son our Savior Jesus Christ; who liveth and reigneth with thee and the Holy Spirit, one God, now and for ever. Amen.

Rite II Liberating God, we thank you most heartily for the steadfast courage of your servant Pauli Murray, who fought long and well: Unshackle us from bonds of prejudice and fear, so that we show forth your reconciling love and true freedom, which you revealed through your Son our Savior Jesus Christ; who lives and reigns with you and the Holy Spirit, one God, now and for ever. Amen.

For Liturgical Celebration: [Common of a Pastor, A14] [Common of a Prophetic Witness, A31] [For the Ministry I, A49]

July 2

Walter Rauschenbusch, *1918,*
Washington Gladden, *1918,*
and Jacob Riis, *1914*
Prophetic Witnesses

Born the son of a German preacher in upstate New York, Walter Rauschenbusch's childhood was steeped in traditional Protestant doctrine and biblical literalism. While attending Rochester Theological Seminary, he came to believe that Jesus died "to substitute love for selfishness as the basis of human society." For Rauschenbusch, the Kingdom of God was "not a matter of getting individuals to heaven, but of transforming life on earth into the harmony of heaven."

In works such as *Theology for the Social Gospel* (1917), Rauschenbusch enumerated the "social sins" which Jesus bore on the cross, including the combination of greed and political power, militarism, and class contempt. In 1892, he and some friends formed the Brotherhood of the Kingdom, a group whose mission was to open the eyes of the Church to the reality of the Kingdom of God on earth.

Like Rauschenbusch, Washington Gladden's ministry was dedicated to the realization of the Kingdom of God in this world. Gladden was the acting religious editor of the *New York Independent*, in which he exposed corruption in the New York political system. Gladden was the first American clergyman to approve of and support labor unions; after meeting W.E.B. Du Bois, he became an early opponent of segregation.

Born in Denmark in 1849, Jacob Riis arrived in New York City in 1870, as multitudes of immigrants flooded the city seeking work following the devastation of the Civil War.

As a police reporter for the *New York Tribune*, Riis witnessed the poorest, most crime-ridden parts of the city. Teaching himself photography, he combined word and image to display the devastating effects of poverty and crime on so many in New York. His work led Theodore Roosevelt, then City Police Commissioner, to close down the police-run poor houses in which Riis had struggled during his first months in New York.

A life-long Lutheran, Riis wrote of consecrating his pen for Christ: "I wish I could honestly say that it has always come up to the high ideal set it then. I can say, though, that it has ever striven toward it, and that scarce a day has passed since that I have not thought of the charge then laid upon it and upon me."

Rite I   Loving God, who dost call us to do justice and love kindness: We offer thanks for the witness of Walter Rauschenbusch, Washington Gladden, and Jacob Riis, reformers of society; and we pray that, following their examples of faithfulness to the Gospel, we may be ever mindful of the suffering of those who are poor and work diligently for the reform of our communities; through Jesus Christ, who with thee and the Holy Spirit liveth and reigneth, one God, for ever and ever. Amen.

Rite II   Loving God, you call us to do justice and love kindness: We thank you for the witness of Walter Rauschenbusch, Washington Gladden, and Jacob Riis, reformers of society; and we pray that, following their examples of faithfulness to the Gospel, we may be ever mindful of the suffering of those who are poor and work diligently for the reform of our communities; through Jesus Christ, who with you and the Holy Spirit lives and reigns, one God, for ever and ever. Amen.

For Liturgical Celebration: [Common of a Prophetic Witness, A31] [Common of a Saint, A23] [For all Baptized Christians, A42] [For Vocation in Daily Work, A61] [For Labor Day, A62] [For Rogation Days II, A56]

July 2

July 6

John (Jan) Hus
Prophetic Witness and Martyr, 1415

John Hus was born at Husinec in Bohemia c. 1369. He was a priest who, influenced by the writings of John Wyclif, became leader of the Bohemian reform movement, which called for a return to Scripture and living out of the word of God in one's life. As preacher at Bethlehem Chapel in Prague, he talked to the people in their native language. Hundreds gathered every day to hear his call for personal and institutional reform.

Clerics he had offended had him exiled from Prague, but he continued his ministry through the written word. Hus took the radical step of appealing directly to Christ rather than to the hierarchy for the justification of his stance.

When the Council of Constance opened in 1414, Hus traveled there, hoping to clear his name of charges of heresy. Hus had been given a pledge of safe conduct from the Emperor, but his enemies persuaded council officials to imprison him on the grounds that "promises made to heretics need not be kept." Although several leaders of the Council of Constance were in favor of moderate church reform, the council's prime objective was the resolution of the Great Western Schism, which had produced three rival popes at the same time. The council therefore tried to secure a speedy recantation and submission from Hus. He maintained that the charges against him were false or twisted versions of his teachings, and he could not recant opinions he had never held. Faced with an ultimatum to recant or die, Hus chose the latter. As he approached the stake on July 6, 1415, he refused a last attempt to get him to recant and said: "The principal intention of my preaching and of all my other acts or writings was solely that I might turn men from sin. And in that truth of the gospel that I wrote, taught, and preached in accordance with the sayings and expositions of the holy doctors, I am willing gladly to die today."

His death did not end the movement, and the Bohemian reformation continued. Hus influenced Martin Luther's reforming ideas. The Moravian Church traces its origins to Hus. Hus' rousing assertion "Truth will conquer!" is the motto of the Czech Republic today.

Rite I Faithful God, who didst give Jan Hus the courage to confess thy truth and recall thy Church to the image of Christ: Enable us, inspired by his example, to bear witness against corruption and never cease to pray for our enemies, that we may prove faithful followers of our Savior Jesus Christ; who liveth and reigneth with thee and the Holy Spirit, one God, for ever and ever. Amen.

Rite II Faithful God, you gave Jan Hus the courage to confess your truth and recall your Church to the image of Christ: Enable us, inspired by his example, to bear witness against corruption and never cease to pray for our enemies, that we may prove faithful followers of our Savior Jesus Christ; who lives and reigns with you and the Holy Spirit, one God, for ever and ever. Amen.

For Liturgical Celebration: [Common of a Martyr, A7] [Common of a Prophetic Witness, A31] [Common of a Pastor, A14] [Of the Holy Cross, A41]

July 11

Benedict of Nursia
Abbot of Monte Cassino, c. 540

Benedict is generally accounted the father of western monasticism. He was born about 480, at Nursia in central Italy, and was educated at Rome. The style of life he found there disgusted him. Rome at this time was overrun by various barbarian tribes; the period was one of considerable political instability, a breakdown of western society, and the beginnings of barbarian kingdoms. Benedict's disapproval of the manners and morals of Rome led him to a vocation of monastic seclusion. He withdrew to a hillside cave above Lake Subiaco, about forty miles west of Rome, where there was already at least one other monk. Gradually, a community grew up around Benedict. Sometime between 525 and 530, he moved south with some of his disciples to Monte Cassino, midway between Rome and Naples, where he established another community, and, about 540, composed his monastic *Rule*. He does not appear to have been ordained or to have contemplated the founding of an "order." He died sometime between 540 and 550 and was buried in the same grave as his sister, Scholastica.

No personality or text in the history of monasticism, it has been said, has occasioned more studies than Benedict and his rule. The major problem for historians is the question of how much of the rule is original. This is closely related to the question of the date of another, very similar but anonymous, rule for monks, known as the "Rule of the Master," which may antedate Benedict's *Rule* by ten years. This does not detract from the fact that Benedict's firm but reasonable rule has been the basic source document from which most later monastic rules were derived. Its average day provides for a little over four hours to be spent in liturgical prayer, a little over five hours in spiritual reading, about six hours of work, one hour for eating, and about eight hours of sleep. The entire Psalter is to be recited in the Divine Office once every week.

At profession, the new monk takes vows of "stability, amendment of life, and obedience." Pope Gregory the Great wrote Benedict's "Life" in the second book of his *Dialogues*. He adopted Benedict's monasticism as an instrument of evangelization when, in 596, he sent Augustine and his companions to convert the Anglo-Saxon people. In the Anglican Communion today, the rules of many religious orders are influenced by Benedict's rule.

Rite I Everlasting God, we give thanks to thee for the purity and humility with which thou didst endow thy servant Benedict: Grant us grace, in union with his example and prayers, to hallow and conform our souls and bodies to the purpose of thy most holy will; through Christ our Lord. Amen.

Rite II Everlasting God, we give you thanks for the purity and humility with which you endowed your servant Benedict: Grant us grace, in union with his example and prayers, to hallow and conform our souls and bodies to the purpose of your most holy will; through Christ our Lord. Amen.

For Liturgical Celebration: [Common of a Monastic or Professed Religious, A20] [Common of a Theologian and Teacher, A17] [Of the Holy Spirit, A38] [Of the Incarnation, A39] [For the Ministry III, A51]

July 12

Nathan Söderblom
Archbishop of Uppsala and Ecumenist, 1931

Nathan Söderblom, Archbishop of Uppsala, is regarded as one of the founders of the modern ecumenical movement. Born at Trönö in Sweden on January 15, 1866, Söderblom attended the University of Uppsala and was ordained a priest in the (Lutheran) Church of Sweden in 1893. From 1894-1901, he served as Pastor of the Swedish Lutheran community in Paris, during which time he took his doctorate in theology at the Sorbonne. He returned to Uppsala in 1902 to teach and lead the School of Theology at the university. He was a highly respected scholar and teacher, a prolific writer, and an early proponent of the study of comparative religions.

To the surprise and dismay of many, he was appointed Archbishop of Uppsala in 1914. It had been centuries since the senior bishops of the Swedish Church had been passed over for the appointment, and this was particularly notable since Söderblom was not a bishop. He served as Archbishop of Uppsala until his death in Uppsala on July 12, 1931.

Söderblom took a great interest in the early liturgical renewal movement among Roman Catholics, Anglicans, and Lutherans. This coincided with his deep commitment to the unity of the churches of Christ and his passion for ecumenical advancement. In 1925 he invited Episcopalian/Anglican, Reformed, Lutheran, and Orthodox leaders to Stockholm, and together they formed the Universal Christian Council on Life and Work. Söderblom worked closely with Charles Henry Brent (March 27) at the First Conference on Faith and Order that Brent organized in 1927 in Lausanne, Switzerland. Because of his effort and his tireless advocacy of Christian unity, Söderblom is numbered among the ecumenists whose efforts led eventually to the formation of the World Council of Churches in 1948. It was Söderblom's advocacy for church unity as a means toward world peace that earned him the Nobel Peace Prize in 1930.

Archbishop Söderblom saw a profound connection between liturgical worship, personal prayer, and social justice. A rich cohesion of these elements was, in his mind, the foundation of a Christian commitment well lived.

Söderblom died in Uppsala, Sweden, in 1931.

Rite I Almighty God, we bless thy Name for the life and work of Nathan Söderblom, Archbishop of Uppsala, who helped to inspire the modern liturgical revival and worked tirelessly for cooperation among Christians. Inspire us by his example, that we may ever strive for the renewal of thy Church in life and worship, for the glory of thy Name; who with Jesus Christ and the Holy Spirit liveth and reigneth, one God, for ever and ever. Amen.

Rite II Almighty God, we bless your Name for the life and work of Nathan Söderblom, Archbishop of Uppsala, who helped to inspire the modern liturgical revival and worked tirelessly for cooperation among Christians. Inspire us by his example, that we may ever strive for the renewal of your Church in life and worship, for the glory of your Name; who with Jesus Christ and the Holy Spirit lives and reigns, one God, for ever and ever. Amen.

For Liturgical Celebration: [Common of a Pastor, A14] [For the Ministry II, A50] [For the Unity of the Church, A48]

July 13

Conrad Weiser
Witness to Peace and Reconciliation, 1760

Conrad Weiser was an eighteenth century American diplomat who worked for peace and reconciliation between the European settlers and the Native peoples of Pennsylvania. Of Lutheran descent, he was the father-in-law of Henry Melchior Muhlenberg (October 7).

Born in Germany in 1696, he immigrated to the United States as a child. At 17, Weiser went to live among the Mohawks in New York in order to learn their language and culture. He later made his way to southeastern Pennsylvania, where he learned customs and language of the Iroquois.

Weiser eventually settled in the area that is now Reading, Pennsylvania. He designed the layout of the city of Reading, is numbered among the founders of Berks County, and served a long tenure as the local judge. Like many people of his time, he had to work at a variety of occupations in order to care for his family: farmer, tanner, merchant, and real estate speculator. For a time, Weiser was enamored with the Seventh Day Baptist movement and took up residence at the Ephrata Cloister.

His knowledge of the Iroquois language and his natural diplomatic gifts made him invaluable during the years of the settlement. He negotiated land deeds and other treaties, not only between Native Americans and European settlers—he also did diplomatic work between the various tribes of Native Americans and was often, but not always, successful in keeping the peace among them. He advised William Penn and Benjamin Franklin on matters related to Native Americans and played an important role in keeping the Iroquois sympathetic to the British cause during the French and Indian Wars.

At the time of Weiser's death in 1760, an Iroquois leader was heard to remark, "We are at a great loss and sit in darkness . . . as since his death we cannot so well understand one another."

Rite I   Almighty God, of thy grace thou didst endue Conrad Weiser with the gift of diplomacy, the insight to understand two different cultures and interpret each to the other with clarity and honesty: As we strive to be faithful to our vocation to commend thy kingdom, help us to proclaim the Gospel to the many cultures around us, that by thy Holy Spirit we may be effective ambassadors for our Savior Jesus Christ; who with thee and the same Holy Spirit liveth and reigneth, one God, now and for ever. Amen.

Rite II Almighty God, of your grace you gave Conrad Weiser the gift of diplomacy, the insight to understand two different cultures and interpret each to the other with clarity and honesty: As we strive to be faithful to our vocation to commend your kingdom, help us to proclaim the Gospel to the many cultures around us, that by your Holy Spirit we may be effective ambassadors for our Savior Jesus Christ; who with you and the same Holy Spirit lives and reigns, one God, now and for ever. Amen.

For Liturgical Celebration: [Common of a Saint, A23] [For Reconciliation and Forgiveness, A68] [For Peace, A55] [For Social Justice, A58] [Common of a Prophetic Witness, A31]

July 14

Samson Occom
Witness to the Faith in New England, 1792

Samson Occom, one of the first ordained Native American ministers, was born a member of the Mohegan Nation near New London, Connecticut, in 1723. By the age of sixteen, Occom had been exposed to the evangelical preaching of the Great Awakening. In 1743, he began studying theology at the school of congregational minister Eleazar Wheelock, later founder of Dartmouth College.

Occom did mission work among the Native Americans in New England and Montauk, Long Island. In 1759, he was ordained a Presbyterian minister. In 1766, at the behest of Eleazar Wheelock, Occom went to England, where he was to raise money for Wheelock's Indian charity school. He preached extensively for over a year, traveling across England and raising over eleven thousand pounds from wealthy patrons, including King George III. When he returned from England, however, his family, supposedly under the care of Wheelock, was found destitute, and the school for which he had labored moved to Hanover, New Hampshire, where it became Dartmouth College. The funds he had raised had been put toward the education of Englishmen rather than of Native Americans.

Following a disagreement with the colonial government of Connecticut over a lack of compensation for lands they had sold, Occom and many other Mohegans moved to the Oneida territory in upstate New York. There, he and his companions founded the Brothertown Community. In his day, Occom was renowned for his eloquence and spiritual wisdom. He was the first Native American to publish his works in English. His work among the Mohegans of Connecticut, many of whom became Christians under his guidance, helped them to avoid later relocation.

Occum died in New Stockbridge, New York, in 1792.

Rite I God, the Great Spirit, whose breath dost give life to the world and whose voice dost thunder in the wind: We give thee thanks for thy servant Samson Occom, strong preacher and teacher among the Mohegan people; and pray that we, cherishing his example, may love learning and by love build up the communities into which thou dost send us; through Jesus Christ our Lord, who with thee and the Holy Spirit liveth and reigneth, one God, now and for ever. Amen.

Rite II God, the Great Spirit, whose breath gives life to the world and whose voice thunders in the wind: We give you thanks for your servant Samson Occom, strong preacher and teacher among the Mohegan people; and pray that we, cherishing his example, may love learning and by love build up the communities into which you send us; through Jesus Christ our Lord, who with you and the Holy Spirit lives and reigns, one God, now and for ever. Amen.

For Liturgical Celebration: [Common of a Missionary, A11] [Common of a Pastor, A14] [For the Ministry I, A49] [For the Mission of the Church, A52]

July 16

"The Righteous Gentiles"

During the Second World War, thousands of Christians and persons of faith made valiant sacrifices, often at the risk of their own lives, to save Jews from the Holocaust. These "Righteous Gentiles" are honored for courageous action in the face of Hitler's reign of terror.

Raoul Wallenberg, a Lutheran, was a Swedish humanitarian and diplomat whose great resourcefulness saved thousands of Hungarian Jews during the Nazi occupation. He issued them Swedish passports so that they could escape, and housed many in Swedish government property in Budapest, thereby protecting them on the basis of diplomatic immunity.

Hiram Bingham IV, an Episcopalian, was an American diplomat in France during the early years of the Nazi occupation. He violated State Department protocol by arranging escape routes for persecuted Jews, and often provided the most wanted with safe haven in his own home. When transferred to Argentina, he devoted considerable effort to tracking the movements of Nazi war criminals.

Carl Lutz, an evangelical, was a Swiss diplomat in Budapest who also worked to save the lives of many Hungarian Jews. Although deeply involved in this endeavor at every level, he is most remembered for negotiating with the Nazis for safe passage from Hungary to Palestine for more than 10,000 Jews.

Chiune Sugihara, an Orthodox Christian, while serving as Japanese Consul in Lithuania, rescued thousands of Jews by providing them with travel credentials so they could escape. In doing so, he violated official diplomatic policy and was removed from his country's foreign service. He lived the rest of his life in disgrace.

André and Magda Trocmé, of the Reformed tradition, were French Christians who saved the lives of several thousand Jews in France during the Nazi occupation. He was the pastor in Le Chambon-sur-Lignon and, together with people in neighboring communities, he created a safe haven for many refugees from the Nazi terror.

These faithful servants, together with more than 23,000 others verified to date, are honored at Yad Vashem, the Holocaust Memorial overlooking Jerusalem, and celebrated there as "the righteous among the nations."

Rite I Lord of the Exodus, who dost deliver thy people with a strong hand and a mighty arm: Strengthen thy Church with the examples of the Righteous Gentiles of World War II to defy oppression for the rescue of the innocent; through Jesus Christ our Lord, who liveth and reigneth with thee and the Holy Spirit, one God, now and for ever. Amen.

Rite II Lord of the Exodus, who delivers your people with a strong hand and a mighty arm: Strengthen your Church with the examples of the Righteous Gentiles of World War II to defy oppression for the rescue of the innocent; through Jesus Christ our Lord, who lives and reigns with you and the Holy Spirit, one God, now and for ever. Amen.

For Liturgical Celebration: [Common of a Saint, A23] [For Social Justice, A58] [Common of a Prophetic Witness, A31]

July 17

William White
Bishop of Pennsylvania, 1836

William White was born in Philadelphia, March 24, 1747, and was educated at the college of that city, graduating in 1765. In 1770, he went to England, was ordained deacon on December 23, and priest on April 25, 1772. On his return home, he became assistant minister of Christ and St. Peter's, 1772–1779, and rector from that year until his death, July 17, 1836. He also served as chaplain of the Continental Congress from 1777 to 1789, and then of the United States Senate until 1800. Chosen unanimously as first Bishop of Pennsylvania, September 14, 1786, he went to England again, with Samuel Provoost, Bishop-elect of New York; and the two men were consecrated in Lambeth Chapel on Septuagesima Sunday, February 4, 1787, by the Archbishops of Canterbury and York and the Bishops of Bath and Wells and of Peterborough.

Bishop White was the chief architect of the Constitution of the American Episcopal Church and the wise overseer of its life during the first generation of its history. He was the Presiding Bishop at its organizing General Convention in 1789 and again from 1795 until his death in Philadelphia, on July 17, 1836.

He was a theologian of no mean ability, and among his proteges, in whose formation he had a large hand, were such leaders of a new generation as John Henry Hobart, Jackson Kemper, and William Augustus Muhlenberg. White's gifts of statesmanship and reconciling moderation steered the American Church through the first decades of its independent life. His influence in his native city made him its "first citizen." To few men has the epithet "venerable" been more aptly applied.

Rite I O Lord, who in a time of turmoil and confusion didst raise up thy servant William White and didst endow him with wisdom, patience, and a reconciling temper, that he might lead thy Church into ways of stability and peace: Hear our prayer, and give us wise and faithful leaders, that, through their ministry, thy people may be blessed and thy will be done; through Jesus Christ our Lord, who liveth and reigneth with thee and the Holy Spirit, one God, for ever and ever. Amen.

Rite II O Lord, in a time of turmoil and confusion, you raised up your servant William White, and endowed him with wisdom, patience, and a reconciling temper, that he might lead your Church into ways of stability and peace: Hear our prayer, and give us wise and faithful leaders, that, through their ministry, your people may be blessed and your will be done; through Jesus Christ our Lord, who lives and reigns with you and the Holy Spirit, one God, for ever and ever. Amen.

For Liturgical Celebration: [Common of a Pastor, A14] [For the Ministry II, A50]

July 18

Bartolomé de las Casas
Friar and Missionary to the Indies, 1566

Bartolomé de las Casas, "The Apostle of the Indies," was a Dominican known for his defense of the rights and dignity of indigenous peoples in the Americas.

Las Casas was born in Seville, Spain, in 1484. He studied both theology and law at the University of Salamanca. As a lawyer, las Casas participated in an expedition in Hispaniola in 1502. As a reward, he was given an *encomienda*, a royal land grant populated with native peoples of the West Indies. Disillusioned by the inhumanity of the colonial system, he began to seek ways to reform it. Las Casas was ordained priest in 1507 in Rome but waited to celebrate his first mass in 1510 at Santo Domingo.

In December of 1511, the Dominican Antonio de Montesinos preached a fiery sermon implicating the colonists in the genocide of the Native peoples. Las Casas gave up his rights to the *encomienda* and no longer possessed slaves; in his own preaching he urged other Spanish colonists to do likewise. Continuing his demand for change, he returned to Spain in 1515 to plead for justice from the Spanish government. The powerful archbishop of Toledo, who named him "Protector of the Indies," took up his cause.

His passionate defense of the Natives before the Spanish Parliament persuaded the emperor, Charles V, to accept las Casas's project of founding "towns of free Indians," communities of both Spaniards and Native Americans who would jointly create a new civilization in the Americas; but the efforts were met with failure. After this, las Casas joined the Dominican order in 1523. Las Casas's work seemed to be crowned with success in 1542 when Charles V signed the "New Laws," which required Spanish colonists to free Indians after a single generation. However, the laws were generally ignored.

Las Casas was made the first bishop of Chiapas, Mexico, in 1544, where he tried to implement the New Laws. In 1545, he decreed in a pastoral letter that all slave owners would be denied absolution unless they freed their slaves and returned their property to them. He renounced his bishopric after the repeal of the New Laws and returned to Spain in 1547. In 1550, he engaged in a public debate against the theologian Juan Gines de Seulvada who argued that war against the Native Americans and their enslavement was justified because of their inferiority. Las Casas argued for the full humanity of the Native peoples and advocated for peaceful evangelism. In 1552, he wrote his most famous work, *A Brief Account of the Destruction of the Indies*, a sensationalist exposé of the oppression inflicted upon the peoples of the West Indies.

Las Casas lived his convictions with such zeal that he often seemed intolerant of others, but he is remembered as a tireless advocate for justice for those oppressed by colonialism and an early proponent of universal human rights.

Las Casas died in Madrid on July 18, 1566.

Rite I   Eternal God, we offer thanks for the witness of Bartolomé de las Casas, whose deep love for thy people caused him to refuse absolution to those who would not free their Indian slaves. Help us, inspired by his example, to work and pray for the freeing of all enslaved people of our world, for the sake of Jesus Christ our Redeemer; who liveth and reigneth with thee and the Holy Spirit, one God, for ever and ever. Amen.

Rite II Eternal God, we give you thanks for the witness of Bartolomé de las Casas, whose deep love for your people caused him to refuse absolution to those who would not free their Indian slaves. Help us, inspired by his example, to work and pray for the freeing of all enslaved people of our world, for the sake of Jesus Christ our Redeemer; who lives and reigns with you and the Holy Spirit, one God, for ever and ever. Amen.

For Liturgical Celebration: [Common of a Monastic or Professed Religious, A20] [Common of a Pastor, A14] [Common of a Prophetic Witness, A31] [For Social Justice, A58]

July 19

Macrina
Monastic and Teacher, 379

Macrina (340–379) was a monastic, theologian, and teacher. She founded one of the earliest Christian communities in the Cappadocian city of Pontus. Macrina left no writings; we know of her through the works of her brother St. Gregory of Nyssa. In his *Life of St. Macrina*, Gregory describes her as both beautiful and brilliant, an authoritative spiritual teacher.

Macrina persuaded her mother Emmelia to renounce their wealthy lifestyle and to help her establish a monastery on the family's estate. Macrina's ideal of community emphasized caring for the poor and ministering to the wider community. She literally picked up young women who lay in the road starving. Many joined her order.

Gregory credits Macrina as the spiritual and theological intelligence behind her siblings' notable careers in the Church. Gregory, and their brothers St. Basil, St. Peter of Sebaste, and Naucratios went to her often for theological counsel. Macrina frequently challenged her celebrated brothers. She told Gregory his fame was not due to his own merit, but to the prayers of his parents. She took Basil in hand when he returned from Athens "monstrously conceited about his skill in rhetoric." Under her influence, Basil and Peter renounced material possessions and turned away from secular academia to become monks and theologians. Basil and Peter wrote a *Rule* for community life, ensuring that Macrina's ideas for Christian community would have lasting authority. Basil, Gregory, and Peter all became bishops, in no small measure because of Macrina's influence, and became leading defenders of the Nicene faith.

Gregory visited Macrina as she lay dying on two planks on the floor. He relates Macrina's last words as a classical Greek farewell oration imbued with Holy Scripture. In both his *Life of St. Macrina* and in his later treatise *Of the Soul and Resurrection*, Gregory presents Macrina admiringly as a Christian Socrates, delivering beautiful deathbed prayers and teachings about the resurrection.

Rite I   Merciful God, thou didst call thy servant Macrina to reveal in her life and her teaching the riches of thy grace and truth: May we, following her example, seek after thy wisdom and live according to her way; through Jesus Christ our Savior, who liveth and reigneth with thee and the Holy Spirit, one God, for ever and ever. Amen.

Rite II Merciful God, you called your servant Macrina to reveal in her life and her teaching the riches of your grace and truth: May we, following her example, seek after your wisdom and live according to her way; through Jesus Christ our Savior, who lives and reigns with you and the Holy Spirit, one God, for ever and ever. Amen.

For Liturgical Celebration: [Common of a Monastic or Professed Religious, A20] [Common of a Theologian and Teacher, A17] [For all Baptized Christians, A42] [Of the Holy Trinity, A37]

July 20

Elizabeth Cady Stanton, *1902;* Amelia Bloomer, *1894;* Sojourner Truth, *1883;* and Harriet Ross Tubman, *1913*
Liberators and Prophets

Elizabeth Cady Stanton 1815–1902

Born on November 12, 1815, into an affluent, strict Calvinist family in Johnstown, New York, Elizabeth, as a young woman, took seriously the Presbyterian doctrines of predestination and human depravity. She became very depressed, but resolved her mental crises through action. She dedicated her life to righting the wrongs perpetrated upon women by the Church and society.

She and four other women organized the first Women's Rights Convention at Seneca Falls, New York, July 19–20, 1848. The event set her political and religious agenda for the next 50 years. She held the Church accountable for oppressing women by using Scripture to enforce subordination of women in marriage and to prohibit them from ordained ministry. She held society accountable for denying women equal access to professional jobs, property ownership, the vote, and for granting less pay for the same work.

In 1881, the Revised Version of the Bible was published by a committee which included no women scholars. Elizabeth founded her own committee of women to write a commentary on Scripture, and applying the Greek she learned as a child from her minister, focused on passages used to oppress and discriminate against women.

Although Elizabeth blamed male clergy for women's oppression, she attended Trinity Episcopal Church in Seneca Falls with her friend Amelia Bloomer. As a dissenting prophet, Elizabeth preached hundreds of homilies and political speeches in pulpits throughout the nation. Wherever she visited, she was experienced as a holy presence and a liberator. She never lost her sense of humor, despite years of contending with opposition, even from friends. In a note to Susan B. Anthony, she said: "Do not feel depressed, my dear friend, what is good in us is immortal, and if the sore trials we have endured are sifting out pride and selfishness, we shall not have suffered in vain." Shortly before she died in New York City, on October 26, 1902, she said: "My only regret is that I have not been braver and bolder and truer in the honest conviction of my soul."

Amelia Jenks Bloomer 1818–1894

Amelia Jenks, the youngest of six children, born in New York on May 27, 1818, to a pious Presbyterian family, early on demonstrated a kindness of heart and strict regard for truth and right. As a young woman, she joined in the temperance, anti-slavery, and women's rights movements.

Amelia Jenks Bloomer never intended to make dress reform a major platform in women's struggle for justice. But, women's fashion of the day prescribed waist-cinching corsets, even for pregnant women, resulting in severe health problems. Faith and fashion collided explosively when she published in her newspaper, *The Lily*, a picture of herself in loose-fitting Turkish trousers, and began wearing them publicly. Clergy, from their pulpits, attacked women who wore them, citing Moses: "Women should not dress like men." Amelia fired back: "It matters not what Moses had to say to the men and women of his time about what they should wear. If clergy really cared about what Moses said about clothes, they would all put fringes and blue ribbons on their garments." Her popularity soared as she engaged clergy in public debate.

She insisted that "certain passages in the Scriptures relating to women had been given a strained and unnatural meaning." And, of St. Paul she said: "Could he have looked into the future and foreseen all the sorrow and strife, the cruel exactions and oppression on the one hand and the blind submission and cringing fear on the other, that his words have sanctioned and caused, he would never have uttered them."
And of women's right to freedom, "The same Power that brought the slave out of bondage will, in His own good time and way, bring about the emancipation of woman, and make her the equal in power and dominion that she was in the beginning."

Later in life, in Council Bluffs, Iowa, a frontier town, she worked to establish churches, libraries, and school houses. She provided hospitality for traveling clergy of all denominations, and for temperance lecturers and reformers. Trinity Episcopal Church, Seneca Falls, New York, where she was baptized, records her as a "faithful Christian missionary all her life." Amelia Jenks Bloomer died in Council Bluffs on December 30, 1894.

Sojourner Truth, "Miriam of the Later Exodus" 1797–8 to 1883

Isabella (Sojourner Truth) was the next-to-youngest child of several born to James and Elizabeth, slaves owned by a wealthy Dutchman in New York, in 1797 or 1798. For the first 28 years of her life she was a slave, sold from household to household.

She fled slavery with the help of Quaker friends, first living in Philadelphia, then New York, where she joined the Mother Zion African Methodist Episcopal Church when African Americans were being denied the right to worship with white members of St. George's Church in Philadelphia. Belle (as Isabella was called) became a street-corner evangelist in poverty-stricken areas of New York City, but quickly realized people needed food, housing, and warm clothing. She focused her work on a homeless shelter for women.

When she was about 46, Belle believed she heard God say to her, "Go east." So, she set out east for Long Island and Connecticut. Stopping at a Quaker farm for a drink of water, she was asked her name. "My name is Sojourner," Belle said. "What is your last name?" the woman asked. Belle thought of all her masters' names she had carried through life. Then the thought came: "The only master I have now is God, and His name is Truth."

Sojourner became a traveling preacher, approaching white religious meetings and campgrounds and asking to speak. Fascinated by her charismatic presence, her wit, wisdom, and imposing six-foot height, they found her hard to refuse. She never learned to read or write, but quoted extensive Bible passages from memory in her sermons. She ended by singing a "home-made" hymn and addressing the crowd on the evils of slavery. Her reputation grew, and she became part of the abolitionist and women's rights speakers' network.

During a women's rights convention in Ohio, Sojourner gave the speech for which she is best remembered: "Ain't I a Woman." She had listened for hours to clergy attack women's rights and abolition, using the Bible to support their oppressive logic: God had created women to be weak and blacks to be a subservient race. In her speech she retorted, "If the first woman God ever made was strong enough to turn the world upside down all alone, these women together ought to be able to turn it back, and get it right side up again! And now they is asking to do it, the men better let them."

Sojourner Truth died on November 26, 1883, in Battle Creek, Michigan.

Harriet Ross Tubman, "Moses of her People" 1820–1913

Slave births were recorded under property, not as persons with names; but we know that Harriet Ross, born sometime during 1820 on a Maryland Chesapeake Bay plantation, was the sixth of eleven children born to Ben Ross and Harriet Green. Although her parents were loving and they enjoyed a cheerful family life inside their cabin, they lived in fear of the children being sold off at any time.

Harriet suffered beatings and a severe injury, but grew up strong and defiant, refusing to appear happy and smiling to her owners. To cope with brutality and oppression, she turned to religion. Her favorite Bible story was about Moses who led the Israelites out of slavery. The slaves prayed for a Moses of their own.

When she was about 24, Harriet escaped to Canada, but could not forget her parents and other slaves she left behind. Working with the Quakers, she made at least 19 trips back to Maryland between 1851 and 1861, freeing over 300 people by leading them into Canada. She was so successful, $40,000 was offered for her capture.

Guided by God through omens, dreams, warnings, she claimed her struggle against slavery had been commanded by God. She foresaw the Civil War in a vision. When it began, she quickly joined the Union Army, serving as cook and nurse, caring for both Confederate and Union soldiers. She served as a spy and scout. She led 300 black troops on a raid which freed over 750 slaves, making her the first American woman to lead troops into military action.

In 1858 – 9, she moved to upstate New York where she opened her home to African American orphans and to helpless old people. Although she was illiterate, she founded schools for African American children. She joined the fight for women's rights, working with Elizabeth Cady Stanton and Susan B. Anthony, but supported African American women in their efforts to found their own organizations to address equality, work, and education. She died on March 10, 1913, in Auburn, New York.

Rite I O God, whose Spirit guideth us into all truth and maketh us free: Strengthen and sustain us as thou didst thy servants Elizabeth, Amelia, Sojourner, and Harriet. Give us vision and courage to stand against oppression and injustice and all that worketh against the glorious liberty to which thou callest all thy children; through Jesus Christ our Savior, who liveth and reigneth with thee and the Holy Spirit, one God, for ever and ever. Amen.

Rite II O God, whose Spirit guides us into all truth and makes us free: Strengthen and sustain us as you did your servants Elizabeth, Amelia, Sojourner, and Harriet. Give us vision and courage to stand against oppression and injustice and all that works against the glorious liberty to which you call all your children; through Jesus Christ our Savior, who lives and reigns with you and the Holy Spirit, one God, for ever and ever. Amen.

For Liturgical Celebration: [Common of a Prophetic Witness, A31]

July 21

Albert John Luthuli
Prophetic Witness in South Africa, 1967

Albert John Mvumbi Luthuli was the first African to receive the Nobel Peace Prize, in recognition of his leadership in South Africa's non-violent struggle against apartheid. A man of noble bearing, charitable, intolerant of hatred, and adamant in his demands for equality and peace among all people, Luthuli forged a philosophical compatibility between two cultures—the Zulu culture of his native Africa and the Christian-democratic culture of Europe.

Born into a Christian family in 1898, Luthuli was educated in mission schools, took a college degree in Durban, and spent the first fifteen years of his working life as a school teacher before taking on the responsibilities of political activism. In 1936, he was elected a Zulu chief and was made responsible for a five thousand person community in the sugar lands of Natal. This led to a number of other elected and appointed positions related to the struggle for civil rights in South Africa, culminating in his election as President of the Natal region of the African National Congress in 1945, becoming National President in 1952. He was awarded the Nobel Peace Prize in 1960 for his work against apartheid.

Luthuli's increasing prominence as a leader of the anti-apartheid movement was met with significant resistance by the white South African government. His movements were restricted, his publications banned, and he was imprisoned on several occasions.

A Methodist lay preacher, Luthuli believed the struggle for civil rights was a Christian struggle and his participation and leadership grew out of his understanding of Christian discipleship. "My own urge because I am a Christian, is to get into the thick of the struggle with other Christians, taking my Christianity with me and praying that it may be used to influence for good the character of the resistance." When confronted by the South African government with an appeal to suspend his activism, Luthuli is reported to have said, "The road to freedom is via the cross."

Although Luthuli's death on July 21, 1967, was nearly a quarter century before the end of apartheid in South Africa, he is remembered as a Christian statesman in the fight against political, racial, and religious oppression.

Rite I God of peace, who didst call thy servant Albert Luthuli to be a leader in the struggle against apartheid: Strengthen thy Church, that in union with his example and prayers, we might resist injustice in all its forms; through Jesus Christ our Lord, who liveth and reigneth with thee and the Holy Spirit, for all time. Amen.

Rite II God of peace, who called your servant Albert Luthuli to be a leader in the struggle against apartheid: Strengthen your Church, that in union with his example and prayers, we might resist injustice in all its forms; through Jesus Christ our Lord, who lives and reigns with you and the Holy Spirit, for all time. Amen.

For Liturgical Celebration: [Common of a Prophetic Witness, A31] [Common of a Saint, A23] [For Reconciliation and Forgiveness, A68]

July 23

John Cassian
Abbot at Marseilles, 435

Born in Romania around 365, John Cassian struggled with the problems of living the Christian life in a time when the world seemed to be falling apart. As a young man he traveled to a monastery in Bethlehem and later moved to Egypt, where he sought the tutelage of the great founders of the ascetic movement of the desert, such as Antony and Macarius.

At the heart of desert monasticism was the idea that the image of God in each person, tarnished by sin but not destroyed, yearns to and has the capacity to love God with the purity of heart with which God loves us. Their aim in desert solitude was to rid themselves of the anxieties and distractions that called their attention away from loving God.

Cassian was initiated into this tradition before political pressures forced him to leave Egypt in about 399. He moved to southern Gaul and, in about 415, founded a house in Marseilles for monks, and later a house for women religious. Though Cassian's goal, like that of his desert mentors, was the perfection of the individual soul, he insisted that no one should embark on a monastic vocation alone. One should enter a house where other monks are pursuing the same goal, live according to a time-tested rule, and thereby gain the guidance and companionship of the community.

Though Cassian remained committed to the desert ideal of individual perfection, his insistence on the necessity of Christian community and loving moderation was the basis for Benedictine monasticism, which eventually became the basic spirituality of the Western Church. It was perhaps a paradox that only in community could the Christian soul: "lose sight of earthly things in proportion to the inspiration of its purity so that . . . with the inner gaze of the soul it sees the glorified Jesus coming in the splendor of His majesty."

Cassian died in Marseilles in about 435.

Rite I   Holy One, whose beloved Son Jesus Christ didst bless the pure in heart: Grant that we, together with thy servant John Cassian and in union with his prayers, may ever seek the purity with which to behold thee as thou art; one God, now and for ever. Amen.

Rite II   Holy One, whose beloved Son Jesus Christ blessed the pure in heart: Grant that we, together with your servant John Cassian and in union with his prayers, may ever seek the purity with which to behold you as you are; one God, now and for ever. Amen.

For Liturgical Celebration: [Common of a Monastic or Professed Religious, A20] [Common of a Theologian and Teacher, A17] [Of the Holy Spirit, A38] [Of the Incarnation, A39]

July 24

Thomas à Kempis
Priest, 1471

The name of Thomas à Kempis is perhaps more widely known than that of any other medieval Christian writer. The *Imitation of Christ*, which he composed or compiled, has been translated into more languages than any other book except the Holy Scriptures. Millions of Christians have found in this manual a treasured and constant source of edification.

His name was Thomas Hammerken, and he was born at Kempen in the Duchy of Cleves about 1380. He was educated at Deventer by the Brethren of the Common Life, and joined their order in 1399 at their house of Mount St. Agnes in Zwolle (in the Low Countries). He took his vows (those of the Augustinian Canons Regular) there in 1407, was ordained a priest in 1415, and was made sub-prior in 1425. He died on July 25, 1471.

The Order of the Brethren of the Common Life was founded by Gerard Groote (1340–1384) at Deventer. It included both clergy and lay members who cultivated a biblical piety of a practical rather than speculative nature, with stress upon the inner life and the practice of virtues. They supported themselves by copying manuscripts and teaching. One of their most famous pupils was the humanist Erasmus. Many have seen in them harbingers of the Reformation; but the Brethren had little interest in the problems of the institutional Church. Their spirituality, known as the "New Devotion" (*Devotio moderna*), has influenced both Catholic and Protestant traditions of prayer and meditation.

Rite I   Holy Father, who hast nourished and strengthened thy Church by the inspired writings of thy servant Thomas à Kempis: Grant that we may learn from him to know what is necessary to be known, to love what is to be loved, to praise what highly pleases thee, and always to seek to know and follow thy will; through Jesus Christ our Lord, who liveth and reigneth with thee and the Holy Spirit, one God, for ever and ever. Amen.

Rite II   Holy Father, you have nourished and strengthened your Church by the inspired writings of your servant Thomas à Kempis: Grant that we may learn from him to know what is necessary to be known, to love what is to be loved, to praise what highly pleases you, and always to seek to know and follow your will; through Jesus Christ our Lord, who lives and reigns with you and the Holy Spirit, one God, for ever and ever. Amen.

For Liturgical Celebration: [Common of a Theologian and Teacher, A17] [Common of a Pastor, A14] [Of the Incarnation, A39]

July 26

Joachim and Anne
Parents of the Blessed Virgin Mary

The gospels tell us little about the home of our Lord's mother. She is thought to have been of Davidic descent and to have been brought up in a devout Jewish family that cherished the hope of Israel for the coming kingdom of God, in remembrance of the promise to Abraham and the forefathers.

In the second century, a devout Christian sought to supply a fuller account of Mary's birth and family, to satisfy the interest and curiosity of believers. An apocryphal gospel, known as the *Protevangelium of James* or *The Nativity of Mary*, appeared. It included legendary stories of Mary's parents Joachim and Anne. These stories were built out of Old Testament narratives of the births of Isaac and of Samuel (whose mother's name, Hannah, is the original form of Anne), and from traditions of the birth of John the Baptist. In these stories, Joachim and Anne—the childless, elderly couple who grieved that they would have no posterity—were rewarded with the birth of a girl, whom they dedicated in infancy to the service of God under the tutelage of the temple priests.

In 550, the Emperor Justinian I erected in Constantinople the first church to Saint Anne. The Eastern Churches observe her festival on July 25. Not until the twelfth century did her feast become known in the West. Pope Urban VI fixed her day, in 1378, to follow the feast of Saint James. Joachim has had several dates assigned to his memory; but the new Roman Calendar of 1969 joins his festival to that of Anne on this day.

Rite I   Almighty God, heavenly Father, we remember in thanksgiving this day the parents of the Blessed Virgin Mary; and we pray that we all may be made one in the heavenly family of thy Son Jesus Christ our Lord; who with thee and the Holy Spirit liveth and reigneth, one God, for ever and ever. Amen.

Rite II   Almighty God, heavenly Father, we remember in thanksgiving this day the parents of the Blessed Virgin Mary; and we pray that we all may be made one in the heavenly family of your Son Jesus Christ our Lord; who with you and the Holy Spirit lives and reigns, one God, for ever and ever. Amen.

For Liturgical Celebration: [Common of a Saint, A23] [Common of the Blessed Virgin Mary, Godbearer, A29]

July 26

Charles Raymond Barnes
1938

Charles Raymond Barnes was an Episcopal priest and martyr, slain for exposing atrocities in the Dominican Reublic under the rule of Rafael Trujillo.

Barnes was born in 1892 and studied at The University of the South, Sewanne, Tennessee, and at Columbia University and General Theological Seminary in New York. After ordination, he served parishes in Harrisburg, Pennsylvania, and in British Honduras, now Belize. In 1936, Barnes travelled to the Dominican Republic to serve as the Vicar of Epiphany Church in the capitol, Santo Domingo.

Economic conditions were poor across the island of Hispaniola, and many Haitians had come to the Dominican Republic to work in the fields; after harsh deportation measures failed to change the situation, the dictator Trujillo ordered a massacre of Haitian immigrants. Barnes learned of the atrocities being committed and secretly wrote articles about the events, hoping to bring international attention to bear on the situation.

After a friend was found with one of the articles in his possession while leaving the country, three plainclothes policemen visited the rectory where Barnes lived on July 26, 1938, and murdered him. He was buried in the chancel of Epiphany Church, now the Episcopal Cathedral of the Epiphany, and is considered the Martyr of the Dominican Episcopal Church.

Rite I　Grant, we beseech thee, merciful God, that thy Church, standing firm in the witness of thy Son and following the good example of thy servant Charles Barnes, may ever speak boldly against evil and confess the truth before the rulers of this world; through thy Son Jesus Christ, who with thee and the Holy Spirit, liveth and reigneth, one God, now and for ever. Amen.

Rite II　Grant, we pray, merciful God, that your Church, standing firm in the witness of your Son and following the good example of your servant Charles Barnes, may ever speak boldly against evil and confess the truth before the rulers of this world; through your Son Jesus Christ, who with you and the Holy Spirit, lives and reigns, one God, now and for ever. Amen.

For Liturgical Celebration: [Common of a Martyr, A7] [Common of a Pastor, A14] [Of the Holy Cross, A41]

July 27

William Reed Huntington
Priest, 1909

"First presbyter of the Church," was the well-deserved, if unofficial, title of the sixth rector of Grace Church, New York City. Huntington provided a leadership characterized by breadth, generosity, scholarship, and boldness. He was the acknowledged leader in the House of Deputies of The Episcopal Church's General Convention during a period of intense stress and conflict within the Church. His reconciling spirit helped preserve the unity of The Episcopal Church in the painful days after the beginning of the schism, led by the Assistant Bishop of Kentucky, which resulted in the formation of the Reformed Episcopal Church.

In the House of Deputies, of which he was a member from 1871 until 1907, Huntington showed active and pioneering vision in making daring proposals. As early as 1871, his motion to revive the primitive order of "deaconesses" began a long struggle, which culminated in 1889 in canonical authorization for that order. Huntington's parish immediately provided facilities for this new ministry, and Huntington House became a training center for deaconesses and other women workers in the Church.

Christian unity was Huntington's great passion throughout his ministry. In his book, *The Church Idea* (1870), he attempted to articulate the essentials of Christian unity. The grounds he proposed as a basis for unity were presented to, and accepted by, the House of Bishops in Chicago in 1886, and, with some slight modification, were adopted by the Lambeth Conference in 1888. The "Chicago-Lambeth Quadrilateral" has become a historic landmark for the Anglican Communion. It is included on pages 876–878 of the Book of Common Prayer, among the Historical Documents of the Church.

In addition to his roles as ecumenist and statesman, Huntington is significant as a liturgical scholar. It was his bold proposal to revise the Prayer Book that led to the revision of 1892, providing a hitherto unknown flexibility and significant enrichment. His Collect for

Monday in Holy Week, now used also for Fridays at Morning Prayer, is itself an example of skillful revision. In it he takes two striking clauses from the exhortation to the sick in the 1662 Prayer Book, and uses them as part of a prayer for grace to follow the Lord in his sufferings.

Rite I O Lord our God, we thank thee for instilling in the heart of thy servant William Reed Huntington a fervent love for thy Church and its mission in the world; and we pray that, with unflagging faith in thy promises, we may make known to all people thy blessed gift of eternal life; through Jesus Christ our Lord, who liveth and reigneth with thee and the Holy Spirit, one God, for ever and ever. Amen.

Rite II O Lord our God, we thank you for instilling in the heart of your servant William Reed Huntington a fervent love for your Church and its mission in the world; and we pray that, with unflagging faith in your promises, we may make known to all people your blessed gift of eternal life; through Jesus Christ our Lord, who lives and reigns with you and the Holy Spirit, one God, for ever and ever. Amen.

For Liturgical Celebration: [Common of a Monastic or Professed Religious, A20] [Common of a Pastor, A14] [For the Ministry III, A51]

July 28

Johann Sebastian Bach, *1750,*
George Frederick Handel, *1759,*
and Henry Purcell, *1695*
Composers

Johann Sebastian Bach was born in Eisenach, Germany, in 1685, into a family of musicians. As a youngster, he studied violin and organ and served as a choirboy at the parish church. By early adulthood, Bach had already achieved an enviable reputation as a composer and performer.

His assignments as a church musician began in 1707 and, a year later, he became the organist and chamber musician for the court of the Duke of Weimar. In 1723, Bach was appointed cantor of the St. Thomas School in Leipzig and parish musician at both St. Thomas and St. Nicholas churches, where he remained until his death in 1750. A man of deep Lutheran faith, Bach's music was an expression of his religious convictions.

George Frederick Handel was also born in 1685, in Halle, Germany. After studying law, he became organist at the Reformed Cathedral in Halle in 1702, and, in 1703, he went to Hamburg to study and compose opera. His interest in opera led him to Italy and then on to England, where he became a citizen in 1726.

Once in England, Handel supported himself with court appointments and private patronage. His energies were devoted to producing Italian operas and English oratorios, large choral works based upon religious themes. Handel's most popular work, *Messiah*, was first performed in Dublin in 1741, and is notable for its powerful musical interpretation of texts from the Holy Scriptures.

A man of great charity and generosity, Handel died in London in 1759 and was buried in the Poets' Corner of Westminster Abbey.

Henry Purcell was born in London in 1659 and became one of the greatest English composers, flourishing in the period that followed the Restoration of the monarchy after the Puritan Commonwealth period.

Purcell spent much of his short life in the service of the Chapels Royal as a singer, composer, and organist. With considerable gifts as a composer, he wrote extensively in a variety of genres for the Church and for popular entertainment. He died in 1695 and is buried adjacent to the organ near the north aisle of Westminster Abbey.

Rite I Almighty God, beautiful in majesty and majestic in holiness, thou gavest to thy musicians Johann Sebastian Bach, George Frederick Handel, and Henry Purcell grace to show forth thy glory in their music: may we also be moved to sound out thy praises as a foretaste of thy eternal glory; through Jesus Christ our Savior, who liveth and reigneth with thee and the Holy Spirit, one God, for ever and ever. Amen.

Rite II Almighty God, beautiful in majesty and majestic in holiness, you gave to your musicians Johann Sebastian Bach, George Frederick Handel, and Henry Purcell grace to show forth your glory in their music: may we be also moved to sound out your praises as a foretaste of your eternal glory; through Jesus Christ our Savior, who lives and reigns with you and the Holy Spirit, one God, for ever and ever. Amen.

For Liturgical Celebration: [Common of an Artist, Writer, or Composer, A27]

July 29

Mary, Martha, and Lazarus of Bethany

Mary, Martha, and Lazarus of Bethany are described in the Gospels According to Luke and John as close and much-loved friends of Jesus. Luke records the well-known story of their hospitality, which made Martha a symbol of the active life and Mary of the contemplative, though some commentators would take the words of Jesus to be a defense of that which Mary does best, and a commendation of Martha for what she does best—neither vocation giving grounds for despising the other.

Jesus raised Lazarus from the dead which, in John's gospel, is a powerful anticipation of resurrection and sign of eternal life for those who claim by faith the resurrection of Jesus. The story of the raising of Lazarus also sheds additional light on Martha. Jesus delays his visit to their home and arrives only after Lazarus is dead. Martha comes out to meet Jesus on the road, and while somewhat terse at first, she is still confident of his power to heal and restore. The exchange between them evokes Martha's deep faith and acknowledgment of Jesus as the Messiah.

John also records the supper at Bethany at which Mary anointed Jesus' feet with fragrant ointment and wiped them with her hair. This tender gesture of love evoked criticism from the disciples. Jesus interpreted the gift as a preparation for his death and burial.

The devotion and friendship of Mary, Martha, and Lazarus have been an example of fidelity and service to the Lord. Their hospitality and kindness, and Jesus' enjoyment of their company, show us the beauty of human friendship and love at its best. And the raising of Lazarus by Jesus is a sign of hope and promise for all who are in Christ.

Rite I Generous God, whose Son Jesus Christ enjoyed the friendship and hospitality of Mary, Martha, and Lazarus of Bethany: Open our hearts to love thee, our ears to hear thee, and our hands to welcome and serve thee in others, through Jesus Christ, our risen Lord; who with thee and the Holy Spirit liveth and reigneth, one God, for ever and ever. Amen.

Rite II Generous God, whose Son Jesus Christ enjoyed the friendship and hospitality of Mary, Martha, and Lazarus of Bethany: Open our hearts to love you, our ears to hear you, and our hands to welcome and serve you in others, through Jesus Christ, our risen Lord; who with you and the Holy Spirit lives and reigns, one God, for ever and ever. Amen.

For Liturgical Celebration: [Common of a Saint, A23] [For all Baptized Christians, A42] [For Vocation in Daily Work, A61]

July 29

First Ordination of Women to the Priesthood in The Episcopal Church
1974

On July 29, 1974, the feast of Martha and Mary of Bethany, eleven women deacons were ordained to the priesthood at the Church of the Advocate, in Philadelphia, Pennsylvania. "We are certain that the Church needs women in priesthood to be true to the gospel understanding of human unity in Christ," explained the eleven ordinands in a public statement.

One year earlier, the General Convention of The Episcopal Church had defeated a resolution to amend the canons on ordination to state that they "shall be equally applicable to men and women." A similar resolution in 1970 had also been narrowly defeated. After the 1973 convention, a group began exploring the possibility of ordaining women without General Convention action.

After months of planning, Merrill Bittner, Alla Bozarth-Campbell, Allison Cheek, Emily Hewitt, Carter Heyward, Suzanne Hiatt, Marie Moorefield, Jeannette Piccard, Betty Bone Schiess, Katrina Welles Swanson, and Nancy Hatch Wittig were ordained by three retired or resigned bishops—Daniel Corrigan, Robert DeWitt, and Edward Welles—in the presence of one active bishop, Antonio Ramos of Costa Rica, and a congregation of about 2000.

Following the ordination, a special session of the House of Bishops, convened on August 14, 1974, determined that the ordinations were not only canonically irregular but also invalid. At their regularly scheduled meeting in October 1974, the bishops affirmed the principle of ordaining women but condemned the bishops who had acted without the church's authorization.

A year later, on September 7, 1975, E. Lee McGee, Alison Palmer, Elizabeth Rosenberg, and Diane Tickell were ordained to the priesthood by retired Bishop George Barrett at the Church of St.

Stephen and the Incarnation in Washington, DC. Two weeks later, the House of Bishops decried this action as well.

On September 16, 1976, the General Convention voted to amend the canons to stipulate that both women and men are eligible for ordination. The House of Bishops determined that each woman ordained before 1977 could function as a priest after a "completion of the ritual acts" performed in Philadelphia or Washington.

Rite I O God, who didst pour thy Spirit from on high to bless and summon these women, who heard the strength of thy call: We beseech thee to equip, guide, and inspire us with wisdom, boldness, and faith to put our trust in thee always, hear thee preach new life to thy Church and stretch out our hands to serve thee, as thou didst create and redeem us in the name of Jesus Christ, who liveth with thee and the Holy Spirit, one God everlasting. Amen.

Rite II O God, you poured your Spirit from on high to bless and summon these women, who heard the strength of your call: Equip, guide, and inspire us with wisdom, boldness, and faith to trust you in all circumstances, hear you preach new life to your Church, and stretch out our hands to serve you, as you created us and redeemed us in the name of Jesus Christ, who lives with you and the Holy Spirit, one God everlasting. Amen.

For Liturgical Celebration: [Common of a Pastor, A14] [Common of a Prophetic Witness, A31] [For the Ministry II, A50]

July 30

William Wilberforce, *1833*, *and* Anthony Ashley-Cooper, Lord Shaftesbury, *1885*
Prophetic Witnesses

William Wilberforce was born into an affluent Yorkshire family in 1759 and received his education at Cambridge. In 1780, he was elected to the House of Commons, serving until 1825. Drawn to the evangelical expression of the Church from 1784, his colleagues convinced him not to abandon his political activism in favor of his newfound piety, but, as a consequence, he refused appointment to high office or to a peerage.

Wilberforce passionately promoted overseas missions, popular education, and the reformation of public manners and morals. He supported parliamentary reform and emancipation for Roman Catholics. Above all, he is remembered for his persistent, uncompromising, and single-minded crusade for the abolition of slavery and the slave trade, for which he received the blessing of John Wesley.

Wilberforce's eloquence as a speaker, his charm in personal address, and his profound religious spirit made him a formidable power for good; and his countrymen came to recognize in him a man of heroic greatness. Wilberforce died in London on July 29, 1833, and was buried in Westminster Abbey.

Anthony Ashley-Cooper was born in 1801, son of the Sixth Earl of Shaftesbury. Given the courtesy title of "Lord Ashley," he was educated at Harrow and Oxford, and became a Member of Parliament at the age of 25, representing the pocket borough of Woodstock that was controlled by the Shaftesbury family.

Inspired by his evangelical convictions, he soon took up the challenge of social reform, with particular concern for the just treatment of factory workers, particularly children. Lord Ashley led the charge in Parliament to limit workers' hours and improve work and safety conditions. He also successfully introduced legislation that regulated the working conditions of women and children in the mines, and restricted the abuse of little boys as chimney sweeps.

Lord Ashley devoted his parliamentary career to issues of injustice at all levels of English society, with particular concern regarding the oppression of women and children. He was an outspoken critic of slavery.

For many years, Lord Ashley was president of the British and Foreign Bible Society. Like Wilberforce, he was a man of prayer and deep faith, and his diaries are filled with profound spiritual reflections. Lord Ashley died on October 1, 1885.

Rite I   Let thy continual mercy, O Lord, kindle in thy Church the never-failing gift of love, that we, following the examples of thy servants William Wilberforce and Anthony Ashley-Cooper, may have grace to defend the poor and maintain the cause of those who have no helper; for the sake of him who didst give his life for us, thy Son, our Savior Jesus Christ, who liveth and reigneth with thee and the Holy Spirit, one God, now and for ever. Amen.

Rite II   Let your continual mercy, O Lord, kindle in your Church the never-failing gift of love, that we, following the examples of your servants William Wilberforce and Anthony Ashley-Cooper, may have grace to defend the poor and maintain the cause of those who have no helper; for the sake of him who gave his life for us, your Son, our Savior Jesus Christ, who lives and reigns with you and the Holy Spirit, one God, now and for ever. Amen.

For Liturgical Celebration: [Common of a Prophetic Witness, A31] [For Social Justice, A58]

July 31

Ignatius of Loyola
Priest and Monastic, 1556

Ignatius was born into a noble Basque family in 1491. In his autobiography, he tells us, "Up to his twenty-sixth year, he was a man given over to the vanities of the world and took special delight in the exercise of arms with a great and vain desire of winning glory." An act of reckless heroism at the Battle of Pamplona in 1521 led to his being seriously wounded. During his convalescence at Loyola, Ignatius experienced a profound spiritual awakening. Following his recovery and an arduous period of retreat, a call to be Christ's knight in the service of God's kingdom was deepened and confirmed.

Ignatius began to share the fruits of his experience with others, making use of a notebook which eventually became the text of the *Spiritual Exercises*. Since his time, many have found the *Exercises* to be a way of encountering Christ as intimate companion and responding to Christ's call: "Whoever wishes to come with me must labor with me."

The fact that Ignatius was an unschooled layman made him suspect in the eyes of church authorities and led him, at the age of 37, to study theology at the University of Paris in preparation for the priesthood. While there, Ignatius gave the *Exercises* to several of his fellow students; and in 1534, together with six companions, he took vows to live lives of strict poverty and to serve the needs of the poor. Thus, what later came to be known as the Society of Jesus was born.

In 1540, the Society was formally recognized, and Ignatius became its first Superior General. According to his journals and many of his letters, a profound sense of sharing God's work in union with Christ made the season of intense activity which followed a time of great blessing and consolation.

Ignatius died on July 31, 1556, in the simple room which served both as his bedroom and chapel, having sought to find God in all things and to do all things for God's greater glory. His life and teaching, as Evelyn Underhill and others have acknowledged, represents the best of the Counter-Reformation.

Rite I   Almighty God, from whom all good things come: Thou didst call Ignatius of Loyola to the service of thy Divine Majesty and to find thee in all things. Inspired by his example and strengthened by his companionship, may we labor without counting the cost and seek no reward other than knowing that we do thy will; through Jesus Christ our Savior, who liveth and reigneth with thee and the Holy Spirit, one God, now and for ever. Amen.

Rite II Almighty God, from whom all good things come: You called Ignatius of Loyola to the service of your Divine Majesty and to find you in all things. Inspired by his example and strengthened by his companionship, may we labor without counting the cost and seek no reward other than knowing that we do your will; through Jesus Christ our Savior, who lives and reigns with you and the Holy Spirit, one God, now and for ever. Amen.

For Liturgical Celebration: [Common of a Monastic or Professed Religious, A20] [Of the Holy Spirit, A38]

AUGUST

1 Joseph of Arimathea
2 Samuel Ferguson, Missionary Bishop for West Africa, 1916
3 George Freeman Bragg, Jr., Priest, 1940
3 William Edward Burghardt Du Bois, Sociologist, 1963
4
5 Albrecht Dürer, 1528, Matthias Grünewald, 1529, and Lucas Cranach the Elder, 1553, Artists
6
7 John Mason Neale, Priest, 1866
7 Catherine Winkworth, Poet, 1878
8 Dominic, Priest and Friar, 1221
9 Herman of Alaska, Missionary to the Aleut, 1837
10 Laurence, Deacon, and Martyr at Rome, 258
11 Clare, Abbess at Assisi, 1253
12 Florence Nightingale, Nurse, Social Reformer, 1910
13 Jeremy Taylor, Bishop of Down, Connor, and Dromore, 1667
14 Jonathan Myrick Daniels, Seminarian and Martyr, 1965
15
16
17 Samuel Johnson, 1772, Timothy Cutler, 1765, and Thomas Bradbury Chandler, 1790, Priests
17 The Baptisms of Manteo, and Virginia Dare, 1587
18 William Porcher DuBose, Priest, 1918
18 Artemisia Bowden, 1969
19
20 Bernard, Abbot of Clairvaux, 1153
21
22

23　Martin de Porres, 1639, Rosa de Lima, 1617, and Toribio de Mogrovejo, 1606, Witnesses to the Faith in South America

24

25　Louis, King of France, 1270

26

27　Thomas Gallaudet, 1902, with Henry Winter Syle, 1890

28　Augustine, Bishop of Hippo, and Theologian, 430

28　Moses the Black, Desert Father and Martyr, c. 400

29　John Bunyan, Writer, 1688

30　Charles Chapman Grafton, Bishop of Fond du Lac, and Ecumenist, 1912

31　Aidan, 651, and Cuthbert, 687, Bishops of Lindisfarne

August 1

Joseph of Arimathea

Joseph of Arimathaea was a secret disciple of our Lord whose intervention with Pilate ensured a burial for Jesus' crucified body. After the Crucifixion, when many of Jesus' disciples went into hiding for fear of the authorities, Joseph courageously came forward to ask Pilate's permission to remove Jesus' body from the cross in accordance with pious Jewish practice, namely, to provide the deceased with a timely and proper burial. Moreover, Joseph freely offered his own newly dug tomb for Jesus, preventing further desecration by humans or animals.

Though we know nothing of his further role in the early Christian movement, legends developed in later centuries about Joseph's possible subsequent leadership. However, Joseph's remembrance does not depend upon such legends; what is known of Joseph with certainty comes from the gospel narratives of Jesus' burial, attesting to his devotion, his generous compassion, and his brave willingness to take action on behalf of another when such action mattered.

Rite I Merciful God, whose servant Joseph of Arimathea with reverence and godly fear prepared the body of our Lord and Savior for burial and laid it in his own tomb: Grant to us, thy faithful people, grace and courage to love and serve Jesus with sincere devotion all the days of our life; through Jesus Christ our Lord, who liveth and reigneth with thee and the Holy Spirit, one God, for ever and ever. Amen.

Rite II Merciful God, whose servant Joseph of Arimathea with reverence and godly fear prepared the body of our Lord and Savior for burial and laid it in his own tomb: Grant to us, your faithful people, grace and courage to love and serve Jesus with sincere devotion all the days of our life; through Jesus Christ our Lord, who lives and reigns with you and the Holy Spirit, one God, for ever and ever. Amen.

For Liturgical Celebration: [Common of a Saint, A23] [For all Baptized Christians, A42]

August 2

Samuel Ferguson
Missionary Bishop for West Africa, 1916

Samuel David Ferguson was the first African American bishop in The Episcopal Church accorded the full honors due his position. While there had been other African American bishops before him, Bishop Ferguson was the first to be seated in the House of Bishops, and he took his role in the House with utmost sincerity and integrity, as an example to those around him. From celebrating the opening Eucharist of the 1910 General Convention to attending society events in the South, Bishop Ferguson modelled a dignity and strength that communicated his equal stature as an Episcopal bishop despite the discrimination he faced.

Ferguson was born in Charleston, South Carolina, on January 1, 1842, but grew up in Liberia, West Africa, having moved there with his family at the age of six. He attended mission schools that were sponsored by The Episcopal Church and eventually became a teacher.

Ferguson was ordained a deacon in 1865 and a priest in 1867, serving first as curate and then as rector of St. Mark's Church, Harper, Liberia. Called to be the fourth bishop of Cape Palmas (later the Diocese of Liberia) in 1885, his ordination to the episcopate took place at Grace Church in New York City. He was the first American-born black to become Bishop of Liberia.

Consistent with his first vocation as a teacher, Ferguson emphasized the importance of education throughout his ministry. He founded schools throughout Liberia, assisted financially by the Women's Auxiliary [later to be the United Thank Offering (UTO) of The Episcopal Church Women], and his passion for education influenced other parts of West Africa.

With the generous support of Robert Fulton Cutting, a wealthy New York financier, who served for a time as the treasurer of the Domestic and Foreign Missionary Society, Bishop Ferguson founded Cuttington College in 1889, where, in addition to basic studies, theological, agricultural, and industrial education were emphasized. Ferguson believed that establishing a strong spiritual and educational foundation was the best way for Liberia's young people to transform society. Although interrupted during the Liberian civil wars of 1989-1996 and 1999-2003, the college, now Cuttington University, resumed its mission to serve the people of Liberia in 2004, thus fulfilling Bishop Ferguson's vision.

Bishop Ferguson remained in Liberia for the rest of his life. He died in Monrovia on August 2, 1916.

Rite I   Almighty God, who didst raise up thy servant Samuel Ferguson and inspire in him a missionary vision of thy Church in education and ministry: Stir up in us through his example a zeal for a Church, alive with thy Holy Word, reaching forth in love and service to all; through Jesus Christ our Lord, who liveth and reigneth with thee and the Holy Spirit, one God, now and for ever. Amen.

Rite II   Almighty God, who raised up your servant Samuel Ferguson and inspired in him a missionary vision of your Church in education and ministry: Stir up in us through his example a zeal for a Church, alive with your Holy Word, reaching forth in love and service to all; through Jesus Christ our Lord, who lives and reigns with you and the Holy Spirit, one God, now and for ever. Amen.

For Liturgical Celebration: [Common of a Missionary, A11] [Common of a Pastor, A14] [For the Ministry II, A50] [For the Mission of the Church, A52] [For Education, A60]

August 3

George Freeman Bragg, Jr.
Priest, 1940

George Freeman Bragg served for 35 years as the secretary of the Conference for Church Workers Among the Colored People and authored important studies, such as *A History of the Afro-American Group of The Episcopal Church* and *Richard Allen and Absalom Jones,* documenting the early history of African Americans in The Episcopal Church.

Bragg was born to slaves of an Episcopal family in Warrenton, North Carolina, in 1863. As a young man he campaigned for the Readjuster Party in Virginia, which advocated for voting rights and state supported higher education for African Americans. He was the editor of the influential black weekly paper *The Lancet*, which he renamed the *Afro-American Churchman* upon his entrance into divinity school in 1885. Through this paper, Bragg called attention to the fact that African Americans were treated as recipients of mission work but were not supported in raising up self-sustaining institutions that would have fostered their presence in the Church.

Ordained a deacon in 1887 in Norfolk, Virginia, Bragg challenged the diocese's policy of requiring black men to remain in deacon's orders for five or more years, much longer than their white counterparts, and in 1888 he was ordained a priest. He served as the rector of St. James' First African Church in Baltimore for 49 years, from 1891 until his death in 1940. He helped establish the Maryland Home for Friendless Colored Children, and did not cease in his advocacy for black Episcopalians and their full inclusion in the larger life of the church, vehemently challenging the exclusion of African Americans from the church's society for mission work. He was instrumental in fostering over twenty priestly vocations in an environment in which black Episcopalians were often left to fend for themselves without the support and resources of the larger Church.

Rite I   O God, whose mighty hand freed thy servant George Freeman Bragg from bondage and blessed him with perseverance and courage: Deliver thy Church from its ignorance and injustice, that, through his example and prayers, all the baptized may share in the work of ministry and, at the last, attain to the perfect freedom of thy Son, our Lord Jesus Christ; who liveth and reigneth with thee and the Holy Spirit, one God, now and for ever. Amen.

Rite II   O God, whose mighty hand freed your servant George Freeman Bragg from bondage and blessed him with perseverance and courage: Deliver your Church from its ignorance and injustice, that, through his example and prayers, all the baptized may share in the work of ministry and, at the last, attain to the perfect freedom of your Son, our Lord Jesus Christ; who lives and reigns with you and the Holy Spirit, one God, now and for ever. Amen.

For Liturgical Celebration: [Common of a Pastor, A14] [Common of a Prophetic Witness, A31] [For the Ministry I, A49]

August 3

William Edward Burghardt Du Bois
Sociologist, 1963

William Edward Burghardt Du Bois was born on February 23, 1868, in Great Barrington, Massachusetts. Du Bois is remembered for his powerful advocacy of the civil rights of African Americans and for his writings on their spiritual life.

Raised as a Congregationalist, Du Bois maintained great affection for The Episcopal Church of his grandparents and, in the 1950s, he attended Holy Trinity Episcopal Church in Brooklyn, New York. Throughout his career, Du Bois invoked the faith of African Americans and the centrality of the Church in their communities as key to overcoming institutionalized racism in the United States. With the publication of *The Souls of Black Folks* in 1903, many African Americans heralded him as a contemporary prophet. In this book, Du Bois dismantled the prevailing cultural and religious assumptions of white Americans that African Americans were spiritually and morally inferior beings. Anticipating black liberation theology, Du Bois articulated an Afrocentric religious perspective in which African Americans were the bearers of spiritual insight from which white Americans must learn. Alongside the Bible, *The Souls of Black Folk* became a touchstone for African American identity in the twentieth century.

In 1906, he worked with others toward "organized determination and aggressive action on the part of men who believe in Negro freedom and growth." The result was the so-called "Niagara Movement" (named for the group's first meeting site, which was shifted to Canada when they were prevented from meeting in the U.S.), the objectives of which were to advocate for civil justice and oppose discrimination. In 1909, most of the group members merged with white supporters, and the National Association for the Advancement of Colored People was formed.

Du Bois had deeply held religious convictions grounded in the liberal Christianity of his era, but he consistently criticized institutional churches, black and white alike, for overweening concern on external displays of religiosity and materialism. In his later years, Du Bois was a Communist and remained a reluctant defender of Joseph Stalin when most on the American Left had denounced him. Yet during these very same years Du Bois maintained that Christianity's vision of justice and peace represented the highest ethical standards for humanity.

A leading participant in the Pan-African movement, Du Bois renounced his American citizenship and moved to Ghana, where he died on August 27, 1963, on the eve of the March on Washington. Martin Luther King Jr. wrote of Du Bois, "His singular greatness lay in his quest for truth about his own people. There were very few scholars who concerned themselves with honest study of the black man, and he sought to fill the immense void."

Rite I   Gracious God, kindle in thy Church a zeal for justice and the dignity of all, that we, following the example of thy servant William Edward Burghardt Du Bois, may have the grace to defend all the oppressed and maintain the cause of those who have been silenced; through Jesus Christ our Lord, who liveth and reigneth with thee and the Holy Spirit, one God, now and for ever. Amen.

Rite II Gracious God, kindle in your Church a zeal for justice and the dignity of all, that we, following the example of your servant William Edward Burghardt Du Bois, may have the grace to defend all the oppressed and maintain the cause of those who have been silenced; through Jesus Christ our Lord, who lives and reigns with you and the Holy Spirit, one God, now and for ever. Amen.

For Liturgical Celebration: [Common of a Prophetic Witness, A31] [For all Baptized Christians, A42]

August 5

Albrecht Dürer, *1528,*
Matthias Grünewald, *1529,*
and Lucas Cranach the Elder, *1553*
Artists

In the turbulent sixteenth century, as the Renaissance and the Reformation changed the cultural, social, political, and religious face of northern Europe from medieval to modern, three artists stand as signs of those revolutions.

Albrecht Dürer was born in 1471 at Nuremberg and is generally regarded as the greatest German artist of the Renaissance. While he produced exquisite, life-like paintings, he is best known for his woodcuts and copperplate engravings. This art form enabled numbers of prints to be made of each work, which could then be sold to satisfy the rising middle class's new demand for affordable art. His production was a sign of the shift in early modern society, especially in Protestant areas, from the church to the home as the center of life and religion.

Little is known of the early life of Matthias Grünewald, the name given to this artist by his seventeenth-century biographer. Presumably born circa 1470, he is known to have been in Strasburg in 1479, already accomplished at portraits and woodcuts. He went to Basel in 1490, where Dürer was his pupil. Later, he moved to what is now Alsace, where he painted his famous Isenheim Altarpiece between 1512 and 1516. This piece was designed to go behind the chapel altar at the hospital in the monastery of the Order of St. Anthony. Grünewald was a deeply religious man who was particularly fascinated by the crucifixion as witnessed by the combination of raw physicality and mysticism that can be observed in the Isenheim Altarpiece.

Lucas Cranach the Elder was born in 1472 in south Germany. In his twenties he moved to Vienna, where he became known in humanist circles. He later moved to Wittenberg, where he became court painter to Frederick III, who was Martin Luther's protector. His work enjoyed great popularity in his day, but history best remembers him for his several portraits of Luther and for the exquisite woodcuts he provided for the first German New Testament in 1522.

Rite I   We give thanks to thee, O Lord, for the vision and skill of Albrecht Dürer, Matthias Grünewald, and Lucas Cranach the Elder, whose artistic depictions helped the peoples of their age understand the full suffering and glory of thine incarnate Son; and we pray that their work may strengthen our faith in Jesus Christ and the mystery of the Holy Trinity; who liveth and reigneth, one God, for ever and ever. Amen.

Rite II We give thanks to you, O Lord, for the vision and skill of Albrecht Dürer, Matthias Grünewald, and Lucas Cranach the Elder, whose artistic depictions helped the peoples of their age understand the full suffering and glory of your incarnate Son; and we pray that their work may strengthen our faith in Jesus Christ and the mystery of the Holy Trinity; for you live and reign, one God, for ever and ever. Amen.

For Liturgical Celebration: [Common of an Artist, Writer, or Composer, A27]

August 7

John Mason Neale
Priest, 1866

John Mason Neale was born in London in 1818, studied at Cambridge, where he also served as tutor and chaplain, and was ordained to the priesthood in 1842. Chronic ill health made parish ministry impracticable, but in 1846, he was made warden of Sackville College, a charitable residence for the poor, which position he held for the rest of his life. Both a scholar and a creative poet, his skills in composing original verse and translating Latin and Greek hymns into effective English lyrics were devoted to the Church and were but one expression of his active support to the Oxford Movement in its revival of medieval liturgical forms. With such familiar words as "Good Christian men, rejoice" (*The Hymnal 1982*, #107), "Come, ye faithful, raise the strain" (#199, 200), "All glory, laud, and honor" (#154, 155), "Sing, my tongue, the glorious battle" (#165, 166), and "Creator of the stars of night" (#60), he greatly enriched our hymnody.

Gentleness combined with firmness, good humor, modesty, patience, devotion, and "an unbounded charity," describe Neale's character. A prolific writer and compiler, his works include *Medieval Hymns and Sequences*, *Hymns of the Eastern Church*, *Liturgiology and Church History*, and a four-volume commentary on the Psalms. He established the Camden Society, later called the Ecclesiological Society, and consistent with Anglo-Catholic principles that wed liturgical piety with compassionate social action, he founded the Sisterhood of St. Margaret for the relief of suffering women and girls.

Neale faced active persecution for his liturgical and theological principles. He was forced to resign his first parish due to disagreements with his bishop. He was physically attacked several times including at a funeral of one of the Sisters. Mobs threatened both him and his family, believing him to be a secret agent of the Vatican attempting to destroy the Church of England from within.

Though his work was little appreciated in England, his contributions were recognized both in the United States and in Russia, where the Metropolitan presented him with a rare copy of the Old Believers' Liturgy. He died on the Feast of the Transfiguration in 1866, at the age of 46, leaving a lasting mark on our worship.

Rite I   Grant unto us, O God, that in all time of our testing we may know thy presence and obey thy will; that, following the example of thy servant John Mason Neale, we may with integrity and courage accomplish what thou givest us to do, and endure what thou givest us to bear; through Jesus Christ our Lord, who liveth and reigneth with thee and the Holy Spirit, one God, for ever and ever. Amen.

Rite II   Grant, O God, that in all time of our testing we may know your presence and obey your will; that, following the example of your servant John Mason Neale, we may with integrity and courage accomplish what you give us to do, and endure what you give us to bear; through Jesus Christ our Lord, who lives and reigns with you and the Holy Spirit, one God, for ever and ever. Amen.

For Liturgical Celebration: [Common of an Artist, Writer, or Composer, A27] [Common of a Pastor, A14] [Of the Holy Trinity, A37]

August 7

Catherine Winkworth
Poet, 1878

Catherine Winkworth is celebrated as the premier translator of German hymns and chorales into English.

Winkworth was born in London in 1827, but grew up in Manchester, where she spent most of her life. Her lifelong fascination with German hymns and chorales began during a yearlong visit to Dresden, Germany, in 1848. Her first set of translations, *Lyra Germanica*, 1855, contained 103 hymns, and a second series under the same title appeared in 1858, and contained 121 hymns. Her translations were immensely successful in expressing the theological richness and spirit of the German texts; *Lyra Germanica* went through numerous editions and reprints and remains today a monumental contribution to the history of hymnody. Among the most well known of Winkworth's translations are "Comfort, comfort ye my people" (*The Hymnal 1982*, #67), "Now thank we all our God" (#396; #397), "Praise to the Lord, the Almighty" (#390), and "Deck thyself, my soul, with gladness" (#339)

In some cases, Winkworth's sturdy translations had been wed with tunes that did not always capture the spirit of the original German chorale. To help rectify this, Winkworth published *The Chorale Book for England* in 1863 that matched her translations with their original tunes. In 1869, she published a commentary that provided biographies of the German hymn writers and other material to make the German hymn and chorale more accessible to the English singers of her masterful translations.

She is also remembered for her advocacy for women's rights and for her efforts to encourage university education for women. In support of her advocacy for women, Winkworth sought inspiration in German literature and made it available in English translation. Notable are her translations of the biographies of two founders of sisterhoods for the poor and the sick: *Life of Pastor Fliedner*, 1861, and *Life of Amelia Sieveking*, 1863.

Winkworth was traveling to an international conference on women's issues when she died of a heart attack on July 1, 1878. She was 51. She was buried at Monnetier, near Geneva. Her life and work has been honored with a monument in Bristol Cathedral.

Rite I Comfort thy people, O God of peace, and prepare a way for us in the desert, that, like thy poet and translator Catherine Winkworth, we may preserve the spiritual treasures of thy saints of former years and sing our thanks to thee with hearts and hands and voices, eternal triune God whom earth and heaven adore; for thou liveth and reigneth for ever and ever. Amen.

Rite II Comfort your people, O God of peace, and prepare a way for us in the desert, that, like your poet and translator Catherine Winkworth, we may preserve the spiritual treasures of your saints of former years and sing our thanks to you with hearts and hands and voices, eternal triune God whom earth and heaven adore; for you live and reign for ever and ever. Amen.

For Liturgical Celebration: [Common of an Artist, Writer, or Composer, A27] [Of the Holy Trinity, A37]

August 8

Dominic
Priest and Friar, 1221

Dominic was the founder of the Order of Preachers, commonly known as Dominicans. In England they were called Black Friars, because of the black mantle they wore over their white habits. Dominic was born circa 1170 in Spain.

Influenced by the contemporary search for a life of apostolic poverty, Dominic is reputed to have sold all his possessions to help the poor during a famine in 1191. Ordained in 1196, he soon became a canon and then sub-prior of the Cathedral of Osma, where a rule of strict discipline was established among the canons.

In 1203 he began a number of preaching tours in Languedoc, a region in Southern France, against the Albigensian heretics, who held Manichaean, dualistic views. He kept himself aloof, however, from the repressive crusade which was instigated against them. In 1214, his plan to found a special preaching order for the conversion of the Albigensians began to take shape, and, in the following year, he took his followers to Toulouse.

At the Fourth Lateran Council in October, 1215, Dominic sought confirmation of his order from Pope Innocent III. This was granted by Innocent's successor, Honorius III, in 1216 and 1217.

Over the next few years, Dominic traveled extensively, establishing friaries, organizing the order, and preaching, until his death on August 6, 1221. He is remembered as a man of austere poverty and heroic sanctity, always zealous to win souls by the preaching of pure doctrine.

The Dominican Constitutions, first formulated in 1216 and revised and codified by the Master-General of the Order, Raymond of Peñafort, in 1241, place a strong emphasis on learning, preaching, and teaching, and, partly through the influence of Francis of Assisi, on absolute poverty. The continuing Dominican apostolate embraces intellectual work and the arts of preaching, their major houses usually situated in university centers, to which they have contributed such notable teachers as Thomas Aquinas. Their Constitutions express the priority this way: "In the cells, moreover, they can write, read, pray, sleep, and even stay awake at night, if they desire, on account of study."

Rite I   Almighty God, whose servant Dominic grew in knowledge of thy truth and formed an order of preachers to proclaim the Good News of Christ: Give to all thy people a hunger for thy Word and an urgent longing to share the Gospel, that the whole world may come to know thee as thou art revealed in thy Son Jesus Christ; who liveth and reigneth with thee and the Holy Spirit, one God, for ever and ever. Amen.

Rite II Almighty God, whose servant Dominic grew in knowledge of your truth and formed an order of preachers to proclaim the Good News of Christ: Give to all your people a hunger for your Word and an urgent longing to share the Gospel, that the whole world may come to know you as you are revealed in your Son Jesus Christ; who lives and reigns with you and the Holy Spirit, one God, for ever and ever. Amen.

For Liturgical Celebration: [Common of a Monastic, 652 or Professed Religious] [For the Unity of the Church, A48] [For the Mission of the Church, A52]

August 9

Herman of Alaska
Missionary to the Aleut, 1837

Herman of Alaska, known in the Russian Orthodox Church as "St. Herman: Wonderworker of All America," was the first saint to be canonized by the Orthodox Church in America.

Herman was born in Russia, near Moscow, in 1756. His baptismal and family names are unknown. He is known by his monastic name. Naturally pious from an early age, Herman entered the Trinity-St. Sergius Hermitage near St. Petersburg at 16 and, drawn to the spiritual charism of Abbot Nasarios, eventually transferred to the Valaam Monastery. He was never ordained. For many years he secured permission to live as a hermit, attending the liturgies of the monastery only on holy days.

In 1793, with a small group of colleagues, Herman set out to do missionary work in Alaska. They settled on Spruce Island, near Kodiak, and named their community "New Valaam" in honor of their home monastery. Herman lived and worked in the area for the remainder of his life.

He advocated for and defended the native Aleut against sometimes-oppressive authorities, particular Russian and European colonists with commercial interests. He cared lovingly and sacrificially for all who came to him, counseling and teaching them, and tirelessly nursing the sick. He especially loved children, for whom he often baked biscuits and cookies.

Even though Herman had minimal education outside of the monastic life, he was regarded among the native Alaskans as a great and compelling teacher. Over time he also developed a reputation as a teacher and sage among the Russian and European settlers in the area. He so captivated his listeners that many would listen to him through the long hours of the night and not leave his company until morning. The people he served often referred to Herman as their North Star.

Herman died at Spruce Island on December 25, 1837, according to the Gregorian calendar then still in use in Alaska.

In the spring of 1969, the Synod of Bishops of the Orthodox Church in America proclaimed Herman a saint. He was glorified in a solemn liturgy on August 9, 1970, at Holy Resurrection Orthodox Cathedral on Kodiak Island, Alaska, with simultaneous rites taking place at other Orthodox centers.

Rite I   Holy God, we bless thy Name for Herman, joyful North Star of Christ's Church, who didst bring the Good News of Christ's love to thy people in Alaska; and we pray that, following his example and admonition, we may love thee, God, above all; through Jesus Christ, who with thee and the Holy Spirit liveth and reigneth, throughout all ages. Amen.

Rite II   Holy God, we bless your Name for Herman, joyful North Star of Christ's Church, who brought the Good News of Christ's love to your people in Alaska; and we pray that, following his example and admonition, we may love you, God, above all; through Jesus Christ, who with you and the Holy Spirit lives and reigns, throughout all ages. Amen.

For Liturgical Celebration: [Common of a Missionary, A11] [Common of a Monastic or Professed Religious, A20] [For the Mission of the Church, A52]

August 10

Laurence
Deacon, and Martyr at Rome, 258

Laurence the Deacon was martyred at Rome during a persecution initiated in 257 by the Emperor Valerian, aimed primarily at the clergy and the laity of the upper classes; all properties used by the Church were confiscated, and assemblies for Christian worship were forbidden. On August 4, 258, Pope Sixtus II and his seven deacons were apprehended in the Roman catacombs and summarily executed, except for the archdeacon, Laurence, who was martyred on the tenth. Though no authentic record of Laurence's ordeal has been preserved, tradition maintains that the prefect demanded information from him about the Church's treasures. Laurence, in reply, assembled the sick and poor to whom, as archdeacon, he had distributed the Church's relief funds, and presented them to the prefect, saying, "These are the treasures of the Church." Laurence is believed to have been roasted alive on a gridiron.

The Emperor Constantine erected a shrine and basilica over Laurence's tomb in a catacomb on the Via Tiburtina. The present Church of St. Laurence Outside the Walls, a beautiful double basilica (damaged in World War II), includes a choir and sanctuary erected by Pope Pelagius II (579–590) and a nave by Pope Honorius III (1216–1227).

Laurence is the subject of a small round glass medallion, probably dating from the fourth century, now in the Metropolitan Museum in New York. It bears the simple inscription, "Live with Christ and Laurence."

The Greek word from which we derive our English word "martyr" simply means "witness;" in the age of the persecutions, before Constantine recognized the Church early in the fourth century, a "martyr" came to be generally understood, as it is to this day, as one who had witnessed even to death. For Laurence, as for all the martyrs, to die for Christ was to live with Christ.

Rite I   Almighty God, by whose grace and power thy servant Laurence didst triumph over suffering and didst despise death: Grant, we pray, that we, steadfast in service to the poor and outcast, may share with him in the joys of thine everlasting kingdom; through Jesus Christ our Lord, who liveth and reigneth with thee and the Holy Spirit, one God, for ever and ever. Amen.

Rite II   Almighty God, by whose grace and power your servant Laurence triumphed over suffering and despised death: Grant, we pray, that we, steadfast in service to the poor and outcast, may share with him in the joys of your everlasting kingdom; through Jesus Christ our Lord, who lives and reigns with you and the Holy Spirit, one God, for ever and ever. Amen.

For Liturgical Celebration: [Common of a Martyr, A7] [For Social Service, A59] [Of the Holy Cross, A41]

August 11

Clare
Abbess at Assisi, 1253

In the latter part of the twelfth century, the Church had fallen on evil days and was weak and spiritually impoverished. It was then that Francis of Assisi renounced his wealth and established the mendicant order of Franciscans. At the first gathering of the order in 1212, Francis preached a sermon that was to make a radical change in the life of an eighteen-year-old young woman named Clare Offreduccio.

The daughter of a wealthy family and a noted beauty, Clare was inspired by Francis' words with the desire to serve God and to give her life to the following of Christ's teaching. She sought out Francis and begged that she might become a member of his order, placing her jewelry and rich outer garments on the altar as an offering. Francis could not refuse her pleas. He placed her temporarily in a nearby Benedictine convent.

When this action became known, friends and relatives tried to take Clare from her retreat. She was adamant. She would be the bride of Christ alone. She prevailed, and soon after was taken by Francis to a poor dwelling beside the Church of St. Damian at Assisi. Several other women joined her. She became Mother Superior of the order, which was called the "Poor Ladies of St. Damian," and, after her death, the "Poor Clares" in tribute to her.

The order's practices were austere. They embraced the Franciscan rule of absolute poverty. Their days were given over to begging and to works of mercy for the poor and the neglected. Clare herself was servant, not only to the poor, but to her nuns.

Clare governed the convent for forty years, caring for the sisters, ready to do whatever Francis directed. She said to him, "I am yours by having given my will to God." Her biographer says that she "radiated a spirit of fervor so strong that it kindled those who but heard her voice."

In 1253, her last illness began. Daily she weakened, and daily she was visited by devoted people, by priests, and even by the Pope. On her last day, as she saw many weeping by her bedside, she exhorted them to love "holy poverty" and to share their possessions. She was heard to say: "Go forth in peace, for you have followed the good road. Go forth without fear, for he that created you has sanctified you, has always protected you, and loves you as a mother. Blessed be God, for having created me."

Rite I   O God, whose blessed Son became poor that we, through his poverty, might be rich: Deliver us, we pray thee, from an inordinate love of this world, that, inspired by the devotion of thy servant Clare, we may serve thee with singleness of heart and attain to the riches of the age to come; through Jesus Christ our Lord, who liveth and reigneth with thee, in the unity of the Holy Spirit, one God, now and for ever. Amen.

Rite II   O God, whose blessed Son became poor that we, through his poverty, might be rich: Deliver us from an inordinate love of this world, that we, inspired by the devotion of your servant Clare, may serve you with singleness of heart and attain to the riches of the age to come; through Jesus Christ our Lord, who lives and reigns with you and the Holy Spirit, one God, for ever and ever. Amen.

For Liturgical Celebration: [Common of a Monastic or Professed Religious, A20] [Of the Incarnation, A39] [For the Ministry III, A51]

August 12

Florence Nightingale
Nurse, Social Reformer, 1910

Florence Nightingale was born to a wealthy English family in Florence, Italy, on May 12, 1820. She was trained as a nurse in a hospital run by a Lutheran order of Deaconesses at Kaiserwerth (1851) and in 1853 became superintendent of a hospital for invalid women in London. In response to God's call and animated by a spirit of service, in 1854 she volunteered for duty during the Crimean War and recruited 38 nurses to join her. With them she organized the first modern nursing service in the British field hospitals of Scutari and Balaclava.

Making late-night rounds to check on the welfare of her charges, a hand-held lantern to aid her, the wounded identified her as "The Lady with the Lamp." By imposing strict discipline and high standards of sanitation she radically reduced the drastic death toll and rampant infection then typical in field hospitals. She returned to England in 1856, and a fund of £ 50,000 was subscribed to enable her to form an institution for the training of nurses at St. Thomas's Hospital and at King's College Hospital. Her school at St. Thomas's Hospital became significant in helping to elevate nursing into a profession. She devoted many years to the question of army sanitary reform, to the improvement of nursing, and to public health in India. Her main work, *Notes on Nursing* (1859), went through many editions.

An Anglican, she remained committed to a personal mystical religion, which sustained her through many years of poor health until her death in 1910. Until the end of her life, although her illness prevented her from leaving her home, she continued in frequent spiritual conversation with many prominent church leaders of the day, including the local parish priest, who regularly brought Communion to her. By the time of her death on August 13, 1910, her accomplishments and legacy were widely recognized, and she is honored throughout the world as the founder of the modern profession of nursing.

Rite I O God, who didst give grace to thy servant Florence Nightingale to bear thy healing love into the shadow of death: Grant unto all who heal the same virtues of patience, mercy, and steadfast love, that thy saving health may be revealed to all; through Jesus Christ, who liveth and reigneth with thee and the Holy Spirit, one God, now and for ever. Amen.

Rite II O God, who gave grace to your servant Florence Nightingale to bear your healing love into the shadow of death: Grant to all who heal the same virtues of patience, mercy, and steadfast love, that your saving health may be revealed to all; through Jesus Christ, who lives and reigns with you and the Holy Spirit, one God, now and for ever. Amen.

For Liturgical Celebration: [Common of a Prophetic Witness, A31] [For the Sick, A57]

August 13

Jeremy Taylor
Bishop of Down, Connor, and Dromore, 1667

Jeremy Taylor, one of the most influential of the "Caroline Divines," was educated at Cambridge and, through the influence of William Laud, became a Fellow of All Souls at Oxford. He was still quite young when he became chaplain to Charles I and, later, during the Civil War, a chaplain in the Royalist army.

The successes of Cromwell's forces brought about Taylor's imprisonment and, after Cromwell's victory, Taylor spent several years in forced retirement as chaplain to the family of Lord Carberry in Wales. It was during this time that his most influential works were written, especially *Holy Living* and *Holy Dying* (1651).

Among his other works, *Liberty of Prophesying* proved to be a seminal work in encouraging the development of religious toleration in the seventeenth century. The principles set forth in that book rank with those of Milton's *Areopagitica* in its plea for freedom of thought.

Despite Taylor's unquestioned literary genius, he was, unfortunately, not asked to have a part in the Prayer Book revision of 1662. The first American Prayer Book, however, incorporated one of his prayers, part of which has been adapted to serve as the Collect of his commemoration; and another has been added in the present Prayer Book.

Taylor's theology has sometimes been criticized, most bitingly by Samuel Taylor Coleridge, who claimed that Taylor seems to "present our own holy life as the grounds of our religious hope, rather than as the fruit of that hope, whose ground is the mercies of Christ." No such complaint, however, was ever made about his prayers, which exemplify the best of Caroline divinity, blended with great literary genius.

In later life, Taylor and his family moved to the northeastern part of Ireland where, after the restoration of the monarchy, he became Bishop of Down and Connor. To this was later added the small adjacent diocese of Dromore. As Bishop, he labored tirelessly to rebuild churches, restore the use of the Prayer Book, and overcome continuing Puritan opposition. As Vice-chancellor of Trinity College, Dublin, he took a leading part in reviving the intellectual life of the Church of Ireland. He remained to the end a man of prayer and a pastor.

Rite I O God, whose days are without end, and whose mercies cannot be numbered: Make us, we beseech thee, like thy servant Jeremy Taylor, deeply sensible of the shortness and uncertainty of human life; and let thy Holy Spirit lead us in holiness and righteousness all our days, through Jesus Christ our Lord, who liveth and reigneth with thee and the Holy Spirit, one God, now and for ever. Amen.

Rite II O God, whose days are without end, and whose mercies cannot be numbered: Make us, like your servant Jeremy Taylor, deeply aware of the shortness and uncertainty of human life; and let your Holy Spirit lead us in holiness and righteousness all our days, through Jesus Christ our Lord, who lives and reigns with you and the Holy Spirit, one God, now and for ever. Amen.

For Liturgical Celebration: [Common of a Theologian and Teacher, A17] [Common of a Pastor, A14] [For the Ministry II, A50]

August 14

Jonathan Myrick Daniels
Seminarian and Martyr, 1965

Jonathan Myrick Daniels was born in Keene, New Hampshire, in 1939. He was shot and killed by an unemployed highway worker in Hayneville, Alabama, August 20, 1965.

Like many young adults, from high school in Keene to graduate school at Harvard, Jonathan wrestled with vocation. Attracted to medicine, ordained ministry, law, and writing, he found himself close to a loss of faith when his discernment was clarified by a profound conversion on Easter Day 1962 at the Church of the Advent in Boston. Jonathan then entered the Episcopal Theological School in Cambridge, Massachusetts.

In March 1965, the televised appeal of Martin Luther King, Jr. to come to Selma to secure for all citizens the right to vote touched Jonathan's passions for the well-being of others, the Christian witness of the Church, and political justice. His conviction was deepened at Evening Prayer during the singing of the Magnificat: "'He hath put down the mighty from their seat and hath exalted the humble and meek. He hath filled the hungry with good things.' I knew that I must go to Selma. The Virgin's song was to grow more and more dear to me in the weeks ahead."

In Selma he found himself in the midst of a time and place where the nation's racism and The Episcopal Church's share in that inheritance were exposed. Greatly moved by what he saw and experienced, he returned to seminary, asked leave to work in Selma while continuing his studies, and returned there under the sponsorship of the Episcopal Society for Cultural and Racial Unity.

After a brief return to Cambridge in May to complete exams, he returned to Alabama to resume his efforts assisting those engaged in the integration struggle. Jailed on August 14 for joining a picket line, Jonathan and his companions resolved to remain together until bail could be posted for all of them, as it was six days later. Released and aware that they were in danger, four of them walked to a small store. As sixteen-year-old Ruby Sales reached the top step of the entrance, a man with a shotgun appeared, cursing her. Jonathan pulled her to one side to shield her from the unexpected threats and was killed instantly by the 12-gauge blast.

Jonathan's letters and papers bear eloquent witness to the profound effect Selma had upon him. He writes, "The doctrine of the creeds, the enacted faith of the sacraments, were the essential preconditions of the experience itself. The faith with which I went to Selma has not changed: it has grown . . . I began to know in my bones and sinews that I had been truly baptized into the Lord's death and resurrection . . . with them, the black men and white men, with all life, in him whose Name is above all the names that the races and nations shout . . . We are indelibly and unspeakably one."

Rite I   O God of justice and compassion, who didst put down the proud and the mighty from their place, and dost lift up the poor and the afflicted: We give thee thanks for thy faithful witness Jonathan Myrick Daniels, who, in the midst of injustice and violence, risked and gave his life for another; and we pray that we, following his example, may make no peace with oppression; through Jesus Christ the just one, who with thee and the Holy Spirit liveth and reigneth, one God, for ever and ever. Amen.

Rite II O God of justice and compassion, you put down the proud and mighty from their place, and lift up the poor and the afflicted: We give you thanks for your faithful witness Jonathan Myrick Daniels, who, in the midst of injustice and violence, risked and gave his life for another; and we pray that we, following his example, may make no peace with oppression; through Jesus Christ the just one, who lives and reigns with you and the Holy Spirit, one God, for ever and ever. Amen.

For Liturgical Celebration: [Common of a Martyr, A7] [Common of a Prophetic Witness, A31] [Of the Holy Cross, A41]

AUGUST 14

August 17

Samuel Johnson, *1772,*
Timothy Cutler, *1765,*
and Thomas Bradbury Chandler, *1790*
Priests

Samuel Johnson, born in Connecticut in 1696, was ordained a Congregational minister in 1719. But ongoing study and his experience of ministry led to an appreciation of episcopal orders and apostolic succession, as well as the ordered liturgy of the Book of Common Prayer. Shortly after his ordination, he and sympathetic others met and discussed the Anglican alternative including Harvard graduate Timothy Cutler, then rector of Yale College. In September of 1722, Johnson, Cutler, and their friend Daniel Browne—the "Yale Apostates"—confronted the trustees of Yale College and announced their intention to seek ordination in the Church of England. In March 1723, they were ordained to the Anglican priesthood by the Bishop of Norwich.

Returning to New England as a missionary for the Society for the Propagation of the Gospel in Foreign Parts (SPG), Johnson became the rector of the first Anglican congregation in Connecticut, at Stratford, where he served until he became the first President of King's College (now Columbia University) in New York. Cutler, after doctoral studies at Oxford and Cambridge, served as rector of Christ Church, Boston, where he tirelessly advocated for the appointment of an Anglican bishop in the colonies until his death on August 17, 1765.

Johnson's pupil, Thomas Bradbury Chandler (April 26, 1726–June 17, 1790), also an ardent advocate for bishops in the colonies, continued the work. Chandler, the father-in-law of Bishop John Henry Hobart, served for 43 years as the rector of St. John's, Elizabethtown (now Elizabeth), New Jersey, and was himself appointed the first Anglican bishop in the Americas, in Nova Scotia, but was unable to accept the appointment due to illness.

Johnson, Cutler, and Chandler were notable exponents of Anglican theology and polity in the formative years of pre-Revolutionary

America, when the diverse "marketplace" of religion in the colonies was in its infancy, but growing robustly in a climate sympathetic to religious freedom. The experience, examples and advocacy of Johnson, Cutler, Chandler, and others like them contributed substantially to the continuation of Anglicanism in post-Revolutionary America, adapting Anglican thought and practice to a newly emerging United States.

Rite I God of a pilgrim people, who didst call Samuel Johnson, Timothy Cutler, and Thomas Chandler to leave their spiritual home and embrace the Anglican way: We give thee thanks for their devoted service in building up thy Church and shepherding thy flock in colonial times; and we pray that, like them, we may follow where thy Spirit leads and be ever eager to feed the hearts and minds of those entrusted to our care, in the Name of Jesus Christ; who liveth and reigneth with thee and the Holy Spirit, one God, now and for ever. Amen.

Rite II God of your pilgrim people, you called Samuel Johnson, Timothy Cutler, and Thomas Chandler to leave their spiritual home and embrace the Anglican way: We give you thanks for their devoted service in building up your Church and shepherding your flock in colonial times; and we pray that, like them, we may follow where your Spirit leads and be ever eager to feed the hearts and minds of those entrusted to our care, in the Name of Jesus Christ; who lives and reigns with you and the Holy Spirit, one God, now and for ever. Amen.

For Liturgical Celebration: [Common of a Pastor, A14] [For the Ministry I, A49]

August 17

Baptisms of Manteo, and Virginia Dare
1587

In the late sixteenth century, Sir Walter Raleigh established three colonies along the northeastern coast of what is now the state of North Carolina. In July 1587, the third and final settlement, consisting of 120 men, women, and children, under the leadership of John White, landed on Roanoke Island, near the present-day community of Nags Head.

With the colonists was Manteo, a Native American of the Algonquian nation and resident of Croatoan, who had traveled to London in an earlier expedition to become a liaison between the English and the Native Americans.

On August 13, 1587, Manteo was baptized, the first recorded baptism of the Church of England in the American colonies and the first recorded baptism of a Native American person in the Church of England. On August 18, Governor White's daughter Eleanor and her husband Ananias Dare celebrated the birth of their first child, Virginia. The first child born to English settlers on the North American continent, Virginia's baptism on August 20 was the second recorded baptism in the Church of England in North America.

Governor White returned to England in late August 1587 to obtain badly needed supplies. It was understood that if the colonists were forced to abandon the settlement in White's absence, they would carve the name of their destination on a tree. If their departure were due to attack, a Maltese cross would be carved beneath. Delayed by events beyond his control, White was unable to return to the colony for three years. It was not until August 18, 1590, that White finally arrived at the site of the village. White found the word "Croatoan," with no carved cross or other signs of distress, carved into a post of the fort. Little certainty surrounds the fate of the English settlers, who remain known to history as the "Lost Colony."

Rite I O God, thou hast created every human being in thine own image, and each one is precious in thy sight: Grant that, in remembering the baptisms of Manteo and Virginia Dare, we may grow in honoring thy gift of diversity in human life; become stronger in living out our baptismal vow to respect the dignity of every human being; and bring into the fellowship of the risen Christ those who come to him in faith, baptizing them in the name of the Father, and of the Son, and of the Holy Spirit. Amen.

Rite II O God, you have created every human being in your image, and each one is precious in your sight: Grant that, in remembering the baptisms of Manteo and Virginia Dare, we may grow in honoring your gift of diversity in human life; become stronger in living out our baptismal vow to respect the dignity of every human being; and bring into the fellowship of the risen Christ those who come to him in faith, baptizing them in the name of the Father, and of the Son, and of the Holy Spirit. Amen.

For Liturgical Celebration: [Common of a Saint, A23] [For all Baptized Christians, A42]

August 18

William Porcher DuBose
Priest, 1918

William Porcher DuBose, probably the most original and creative thinker the American Episcopal Church has ever produced, spent most of his life as a professor at The University of the South, in Sewanee, Tennessee. He was not widely traveled, and not widely known, until, at the age of 56, he published the first of several books on theology that made him respected, not only in his own country, but also in England and France.

DuBose was born in 1836 in South Carolina, into a wealthy and cultured Huguenot family. At the University of Virginia, he acquired a fluent knowledge of Greek and other languages, which helped him lay the foundation for a profound understanding of the New Testament. His theological studies were begun at the Episcopal seminary in Camden, South Carolina. He was ordained in 1861, and became an officer and chaplain in the Confederate Army.

Doctrine and life were always in close conversation for DuBose. In a series of books he probed the inner meaning of the Gospels, the Epistles of Paul, and the Epistle to the Hebrews. He treated life and doctrine as a dramatic dialogue, fusing the best of contemporary thought and criticism with his own strong inner faith. The result was both a personal and scriptural catholic theology. He reflected, as he acknowledged, the great religious movements of the nineteenth century: the Tractarianism of Oxford; the liberalism of F.D. Maurice; the scholarship of the Germans; and the evangelical spirit that was so pervasive at the time.

The richness and complexity of DuBose's thought are not easily captured in a few words, but the following passage, written shortly before his death in 1918, is a characteristic sample of his theology: "God has placed forever before our eyes, not the image but the Very Person of the Spiritual Man. We have not to ascend into Heaven to bring Him down, nor to descend into the abyss to bring Him up, for

He is with us, and near us, and in us. We have only to confess with our mouths that He is Lord, and believe in our hearts that God has raised Him from the dead—and raised us in Him—and we shall live."

Rite I Almighty God, who didst give to thy servant William Porcher DuBose special gifts of grace to understand the Scriptures and to teach the truth as it is in Christ Jesus: Grant that by this teaching we may know thee, the one true God, and Jesus Christ whom thou hast sent; who liveth and reigneth with thee and the Holy Spirit, one God, now and for ever. Amen.

Rite II Almighty God, you gave to your servant William Porcher DuBose special gifts of grace to understand the Scriptures and to teach the truth as it is in Christ Jesus: Grant that by this teaching we may know you, the one true God, and Jesus Christ whom you have sent; who lives and reigns with you and the Holy Spirit, one God, now and for ever. Amen.

For Liturgical Celebration: [Common of a Theologian and Teacher, A17] [Common of a Pastor, A14] [For the Ministry I, A49] [For Education, A60]

August 18
Artemisia Bowden
1969

The Rt. Rev. James Steptoe Johnston, Bishop of the Missionary District of Western Texas (1888–1916), desired to provide education and skill development for newly emancipated blacks in the mission field. Bishop Johnston traveled to Raleigh, North Carolina, in search of a young, black, female teacher. In 1902, Ms. Artemisia Bowden courageously accepted Bishop Johnston's invitation and assumed leadership of the St. Philip's Vocational Day School for Colored Children in San Antonio, Texas.

She began with less than ten students. After leading the school for 52 years, a small day school was transformed into a fully accredited junior college offering over 100 degree and certificate programs. In 2016, St. Philip's College has an enrollment of over 11,000 students. St. Philip's College carries the dual designation of being a Historically Black College and a Hispanic Serving Institution Bowden's work, which began more than 110 years ago, continues to be an essential piece of the educational system in South Texas.

Her participation in various social causes included the Texas Commission on Interracial Relations, the Negro Business and Professional Women's Club, the City Federation of Clubs, the Southern Conference of Christians and Jews, the Coordination Council of Juvenile Delinquency in the Texas Social Welfare Association, the American Friends Service Commission, the Texas T.B. Association of Bexar County, and the National Association of College Women's Clubs.

Her visionary leadership at St. Philip's, as well as in the community, earned her honorary degrees, and recognition as one of ten outstanding women in the field of education by the National Council of Negro Women in 1946; she was honored as Zeta Phi Beta's Woman of the Year in 1955. Dr. Bowden died in 1969, after a full and rich life of faith in Christ and fidelity to Christ's Church, having served both the School and St. Philip's Church in the Diocese of West Texas for more than sixty-seven years.

Rite I O God, by thy Holy Spirit thou dost give gifts to thy people so that they might faithfully serve thy Church and the world: We give praise to thee for the gifts of perseverance, teaching, and wisdom made manifest in thy servant, Artemisia Bowden, whom thou didst call far from home for the sake of educating the daughters and granddaughters of former slaves in Texas. We give thanks to thee for thy blessing and prospering of her life's work, and pray that, following her example, we may be ever mindful of the call to serve where thou dost send us; through Jesus Christ our Lord, who with thee and the Spirit, liveth and reigneth, one God, for ever and ever. Amen.

Rite II O God, by your Holy Spirit, you give gifts to your people so that they might faithfully serve your Church and the world: We give you praise for the gifts of perseverance, teaching, and wisdom made manifest in your servant, Artemisia Bowden, whom you called far from home for the sake of educating the daughters and granddaughters of former slaves in Texas. We thank you for blessing and prospering her life's work, and pray that, following her example, we may be ever mindful of the call to serve where you send us; through Jesus Christ our Lord, who with you and the Spirit, lives and reigns, one God, for ever and ever. Amen.

For Liturgical Celebration: [Common of a Prophetic Witness, A31] [For Education, A60]

August 20

Bernard, Abbot of Clairvaux
1153

Bernard was the son of a knight and landowner who lived near Dijon, France. He was born in 1090 and given a secular education, but in 1113 he entered the Benedictine Abbey of Citeaux. His family was not pleased with his choice of a monastic life, but he nevertheless persuaded four of his brothers and about twenty-six of his friends to join him. After only three years, the abbot of Citeaux deployed Bernard and a small company of monks to establish a monastery at Clairvaux in 1115.

The work at Clairvaux, and the extreme rigors of the Benedictine rule practiced by the Cistercian community, were taxing. Tasked with much, Bernard denied himself sleep to the detriment of his health that he might have time to write letters and sermons. He preached so persuasively that sixty new abbeys were founded, all affiliated with Clairvaux. Famed for the ardor with which he preached love for God "without measure," he fulfilled his own definition of a holy man: "seen to be good and charitable, holding back nothing for himself, but using his every gift for the common good."

By 1140, his writings had made him one of the most influential figures in Christendom. His guidance was sought by prelates and princes, drawing him into active participation in all manner of controversy involving the Church, from settling disputes among secular rulers to sorting contentious theological debates. An ardent opponent of a growing movement of his time to reconcile inconsistencies of doctrine by reason, he felt that such an approach was a downgrading of the mysteries. This conflict took particular expression in his fierce opposition to the formidable theologian, Abelard.

When a former monk of Clairvaux was elected Pope Eugenius III, papal reliance upon Bernard grew. Commissioned by the Pope, Bernard preached the Crusade against the Albigensians and the Second Crusade to liberate Jerusalem, winning much support for the latter in

France and Germany. When that Crusade ended in disaster, Bernard was roundly attacked for having supported it. He died soon after in 1153.

Among Bernard's writings are treatises on papal duty, on love, on the veneration of Mary, and a commentary on the Song of Songs. Among well known hymns, he is credited with having written "O sacred head sore wounded" (*The Hymnal 1982*, #168; #169), "Jesus, the very thought of thee" (#642) and "O Jesus, joy of loving hearts" (#649; #650).

Rite I   O God, by whose grace thy servant Bernard of Clairvaux, kindled with the flame of thy love, became a burning and a shining light in thy Church: Grant that we also may be aflame with the spirit of love and discipline and walk before thee as children of light; through Jesus Christ our Lord, who liveth and reigneth with thee and the Holy Spirit, one God, now and for ever. Amen.

Rite II O God, by whose grace your servant Bernard of Clairvaux, kindled with the flame of your love, became a burning and a shining light in your Church: Grant that we also may be aflame with the spirit of love and discipline and walk before you as children of light; through Jesus Christ our Lord, who lives and reigns with you and the Holy Spirit, one God, now and for ever. Amen.

For Liturgical Celebration: [Common of a Monastic or Professed Religious, A20] [Common of a Theologian and Teacher, A17] [Of the Incarnation, A39]

August 23

Martin de Porres, *1639,* Rosa de Lima, *1617,* and Toribio de Mogrovejo, *1606*
Witnesses to the Faith in South America

Toribio de Mogrovejo, born in Spain in 1538 and a brilliant student of law and theology, was called in 1580 to serve as archbishop of Lima. He objected that he was a layman but was overruled, ordained priest and bishop, and arrived in Peru in 1581 as archbishop. Confronted with the worst of colonialism, Toribio fought injustice in both the church and the civil order. He baptized and confirmed many thousands of souls and founded many churches, religious houses, hospitals, and the first seminary in the Western hemisphere, at Lima in 1591. Among his flock were Martin de Porres and Rosa de Lima.

Martin de Porres was born in Lima, Peru, on December 9, 1579, the illegitimate son of a Spanish nobleman and a young black former slave. Because Martin inherited the dark skin of his mother, his father abandoned the family. Martin apprenticed to a barber-surgeon and, after learning the trade, he applied to the Dominicans to be a "lay helper." Placed in charge of the infirmary, his tender care of the sick and his reputation as a healer led the community to request his religious profession, despite a long-standing policy that "no black person may be received to the holy habit or profession of our Order." That policy was rescinded and Martin took vows as a Dominican brother in 1603.

Rosa de Lima, born in 1586 and friend of Martin, shared his passion for the sick and the poor. Rosa was exceedingly beautiful, but because of her family's fading fortunes, she feared being married off to a wealthy man, her looks a compensation for the lack of suitable dowry. To sabotage this possibility, Rosa disfigured her face and, to contribute to her family's upkeep, took in sewing and worked as a gardener. An abiding passion for the poor eventually led her to the Third Order of St. Dominic and a reclusive life of prayer that sustained her works of mercy for the poorest of the poor, particularly for indigenous peoples, slaves, and others on the margins of society, until her death in 1617.

These three, bound in baptism, community, and friendship, testify to the power of baptismal relationship and communion, and Christian faith transmitted from generation to generation incarnate in works of service and mercy.

Rite I   Merciful God, who didst send thy Gospel to the people of Peru through Martin de Porres, who brought its comfort even to slaves; through Rosa de Lima, who worked among the poorest of the poor; and through Toribio de Mogrovejo, who founded the first seminary in the Americas and baptized many: Help us to follow their example in bringing fearlessly the comfort of thy grace to all downtrodden and outcast people, that thy Church may be renewed with songs of salvation and praise; through Jesus Christ, who with thee and the Holy Spirit liveth and reigneth, one God, now and for ever. Amen.

Rite II   Merciful God, you sent your Gospel to the people of Peru through Martin de Porres, who brought its comfort even to slaves; through Rosa de Lima, who worked among the poorest of the poor; and through Toribio de Mogrovejo, who founded the first seminary in the Americas and baptized many: Help us to follow their example in bringing fearlessly the comfort of your grace to all downtrodden and outcast people, that your Church may be renewed with songs of salvation and praise; through Jesus Christ, who with you and the Holy Spirit lives and reigns, one God, now and for ever. Amen.

For Liturgical Celebration: [Common of a Monastic or Professed Religious, A20] [Common of a Prophetic Witness, A31] [For Social Service, A59]

August 25
Louis, King of France
1270

Louis IX was born at Poissy on April 25, 1214. His father, Louis VIII, died when Louis IX was 11 years old; he was crowned King at Rheims on November 29, 1226. His mother and regent, Blanche of Castile, inspired his early religious exercises of devotion and asceticism. At age 20, Louis married Margaret of Provence, who bore him 11 children, 9 of whom lived past infancy. Blanche remained a major influence on her son Louis IX until her death in 1252.

A man of unusual purity of life and manners, he was sincerely committed to his faith and to its moral demands. Living simply, dressing plainly, visiting hospitals, helping the poor, and acting with integrity and honesty, Louis IX believed that the crown was given him by God and God would hold him accountable for his reign.

During a campaign in 1242, King Louis became very ill. In an act customary of the piety and politics of his time and culture, he vowed if he recovered that he would lead a Crusade against the Muslims. Leaving his mother Blanche in charge of the kingdom, Louis led the Seventh Crusade (1248-1254).After an unsuccessful struggle, including capture by Egyptian forces, Louis IX went home to France.

Back in France, Louis's piety inspired his patronage of the arts and encouraged the spread of Gothic architecture. One of his most notable commissions is Sainte-Chapelle ("Holy Chapel"), erected as a shrine for the Crown of Thorns and a fragment of the True Cross, precious relics of the Passion of Jesus that Louis had purchased in 1239–41 for a sum twice the total cost of the chapel itself.

A deplorable aspect of medieval Christianity was its anti-semitism, and despite his attempts to cultivate holiness, Louis IX was complicit in official action against Jewish believers. Louis ordered the expulsion of all Jews engaged in usury and the confiscation of their property to finance his crusade. At the urging of Pope Gregory IX, Louis also ordered the burning in Paris in 1243 of some 12,000 manuscript copies of the Talmud and other Jewish books and increased the power and authority of the Inquisition in France.

In 1270, Louis IX led the Eighth Crusade to Tunis. There, Louis developed "flux of the stomach" and died August 25, 1270.

Rite I   O God, who didst call thy servant Louis of France to an earthly throne that he might advance thy heavenly kingdom, and gave him zeal for thy Church and love for thy people: Mercifully grant that we who commemorate him this day may be fruitful in good works and attain to the glorious crown of thy saints; through Jesus Christ our Lord, who liveth and reigneth with thee and the Holy Spirit, one God, for ever and ever. Amen.

Rite II O God, you called your servant Louis of France to an earthly throne that he might advance your heavenly kingdom, and gave him zeal for your Church and love for your people: Mercifully grant that we who commemorate him this day may be fruitful in good works and attain to the glorious crown of your saints; through Jesus Christ our Lord, who lives and reigns with you and the Holy Spirit, one God, for ever and ever. Amen.

For Liturgical Celebration: [Common of a Saint, A23] [For Vocation in Daily Work, A61]

August 27

Thomas Gallaudet, 1902, with
Henry Winter Syle, 1890

Ministry to the deaf in The Episcopal Church begins with Thomas Gallaudet and his protégé, Henry Winter Syle. Without Gallaudet's genius and zeal for the spiritual well-being of deaf persons, it is improbable that a history of ministry to the deaf in The Episcopal Church could be written. He has been called "The Apostle to the Deaf."

Gallaudet was born June 3, 1822, in Hartford, Connecticut, the eldest son of Thomas Hopkins Gallaudet, founder of the West Hartford School for the Deaf, whose wife, Sophia, was a deaf-mute.

After graduating from Trinity College in Hartford, Thomas announced his intention of being confirmed and becoming a priest in The Episcopal Church. His father prevailed upon him to postpone a final decision, and to accept a teaching position in the New York Institution for Deaf-Mutes. There he met and married Elizabeth Budd, a deaf-mute. Gallaudet was ordained deacon in 1850 and served his diaconate at St. Stephen's Church, where he established a Bible class for deaf persons.

Ordained a priest in 1851, Gallaudet became Assistant Rector at St. Ann's Church, where he conceived a plan for establishing a church that would be a spiritual home for deaf people. This became a reality the following year, with the founding of St. Ann's Church for Deaf-Mutes. The congregation was able to purchase a church building in 1859, and it became a center for missionary work to the deaf continuing into its merger with the parish of Calvary-St. George in 1976. As a result of this ministry, mission congregations were established in many cities. Gallaudet died on August 27, 1902.

One fruit of Gallaudet's ministry was Henry Winter Syle, who had lost his hearing as the result of scarlet fever. Educated at Trinity College, Hartford; St. John's College, Cambridge, England; and Yale; Syle was a brilliant student, who persisted in his determination to obtain an education, despite his handicap and fragile health. He was encouraged by Gallaudet to seek Holy Orders, and, having moved to Philadelphia, was supported by Bishop Stevens, against the opposition of many who believed that the impairment of one of the senses was an impediment to ordination. Syle was ordained in 1876, the first deaf person to receive Holy Orders in this Church. In 1888, he built All Souls Church for the Deaf in Philadelphia, the first Episcopal church constructed especially for deaf persons. He died on January 6, 1890.

Rite I O Loving God, whose will it is that everyone shouldst come to thee and be saved: We bless thy holy Name for thy servants Thomas Gallaudet and Henry Winter Syle, and we pray that thou wilt continually move thy Church to respond in love to the needs of all people; through Jesus Christ, who liveth and reigneth with thee and the Holy Spirit, one God, now and for ever. Amen.

Rite II O Loving God, whose will it is that everyone should come to you and be saved: We bless your holy Name for your servants Thomas Gallaudet and Henry Winter Syle, and we pray that you will continually move your Church to respond in love to the needs of all people; through Jesus Christ, who lives and reigns with you and the Holy Spirit, one God, now and for ever. Amen.

For Liturgical Celebration: [Common of a Missionary, A11] [Common of a Prophetic Witness, A31] [For the Mission of the Church, A52]

August 28

Augustine
Bishop of Hippo, and Theologian, 430

Augustine, perhaps the greatest theologian in the history of Western Christianity, was born in 354 at Tagaste in North Africa. In his restless search for truth, he was attracted by Manichaeism and Neoplatonism, and was constantly engaged in an inner struggle with his personal morals. Finally, under the influence of his mother Monnica, Augustine surrendered to the Christian faith in the late summer of 386. He was baptized by Ambrose, Bishop of Milan, on Easter Eve in 387. After returning to North Africa in 391, Augustine found himself unexpectedly chosen by the people of Hippo to be a presbyter. Four years later he was chosen bishop of that city. His spiritual autobiography, *The Confessions of St. Augustine*, written shortly before 400 in the form of an extended prayer, is a classic of Western spirituality.

Augustine wrote countless treatises, letters, and sermons. They have provided a rich source of new and fresh insights into Christian truth.

The Manichaeans had attempted to solve the problem of evil by positing the existence of an independent agency eternally opposed to God. In refutation, Augustine affirmed that all creation is essentially good, having been created by God, and that evil is, properly speaking, the privation of good. A rigorist sect, the Donatists, had split from the Great Church after the persecution of Diocletian in the early fourth century. Against them, Augustine asserted that the Church was "holy," not because its members could be proved holy, but because holiness was the purpose of the Church, to which all its members are called.

Stirred by Alaric the Visigoth's sack of Rome in 410, Augustine wrote his greatest work, *The City of God*. In it he writes: "Two cities have been formed by two loves: the earthly by love of self, even to the contempt of God, the heavenly by the love of God, even to the contempt of self. The earthly city glories in itself, the heavenly city glories in the Lord . . . In the one, the princes, and the nations it subdues, are ruled by the love of ruling; in the other, the princes and the subjects serve one another in love."

Augustine died on August 28, 430, as the Vandals were besieging his own earthly city of Hippo.

Rite I   Lord God, the light of the minds that know thee, the life of the souls that love thee, and the strength of the hearts that serve thee: Help us, following the example of thy servant, Augustine of Hippo, so to know thee that we may truly love thee, and so to love thee that we may fully serve thee, whom to serve is perfect freedom; through Jesus Christ our Lord, who liveth and reigneth with thee and the Holy Spirit, one God, now and for ever. Amen.

Rite II Lord God, the light of the minds that know you, the life of the souls that love you, and the strength of the hearts that serve you: Help us, following the example of your servant, Augustine of Hippo, so to know you that we may truly love you, and so to love you that we may fully serve you, whom to serve is perfect freedom; through Jesus Christ our Lord, who lives and reigns with you and the Holy Spirit, one God, now and for ever. Amen.

For Liturgical Celebration: [Common of a Theologian and Teacher, A17] [Common of a Pastor, A14] [Of the Holy Trinity, A37] [For the Ministry II, A50]

August 28

Moses the Black
Desert Father and Martyr, c. 400

Moses of Ethiopia, sometimes called Moses the Black, was a fifth century monk who lived in one of several isolated desert monasteries near Scete in Lower Egypt. He was described as being tall, strong, "black of body," and in his early life, the hot-blooded leader of a marauding robber band.

Little is known of his actual life, but an imaginative collection of religious legends has accumulated about him. Such tales point to the deep struggles of a Christian soul seeking salvation in difficult settings. Moses was portrayed as a person of excesses, a slave who was both a thief and a murderer, a perennial fornicator who, after he became a monk, still struggled for several years with sexual fantasies. To rid himself of sexual temptation, he reportedly stood all night in his cell with his eyes open. This struggle endured for seven years, after which the temptations went away.

He led an ascetic life, lived in a simple cell, and ate only ten ounces of dry bread each day. Once, when the monks gathered to judge a member who had sinned, Brother Moses arrived carrying a leaky basket filled with sand on his back. He explained that what he was holding behind him represented his own many sins, now hidden from his own view. "And now I have come to judge my brother for a small fault," he remarked. The other monks then each personally forgave their erring brother and returned to their cells.

Moses was not ordained until late in life; also in his later years, he founded his own monastery. At about age 75, he was warned that an armed band of raiders was approaching to slay him. "They who live by the sword shall die by the sword" (Matthew 26:52), the former robber-murderer calmly replied. He and six other brothers waited patiently, and were slain, after which, according to the monastic account *St. Moses the Ethiopian*, seven crowns descended from heaven over the place where they were martyred.

Rite I   Almighty God, whose blessed Son dost guide our footsteps into the way of peace: Deliver us from paths of hatred and violence, that we, following the example of thy servant Moses, may serve thee with singleness of heart and attain to the tranquility of the world to come; through Jesus Christ our Lord, who liveth and reigneth with thee in the unity of the Holy Spirit, one God, now and for ever. Amen.

Rite II Almighty God, whose blessed Son guides our footsteps in the way of peace: Deliver us from paths of hatred and violence, that we, following the example of your servant Moses, may serve you with singleness of heart and attain to the tranquility of the world to come; through Jesus Christ our Lord, who lives and reigns with you in the unity of the Holy Spirit, one God, now and for ever. Amen.

For Liturgical Celebration: [Common of a Martyr, A7] [Common of a Monastic or Professed Religious, A20] [Of the Holy Cross, A41] [Of the Incarnation, A39]

August 29

John Bunyan
Writer, 1688

John Bunyan was born in 1628 at Elstow in Bedfordshire, England. Little is known about his early life. His parents were poor; his father was a brazier, a trade that Bunyan also followed for a time. Bunyan had little to no formal education, and he may have learned to read English from reading the Bible. He served as a soldier in the Parliamentary army during the English Civil War, after which he married. His wife introduced him to Arthur Dent's *Plain Man's Pathway to Heaven* and Bishop Lewis Bayly's *Practice of Piety*, devotional books that set him on the religious path.

In 1653, he was baptized in the Bedford Baptist (Independent) Church, and was soon thereafter recognized as a preacher, a vocation at which he excelled. He claimed to have had visions similar to those of Teresa of Avila. After the Restoration of the monarchy in 1660, Bunyan was targeted and slandered by the new royalist government, along with many others who had supported the revolutionary cause during the Civil War. Under the laws of the restored Stuart regime, congregational meeting houses were closed and citizens were required to attend their Anglican parishes. It was punishable by law for anyone, except those who had been ordained according to Anglican orders, to conduct services or preach. Bunyan was arrested while preaching in 1660 and spent most of the next twelve years imprisoned in Bedford.

While imprisoned, Bunyan wrote the first part of his most famous work, *The Pilgrim's Progress*, an allegorical story that was completed in 1684. *The Pilgrim's Progress* tells the story of Christian, a lonely pilgrim who must cross such treacherous terrain as the Slough of Despond and the River of Death before finally reaching the Land of Beulah. Along with John Milton's *Paradise Lost*, it was one of the most influential works of the seventeenth century, and retained its influence for several centuries thereafter. Bunyan died August 31, 1688.

Rite I   God of peace, who didst call John Bunyan to be valiant for truth: Grant that we, having endured as strangers and pilgrims on this earth, may at last rejoice with all the faithful in thy heavenly city; through Jesus Christ our Savior, who with thee and the Holy Spirit liveth and reigneth, one God, for ever and ever. Amen.

Rite II   God of peace, you called John Bunyan to be valiant for truth: Grant that we, having endured as strangers and pilgrims on this earth, may at last rejoice with all the faithful in your heavenly city; through Jesus Christ our Savior, who with you and the Holy Spirit lives and reigns, one God, for ever and ever. Amen.

For Liturgical Celebration: [Common of an Artist, Writer, or Composer, A27] [Of the Holy Spirit, A38]

August 30

Charles Chapman Grafton
Bishop of Fond du Lac, and Ecumenist, 1912

Under the influence of the Oxford and Cambridge Movements, Charles Chapman Grafton became a major figure in the renewal of liturgical life in The Episcopal Church.

Grafton was born April 12, 1830, in Boston, and attended Harvard Law School. He was confirmed at Church of the Advent—then a leading parish implementing the principles of the Oxford Movement—where he began seriously to explore his vocation. After graduation, he moved to Maryland to study with the Tractarian Bishop William Whittington, who eventually ordained him deacon on December 23, 1855, and priest on May 30, 1858.

Grafton served a number of parishes in Maryland but experienced a growing attraction to the religious life. In 1865, he left for England specifically to meet a leading proponent of the Oxford Movement, Edward Bouverie Pusey. In the following year, after a series of meetings held at All Saints, Margaret Street, in London, Grafton and two others took religious vows and the Society of St. John the Evangelist had its beginning. Grafton returned to America in 1872 and was elected fourth Rector of the Church of the Advent, Boston. In 1882, he founded the Sisterhood of the Holy Nativity based in Ripon, Wisconsin.

In 1888, Grafton was elected second bishop of Fond du Lac. His consent process was difficult, as many thought him too ritualistic, but he soon became known not only as an Anglo-Catholic but also as an ecumenist, deeply committed to improving relations with the Orthodox and Old Catholics.

Perhaps the most famous event during Grafton's long episcopate was the ordination of his eventual successor as bishop co-adjutor in 1900. He invited the Russian Orthodox Bishop Tikhon and the Old Catholic Bishop Anthony Kozlowski to participate. The service stirred up furor across the country with the publication of a photograph (called derisively "The Fond du Lac Circus") that showed all eight

Episcopal bishops and the two visiting bishops in cope and miter. It caused a church-wide controversy over ritual and vestments that lasted for more than six months, with accusations and threats of ecclesiastical trial flying from all corners, and with scurrilous attacks and virulent justifications. When the dust finally settled, the legitimacy of traditional catholic ritual and vestments had gained a permanent place in the liturgy of The Episcopal Church.

Bishop Grafton died August 30, 1912.

Rite I   Loving God, who didst call Charles Chapman Grafton to be a bishop in thy Church, endowing him with a burning zeal for souls: Grant that, following his example, we may ever live for the extension of thy kingdom, that thy glory may be the chief end of our lives, thy will the law of our conduct, thy love the motive of our actions, and Christ's life the model and mold of our own; through the same Jesus Christ, who liveth and reigneth with thee and the Holy Spirit, one God, throughout all ages. Amen.

Rite II Loving God, you called Charles Chapman Grafton to be a bishop in your Church and endowed him with a burning zeal for souls: Grant that, following his example, we may ever live for the extension of your kingdom, that your glory may be the chief end of our lives, your will the law of our conduct, your love the motive of our actions, and Christ's life the model and mold of our own; through the same Jesus Christ, who lives and reigns with you and the Holy Spirit, one God, throughout all ages. Amen.

For Liturgical Celebration: [Common of a Pastor, A14] [For the Ministry II, A50] [For the Unity of the Church, A48]

August 31

Aidan, 651, and Cuthbert, 687
Bishops of Lindisfarne

The gospel first came to the northern English in 627, when King Edwin of Northumbria was converted by missionaries from Canterbury. Edwin's death in battle in 632 was followed by a severe pagan reaction. A year later, Edwin's exiled nephew Oswald gained the kingdom, and proceeded at once to restore the Christian mission.

During his exile, Oswald had lived at Columba's monastery of Iona, where he had been converted and baptized. Hence he sent to Iona, rather than to Canterbury, for missionaries. The head of the new mission was a gentle monk named Aidan, who centered his work on Lindisfarne, an island off the northeast coast of England. Aidan and his companions restored Christianity in Northumbria and extended the mission through the Midlands as far south as London.

Aidan (whose birth date is unrecorded) died at Bamborough on August 31, 651. Bede said of him: "He neither sought nor loved anything of this world, but delighted in distributing immediately to the poor whatever was given him by kings or rich men of the world. He traversed both town and country on foot, never on horseback, unless compelled by some urgent necessity. Wherever in his way he saw any, either rich or poor, he invited them, if pagans, to embrace the mystery of the faith; or if they were believers, to strengthen them in the faith and stir them up by words and actions to alms and good works."

Cuthbert was the most popular saint of the pre-Conquest Anglo-Saxon Church. He was born about 625. In response to a vision of the death of Aidan of Lindisfarne, Cuthbert entered religious life and was formed in the austere traditions of Celtic monasticism. He was Prior of Melrose Abbey from 651-664 and was then Prior of Lindisfarne.

Although he had been formed in the Celtic tradition and customs, Cuthbert humbly accepted the decisions of the Synod of Whitby in 663 that brought the usages of the English Church in line with Roman practice introduced into Canterbury by Augustine. He was, therefore, a "healer of the breach" between Celtic and Roman factions; his example hastened and strengthened the transition.

Made Bishop of Hexham in 684, Cuthbert much preferred a solitary life, so exchanged bishoprics with his former abbot, Eata, then bishop of Lindisfarne. Two years later, Cuthbert retired and withdrew to the nearby island of Farne, where he died at his hermitage on March 20, 687.

Rite I   Everliving God, who didst call thy servants Aidan and Cuthbert to proclaim the gospel in northern England and endued them with loving hearts and gentle spirits: Grant us grace to live as they did, in simplicity, humility, and love for the poor; through Jesus Christ, who came among us as one who serves and who liveth and reigneth with thee and the Holy Spirit, one God, now and for ever. Amen.

Rite II   Everliving God, you called your servants Aidan and Cuthbert to proclaim the gospel in northern England and gave them loving hearts and gentle spirits: Grant us grace to live as they did, in simplicity, humility, and love for the poor; through Jesus Christ, who came among us as one who serves and who lives and reigns with you and the Holy Spirit, one God, now and for ever. Amen.

For Liturgical Celebration: [Common of a Pastor, A14] [Common of a Monastic or Professed Religious, A20] [For the Ministry II, A50] [Of the Reign of Christ, A46]

SEPTEMBER

1 David Pendleton Oakerhater, Deacon and Missionary, 1931
2 The Martyrs of New Guinea, 1942
3 Prudence Crandall, Teacher and Prophetic Witness, 1890
4 Paul Jones, 1941
4 Albert Schweitzer, 1965
5 Gregorio Aglipay, Priest and Founder of the Philippine Independent Church, 1940
6
7 Elie Naud, Huguenot Witness to the Faith, 1722
8 Nikolai Grundtvig, Bishop and Hymnwriter, 1872
8 Søren Kierkegaard, Teacher and Philosopher, 1855
9 Constance, Nun, and Her Companions, 1878
10 Alexander Crummell, 1898
11 Harry Thacker Burleigh, Composer, 1949
12 John Henry Hobart, Bishop of New York, 1830
13 John Chrysostom, Bishop of Constantinople, 407
14
15 Cyprian, Bishop and Martyr of Carthage, 258
15 James Chisholm, Priest, 1855
16 Ninian, Bishop in Galloway, c. 430
17 Hildegard, 1179
18 Edward Bouverie Pusey, Priest, 1882
18 Dag Hjalmar Agne Carl Hammarskjöld, 1961
19 Theodore of Tarsus, Archbishop of Canterbury, 690
20 John Coleridge Patteson, Bishop of Melanesia, and his Companions, Martyrs, 1871
21
22 Philander Chase, Bishop of Ohio, and of Illinois, 1852

23 Thecla
24 Anna Ellison Butler Alexander, 1947
25 Sergius, Abbot of Holy Trinity, Moscow, 1392
26 Lancelot Andrewes, Bishop of Winchester, 1626
26 Wilson Carlile, Priest, 1942
27 Vincent de Paul, Religious, and Prophetic Witness, 1660
27 Thomas Traherne, Priest, 1674
28 Richard Rolle, 1349, Walter Hilton, 1396, and Margery Kempe, c. 1440, Mystics
29
30 Jerome, Priest, and Monk of Bethlehem, 420

September 1

David Pendleton Oakerhater
Deacon and Missionary, 1931

"God's warrior" is an epithet by which David Pendleton Oakerhater is known among the Cheyenne Indians of Oklahoma. The title is an apt one, for this apostle of Christ to the Cheyenne was originally a soldier who fought against the United States government with warriors of other tribes in the disputes over Indian land rights. Born circa 1851, by the late 1860s Oakerhater had distinguished himself for bravery and leadership as an officer in an elite corps of Cheyenne fighters. In 1875, after a year of minor uprisings and threats of major violence, he and twenty-seven other warrior leaders were taken prisoner by the U.S. Army, charged with inciting rebellion, and sent to a disused military prison in Florida.

Under the influence of a concerned Army captain, who sought to educate the prisoners, Oakerhater and his companions learned English, gave art and archery lessons to the area's many visitors, and had their first encounter with the Christian faith. The captain's example, and that of other concerned Christians from as far away as New York, had their effect on the young warrior. He was moved to answer the call to transform his leadership in war into a lifelong ministry of peace.

With sponsorship from the Diocese of Central New York and financial help from a Mrs. Pendleton of Cincinnati, he and three other prisoners went north to study for the ministry. At his baptism in Syracuse in 1878, he took the name David Pendleton Oakerhater, in honor of his benefactress.

Soon after his ordination to the diaconate in 1881, Oakerhater returned to Oklahoma. There, he was instrumental in founding and operating schools and missions, through great personal sacrifice and often in the face of apathy from the Church hierarchy and resistance from the government. He continued his ministry of service, education, and pastoral care among his people until his death on August 31, 1931.

Half a century before, the young deacon had told his people: "You all know me. You remember when I led you out to war I went first, and what I told you was true. Now I have been away to the East and I have learned about another captain, the Lord Jesus Christ, and he is my leader. He goes first, and all he tells me is true. I come back to my people to tell you to go with me now in this new road, a war that makes all for peace."

Rite I   O God of unsearchable wisdom and mercy, thou didst choose a captive warrior, David Oakerhater, to be thy servant, and didst send him to be a missionary to his own people and to execute the office of deacon among them: Liberate us, who commemorate him today, from bondage to self, and empower us for service to thee and to the neighbors thou hast given us; through Jesus Christ, the captain of our salvation; who liveth and reigneth with thee and the Holy Spirit, one God for ever and ever. Amen.

Rite II   O God of unsearchable wisdom and mercy, you chose a captive warrior, David Oakerhater, to be your servant, and sent him to be a missionary to his own people, and to execute the office of deacon among them: Liberate us, who commemorate him today, from bondage to self, and empower us for service to you and to the neighbors you have given us; through Jesus Christ, the captain of our salvation; who lives and reigns with you and the Holy Spirit, one God for ever and ever. Amen.

For Liturgical Celebration: [Common of a Missionary, A11] [For the Mission of the Church, A52] [For Reconciliation and Forgiveness, A68]

SEPTEMBER 1

September 2

The Martyrs of New Guinea
1942

New Guinea, the second largest island in the world, is still one of the main frontiers of Christian mission, because of its difficult terrain and the cultural diversity of its peoples, who speak some 500 distinct languages. Christian missionaries first began work there in the 1860s and 1870s, with only limited success. The Anglican mission began in 1891, and the first bishop was consecrated in 1898.

During World War II, the suffering of missionaries and of native people was severe. One historian reckons the total number of martyrs from all Christian denominations during this period at around 330. This feast day, observed in the Diocese of New Guinea and in many dioceses of the Church of Australia, marks the witness of nine Australian missionaries and two Papuan martyrs who died while serving those who needed them.

The missionaries were determined to stay with their flocks during the Japanese invasion, and to continue their work of healing, teaching, and evangelism. Once the invasion occurred, they realized that their presence was a danger to the local people with whom they stayed; any people of European descent were considered enemy combatants and villages harboring them were severely punished. Two of the missionaries, one Australian and one Papuan, were evacuating with the villagers with whom they ministered when their boat was strafed and sunk by sea-planes. The remaining missionaries were captured in the bush. Some were executed by soldiers, others by locals who feared retribution for their presence.

One of the Papuan martyrs, Lucian Tapiedi, is among one of the ten 20th century martyrs honored with a statue above the west door of Westminster Abbey in London. While accompanying his Australian companions as a guide, he was separated from the group and killed by a local Orokaiva named Hivijapa. After the war, Hivijapa converted to Christianity, was baptized as Hivijapa Lucian, and built a church at Embi in memory of the evangelist he had slain.

In 1950, the Primate of the Anglican Church in Japan gave several bamboo crosses to be erected at the parish churches of the martyrs as a mark of contrition.

In addition to remembering those who gave up their lives, the day also includes remembrance of the faith and devotion of Papuan Christians of all churches, who risked their own lives to care for the wounded, and to save the lives of many who otherwise would have perished.

Rite I Almighty God, we remember before thee this day the blessed martyrs of New Guinea, who, following the example of their Savior, laid down their lives for their friends; and we pray that we who honor their memory may imitate their loyalty and faith; through Jesus Christ our Lord, who liveth and reigneth with thee and the Holy Spirit, one God, for ever and ever. Amen.

Rite II Almighty God, we remember before you this day the blessed martyrs of New Guinea, who, following the example of their Savior, laid down their lives for their friends; and we pray that we who honor their memory may imitate their loyalty and faith; through Jesus Christ our Lord, who lives and reigns with you and the Holy Spirit, one God, for ever and ever. Amen.

For Liturgical Celebration: [Common of a Martyr, A7] [Of the Holy Cross, A41] [On the Anniversary of a Disaster, A67]

September 3

Prudence Crandall
Teacher and Prophetic Witness, 1890

Born to a Quaker family in Rhode Island in 1803, Prudence Crandall was educated in arithmetic, the sciences, and Latin at the New England Friends' Boarding School in Rhode Island. The Religious Society of Friends, or "Quakers," believed that women should be educated, and it was in the environment of the Friends' Boarding School that Prudence Crandall's passion for teaching was first awakened.

In 1831, Crandall started a girl's school in Canterbury, Connecticut, where she educated the daughters of the town's wealthy families. In 1833 she admitted to her school a young African American girl named Sarah Harris, who wanted an education so that she could in turn teach other African American children. The parents of the white children at Crandall's school were outraged and demanded Harris's expulsion, but Crandall refused and decided to open a new school for African American girls.

Despite repeated attempts by town members to close the school, and even threats to destroy it, Crandall persevered in her labors. She enlisted the help of William Lloyd Garrison, editor of *The Liberator*, the nation's major antislavery newspaper. Through his paper and advocacy, Garrison spread awareness of her cause all over the nation.

However, later in 1833, the state legislature passed the so-called "Black Law," which made it a crime to open a school that taught African American children from any state other than Connecticut. Crandall, who had received pupils from other states, was arrested, jailed, and tried. She was eventually convicted, but a higher court reversed the decision. Far from subsiding, the harassment she endured grew worse, and, fearing for the safety of her students, she closed her school in 1834, and settled with her husband in LaSalle County, Illinois, on a farm. She opened a school there, and worked for Women's Suffrage and the Temperance movement.

After her husband died in 1874, Crandall moved to Elk Falls, Kansas. In 1886 a petition endorsed by Mark Twain and signed by more than a hundred citizens of that state, expressing their regret and shame over her treatment, persuaded the Connecticut state legislature to award her a pension. Prudence Crandall died in 1890, and today she is recognized as the official State Heroine of Connecticut.

Rite I God, the wellspring of justice and strength: We thank thee for raising up in Prudence Crandall a belief in education and a resolute will to teach girls of every color and race, that, alongside her, they might take their place in working for the nurture and well-being of all society, undaunted by prejudice or adversity. Grant that we, following her example, may participate in the work of building up the human family in Christ, thy Word and Wisdom; who with thee and the Holy Spirit liveth and reigneth, one God, now and for ever. Amen.

Rite II God, the wellspring of justice and strength: We thank you for raising up in Prudence Crandall a belief in education and a resolute will to teach girls of every color and race, that, alongside her, they might take their place in working for the nurture and well-being of all society, undaunted by prejudice or adversity. Grant that we, following her example, may participate in the work of building up the human family in Christ, your Word and Wisdom; who with you and the Holy Spirit lives and reigns, one God, now and for ever. Amen.

For Liturgical Celebration: [Common of a Saint, A23] [For Education, A60] [Common of a Prophetic Witness, A31]

September 4

Paul Jones
1941

Paul Jones was born in 1880 in the rectory of St. Stephen's Church, Wilkes-Barre, Pennsylvania. After graduating from Yale University and the Episcopal Theological School in Cambridge, Massachusetts, he accepted a call to serve a mission in Logan, Utah. In 1914, Paul Jones was appointed Archdeacon of the Missionary District of Utah and, later that year, was elected its Bishop. Meanwhile, World War I had begun.

As Bishop of Utah, Paul Jones did much to expand the Church's mission stations and to strengthen diocesan institutions. At the same time, he spoke openly about his opposition to war.

With the entry of the United States into the war, the Bishop of Utah's views became increasingly controversial. At a meeting of the Fellowship of Reconciliation in Los Angeles in 1917, Bishop Jones expressed his belief that "war is unchristian," for which he was attacked with banner headlines in the Utah press.

As a result of the speech and the reaction it caused in Utah, a commission of the House of Bishops was appointed to investigate the situation. In their report, the commission concluded that "The underlying contention of the Bishop of Utah seems to be that war is unchristian. With this general statement the Commission cannot agree . . . " The report went on to recommend that "The Bishop of Utah ought to resign his office," thus rejecting Paul Jones' right to object to war on grounds of faith and conscience.

In the spring of 1918, Bishop Jones, yielding to pressure, resigned as Bishop of Utah. In his farewell to the Missionary District of Utah in 1918, Bishop Jones said: "Where I serve the Church is of small importance, so long as I can make my life count in the cause of Christ . . . Expediency may make necessary the resignation of a bishop at this time, but no expedience can ever justify the degradation of the ideals of the episcopate which these conclusions seem to involve."

For the rest of his life, he continued a ministry within the Church dedicated to peace and conscience, speaking always with a conviction and gentleness rooted in the gospel. Bishop Jones died on September 4, 1941.

Rite I   Merciful God, who didst send thy beloved Son to preach peace to those who are far off and to those who are near: Raise up in this and every land witnesses, who, after the example of thy servant Paul Jones, will stand firm in proclaiming the Gospel of the Prince of Peace, our Savior Jesus Christ, who liveth and reigneth with thee and the Holy Spirit, one God, now and for ever. Amen.

Rite II   Merciful God, you sent your beloved Son to preach peace to those who are far off and to those who are near: Raise up in this and every land witnesses who, after the example of your servant Paul Jones, will stand firm in proclaiming the Gospel of the Prince of Peace, our Savior Jesus Christ, who lives and reigns with you and the Holy Spirit, one God, now and for ever. Amen.

For Liturgical Celebration: [Common of a Pastor, A14] [For the Ministry II, A50] [For Peace, A55]

September 4
Albert Schweitzer
1965

Albert Schweitzer was an accomplished musician, an insightful theologian, a pioneering medical doctor, and noted humanitarian.

Schweitzer was born on January 14, 1875, in Kayserburg in the disputed Alsace-Lorraine region, the son of a Lutheran pastor. He began studying music at an early age, and took to the organ. At the age of 18, he began studying with the noted French organist Charles-Marie Widor, with whom he studied the music and theology of Johann Sebastian Bach (July 28). Widor and Schweitzer founded the Paris Bach Society in 1905 and laid the foundations for the Bach revival of the 20th century.

Schweitzer entered an almost unimaginably productive time of life between 1899 and 1912. Schweitzer earned three doctoral degrees from Strasbourg faculties: philosophy (1899), theology (1901), and medicine (1913). He served as a Lutheran pastor in St. Nicholas Church in Strasbourg, taught in the theology faculty, performed regular concerts for the Bach Society, and wrote many of his most important books. Schweitzer was a prolific author whose work included a pamphlet on the art of organ-building and playing that kicked off a sweeping reform of organ building practices, a two-volume work on J. S. Bach, a dissertation on Immanuel Kant's philosophy of religion, and two books that revolutionized the study of the New Testament: *The Quest of the Historical Jesus* and *The Mysticism of Paul the Apostle*.

Schweitzer's philosophical and theological study crystalized around the importance of ethics. Knowledge, in his view, was incomplete if it did not lead to direct action. As a result, Schweitzer decided to earn a medical degree in order to relieve human suffering. After receiving the M.D. degree in 1913, he travelled to Gabon and served as a medical doctor there as an embodiment of his commitment to follow Christ. He and his wife, physician and researcher Hélène Bresslau, established a medical clinic in Lambaréné, Gabon, in 1913, where he served the local population. When World War I broke out, Schweitzer and his wife were forced to leave the hospital and, after recuperating, continued fund-raising efforts to keep the hospital going. Even after returning in 1924, Schweitzer periodically raised money for the mission with organ recordings and concert tours throughout Europe and the United States. He served as chief doctor at Lambaréné for almost fifty years until his death there at the age of 90 on September 4, 1965.

He received the Nobel Peace Prize in 1952 for his "ethic of reverence for life." He explained this ethic as "the universal, encompassing ethic of love. It is the perceived ethic of Jesus expressed in necessarily thoughtful form." The chief calling of Christians was to work in the spirit of Jesus in order to make present the Kingdom of God. Schweitzer lived this understanding through his tireless efforts on behalf of his patients, in his public criticism of European colonialism in Africa, and in his appeals for the abolishment of nuclear tests and weapons.

Rite I O God, who didst endow thy servant Albert Schweitzer with a multitude of gifts for learning, beauty, and service: Inspire thy Church that we, following his example, may be utterly dedicated to thee, that all our works might be done to thy glory and the welfare of thy people; through Christ our Lord, who liveth and reigneth with thee and the Holy Spirit, one God, now and for ever. Amen.

Rite II O God, who endowed your servant Albert Schweitzer with a multitude of gifts for learning, beauty, and service: Inspire your Church that we, following his example, may be utterly dedicated to you, that all our works might be done to your glory and the welfare of your people; through Christ our Lord, who lives and reigns with you and the Holy Spirit, one God, now and for ever. Amen.

For Liturgical Celebration: [Common of a Saint, A23] [Common of a Theologian and Teacher, A17] [Common of an Artist, Writer, or Composer, A27] [For the Ministry III, A51] [For the Sick, A57] [For the Mission of the Church, A52]

SEPTEMBER 4

September 5

Gregorio Aglipay
Priest and Founder of the Philippine Independent Church, 1940

Gregorio Aglipay was the principal founder and first Supreme Bishop of the Philippine Independent Church.

Aglipay was born in 1860 and orphaned at an early age. As a boy, he worked in the tobacco fields during the Spanish occupation of his homeland, and for the rest of his life bore hard feelings toward the Spanish colonialists. He took a degree in law before embarking on theological studies in preparation for the priesthood. He was ordained in 1890, but seems to have been something of a free spirit from the beginning, illustrated by his joining the Freemasons, an affiliation that was forbidden to Catholic priests.

In 1898, the Philippine Revolution began to bring an end to Spanish colonization. Because church and state were deeply intertwined, any revolutionary activity in the state was destined to have impact as well on the church. Matters were compounded by the fact that the Spanish hierarchy did not allow native Filipinos to rise through the ranks of their own church. Aglipay quickly took the side of the Filipino nationalists and recognized that national independence would also mean independence from the Roman Catholic Church, because it was strongly allied with Spanish interests. Aglipay called upon his fellow Catholic priests to occupy the parishes and support the revolution. Many followed his lead.

At first, Aglipay was threatened with excommunication, and later he was tempted with a deal that would have made him a Roman Catholic bishop with enormous resources at his personal disposal. Aglipay refused the deal. When Isobelo Delos Reyes, Sr. and those working with him established the new Philippine Independent Church, Aglipay was elected its first Supreme Bishop. Subsequently, Aglipay and the whole of the Philippine Independent Church were excommunicated from the Roman Catholic Church.

Aglipay died in 1940.

In 1960, the Philippine Independent Church entered into full communion with The Episcopal Church and, through that affiliation, is recognized as being in full communion with the churches of the Anglican Communion.

Rite I   Eternal God, who didst call Gregorio Aglipay to witness to thy truth in the renewal of thy Church in the Philippines: Help us, like him, to be guided by thy Holy Spirit, that people everywhere may hear the saving words of our Savior, so that all may believe and find eternal life; through the same Jesus Christ who, with thee and the Holy Spirit, liveth and reigneth, one God, for ever and ever. Amen.

Rite II Eternal God, you called Gregorio Aglipay to witness to your truth in the renewal of your Church in the Philippines: Help us, like him, to be guided by your Holy Spirit, that people everywhere may hear the saving words of our Savior, so that all may believe and find eternal life; through the same Jesus Christ who, with you and the Holy Spirit, lives and reigns, one God, for ever and ever. Amen.

For Liturgical Celebration: [Common of a Pastor, A14] [For the Ministry II, A50]

September 7

Elie Naud
Huguenot Witness to the Faith, 1722

Elie Naud (also known as Elias Neau) was a French Huguenot (French Reformed) born in 1661. It was an era when French Roman Catholicism was increasingly dominant and the persecution of Protestants was becoming more violent. Naud fled France and landed in England, where he sojourned briefly before settling permanently in New York City. During his early years in New York, he traveled frequently to Europe to raise money for Huguenot causes, having to take passage in steerage because he was not a Roman Catholic. His unwillingness to renounce his French Reformed faith resulted in his imprisonment for nearly two years in the infamous Chateau d'If.

In New York City, Naud became a member of L'Eglise du Saint-Esprit, a French-speaking parish which eventually joined The Episcopal Church, and later of Trinity Church, Wall Street, where he served for fifteen years as a catechist among slaves and Native Americans, preparing them for baptism.

Naud founded a school for the children of the poor and for the children of slaves. Upon the recommendation of the Rector of Trinity Church, the Bishop of London, acting for the Society for the Propagation of the Gospel (SPG), licensed Naud as a missioner "to slaves and ragged people in the New World." Naud also worked to influence Parliament for the passage of British laws that would demand Christian instruction for the children of slaves and Native Americans and schools for their education. Only through these means, he believed, could an equal and free society be created. During the New York City slave riot of 1712, Naud remained faithful to his vision despite threats of death from those who believed education of slaves fueled such uprisings.

Naud continued to write hymns and poetry in his native French throughout his life. He died on September 7, 1722, and was buried in the churchyard at Trinity Church, Wall Street.

Rite I   Blessed God, whose Son Jesus knelt to serve his disciples: We honor thee for the witness of thy servant Elie Naud; and pray that we, with him, may proclaim Christ in service to those deemed by the world to be littlest and least, following Jesus, who came not to be ministered to but to minister; who liveth and reigneth with thee and the Holy Spirit, one God, to whom be honor and glory for ever and ever. Amen.

Rite II Blessed God, whose Son Jesus knelt to serve his disciples: We honor you for the witness of your servant Elie Naud; and pray that we, with him, may proclaim Christ in service to those deemed by the world to be littlest and least, following Jesus, who came not to be ministered to but to minister; who lives and reigns with you and the Holy Spirit, one God, to whom be honor and glory for ever and ever. Amen.

For Liturgical Celebration: [Common of a Saint, A23] [For Social Service, A59] [Common of a Prophetic Witness, A31]

September 8

Nikolai Grundtvig
Bishop and Hymnwriter, 1872

Nikolai Grundtvig was among the most influential Danes of the nineteenth century in theological and philosophical circles and in civic life.

Born in 1783, the son of a Lutheran pastor, Grundtvig inherited from his father a lifelong appreciation for classical Lutheran orthodoxy rooted in sacramental practice, a stark contrast from the dry rationalism common to Danish Lutheranism at the time. From his mother, Grundtvig received a fascination with the literature, legends, and poetry of the Norse.

Grundtvig was a student all his life. His academic passions were largely in history and theology, but education, he believed, opened one's heart and mind to a vigorous love of life. Grundtvig also believed in the power of poetry. He thought that poetry had the capacity to speak to the souls of human beings more deeply than prose, particularly in matters of the heart and the life of faith. During his lifetime, he composed more than a thousand hymns, a number of which are still sung today: "Built on a rock the Church doth stand," "O day full of grace," and "God's word is our great heritage."

Grundtvig's father was pastor of a large congregation and, as he aged, he needed assistance. Grundtvig preached a trial sermon at his father's church during which he launched a scathing attack on Danish rationalism. The sermon met with a severe response and he was widely denounced. Nonetheless, he survived the resulting spiritual crisis and was ordained in 1811. He served as his father's curate until his father's death in 1813. After a long season with no work, Grundtvig served several short-term pastorates that usually came to an end because of his commitment to a Lutheran orthodoxy rooted in sacraments and liturgy. He believed that the dry, rational, almost gloomy approach favored at the time did not penetrate the depths of the human soul.

Toward the end of his life, Grundtvig's vision was taking hold, and his influence upon both church and nation continued to increase. He was made a bishop in 1861. He died in 1872.

Rite I Almighty God, who didst build thy Church upon a rock: Help us remember, with thy hymn writer Nikolai Grundtvig, that though steeples may fall and buildings made by hands may crumble, Jesus makes our bodies his temple through the indwelling of the Holy Spirit. Help us to recognize Christ as the Way, the Truth, and the Life, that we may join our voices to the eternal alleluia; through the same Jesus Christ, who with thee and the Holy Spirit liveth and reigneth, one God, in glory everlasting. Amen.

Rite II Almighty God, you built your Church upon a rock: Help us remember, with your hymn writer Nikolai Grundtvig, that though steeples may fall and buildings made by hands may crumble, Jesus makes our bodies his temple through the indwelling of the Holy Spirit. Help us to recognize Christ as the Way, the Truth, and the Life, that we may join our voices to the eternal alleluia; through the same Jesus Christ, who with you and the Holy Spirit lives and reigns, one God, in glory everlasting. Amen.

For Liturgical Celebration: [Common of an Artist, Writer, or Composer, A27] [Common of a Pastor, A14] [Of the Holy Trinity, A37] [For the Ministry II, A50]

September 8

Søren Kierkegaard
Teacher and Philosopher, 1855

One of the most influential philosophers of the nineteenth century, Søren Kierkegaard, the son of a devout Lutheran, born in 1813, spent most of his life in Copenhagen. As a young man, he studied Latin, history, and theology, though he was particularly drawn to philosophy and literature, and his works are remarkable in part for his deft blending and treatment of theological, literary, and philosophical themes.

In 1841, he proposed to Regine Olsen, but self-doubt about his suitability for marriage led him to break off the engagement. The event was greatly influential on his life and his works. From 1843 until his death in 1855, Kierkegaard was a prolific writer. Sometimes referred to as the "Father of Existentialism," Kierkegaard is known for his concept of "the leap of faith," his understanding of how a person's beliefs and actions are based not on evidence, of which there can never be enough, but on the willingness to take the leap despite that lack of evidence. He explored this theme in works such as *Fear and Trembling*, *Repetition*, and *Stages on Life's Way*.

For most of his life, Kierkegaard was critical of established religion, which he felt substituted human desire for God's law. In 1854, he published several articles which attacked what he saw as the selfishness of many leaders of the institutional church. His criticism of the Church as an institution, however, should not be confused with the absence of faith or the lack of trust in the ethical teachings of the Christian gospel.

His religious and theological works, such as *Christian Discourses* and *Practice in Christianity*, though sometimes overlooked, show his profound understanding of the significance of the teaching and sacrificial death of Jesus Christ and of the human call to live in imitation of the selfless, sacrificial life of Jesus. His work was influential on philosophers such as Martin Heidegger and on theologians such as Karl Barth. His challenges to the Church remain powerful reminders of the institution's call to pattern its common life according to the teaching of Jesus Christ.

Rite I   Heavenly Father, whose beloved Son Jesus Christ felt sorrow and dread in the Garden of Gethsemane: Help us to remember that though we walk through the valley of the shadow, thou art always with us, that, with thy philosopher Søren Kierkegaard, we may believe what we have not seen and trust where we cannot test, and so come at length to the eternal joy which thou hast prepared for those who love thee; through the same Jesus Christ our Savior, who liveth and reigneth with thee and the Holy Spirit, one God, in glory everlasting. Amen.

Rite II   Heavenly Father, whose beloved Son Jesus Christ felt sorrow and dread in the Garden of Gethsemane: Help us to remember that though we walk through the valley of the shadow, you are always with us, that, with your philosopher Søren Kierkegaard, we may believe what we have not seen and trust where we cannot test, and so come at length to the eternal joy which you have prepared for those who love you; through the same Jesus Christ our Savior, who lives and reigns with you and the Holy Spirit, one God, in glory everlasting. Amen.

For Liturgical Celebration: [Common of a Theologian and Teacher, A17] [Of the Holy Trinity, A37]

September 9

Constance
Nun, and Her Companions, 1878

In August, 1878, yellow fever invaded the city of Memphis, Tennessee, for the third time in ten years. By the month's end, the disease had become epidemic and a quarantine was ordered. While more than 25,000 citizens had fled in terror, nearly 20,000 more remained to face the pestilence. As cases multiplied, death tolls averaged 200 daily. When the worst was over, ninety percent of the people who remained had contracted the fever; more than 5,000 people had died.

In that time of panic and flight, many brave men and women, both lay and ordained, remained at their posts of duty or came as volunteers to assist despite the terrible risk. Notable among these heroes were Constance, Superior of the Sisters of St. Mary in Memphis, and her Companions. The Sisters had come to Memphis in 1873, at Bishop Quintard's request, to found a girls' school adjacent to St. Mary's Cathedral. When the 1878 epidemic began, George C. Harris, the Cathedral Dean, and Sister Constance immediately organized relief work among the stricken. Helping were six of Constance's fellow Sisters of St. Mary; Sister Clare from St. Margaret's House, Boston, Massachusetts; the Reverend Charles C. Parsons, Rector of Grace and St. Lazarus Church, Memphis; and the Reverend Louis S. Schuyler, assistant at Holy Innocents, Hoboken, New Jersey. The Cathedral group also included three physicians, two of whom were ordained Episcopal priests, the Sisters' two matrons, and several volunteer nurses from New York. They have ever since been known as "The Martyrs of Memphis," as have those of other Communions who ministered in Christ's name during this time of desolation.

The Cathedral buildings were located in the most infected region of Memphis. Here, amid sweltering heat and scenes of indescribable horror, these men and women of God gave relief to the sick, comfort to the dying, and homes to the many orphaned children. Only two of the workers escaped the fever. Among those who died were Constance, Thecla, Ruth, and Frances, and the Reverend Charles Parsons and the Reverend Louis Schuyler. The six martyred Sisters and priests are buried at Elmwood Cemetery. The monument marking the joint grave of Fathers Parsons and Schuyler bears the inscription: "Greater Love Hath No Man." The beautiful High Altar in St. Mary's Cathedral, Memphis, is a memorial to the four Sisters.

Rite I We give thee thanks and praise, O God of compassion, for the heroic witness of Constance and her companions, who, in a time of plague and pestilence, were steadfast in their care for the sick and dying, and loved not their own lives, even unto death; Inspire in us a like love and commitment to those in need, following the example of our Savior Jesus Christ; who with thee and the Holy Spirit liveth and reigneth, one God, now and for ever. Amen.

Rite II We give you thanks and praise, O God of compassion, for the heroic witness of Constance and her companions, who, in a time of plague and pestilence, were steadfast in their care for the sick and dying, and loved not their own lives, even unto death; Inspire in us a like love and commitment to those in need, following the example of our Savior Jesus Christ; who with you and the Holy Spirit lives and reigns, one God, now and for ever. Amen.

For Liturgical Celebration: [Common of a Martyr, A7] [Common of a Monastic or Professed Religious, A20] [Of the Holy Cross, A41] [For Social Service, A59] [For the Sick, A57]

September 10

Alexander Crummell
1898

Born March 3, 1819, in New York City, Alexander Crummell struggled against racism all his life. As a young man of color, he was driven out of an academy in New Hampshire, dismissed as a candidate for Holy Orders in New York, and rejected for admittance to General Seminary. Ordained in 1844 as a priest in the Diocese of Massachusetts, he left for England after being excluded from participating in diocesan convention.

After receiving a degree from Cambridge University, he went to Liberia as a missionary. Africans, Crummell believed, possessed a "warm, emotional, and impulsive energy," which in America had been corrupted by oppression. A model Christian republic seemed possible in Liberia. European education and technology, combined with traditional African communal culture, and undergirded by a national Episcopal Church headed by a black bishop, was the vision espoused by Crummell. He traveled extensively in the United States urging blacks to emigrate to Liberia and support the work of the Church there.

On returning to Liberia, he worked to establish a national Episcopal Church. Political opposition and a loss of funding finally forced him to return to the United States, where he concentrated his efforts on establishing a strong urban presence of independent black congregations that would be centers of worship, education, and social service. When Southern bishops proposed that a separate missionary district be created for black congregations, Crummell created a national convocation to defeat the proposal. The Union of Black Episcopalians is an outgrowth of that organization.

Crummell's ministry spanned more than half a century and three continents. Everywhere, at all times, he labored to prepare black people and to build institutions that would serve them and provide scope for the exercises of their gifts in leadership and creativity. His faith in God, his perseverance in spite of repeated discouragement, his perception that the Church transcended the racism and limited vision of its leaders, and his unfailing belief in the goodness and greatness of black people are the legacy of this African American pioneer.

He died in Red Bank, New Jersey, in 1898.

Rite I   Almighty and everlasting God, we thank thee for thy servant Alexander Crummell, whom thou didst call to preach the gospel to those who were far off and to those who were near. Raise up, we beseech thee, in this and every land, evangelists and heralds of thy kingdom, that thy Church may proclaim the unsearchable riches of our Savior Jesus Christ, who liveth and reigneth with thee and the Holy Spirit, one God, now and for ever. Amen.

Rite II Almighty and everlasting God, we thank you for your servant Alexander Crummell, whom you called to preach the gospel to those who were far off and to those who were near. Raise up, in this and every land, evangelists and heralds of your kingdom, that your Church may proclaim the unsearchable riches of our Savior Jesus Christ, who lives and reigns with you and the Holy Spirit, one God, now and for ever. Amen.

For Liturgical Celebration: [Common of a Missionary, A11] [Common of a Pastor, A14] [For the Ministry I, A49] [For the Mission of the Church, A52]

September 11

Harry Thacker Burleigh
Composer, 1949

Henry (Harry) Thacker Burleigh was an American singer, composer, and arranger who did more than anyone else up to his time to make available the riches of the American Negro spiritual to vast audiences.

Burleigh was born in Erie, Pennsylvania, in 1866. His grandfather, Hamilton Waters, had been a slave who had been blinded by a savage beating but passed along old songs by singing them to his grandson, Harry. Burleigh had a natural voice for singing and sang when and where he could. In 1892, with some difficulty, he won admission to the National Conservatory of Music, where he studied voice and music theory. Although never directly a pupil of Antonín Dvořák, the director of the Conservatory at the time, he worked for Dvořák copying orchestral parts. It was Burleigh who suggested to Dvořák some of the themes that would become Dvorak's *Symphony No. 9: From the New World*.

To support himself while at Conservatory, Burleigh became the baritone soloist at St. George's Episcopal Church in New York City. The presence of a black man in the choir initially caused dissension, but it died down when J. Pierpont Morgan, a member of the parish, took a clear stand on the matter. Even after gaining other employment and becoming a successful composer, Burleigh continued to sing in the choir at St. George's for many years and became a beloved part of the congregation.

Burleigh composed original music, mostly for voice, and was a well-respected arranger and music editor in New York. His art songs were musical settings of the poetry of such great African American poets as Langston Hughes and James Weldon Johnson, among others. His greatest achievement, and that for which he will always be celebrated, was recovering and arranging many Negro spirituals for solo voice and piano so that they could be widely heard on the concert stage. Various choral versions of the spirituals had been well known in the black churches, but it was Burleigh's arrangements that made this distinctively American music available to the masses.

Burleigh died on September 12, 1949.

Rite I   God, our strong deliverer: We bless thy Name for the grace given to Harry Thacker Burleigh, who didst lift up in song the struggles of thy people. Let that Spirit of love which spurred him draw us and thy whole Church to raise our distinct voices into one great harmony of praise; through the same Jesus Christ, who with thee and the Holy Spirit liveth and reigneth, one God, now and for ever. Amen.

Rite II God, our strong deliverer: We bless your Name for the grace given to Harry Thacker Burleigh, who lifted up in song the struggles of your people. Let that Spirit of love which spurred him draw us and your whole Church to raise our distinct voices into one great harmony of praise; through the same Jesus Christ, who with you and the Holy Spirit lives and reigns, one God, now and for ever. Amen.

For Liturgical Celebration: [Common of an Artist, Writer, or Composer, A27]

September 12

John Henry Hobart
Bishop of New York, 1830

John Henry Hobart was one of the leaders who revived The Episcopal Church, following the first two decades of its independent life after the American Revolution, a time that has been described as one of "suspended animation." Born in Philadelphia, September 14, 1775, Hobart was educated at the Universities of Pennsylvania and Princeton, graduating from the latter in 1793. Bishop William White, his longtime friend and adviser, ordained him deacon in 1798 and priest in 1801.

After serving parishes in Pennsylvania, New Jersey, and Long Island, Hobart became assistant minister of Trinity Church, New York City, in 1800. He was consecrated Assistant Bishop of New York on May 29, 1811. Five years later he succeeded Bishop Benjamin Moore, both as diocesan bishop and as rector of Trinity Church. He died at Auburn, New York, September 12, 1830, and was buried beneath the chancel of Trinity Church in New York City.

Within his first four years as bishop, Hobart doubled the number of his clergy and quadrupled the number of missionaries. Before his death, he had planted a church in almost every major town of New York State and had opened missionary work among the Oneida tribe of Native Americans. He was one of the founders of the General Theological Seminary, and the reviver of Geneva, now Hobart, College.

A strong and unbending upholder of Church standards, Hobart established the Bible and Common Prayer Book Society of New York, and was one of the first American scholars to produce theological and devotional manuals for the laity. These "tracts," as they were called, and the personal impression he made on the occasion of a visit to Oxford, were an influence on the development of the Tractarian Movement in England. Both friends and foes respected Hobart for his staunch faith, his consuming energy, his personal integrity, and his missionary zeal.

Rite I   Revive thy Church, Lord God of hosts, whenever it falls into complacency and sloth, by raising up devoted leaders, like thy servant John Henry Hobart, whom we remember today; and grant that their faith and vigor of mind may awaken thy people to thy message and their mission; through Jesus Christ our Lord, who liveth and reigneth with thee and the Holy Spirit, one God, for ever and ever. Amen.

Rite II   Revive your Church, Lord God of hosts, whenever it falls into complacency and sloth, by raising up devoted leaders, like your servant John Henry Hobart, whom we remember today; and grant that their faith and vigor of mind may awaken your people to your message and their mission; through Jesus Christ our Lord, who lives and reigns with you and the Holy Spirit, one God, for ever and ever. Amen.

For Liturgical Celebration: [Common of a Pastor, A14] [For the Ministry II, A50] [For Education, A60]

September 13

John Chrysostom
Bishop of Constantinople, 407

John Chrysostom, Patriarch of Constantinople, is one of the great saints of the Eastern Church. He was born about 354 in Antioch, Syria. As a young man, he responded to the call of desert monasticism until his health was impaired. He returned to Antioch after six years, and was ordained a priest. In 397, he became Patriarch of Constantinople. His episcopate was short and tumultuous. Many criticized his ascetical life in the episcopal residence, and he incurred the wrath of the Empress Eudoxia, who believed that he had called her a "Jezebel." He was twice exiled, and he died during the second period of banishment, on September 14, 407. Thirty-one years later, his remains were brought back to Constantinople, and buried on January 27.

John, called "Chrysostom," which means "the golden-mouthed," was one of the greatest preachers in the history of the Church. People flocked to hear him. His eloquence was accompanied by an acute sensitivity to the needs of people. He saw preaching as an integral part of pastoral care, and as a medium of teaching. He warned that if a priest had no talent for preaching the Word, the souls of those in his charge "will fare no better than ships tossed in the storm."

His sermons provide insights into the liturgy of the Church, and especially into eucharistic practices. He describes the liturgy as a glorious experience, in which all of heaven and earth join. His sermons emphasize the importance of lay participation in the Eucharist. "Why do you marvel," he wrote, "that the people anywhere utter anything with the priest at the altar, when in fact they join with the Cherubim themselves, and the heavenly powers, in offering up sacred hymns?"

His treatise, *Six Books on the Priesthood*, is a classic manual on the priestly office and its awesome demands. The priest, he wrote, must be "dignified, but not haughty; awe-inspiring, but kind; affable in his authority; impartial, but courteous; humble, but not servile, strong but gentle ... "

Rite I O God, who didst give thy servant John Chrysostom grace eloquently to proclaim thy righteousness in the great congregation, and fearlessly to bear reproach for the honor of thy Name: mercifully grant to all bishops and pastors such excellence in preaching, and fidelity in ministering thy Word, that thy people may be partakers with them of the glory that shall be revealed; through Jesus Christ our Lord, who liveth and reigneth with thee and the Holy Spirit, one God for ever and ever. Amen.

Rite II O God, you gave your servant John Chrysostom grace eloquently to proclaim your righteousness in the great congregation, and fearlessly to bear reproach for the honor of your Name: mercifully grant to all bishops and pastors such excellence in preaching, and faithfulness in ministering your Word, that your people may be partakers with them of the glory that shall be revealed; through Jesus Christ our Lord, who lives and reigns with you and the Holy Spirit, one God for ever and ever. Amen.

For Liturgical Celebration: [Common of a Theologian and Teacher, A17] [Common of a Pastor, A14] [For the Ministry II, A50] [Of the Holy Trinity, A37] [Common of a Prophetic Witness, A31]

September 15

Cyprian
Bishop and Martyr of Carthage, 258

Cyprian was a rich, aristocratic, and cultivated rhetorician in North Africa. He was converted to Christianity about 246, and by 248 was chosen Bishop of Carthage. A year later, in the persecution under the Emperor Decius, Cyprian went into hiding. For this he was severely criticized. Nonetheless, he kept in touch with his Church by letter, and directed it with wisdom and compassion. In the controversy over what to do with those who had lapsed during the persecution, Cyprian held that they could be reconciled to the Church after suitable periods of penance, the gravity of the lapse determining the length of the penance. His moderate position was the one that generally prevailed in the Church, over that of the rigorist Novatian, who led a group into schism at Rome and Antioch over this question. In another persecution, under the Emperor Valerian, Cyprian was placed under house arrest in Carthage, and, on September 14, 258, he was beheaded.

Many of Cyprian's writings have been preserved. His *Letter No. 63* contains one of the earliest affirmations that the priest, in offering the Eucharist ("the sacrifice"), acts in the place of Christ, imitating his actions.

In his treatise, *On the Lord's Prayer*, he wrote: "We say 'Hallowed be thy Name,' not that we want God to be made holy by our prayers, but because we seek from the Lord that his Name may be made holy in us, . . . so that we who have been made holy in Baptism may persevere in what we have begun to be."

Although there is some question whether his book, *On the Unity of the Catholic Church*, affirms papal primacy, there is no question about the clarity of his statements on the unity of the college of bishops and the sin of schism. "The episcopate is a single whole," he wrote, "in which each bishop's share gives him a right to, and a responsibility for, the whole. So is the Church a single whole, though she spreads far and wide into a multitude of Churches . . . If you leave the Church of Christ you will not come to Christ's rewards, you will be an alien, an outcast, an enemy. You cannot have God for your Father unless you have the Church for your Mother."

Rite I   Almighty God, who gave to thy servant Cyprian boldness to confess the Name of our Savior Jesus Christ before the rulers of this world and courage to die for this faith: Grant that we may always be ready to give a reason for the hope that is in us and to suffer gladly for the sake of our Lord Jesus Christ; who liveth and reigneth with thee and the Holy Spirit, one God, for ever and ever. Amen.

Rite II   Almighty God, who gave to your servant Cyprian boldness to confess the Name of our Savior Jesus Christ before the rulers of this world and courage to die for this faith: Grant that we may always be ready to give a reason for the hope that is in us and to suffer gladly for the sake of our Lord Jesus Christ; who lives and reigns with you and the Holy Spirit, one God, for ever and ever. Amen.

For Liturgical Celebration: [Common of a Martyr, A7] [Common of a Pastor, A14] [Common of a Theologian and Teacher, A17] [Of the Holy Cross, A41] [For the Unity of the Church, A48] [For the Ministry II, A50]

September 15

James Chisholm
Priest, 1855

James Chisholm, born in 1815, was the rector of St. John's Episcopal Church in Portsmouth, Virginia, when, in 1855, an aggressive yellow fever epidemic swept through tidewater Virginia. Many of the region's wealthy citizens were able to escape the area to avoid exposure and fears of contamination. In most cases, the physicians and clergy who served them departed as well. This left the area's poor bereft of doctors, caregivers, and, in some cases, the basic provisions of food and water to sustain life.

James Chisholm sent his family away to safety, staying behind to provide whatever care for the sick he could. Chisholm provided food, amateur medical assistance, and pastoral care. He was even known to have dug graves for those who had died.

As the ravages of the plague were beginning to subside, Chisholm, weary to the point of exhaustion from his faithful priestly service, contracted the fever, and died the same year.

An account of Chisholm's sacrifice, written only months after his death, marvels at the inner strength that Chisholm discovered that enabled him to stay behind and serve the people, many of whom were only waiting to die. Before the crisis, Chisholm was described as having been retiring to the point of bashfulness, delicate, weak, and lacking much fortitude. When faced, however, with the call of these priestly duties in the face of great hardship, Chisholm showed a strength and courage few knew he possessed.

Rite I Merciful God, who didst call thy priest James Chisholm to sacrifice his life while working amid great suffering and death: Help us, like him, to live by the faith we profess, following in the footsteps of Jesus Christ our Lord; who with the Father and the Holy Spirit liveth and reigneth, one God, in glory everlasting. Amen.

Rite II Merciful God, you called your priest James Chisholm to sacrifice his life while working amid great suffering and death: Help us, like him, to live by the faith we profess, following in the footsteps of Jesus Christ our Lord; who with the Father and the Holy Spirit lives and reigns, one God, in glory everlasting. Amen.

For Liturgical Celebration: [Common of a Pastor, A14] [For the Ministry III, A51] [For Social Service, A59] [For the Sick, A57]

September 16

Ninian
Bishop in Galloway, c. 430

The dates of Ninian's life, and the exact extent of his work, are much disputed. The earliest, and possibly the best, account is the brief one in the Venerable Bede's *Ecclesiastical History*.

Ninian was a Romanized Briton, born in the latter half of the fourth century in southern Scotland. He is said to have been educated in Rome and to have received episcopal ordination. But the main influence on his life was Martin of Tours, with whom he spent some time, and from whom he gained his ideals of an episcopal-monastic structure designed for missionary work.

About the time of Martin's death in 397, Ninian established his base at a place called Candida Casa ("White House") or Whithorn in Galloway, which he dedicated to Martin. Traces of place names and church dedications suggest that his work covered the Solway Plains and the Lake District of England. Ninian seems also to have converted many of the Picts of northern Scotland, as far north as the Moray Firth.

Ninian, together with Patrick, is one of the links of continuity between the ancient Roman-British Church and the developing Celtic Christianity of Ireland and Scotland.

Rite I O God, who by the preaching of thy blessed servant and bishop Ninian didst cause the light of the Gospel to shine in the land of Britain: Grant, we beseech thee, that, having his life and labors in remembrance, we may show forth our thankfulness by following the example of his zeal and patience; through Jesus Christ our Lord, who liveth and reigneth with thee and the Holy Spirit, one God, for ever and ever. Amen.

Rite II O God, by the preaching of your blessed servant and bishop Ninian you caused the light of the Gospel to shine in the land of Britain: Grant, we pray, that having his life and labors in remembrance we may show our thankfulness by following the example of his zeal and patience; through Jesus Christ our Lord, who lives and reigns with you and the Holy Spirit, one God, for ever and ever. Amen.

For Liturgical Celebration: [Common of a Missionary, A11] [Common of a Monastic or Professed Religious, A20] [Common of a Pastor, A14] [For the Ministry II, A50] [For the Mission of the Church, A52]

September 17

Hildegard
1179

Hildegard of Bingen, born in 1098 in the lush Rhineland Valley, was a mystic, poet, composer, dramatist, doctor, and scientist. Her parents' tenth child, she was tithed to the Church and raised by the anchoress Jutta in a cottage near the Benedictine monastery of Disibodenberg.

Drawn by the life of silence and prayer, other women joined them, finding the freedom, rare outside women's religious communities, to develop their intellectual gifts. They organized as a convent under the authority of the abbot of Disibodenberg, with Jutta as abbess. When Jutta died, Hildegard, then 38, became abbess. Later she founded independent convents at Bingen (1150) and Eibingen (1165), with the Archbishop of Mainz as her only superior.

From childhood, Hildegard experienced dazzling spiritual visions. At 43, a voice commanded her to tell what she saw. So began an outpouring of extraordinarily original writings illustrated by unusual and wondrous illuminations. These works abound with feminine imagery for God and God's creative activity.

In 1147, Bernard of Clairvaux recommended her first book of visions, *Scivias*, to Pope Eugenius III, leading to papal authentication at the Synod of Trier. Hildegard became famous, eagerly sought for counsel, a correspondent of kings and queens, abbots and abbesses, archbishops and popes.

She carried out four preaching missions in northern Europe, unprecedented activity for a woman. She practiced medicine, focusing on women's needs; published treatises on natural science and philosophy; and wrote a liturgical drama, *The Play of the Virtues*, in which personified virtues sing their parts and the devil, condemned to live without music, can only speak. For Hildegard, music was essential to worship. Her liturgical compositions, unusual in structure and tonality, were described by contemporaries as "chant of surpassing sweet melody" and "strange and unheard-of music."

Hildegard lived in a world accustomed to male governance. Yet, within her convents, and to a surprising extent outside them, she exercised a commanding spiritual authority based on confidence in her visions and considerable political astuteness. When she died in 1179, at 81, she left a rich legacy which speaks eloquently across the ages.

Rite I   God of all times and seasons: Give us grace that we, after the example of thy servant Hildegard, may both know and make known the joy and jubilation of being part of thy creation, and show forth thy glory, not only with our lips but in our lives; through Jesus Christ our Savior, who liveth and reigneth with thee and the Holy Spirit, one God, for ever and ever. Amen.

Rite II   God of all times and seasons: Give us grace that we, after the example of your servant Hildegard, may both know and make known the joy and jubilation of being part of your creation, and show forth your glory, not only with our lips but in our lives; through Jesus Christ our Savior, who lives and reigns with you and the Holy Spirit, one God, for ever and ever. Amen.

For Liturgical Celebration: [Common of a Monastic or Professed Religious, A20] [Common of an Artist, Writer, or Composer, A27] [Common of a Theologian and Teacher, A17] [Of the Incarnation, A39]

September 18

Edward Bouverie Pusey
Priest, 1882

The revival of High Church teachings and practices in the Anglican Communion, known as the Oxford Movement, found its acknowledged leader in Edward Bouverie Pusey. Born near Oxford, August 22, 1800, Pusey spent all his scholarly life in that University as Regius Professor of Hebrew and as Canon of Christ Church. At the end of 1833, he joined John Keble and John Henry Newman in producing the *Tracts for the Times*, which gave the Oxford Movement its popular name of Tractarianism.

His most influential activity, however, was his preaching—catholic in content, evangelical in his zeal for souls. But to many of his more influential contemporaries, it seemed dangerously innovative. A sermon preached before the University in 1843 on "The Holy Eucharist, a Comfort to the Penitent" was condemned without his being given an opportunity to defend it, and he himself was suspended from preaching for two years—a judgment he bore most patiently. His principles were thus brought before the public, and attention was drawn to the doctrine of the Real Presence of Christ in the Eucharist. From another University sermon, on "The Entire Absolution of the Penitent," may be dated the revival of private confession in the Anglican Communion.

When Newman was received into the Roman Catholic Church in 1845, Pusey's adherence to the Church of England kept many from following, and he defended them in their teachings and practices.

After the death of his wife in 1839, Pusey devoted much of his family fortune to the establishment of churches for the poor and much of his time and care to the establishment of sisterhoods. In 1845, he established the first Anglican sisterhood since the Reformation. It was at this community's convent, Ascot Priory in Berkshire, that Pusey died on September 16, 1882. His body was brought back to Christ Church and buried in the cathedral nave. Pusey House, a house of studies founded after his death, perpetuates his name at Oxford. His own erudition and integrity gave stability to the Oxford Movement and won many to its principles.

Rite I Grant unto us, O God, that in all time of our testing we may know thy presence and obey thy will; that, following the example of thy servant Edward Bouverie Pusey, we may with integrity and courage accomplish what thou givest us to do, and endure what thou givest us to bear; through Jesus Christ our Lord, who liveth and reigneth with thee and the Holy Spirit, one God, for ever and ever. Amen.

Rite II Grant, O God, that in all time of our testing we may know your presence and obey your will; that, following the example of your servant Edward Bouverie Pusey, we may with integrity and courage accomplish what you give us to do, and endure what you give us to bear; through Jesus Christ our Lord, who lives and reigns with you and the Holy Spirit, one God, for ever and ever. Amen.

For Liturgical Celebration: [Common of a Theologian and Teacher, A17] [Common of a Pastor, A14] [Of the Holy Eucharist, A40] [For the Ministry II, A50]

September 18

Dag Hjalmar Agne Carl Hammarskjöld,
1961

Dag Hjalmar Agne Carl Hammarskjöld was a Swedish diplomat, economist, and author, known particularly for the way in which his Christian faith informed his global peacemaking.

Hammarskjöld was born into a family who had served the Swedish crown for centuries; his father became Prime Minister a few years after Dag's birth. Even before graduating from Uppsala University with a law degree, Hammarskjöld was serving as assistant secretary of the unemployment committee. His career included several positions at the Riksbank and in the Swedish Ministries of Finance and Foreign Affairs. He was widely respected for his integrity and principled decisions.

Hammarskjöld was elected the second Secretary-General of the United Nations, serving from April 1953 until his death on September 18, 1961. He insisted that a central role of the United Nations was to preserve the interests of small nations in relation to the major world powers. His work included peace negotiations in the Middle East, rescuing American servicemen taken prisoner in the Korean War, establishing the UN's peacekeeping forces, and peace negotiations in Africa during the collapse of colonialism. He is also responsible for creating the "meditation room" in the UN Headquarters, where people of any faith could retire for spiritual refreshment.

Hammarskjöld was killed pursuing peace in the Congo, when his plane mysteriously crashed on September 18, 1961. Many people—including President Truman—believed that the plane had been deliberately shot down. He was posthumously awarded the Nobel Peace Prize.

Hammarskjöld's ministry provides a powerful witness to the integration of action and contemplation. Informed in his spiritual life by contemplatives and medieval mystics Meister Eckhart and Jan van Ruysbroek, Hammarskjöld is also well-known for the way in which his life exemplified his oft-quoted statement, "In our age, the road to holiness necessarily passes through the world of action." The witness of those saints who demonstrate integrity in putting service to a common human good above their own self-interest is especially vital to the continued ability of God's people to proclaim the Good News in an increasingly polarized and dangerous world.

Rite I   Almighty God, who hast exalted thy humble Christ as King of Kings and Lord of Lords: Enkindle within the hearts of the leaders of this world a yearning for peace with justice, as thou didst within thy servant Dag Hammarskjöld, and, following his good example, ever guide our feet into the way of peace; through the same Jesus Christ our Lord, who livest and reignest with thee and the Holy Spirit, one God, now and for ever. Amen.

Rite II Almighty God, who exalted your humble Christ as King of Kings and Lord of Lords: Kindle within the hearts of the leaders of this world a yearning for peace with justice, as you did within your servant Dag Hammarskjöld, and, following his good example, ever guide our feet into the way of peace; through the same Jesus Christ our Lord, who lives and reigns with you and the Holy Spirit, one God, now and for ever. Amen.

For Liturgical Celebration: [Common of a Martyr, A7] [Common of a Saint, A23] [Of the Holy Cross, A41] [For all Baptized Christians, A42] [For Peace, A55]

September 19

Theodore of Tarsus
Archbishop of Canterbury, 690

Theodore was born in Asia Minor in 602 in Saint Paul's native city, Tarsus. He was ordained Archbishop of Canterbury by Pope Vitalian on March 26, 668.

A learned monk of the East, Theodore was residing in Rome when the English Church, decimated by plague and torn with strife over rival Celtic and Roman customs, was in need of strong leadership. Theodore provided this for a generation, beginning his episcopate at an age when most people are ready to retire.

When Theodore came to England, he established a school at Canterbury that gained a reputation for excellence in all branches of learning and where many leaders of both the Irish and the English Churches were trained. His effective visitation of all England brought unity to the two strains of tradition among the Anglo-Saxon Christians. For example, he recognized Chad's worthiness and regularized his episcopal ordination.

Theodore gave definitive boundaries to English dioceses, so that their bishops could give better pastoral attention to their people. He presided over synods that brought about reforms, according to established rules of canon law. He also laid the foundations of the parochial organization that still obtains in the English Church.

According to Bede, Theodore was the first archbishop whom all the English obeyed, and possibly to no other leader does English Christianity owe so much. He died in his eighty-eighth year on September 19, 690, and was buried, with Augustine and the other early English archbishops, in the monastic Church of Saints Peter and Paul at Canterbury.

Rite I   Almighty God, who didst call thy servant Theodore of Tarsus from Rome to the see of Canterbury and didst give him gifts of grace and wisdom to establish unity where there had been division and order where there had been chaos: Create in thy Church, we pray thee, by the operation of the Holy Spirit, such godly union and concord that it may proclaim, both by word and example, the Gospel of the Prince of Peace; who liveth and reigneth with thee and the Holy Spirit, one God, for ever and ever. Amen.

Rite II Almighty God, you called your servant Theodore of Tarsus from Rome to the see of Canterbury and gave him gifts of grace and wisdom to establish unity where there had been division and order where there had been chaos: Create in your Church, by the operation of the Holy Spirit, such godly union and concord that it may proclaim, both by word and example, the Gospel of the Prince of Peace; who lives and reigns with you and the Holy Spirit, one God, for ever and ever. Amen.

For Liturgical Celebration: [Common of a Pastor, A14] [For the Ministry II, A50]

September 20

John Coleridge Patteson, Bishop of Melanesia, and his Companions
Martyrs, 1871

The death of Bishop Patteson and his companions at the hands of Melanesian islanders, whom Patteson had sought to protect from slave-traders, aroused the British government to take serious measures to prevent piratical man-hunting in the South Seas. Their martyrdom was the seed that produced the strong and vigorous Church which flourishes in Melanesia today.

Patteson was born in London, April 1, 1827, of a Devonshire family. He attended Balliol College, Oxford, where he took his degree in 1849. After travel in Europe and a study of languages, at which he was adept, he became a Fellow of Merton College in 1852 and was ordained the following year.

While serving as a curate of Alphington, Devonshire, near his family home, he responded to Bishop G. A. Selwyn's call in 1855 for helpers in New Zealand. He established a school for boys on Norfolk Island to train native Christian workers. It is said that he learned to speak some twenty-three of the languages of the Melanesian people. On February 24, 1861, he was consecrated Bishop of Melanesia.

On a visit to the island of Nakapu, in the Santa Cruz group, Patteson was stabbed five times in the breast, in mistaken retaliation for the brutal outrages committed some time earlier by slave-traders. In the attack, several of Patteson's company were also killed or wounded. Bishop Selwyn later reconciled the natives of Melanesia to the memory of one who came to help and not to hurt.

Rite I   Almighty God, who didst call thy faithful servant John Coleridge Patteson and his companions to be witnesses and martyrs in the islands of Melanesia and by their labors and sufferings didst raise up a people for thine own possession: Pour out thy Holy Spirit upon thy Church in every land, that, by the service and sacrifice of many, thy holy Name may be glorified and thy kingdom enlarged; through Jesus Christ our Lord, who liveth and reigneth with thee and the Holy Spirit, one God, for ever and ever. Amen.

Rite II Almighty God, you called your faithful servant John Coleridge Patteson and his companions to be witnesses and martyrs in the islands of Melanesia and by their labors and sufferings raised up a people for your own possession: Pour out your Holy Spirit upon your Church in every land, that, by the service and sacrifice of many, your holy Name may be glorified and your kingdom enlarged; through Jesus Christ our Lord, who lives and reigns with you and the Holy Spirit, one God, for ever and ever. Amen.

For Liturgical Celebration: [Common of a Martyr, A7] [Common of a Missionary, A11] [Common of a Pastor, A14] [Of the Holy Cross, A41] [For the Ministry II, A50] [For the Mission of the Church, A52]

September 22

Philander Chase
Bishop of Ohio and of Illinois, 1852

Born the youngest of fifteen children on December 14, 1775, in Cornish, New Hampshire, Philander Chase attended Dartmouth College, where he prepared to become a Congregationalist minister. While at Dartmouth, he happened upon a copy of the Book of Common Prayer. Next to the Bible, he thought it was the most excellent book he had ever studied and believed that it was surely inspired by God. At the age of nineteen he was confirmed in The Episcopal Church.

Following graduation from Dartmouth, Chase worked as a schoolteacher in Albany, New York, and read for Holy Orders. Ordained a deacon in 1798, he began mission work on the northern and western frontiers among the pioneers and the Mohawk and Oneida peoples. The first of the many congregations he founded was at Lake George in New York State.

Ordained a priest in 1799, at the age of twenty-three, Chase served as rector of Christ Church, Poughkeepsie, New York, until 1805. He then moved to New Orleans, where he organized the first Protestant congregation in Louisiana. That parish now serves as the cathedral church for the Diocese of Louisiana. In 1810, he returned north to Hartford, Connecticut, where he served for six years as rector of Christ Church, now the cathedral church of the Diocese of Connecticut. In 1817, he accepted a call to be the first rector of St. John's Church in Worthington, Ohio. A year later he was elected the first Bishop of Ohio. He immediately began founding congregations and organizing the diocese. He also established Kenyon College and Bexley Hall Seminary.

In 1831, Chase resigned as Bishop of Ohio and began ministering to Episcopalians and the unchurched in southern Michigan. In 1835, he was elected the first Bishop of Illinois and served in this office until he died on September 20, 1852. During his time in Illinois, he founded numerous congregations, together with Jubilee College, which included a seminary. As the senior bishop in The Episcopal Church, he served as the Presiding Bishop from 1843 until his death.

Rite I Almighty God, whose Son Jesus Christ is the pioneer and perfecter of our faith: We give thee heartfelt thanks for the pioneering spirit of thy servant Philander Chase and for his zeal in opening new frontiers for the ministry of thy Church. Grant us grace to minister in Christ's name in every place, led by bold witnesses to the Gospel of the Prince of Peace, even Jesus Christ our Lord, who liveth and reigneth with thee and the Holy Spirit, one God, for ever and ever. Amen.

Rite II Almighty God, whose Son Jesus Christ is the pioneer and perfecter of our faith: We give you heartfelt thanks for the pioneering spirit of your servant Philander Chase and for his zeal in opening new frontiers for the ministry of your Church. Grant us grace to minister in Christ's name in every place, led by bold witnesses to the Gospel of the Prince of Peace, Jesus Christ our Lord, who lives and reigns with you and the Holy Spirit, one God, for ever and ever. Amen.

For Liturgical Celebration: [Common of a Pastor, A14] [For the Ministry II, A50]

September 23

Thecla
Apostle and Proto-martyr among Women, c. 70

Thecla, widely known as a disciple of the apostle Paul, was one of the most popular female saints in the early Church. Her story is told in the second-century *Acts of Paul and Thecla*. According to this narrative, upon hearing Paul preach the gospel, Thecla abandoned her plans for marriage and followed Paul. Condemned to burn at the stake, her life was saved by a miraculous thunderstorm. As her adventures continued, she was thrown to the beasts in the local arena. There she was protected by a fierce lioness. Finally, thinking this was her last chance to be baptized, she threw herself into a pool with ravenous seals and baptized herself in the water, while the seals were struck dead by lightning. The governor then released her, and she went on to travel and preach the gospel.

According to Tertullian (writing in about the year 200), early Christian women appealed to Thecla's example to defend women's freedom to teach and to baptize. A shrine to Thecla in Seleucia (Asia Minor) became a popular pilgrimage site in the fourth and fifth centuries. Devotion to Thecla from Gaul to Palestine is also evident in literature, art, and the practice of naming children after her. Her image appeared on wall paintings, clay flasks, oil lamps, stone reliefs, textile curtains, and other media.

Rite I   O God of liberating power, who didst raise up thine apostle Thecla, permitting no obstacle or peril to inhibit her from bearing witness to new life in Jesus Christ: Empower courageous evangelists among us, that men and women everywhere may know the freedom which thou dost offer; through Jesus Christ our Lord, who liveth and reigneth with thee and the Holy Spirit, one God, for ever and ever. Amen.

Rite II God of liberating power, you raised up your apostle Thecla, who allowed no obstacle or peril to inhibit her from bearing witness to new life in Jesus Christ: Empower courageous evangelists among us, that men and women everywhere may experience the freedom you offer; through Jesus Christ our Lord, who lives and reigns with you and the Holy Spirit, one God, for ever and ever. Amen.

For Liturgical Celebration: [Common of a Martyr, A7] [Of the Holy Cross, A41]

September 24

Anna Ellison Butler Alexander
1947

The first African American deaconess in The Episcopal Church, teacher and minister in southern Georgia, Anna Ellison Butler Alexander was born to recently emancipated slaves on Butler Plantation in MacIntosh County, Georgia, in 1865. She was the first African American set aside as a deaconess in The Episcopal Church in 1907. She founded Good Shepherd Church in rural Glynn County's Pennick community, where she taught children to read—by tradition, from the Book of Common Prayer and the Bible—in a one-room schoolhouse. The school was later expanded to two rooms with a loft where Anna lived. She ministered in Pennick for 53 years, leaving a legacy of love and devotion still felt in Glynn County.

Deaconess Alexander served in difficult times, however. The Diocese of Georgia segregated her congregations in 1907 and African American congregations were not invited to another diocesan convention until 1947. Similarly, it was only in 1970 that the General Convention officially recognized deaconesses as being in deacon's orders. However, her witness—wearing the distinctive dress of a deaconess, traveling by foot from Brunswick through Darien to Pennick, showing care and love for all whom she met—represents the best in Christian witness.

Rite I   O God, who didst call Anna Alexander as a deaconess in thy Church, sending her as a teacher and evangelist to the people of Georgia: Grant us the humility to go wherever thou dost send and the wisdom to teach the word of Christ to whomever we meet, that all may come to the enlightenment thou dost intend for thy people; through Jesus Christ, our Teacher and Savior. Amen.

Rite II   O God, you called Anna Alexander as a deaconess in your Church and sent her as teacher and evangelist to the people of Georgia: Grant us the humility to go wherever you send and the wisdom to teach the word of Christ to whomever we meet, that all may come to the enlightenment which you intend for your people; through Jesus Christ, our Teacher and Savior. Amen.

For Liturgical Celebration: [Common of a Prophetic Witness, A31] [For Social Service, A59]

September 25

Sergius
Abbot of Holy Trinity, Moscow, 1392

To the people of Russia, Sergius is a national hero and their patron saint. He was born at Rostov, about 1314.

Civil war in Russia forced Sergius' family to leave the city and to live by farming at Radonezh near Moscow. At the age of twenty, he and his brother began a life of seclusion in a nearby forest, from which developed the Monastery of the Holy Trinity, a center of revival of Russian Christianity. There Sergius remained for the rest of his life, refusing higher advancement, such as the see of Moscow in 1378.

Sergius' firm support of Prince Dimitri Donskoi helped to rally the Russians against their Tartar overlords. Dimitri won a decisive victory against them at the Kulikovo Plains in 1380 and laid the foundation of his people's independent national life.

Sergius was simple and gentle in nature, mystical in temperament, and eager to ensure that his monks should serve the needs of their neighbors. He was able to inspire intense devotion to the Orthodox faith. He died in 1392, and pilgrims still visit his shrine at the monastery of Sergiyev Posad (known as Zagorsk in the Soviet era), which he founded in 1340. The city, located some forty-three miles northwest of Moscow, contains several splendid cathedrals and is the residence of the Patriarch of Moscow.

The Russian Church observes Sergius' memory on September 25. His name is familiar to Anglicans from the Fellowship of St. Alban and St. Sergius, a society established to promote closer relations between the Anglican and Russian Churches.

Rite I   O God, whose blessed Son became poor that we, through his poverty, might be rich: Deliver us from an inordinate love of this world, that we, inspired by the devotion of thy servant Sergius of Moscow, may serve thee with singleness of heart and attain to the riches of the age to come; through Jesus Christ our Lord, who liveth and reigneth with thee and the Holy Spirit, one God, for ever and ever. Amen.

Rite II   O God, whose blessed Son became poor that we, through his poverty, might be rich: Deliver us from an inordinate love of this world, that we, inspired by the devotion of your servant Sergius of Moscow, may serve you with singleness of heart and attain to the riches of the age to come; through Jesus Christ our Lord, who lives and reigns with you and the Holy Spirit, one God, for ever and ever. Amen.

For Liturgical Celebration: [Common of a Monastic or Professed Religious, A20] [Of the Holy Trinity, A37]

September 26

Lancelot Andrewes
Bishop of Winchester, 1626

Lancelot Andrewes, born in 1555, was the favorite preacher of King James I. He was the author of a great number of eloquent sermons, particularly on the Nativity and the Resurrection. They are witty, grounded in the Scriptures, and characterized by the kind of massive learning that the King loved. This makes them difficult reading for modern people, but they repay careful study. T. S. Eliot used the opening of one of Andrewes' Epiphany sermons as the inspiration for his poem, "The Journey of the Magi":

> A cold coming we had of it,
> Just the worst time of the year
> For a Journey, and such a long journey:
> The way deep and the weather sharp,
> The very dead of winter.

Andrewes was also a distinguished biblical scholar, proficient in Hebrew and Greek, and was one of the translators of the Authorized (King James) Version of the Bible. He was Dean of Westminster and headmaster of the school there before he became a bishop and was influential in the education of a number of noted churchmen of his time, in particular, the poet George Herbert.

Andrewes was a very devout man, and one of his most admired works is his *Preces Privatae* ("Private Devotions"), an anthology from the Scriptures and the ancient liturgies, compiled for his own use. It illustrates his piety and throws light on the sources of his theology. He vigorously defended the catholicity of the Church of England against Roman Catholic critics. He was respected by many as the very model of a bishop at a time when bishops were held in low esteem. As his student, John Hacket, later Bishop of Lichfield, wrote about him: "Indeed he was the most Apostolical and Primitive-like Divine, in my Opinion, that wore a Rochet in his Age; of a most venerable Gravity, and yet most sweet in all Commerce; the most Devout that I ever saw, when he appeared before God; of such a Growth in all kind of Learning that very able Clerks were of a low Stature to him."

He died in 1626.

Rite I   Almighty God, who gavest thy servant Lancelot Andrewes the gift of thy Holy Spirit and made him a man of prayer and a faithful pastor of thy people: Perfect in us what is lacking of thy gifts, of faith, to increase it; of hope, to establish it; of love, to kindle it; that we may live in the life of thy grace and glory; through Jesus Christ thy Son our Lord, who liveth and reigneth with thee and the same Holy Spirit, one God, now and for ever. Amen.

Rite II Almighty God, you gave your servant Lancelot Andrewes the gift of your Holy Spirit and made him a man of prayer and a faithful pastor of your people: Perfect in us what is lacking in your gifts, of faith, to increase it; of hope, to establish it; of love, to kindle it; that we may live in the life of your grace and glory; through Jesus Christ your Son our Lord, who lives and reigns with you and the same Holy Spirit, one God, now and for ever. Amen.

For Liturgical Celebration: [Common of a Theologian and Teacher, A17] [Common of a Pastor, A14] [For the Ministry II, A50] [For all Baptized Christians, A42]

September 26

Wilson Carlile
Priest, 1942

Born in 1847 in Brixton, England, Wilson Carlile was, from an early age, afflicted with spinal disease, which made his education difficult. He entered his grandfather's business at the age of thirteen and soon became fluent in French, which he used in his own silk trading endeavors in Paris. His business was eventually ruined in the economic depression of the 1870's. The collapse of his business resulted in physical and emotional distress, and it was during this time that Carlile turned to religion for comfort and a new sense of direction.

After serving as an organist in Dwight L. Moody's evangelistic missions, Carlile was ordained a priest in 1881, serving his curacy at St. Mary Abbots, the parish church in Kensington. He had long been concerned with the Church's lack of presence among the poor and working classes, and as a curate, he encouraged soldiers, grooms, coachmen, and other working laymen to preach the gospel among the residents of some of the worst slums of London. Many among the Church establishment accused Carlile of "dragging the Church into the gutter."

In 1882, he resigned his curacy and devoted himself to the formal establishment of the Church Army, an organization dedicated to the proclamation of the gospel among the least of society. Despite great resistance, he sought official approval for his organization and its work from the Church of England Congress in 1883. In 1885, the Upper Convocation of Canterbury passed a resolution officially approving and recognizing the Church Army. Carlile served as rector of St. Mary-at-Hill, Eastcheap, London, from 1892-1926, where he continued his administration of the Army's ministry. In 1905, he was honored as a Prebendary of St. Paul's Cathedral, London, England.

Today, the Church Army has eight independent geographically based societies across the Anglican Communion and is active in fifteen countries, continuing Carlile's work.

Rite I   God of boundless energy and light: We offer thanks for the courage and passion of Wilson Carlile who, after the example of thy Son, sought new ways to open thy Church to diverse leaders as beacons of the Gospel of Christ. Quicken our hearts to give bold witness to Jesus Christ; who with thee and the Holy Spirit, liveth and reigneth, one God, now and for ever. Amen.

Rite II God of boundless energy and light: We thank you for the courage and passion of Wilson Carlile who, after the example of your Son, sought new ways to open your Church to diverse leaders as beacons of the Gospel of Christ. Quicken our hearts to give bold witness to Jesus Christ; who with you and the Holy Spirit, lives and reigns, one God, now and for ever. Amen.

For Liturgical Celebration: [Common of a Missionary, A11] [Of the Holy Spirit, A38] [For the Ministry III, A51] [For the Mission of the Church, A52]

September 27

Vincent de Paul
Religious, and Prophetic Witness, 1660

Born in France in 1580 to a peasant family, Vincent took his theological studies at Toulouse and was ordained in 1600.

When called to hear the confession of a dying man, Vincent was shocked by the spiritual naiveté of the penitent. In response, Vincent preached sermons on confession in the village chapel of Folleville, calling people to the necessity of repentance. So persuasive were his sermons, that villagers stood in line to go to confession. Vincent had underestimated their spiritual hunger. In 1626, Vincent and three priests pledged to "aggregate and associate to ourselves and to live together as a Congregation . . . and to devote ourselves to the salvation of the people."

Vincent devoted great energy to conducting retreats for clergy because of the widespread deficiencies in theological education and priestly formation. He was a pioneer in the renewal of theological education and was instrumental in establishing seminaries.

For Vincent, charity was a predominant virtue that was to be extended to all. He established charitable confraternities to serve the spiritual and physical needs of the poor and sick. He called upon the women of means in Paris to collect funds for his missionary projects, particularly hospitals to serve the poor.

Vincent was, by temperament, a very irascible person. He said that except for the grace of God he would have been "hard and repulsive, rough and cross." But he became tender and affectionate, very sensitive to the needs of others. He had an extraordinary capacity to connect with all types of people and to move them to be empowered by the gospel of Jesus. In the midst of the most distracting occupations his soul was always intimately united with God. Though honored by the great ones of the world, he remained deeply rooted in humility.

At Vincent's funeral, the preacher declared that Vincent had just about "transformed the face of the Church." "The Apostle of Charity" breathed his last in Paris, on September 27, 1660, at the age of eighty.

He is honored in the tradition as the patron saint of charitable causes.

Rite I   Loving God, we offer thanks for thy servant Vincent de Paul, who gave himself to training clergy to work among the poor and provided many institutions to aid the sick, orphans, and prisoners. May we, like him, encounter Christ in the needy, the outcast, and the friendless, that we may come at length into thy kingdom where thou reignest, one God, holy and undivided Trinity, for ever and ever. Amen.

Rite II   Loving God, we thank you for your servant Vincent de Paul, who gave himself to training clergy to work among the poor and provided many institutions to aid the sick, orphans, and prisoners. May we, like him, encounter Christ in the needy, the outcast, and the friendless, that we may come at length into your kingdom where you reign, one God, holy and undivided Trinity, for ever and ever. Amen.

For Liturgical Celebration: [Common of a Prophetic Witness, A31] [Common of a Pastor, A14] [For Social Service, A59]

September 27

Thomas Traherne
Priest, 1674

Though not as well known as John Donne or George Herbert, Thomas Traherne was one of the seventeenth century's most searching, inventive poets and theologians.

Traherne was among about twelve Anglican lyricists dubbed by the rather prosaic Samuel Johnson as "the Metaphysical Poets." Johnson meant this to imply that their poetry was pretentious and obscure. What he missed was not only their erudition but their subtlety and their profound awareness of the depths of Divine Mystery through which they tried to articulate the Christian Faith in a world which was changing from the sure faith of the Middle Ages to the bewildering maze of conflicting opinion which was the "Modern."

Born in 1637, the son of a humble shoemaker in Hereford, Traherne went to Oxford thanks to the generosity of a prosperous relative. He was awarded the B.A. in 1656 and later the M.A. and B.D. He was ordained priest in 1660. From 1667 on he was the chaplain to Sir Orlando Bridgeman, Keeper of the Great Seal. At 37 he died in his patron's house.

Traherne's poetry was unpublished and unknown until it was found in manuscript in a London bookseller's stall at the beginning of the twentieth century. In all the Metaphysical Poets we find the attempt, often through startling images and seemingly contradictory metaphors, to express the inter-penetration of the sacred and the profane, the mortal human and the immortal divine, the verities of the new sciences and the eternal verities of God's revelation in the Incarnation of Jesus Christ. Traherne was particularly taken with the paradox that the naive grandiosity and self-centeredness of a small child was, in fact, a kind of window into the Divine Being. In reading his poetry it is sometimes not clear whether he is speaking of himself as a small child or of the Christ-Child. In fact, he is often inferring both, by which he means us to understand that in the Incarnation, God assumed our humanity and so our humanity is in fact, our blessed access to God.

Rite I   Creator of wonder and majesty, who didst inspire thy poet Thomas Traherne with mystical insight to see thy glory in the natural world and in the faces of men and women around us: Help us to know thee in thy creation and in our neighbors, and to understand our obligations to both, that we may ever grow into the people thou hast created us to be; through our Savior Jesus Christ, who with thee and the Holy Spirit liveth and reigneth, one God, in everlasting light. Amen.

Rite II   Creator of wonder and majesty, you inspired your poet Thomas Traherne with mystical insight to see your glory in the natural world and in the faces of men and women around us: Help us to know you in your creation and in our neighbors, and to understand our obligations to both, that we may ever grow into the people you have created us to be; through our Savior Jesus Christ, who with you and the Holy Spirit lives and reigns, one God, in everlasting light. Amen.

For Liturgical Celebration: [Common of an Artist, Writer, or Composer, A27] [Common of a Pastor, A14]

September 28

Richard Rolle, *1349,* Walter Hilton, *1396, and* Margery Kempe, *c. 1440*
Mystics

Richard Rolle, Walter Hilton, and Margery Kempe were three early and prominent figures associated with Christian mysticism in England.

Richard Rolle, born 1290, was an English hermit about whose early life we know little. At the age of 18, he gave up his studies at Oxford for the ascetic life, out of which grew a ministry of prayer, writing, and spiritual direction. Rolle lived his final years near the Cistercian convent near Hampole, a village in south Yorkshire. Among his chief writings are several scriptural commentaries; some theological writings, originally written in Latin and translated into English; and many poems. Though criticized by many for promoting a highly subjective form of religion, he was an ardent defender of the contemplative life he practiced.

Similarly, though we know little of the early life of Walter Hilton beyond his birth in 1340, evidence suggests he studied at Cambridge. Hilton spent time as a hermit before becoming an Augustinian canon at Thurgarton Priory in Nottinghamshire late in the fourteenth century. In his great work, *The Scale of Perfection*, he develops his understanding of the "luminous darkness" which marks the transition between self-love and the love of God. Similarities between his work and the anonymous *The Cloud of Unknowing* have convinced some to attribute that latter work to him.

Born circa 1373, Margery Kempe, though illiterate, dictated to a priest the *Book of Margery Kempe,* from which we attain most of our knowledge of her. A mystic who experienced intense visions followed by a period of emotional disturbance, subsequent to which she went on pilgrimage to Canterbury, she later made pilgrimages to the Holy Land and to Santiago de Compostela and was encouraged in her efforts by Julian of Norwich. She describes these travels as well as her mystical experiences and her deep compassion for sinners.

Rite I   Gracious God, we offer thanks for the lives and work of Richard Rolle, Walter Hilton, and Margery Kempe, hermits and mystics, who, passing through the cloud of unknowing, beheld thy glory. Help us, after their examples, to see thee more clearly and love thee more dearly, in the Name of Jesus Christ our Savior; who with thee and the Holy Spirit liveth and reigneth, one God, for ever and ever. Amen.

Rite II Gracious God, we give you thanks for the lives and work of Richard Rolle, Walter Hilton, and Margery Kempe, hermits and mystics, who, passing through the cloud of unknowing, beheld your glory. Help us, after their examples, to see you more clearly and love you more dearly, in the Name of Jesus Christ our Savior; who with you and the Holy Spirit lives and reigns, one God, for ever and ever. Amen.

For Liturgical Celebration: [Common of a Theologian and Teacher, A17] [Of the Incarnation, A39]

September 30

Jerome
Priest, and Monk of Bethlehem, 420

Jerome was the foremost biblical scholar of the ancient Church. His Latin translation of the Bible from early Hebrew and Greek texts, known as the Vulgate version, along with his commentaries and homilies on the biblical books, have made him a major intellectual force in the Western Church.

Jerome was born in Stridon, in the Roman province of Dalmatia, about 347, and was converted and baptized during his student days in Rome. On a visit to Trier, in the Rhineland, he found himself attracted to the monastic life, which he tested in a brief but unhappy experience as a hermit in the Syrian desert of Syria. At Antioch in 378, he reluctantly allowed himself to be ordained a presbyter, and there continued his studies in Hebrew and Greek. The following year, he was in Constantinople as a student of Gregory of Nazianzus. From 382 to 384, he was secretary to Pope Damasus I in Rome and spiritual director of many noble Roman ladies, who were becoming interested in the monastic life. It was Damasus who set him to the task of making a new translation of the Bible into Latin—the *vulgus* tongue used by the common people, as distinguished from the classical Greek—hence the name of his translation, the Vulgate.

After the Pope's death, Jerome returned to the East and established a monastery at Bethlehem, where he lived and worked until his death on September 30, 420. He was buried in a chapel beneath the Church of the Nativity, near the traditional place of our Lord's birth.

Jerome's irascible disposition, pride of learning, and extravagant promotion of asceticism involved him in many bitter controversies over both theological and exegetical questions. Yet he was candid at times in admitting his failings, never ambitious for churchly honors, a militant champion of orthodoxy, an indefatigable worker, and a literary stylist with rare gifts.

Rite I   O God, who didst give us the holy Scriptures for a light to shine upon our path: Grant us, after the example of thy servant Jerome, so to learn of thee according to thy Holy Word, that we may find the light that shines more and more to the perfect day; through Jesus Christ our Lord, who liveth and reigneth with thee and the Holy Spirit, one God, now and for ever. Amen.

Rite II   O God, who gave us the holy Scriptures for a light to shine upon our path: Grant us, after the example of your servant Jerome, so to learn of you according to your Holy Word, that we may find the light that shines more and more to the perfect day; through Jesus Christ our Lord, who lives and reigns with you and the Holy Spirit, one God, now and for ever. Amen.

For Liturgical Celebration: [Common of a Monastic or Professed Religious, A20] [Common of a Theologian and Teacher, A17] [Of the Holy Trinity, A37] [Of the Reign of Christ, A46]

OCTOBER

1   Remigius, Bishop of Rheims, c. 530
2
3   John Raleigh Mott, Evangelist and Ecumenical Pioneer, 1955
4   Francis of Assisi, Friar, 1226
5
6   William Tyndale, 1536, and Miles Coverdale, 1568, Translators of the Bible
7   Henry Melchior Muhlenberg, Lutheran Pastor in North America, 1787
8   William Dwight Porter Bliss, Priest, 1926, and Richard Theodore Ely, Economist, 1943
9   Wilfred Thomason Grenfell, Medical Missionary, 1940
10 Vida Dutton Scudder, Educator and Witness for Peace, 1954
11 Philip, Deacon and Evangelist
12
13
14 Samuel Isaac Joseph Scherechewsky, Bishop of Shanghai, 1906
15 Teresa of Avila, Nun, 1582
16 Hugh Latimer and Nicholas Ridley, Bishops and Martyrs, 1555
17 Ignatius, Bishop of Antioch, and Martyr, c. 115
18
19 Henry Martyn, Priest, and Missionary to India and Persia, 1812
19 William Carey, Missionary to India, 1834
20
21
22
23
24 Hiram Hisanori Kano, 1986

25

26 Alfred the Great, King of the West Saxons, 899

27

28

29 James Hannington, Bishop of Eastern Equatorial Africa, and his Companions, Martyrs, 1885

30 John Wyclif, Priest and Prophetic Witness, 1384

31 Paul Shinji Sasaki, Bishop of Mid-Japan, and of Tokyo, 1946, and Philip Lindel Tsen, Bishop of Honan, China, 1954

October 1

Remigius
Bishop of Rheims, c. 530

Remigius, also known as Remi, one of the patron saints of France, was born about 438, the son of the Count of Laon. At the age of twenty-two he became Bishop of Rheims.

Noted for his learning and holiness of life, Remigius is chiefly remembered because he converted and baptized King Clovis of the Franks on Christmas Day, 496. This event changed the religious history of Europe. Clovis, by becoming Catholic instead of Arian, as were most of the Germanic people of the time, was able to unite the Gallo-Roman population and their Christian leaders behind his expanding hegemony over the Germanic rulers of the West and to liberate Gaul from Roman domination. His conversion also made possible the cooperation the Franks gave later to Pope Gregory the Great in his evangelistic efforts for the English.

Certainly, Clovis' motives in accepting Catholic Christianity were mixed, but there is no doubt of the sincerity of his decision, nor of the important role of Remigius in bringing it to pass. When Clovis was baptized, together with 3,000 of his followers, Remigius gave him the well-known charge, "Worship what you have burned, and burn what you have worshiped."

The feast of Remigius is observed at Rheims on January 13, possibly the date of his death. The later date of October 1 is derived from the translation of his relics to a new abbey church by Pope Leo IX in 1049.

Rite I   O God, who by the teaching of thy faithful servant and bishop Remigius didst turn the nation of the Franks from vain idolatry to the worship of thee, the true and living God, in the fullness of the catholic faith: Grant that we who glory in the name of Christian may show forth our faith in worthy deeds; through Jesus Christ our Lord, who liveth and reigneth with thee and the Holy Spirit, one God, for ever and ever. Amen.

Rite II O God, by the teaching of your faithful servant and bishop Remigius you turned the nation of the Franks from vain idolatry to the worship of you, the true and living God, in the fullness of the catholic faith: Grant that we who glory in the name of Christian may show forth our faith in worthy deeds; through Jesus Christ our Lord, who lives and reigns with you and the Holy Spirit, one God, for ever and ever. Amen.

For Liturgical Celebration: [Common of a Missionary, A11] [Common of a Pastor, A14] [For the Ministry II, A50] [For the Mission of the Church, A52]

October 3

John Raleigh Mott
Evangelist and Ecumenical Pioneer, 1955

A dedicated missionary for the worldwide spread of the gospel, John Raleigh Mott connected ecumenism and evangelism as related tasks for modern Christianity.

John Mott was born in Livingston Manor, New York, on May 25, 1865, and moved with family to Iowa in September of that same year. After graduating from Cornell University in 1888, Mott became student secretary of the International Committee of the YMCA and chairman of the executive committee of the Student Volunteer Movement. In 1895, he became General Secretary of the World Student Christian Federation, and, in 1901, he was appointed the Assistant General Secretary of the YMCA. During World War I, President Woodrow Wilson appointed him to the National War Work Council, for which he received the Distinguished Service Medal.

His ecumenical work was rooted in the missionary slogan "The Evangelization of the World in this Generation." Convinced of the need for better cooperation among Christian communions in the global mission field, he served as chairman of the committee that organized the International Missionary Conference in Edinburgh in 1910, over which he also presided. Considered to be the broadest gathering of Christians up to that point, the Conference marked the beginning of the modern ecumenical movement. Speaking before that Conference, Mott summed up his view of Christian missions: "It is a startling and solemnizing fact that even as late as the twentieth century, the Great Command of Jesus Christ to carry the Gospel to all mankind is still so largely unfulfilled . . . The church is confronted today, as in no preceding generation, with a literally worldwide opportunity to make Christ known." Mott continued his involvement in the developing ecumenical movement, participating in the Faith and Order Conference at Lausanne in 1927, and was Vice-President of the Second World Conference on Faith and Order in Edinburgh (1937). He also served as Chairman of the Life and Work Conference in Oxford, also held in 1937.

In 1946, he received the Nobel Peace Prize for his work in establishing and strengthening international organizations which worked for peace. The World Council of Churches, the founding of which was largely driven by Mott's efforts, elected him its life-long Honorary President in 1948. Although Mott was a Methodist, the Episcopal Church recognized his work by making him an honorary canon of the National Cathedral.

Mott died in 1955.

Rite I   O God, the shepherd of all, we offer thanks for the lifelong commitment of thy servant John Raleigh Mott to the Christian nurture of students in many parts of the world; and we pray that, after his example, we may strive for the weaving together of all peoples in friendship, fellowship, and cooperation, and, while life lasts, be evangelists for Jesus Christ, in whom alone is our peace; and who with thee and the Holy Spirit liveth and reigneth, one God, now and for ever. Amen.

Rite II O God, the shepherd of all, we give you thanks for the lifelong commitment of your servant John Raleigh Mott to the Christian nurture of students in many parts of the world; and we pray that, after his example, we may strive for the weaving together of all peoples in friendship, fellowship, and cooperation, and, while life lasts, be evangelists for Jesus Christ, in whom alone is our peace; and who with you and the Holy Spirit lives and reigns, one God, now and for ever. Amen.

For Liturgical Celebration: [Common of a Saint, A23] [For Vocation in Daily Work, A61] [For the Unity of the Church, A48]

October 4

Francis of Assisi
Friar, 1226

Francis, the son of a prosperous merchant of Assisi, was born in 1182. His early youth was spent in harmless revelry and fruitless attempts to win military glory.

Various encounters with beggars and lepers pricked the young man's conscience, and he decided to embrace a life devoted to Lady Poverty. Despite his father's intense opposition, Francis totally renounced all material values and devoted himself to serve the poor. In 1210, Pope Innocent III confirmed the simple Rule for the Order of Friars Minor, a name Francis chose to emphasize his desire to be numbered among the "least" of God's servants.

The order grew rapidly all over Europe. But, by 1221, Francis had lost control of it, since his ideal of strict and absolute poverty, both for the individual friars and for the order as a whole, was found to be too difficult to maintain. His last years were spent in much suffering of body and spirit, but his unconquerable joy never failed.

Not long before his death, during a retreat on Mount La Verna, Francis received, on September 14, Holy Cross Day, the marks of the Lord's wounds, the stigmata, in his own hands and feet and side. Pope Gregory IX, a former patron of the Franciscans, canonized Francis in 1228 and began the erection of the great basilica in Assisi where Francis is buried.

Of all the saints, Francis is the most popular and admired but probably the least imitated; few have attained to his total identification with the poverty and suffering of Christ. Francis left few writings; but, of these, his spirit of joyous faith comes through most truly in the "Canticle of the Sun," which he composed at Clare's convent of St. Damian. The version in *The Hymnal* begins (*The Hymnal 1982*, #406; #407):

Most High, omnipotent, good Lord,
To thee be ceaseless praise outpoured, —
And blessing without measure.
Let creatures all give thanks to thee
And serve in great humility.

Rite I Most high, omnipotent, good Lord, grant thy people grace to renounce gladly the vanities of this world; that, following the way of blessed Francis, we may, for love of thee, delight in thy whole creation with perfectness of joy; through Jesus Christ our Lord, who lives and reigns with thee and the Holy Spirit, one God, for ever and ever. Amen.

Rite II Most high, omnipotent, good Lord, grant your people grace to renounce gladly the vanities of this world; that, following the way of blessed Francis, we may, for love of you, delight in your whole creation with perfectness of joy; through Jesus Christ our Lord, who lives and reigns with you and the Holy Spirit, one God, for ever and ever. Amen.

For Liturgical Celebration: [Common of a Monastic or Professed Religious, A20] [Common of a Theologian and Teacher, A17] [Common of a Prophetic Witness, A31] [Of the Incarnation, A39] [For the Goodness of God's Creation, A65] [For Social Service, A59]

October 6

William Tyndale, 1536, and Miles Coverdale, 1568
Translators of the Bible

William Tyndale was born about 1495 near the Welsh border. He received bachelors and masters degrees from Oxford and also studied at Cambridge. Ordained about 1521, he spent his early ministry as a domestic chaplain and tutor in Gloucestershire and London.

Tyndale was a man with a single passion—to translate the holy Scriptures into English. Lacking official sanction, he went to Germany in 1524. Strongly opposed to his work, King Henry VIII, Cardinal Wolsey, and others sought to destroy his work and put him to death. He was betrayed by a friend and was strangled and burned at the stake on October 6, 1536, in Brussels.

By the time of Tyndale's death, he had completed his translation of the New Testament and major parts of the Old Testament, particularly the Pentateuch. It is estimated that about eighty percent of Tyndale's work found its way into later translations, notably the Authorized Version of 1611 (King James).

Miles Coverdale was born in Yorkshire around 1488. He studied at Cambridge and was ordained in 1514 and soon thereafter joined the Augustinian Friars. Passionate about scriptural translation, he left the monastery in 1526 and eventually went to the Continent, where the work of translation enjoyed strong support.

He completed the first translation into English of the whole Bible in 1535, which was issued as "The Great Bible" in 1539. Archbishop Cranmer adopted Coverdale's translation of the Psalter for the Book of Common Prayer.

Between times of unrest and relative calm, Coverdale shuttled between England and the Continent. He served as a Lutheran pastor while in exile from 1543-1547. He became Bishop of Exeter in 1551 but was deprived of that office at the accession of Queen Mary, due to his Protestant convictions. He again escaped to the Continent, where he lived until the accession to the throne of Elizabeth I in 1559. He is remembered as an outstanding preacher, an uncommonly gifted linguist and translator, and a leader of the Puritan wing of the Church of England.

Rite I Almighty God, who didst plant in the heart of thy servants William Tyndale and Miles Coverdale a consuming passion to bring the Scriptures to people in their native tongue and didst endow them with the gift of powerful and graceful expression and with strength to persevere against all obstacles: Reveal to us, we pray thee, thy saving Word, as we read and study the Scriptures and hear them calling us to repentance and life; through Jesus Christ our Lord, who liveth and reigneth with thee and the Holy Spirit, one God, for ever and ever. Amen.

Rite II Almighty God, you planted in the heart of your servants William Tyndale and Miles Coverdale a consuming passion to bring the Scriptures to people in their native tongue and endowed them with the gift of powerful and graceful expression and with strength to persevere against all obstacles: Reveal to us your saving Word, as we read and study the Scriptures and hear them calling us to repentance and life; through Jesus Christ our Lord, who lives and reigns with you and the Holy Spirit, one God, for ever and ever. Amen.

For Liturgical Celebration: [Common of an Artist, Writer, or Composer, A27] [Common of a Pastor, A14] [For the Ministry III, A51]

October 7

Henry Melchior Muhlenberg
Lutheran Pastor in North America, 1787

Henry Melchior Muhlenberg is regarded as the patriarch of Lutheranism in North America.

Muhlenberg, born near Hannover, Germany, in 1711, received his education in Göttingen and Halle before immigrating to the American colonies in 1742. Lutherans came to the colonies from a variety of regional and ethnic backgrounds and tended to build churches wherever they settled, sometimes with Lutherans of different origins settling in closer proximity to each other. There was little organization among these disparate groups until the arrival of Muhlenberg.

Upon his arrival, Muhlenberg visited Lutherans in coastal Carolina and Georgia before making his way to Philadelphia. With enormous energy and unflagging patience, Muhlenberg began to call together the Lutherans, first the Germans, then the Swedes, until the formation of the first Lutheran synod in America in 1748, the Ministerium of Pennsylvania. At the inaugural synod, Muhlenberg offered a common liturgy for use among Lutherans. The liturgy was adopted and became the essential element in unifying the Lutherans in America for several generations. Muhlenberg's axiom, "one book, one church," has been a benchmark for liturgical revision among North American Lutherans to the present day.

Muhlenberg also recognized the pastoral challenges of organizing a new church in the New World. In the old countries, the church was closely allied with the state. Taxes to support the churches were collected by the state, and Christian education was part of the curriculum in every school. In the New World, the churches were to be voluntary, self-supporting associations, and education in matters of Christian faith was to be the concern of church and home.

Muhlenberg's family played prominent roles in the birth of the new nation. One of his sons served as a brigadier general in the Revolution, while another was a member of the Continental Congress and later the first speaker of the House of Representatives. His great-grandson, William Augustus Muhlenberg, was a priest who shaped The Episcopal Church in the mid-nineteenth century (see April 8).

Henry Melchior Muhlenberg died on October 7, 1787.

Rite I Loving God, shepherd of thy people: We give thanks to thee for the ministry of Henry Melchior Muhlenberg, who left his native land to minister where called. Make us mindful of our own vocation to serve where thou dost call us; in the Name of Jesus Christ our Lord, who liveth and reigneth with thee and the Holy Spirit, one God, for ever and ever. Amen.

Rite II Loving God, shepherd of your people, we thank you for the ministry of Henry Melchior Muhlenberg, who left his native land to minister where called; make us mindful of our own vocation to serve where you call us; in the Name of Jesus Christ our Lord, who lives and reigns with you and the Holy Spirit, one God, for ever and ever. Amen.

For Liturgical Celebration: [Common of a Pastor, A14] [For the Ministry I, A49]

October 8

William Dwight Porter Bliss, Priest, 1926, and Richard Theodore Ely, Economist, 1943

Richard Theodore Ely was born in 1854 in Ripley, New York. The son of Presbyterians, he became an Episcopalian while working on his undergraduate degree at Columbia. After receiving his doctorate in economics at the University of Heidelberg, Germany, he taught at Johns Hopkins University and then at the University of Wisconsin, Madison. He was appointed Professor of Economics at Northwestern in 1925.

In 1894, Ely was accused of teaching socialist principles, and an effort was made to remove him from this professorship. Ely, who rejected the extremes of both capitalism and socialism, argued for competition with regulation that would raise the moral and ethical level of economic practice.

Ely claimed that the gospel was social rather than individualistic in nature, and he consistently called The Episcopal Church to reform capitalism for the rights and dignity of the American worker. He was one of the founders of the Christian Social Union, and served as its Secretary. Ely's principles influenced his friend Walter Rauschenbusch, a major figure in the Social Gospel Movement. Ely also advocated for more frequent celebration and reception of the Eucharist, seeing a direct connection between his social views and their sacramental grounding.

Ely died in Old Lyme, Connecticut, on October 4, 1943.

William Dwight Porter Bliss was born in Constantinople, Turkey, on August 20, 1856, the son of Christian missionaries. Like R.T. Ely, Bliss believed that the Church was called to work for economic justice, the principles of which were grounded in the gospel. Originally ordained a Congregationalist minister, in 1886 he became an Episcopal deacon and was ordained to the priesthood the next year. He served parishes in Massachusetts, California, and New York before organizing the first Christian Socialist Society in the United States in 1899. Bliss consistently claimed that economic justice, for which all Christians were responsible, was "rooted and grounded in Christ, the liberator, the head of humanity."

Bliss wrote widely on the relationship between faith and economic justice. Among his written works are *The Encyclopedia of Social Reform* (1898) and *The Hand-Book of Socialism* (1895).

In 1914, he travelled to Switzerland on behalf of the YMCA and served there as a pastor until 1921.

Bliss died on October 8, 1926.

———

Rite I Blessed God, whose Son Jesus came as servant to all: We offer thanks for William Bliss and Richard Ely, whose dedication to the commonweal through economic justice led them to be bold reformers of the world and the Church; and we pray that we, with them, may find our true happiness through self-sacrifice in service of thy reign, where all the hungry are fed and the downtrodden are raised up, through Jesus Christ our Liberator; who with thee and the Holy Spirit liveth and reigneth, one God, now and for ever. Amen.

Rite II Blessed God, whose Son Jesus came as servant to all: We thank you for William Bliss and Richard Ely, whose dedication to the commonweal through economic justice led them to be bold reformers of the world and the Church; and we pray that we, with them, may find our true happiness through self-sacrifice in service of your reign, where all the hungry are fed and the downtrodden are raised up, through Jesus Christ our Liberator; who with you and the Holy Spirit lives and reigns, one God, now and for ever. Amen.

For Liturgical Celebration: [Common of a Prophetic Witness, A31] [For Labor Day, A62] [For Rogation Days II, A56]

October 9

Wilfred Thomason Grenfell
Medical Missionary, 1940

Wilfred Thomason Grenfell was born in Cheshire, England, in 1865, the second of four sons of the Reverend Algernon Sidney Grenfell, headmaster of Mostyn House School, Parkgate, and his wife Jane Georgina Hutchinson. While studying medicine at the London Hospital Medical School, he came under the influence of the American revivalist Dwight L. Moody. An athlete skilled in boxing, cricket, rugby, and rowing, he was an early exponent of the "muscular Christianity" made famous by Charles Kingsley.

In 1887, as a qualified doctor, he joined the Royal National Mission to Deep-Sea Fisherman as a medical missionary, serving in Iceland and the Bay of Biscay. During a visit to Labrador in 1892, Grenfell was appalled by the near-starvation, poverty, and ill health of the British workers there. Devoting himself to their nurture and improvement, be built the first hospital of the Labrador Medical Mission in 1893, eventually opening boarding schools, hospital ships, clothing distribution centers, and the Seaman's Institute at St. John's, Newfoundland, often with money he raised himself with speaking tours and books. Many benefactors from New York and New England enabled his relief efforts. Several of Grenfell's books about Labrador and his religious writings appealed to those with whom he worked due to his modest and simple style.

In 1912, he organized the International Grenfell Association, with branches in the United States, Newfoundland, and other parts of Canada, and this organization supported his work and ministry for the remainder of his career. He was knighted for his work in 1927.

Sir William retired from his work in 1935, due to ill health. He died in Vermont in October of 1940.

Rite I Compassionate God, whose Son Jesus Christ taught that by ministering to the least of our brothers and sisters, we minister to him: Make us ever ready to respond to the needs of others, that, inspired by the ministry of Wilfred Grenfell to the sick and to seafarers in Labrador and northern Newfoundland, our actions may witness to the love of our Savior Jesus Christ; who with thee and the Holy Spirit liveth and reigneth, one God, for ever and ever. Amen.

Rite II Compassionate God, whose Son Jesus Christ taught that by ministering to the least of our brothers and sisters, we minister to him: Make us ever ready to respond to the needs of others, that, inspired by the ministry of Wilfred Grenfell to the sick and to seafarers in Labrador and northern Newfoundland, our actions may witness to the love of our Savior Jesus Christ; who with you and the Holy Spirit lives and reigns, one God, for ever and ever. Amen.

For Liturgical Celebration: [Common of a Missionary, A11] [Common of a Pastor, A14] [For Social Service, A59] [For the Sick, A57] [For the Mission of the Church, A52]

October 10

Vida Dutton Scudder
Educator and Witness for Peace, 1954

Vida Dutton Scudder exemplifies the marriage of contemplation and action within an engaged Christian spirituality. As a contemplative laywoman, Scudder was a champion for peace, social action, and women throughout her life.

Scudder was born on December 15, 1861, the child of Congregationalist missionaries in India. In the 1870s, Vida and her mother were prepared for confirmation in The Episcopal Church by Phillips Brooks, then Rector of Trinity Chuch, Copley Square, Boston, and later Bishop of Massachusetts. After studying English literature at Smith College and Oxford University, Scudder began teaching at Wellesley College. Her love of scholarship was matched by her social conscience and deep spirituality. As a young woman, Scudder founded the College Settlements Association, joined the Society of Christian Socialists, and, in 1889, began a lifelong association with the Society of the Companions of the Holy Cross, a community living in the world and devoted to intercessory prayer.

In 1893, Scudder took a leave of absence from Wellesley to work with Helena Stuart Dudley in founding Denison House in Boston, a "college settlement," where wealthy college-educated women provided social services to poor immigrant neighbors, in conversation with the local parish priest. Stresses from teaching and her activism led to a breakdown in 1901. After two years' recuperation in Italy, she returned renewed and became even more active in Church and socialist groups; she started a group for Italian immigrants at Denison House and took an active part in organizing the Women's Trade Union League. In 1911, Scudder founded The Episcopal Church Socialist League, and formally joined the Socialist party. Her support of the Lawrence, Massachusetts, textile workers' strike in 1912 drew a great deal of criticism and threatened her teaching position. Though she initially supported World War I, she joined the Fellowship of Reconciliation in 1923, and by the 1930s was a firm pacifist.

Throughout her life, Scudder's primary relationships and support network were women. After retirement, she authored 16 books on religious and political subjects, combining her intense activism with an equally vibrant spirituality. "If prayer is the deep secret creative force that Jesus tells us it is, we should be very busy with it," she wrote characteristically, adding that there was one sure way "of directly helping on the Kingdom of God. That way is prayer. Social intercession may be the mightiest force in the world." Vida Scudder died on October 9, 1954.

Rite I Most gracious God, who didst send thy beloved Son to preach peace to those who are far off and to those who are near: Raise up in thy Church witnesses who, after the example of thy servant Vida Dutton Scudder, stand firm in proclaiming the power of the gospel of Jesus Christ, who liveth and reigneth with thee and the Holy Spirit, one God, now and for ever. Amen.

Rite II Most gracious God, you sent your beloved Son to preach peace to those who are far off and to those who are near: Raise up in your Church witnesses who, after the example of your servant Vida Dutton Scudder, stand firm in proclaiming the power of the gospel of Jesus Christ, who lives and reigns with you and the Holy Spirit, one God, now and for ever. Amen.

For Liturgical Celebration: [Common of a Prophetic Witness, A31] [For Peace, A55] [For Education, A60]

October 11

Philip
Deacon and Evangelist

Philip, who has been traditionally referred to as a Deacon and an Evangelist, was one of seven honest men appointed, some sources say ordained, by the apostles to distribute bread and alms to the widows and the poor in Jerusalem.

After the martyrdom of Stephen, Philip went to Samaria to preach the gospel. In his travels south to Gaza, he encountered an Ethiopian eunuch, a servant of the Ethiopian queen, reading the Isaiah text on the Suffering Servant. They traveled together, and, in the course of their journey, the Ethiopian was converted and baptized by Philip.

Subsequently, Philip traveled as a missionary from Ashdod northwards and settled in Caesarea. It was in Caesarea that he hosted St. Paul. Philip's activities at the end of his life are the subject of speculation, but some sources place him as a bishop at Lydia in Asia Minor. His feast day in the Eastern Church is October 11, and in the West usually June 6. Other provinces of the Anglican Communion also keep his feast on October 11.

Rite I   O God, who hast made of one blood all the peoples of the earth and sent thy Son to preach peace to those who are far off and to those who are near: Grant that we, following the example of thy servant Philip, may bring thy Word to those who seek thee, for the glory of thy Name; through Jesus Christ our Lord, who liveth and reigneth with thee in the unity of the Holy Spirit, one God, now and for ever. Amen.

Rite II O God, who has made of one blood all the peoples of the earth and sent your Son to preach peace to those who are far off and to those who are near: Grant that we, following the example of your servant Philip, may bring your Word to those who seek you, for the glory of your Name; through Jesus Christ our Lord, who lives and reigns with you in the unity of the Holy Spirit, one God, now and for ever. Amen.

For Liturgical Celebration: [Common of a Missionary, A11] [For the Mission of the Church, A52]

October 14

Samuel Isaac Joseph Scherechewsky
Bishop of Shanghai, 1906

The story of Joseph Schereschewsky is unique in the annals of the Church. He was born on May 6, 1831, of Jewish parents, in the Lithuanian town of Tauroggen. His early education was directed toward the rabbinate, but, during graduate studies in Germany, he became interested in Christianity through missionaries of the London Society for Promoting Christianity Amongst the Jews and through his own reading of a Hebrew translation of the New Testament.

In 1854, Schereschewsky immigrated to America and entered the Western Theological Seminary in Pittsburgh to train for the ministry of the Presbyterian Church. After two years, he decided to become an Episcopalian, and to finish his theological studies at the General Theological Seminary in New York City, from which he graduated in 1859.

After ordination, and in response to Bishop Boone's call for helpers in China, Schereschewsky left for Shanghai. Always facile in languages, he learned to write Chinese during the voyage. From 1862 to 1875, he lived in Peking and translated the Bible and parts of the Prayer Book into Mandarin. After Bishop Williams was transferred to Japan, Schereschewsky was elected Bishop of Shanghai in 1877 and was consecrated in Grace Church, New York City. He established St. John's University in Shanghai, and began his translation of the Bible and other works into Wenli. Stricken with paralysis, he resigned his see in 1883.

Schereschewsky was determined to continue his translation work, and, after many difficulties in finding support, he was able to return to Shanghai in 1895. Two years later, he moved to Tokyo. There he died on October 15, 1906.

With heroic perseverance, Schereschewsky completed his translation of the Bible, typing some 2,000 pages with the middle finger of his partially crippled hand. Four years before his death, he said, "I have sat in this chair for over twenty years. It seemed very hard at first. But God knew best. He kept me for the work for which I am best fitted." He is buried in the Aoyama Cemetery in Tokyo, next to his wife, who supported him constantly during his labors and illness.

Rite I O God, in thy providence thou didst call Joseph Schereschewsky to the ministry of this Church and upheld him in his infirmity, that he might translate the Holy Scriptures into Chinese languages: Inspire us, by his example and prayers, to commit our talents to thy service, confident that thou dost uphold those whom thou dost call; through Jesus Christ our Lord, who liveth and reigneth with thee and the Holy Spirit, one God, for ever and ever. Amen.

Rite II O God, in your providence you called Joseph Schereschewsky to the ministry of this Church and upheld him in his infirmity, that he might translate the Holy Scriptures into Chinese languages: Inspire us, by his example and prayers, to commit our talents to your service, confident that you uphold those whom you call; through Jesus Christ our Lord, who lives and reigns with you and the Holy Spirit, one God, for ever and ever. Amen.

For Liturgical Celebration: [Common of a Missionary, A11] [Common of a Pastor, A14] [For the Ministry II, A50] [For the Mission of the Church, A52]

October 15

Teresa of Avila
Nun, 1582

Teresa was one of two women declared a "Doctor of the Church" in 1970 by the Roman Catholic Church, primarily because of her two mystical contemplative works, *The Way of Perfection* and *Interior Castle*. She was a close spiritual and personal friend of St. John of the Cross.

Teresa was born near Avila. Even in her childhood, she took much pleasure in the study of saints' lives, and she used to delight in spending times of contemplation, repeating over and over, "For ever, for ever, for ever, for ever, they shall see God."

In her autobiography, Teresa tells that, following her mother's death, she became quite worldly. To offset this, her father placed her in an Augustinian convent to be educated, but serious illness ended her studies. During convalescence, she determined to enter the religious life; and, though opposed by her father, she became a postulant at a Carmelite convent. Again, illness forced her to return home. After three years, she returned to the convent.

The easygoing life of the "mitigated" Carmelite rule distracted her from her customary prayer life, to which she returned. Taking recourse in two great penitents, Augustine of Hippo and Mary Magdalene, she became increasingly meditative. She began to receive visions—whether from God or the Devil she could not know—and struggled to reject them.

Teresa set out to establish a reformed Carmelite order of the "discalced" religious, who wore sandals or went unshod. Despite many setbacks, she traveled for 25 years through Spain. Energetic, practical, efficient, as well as being a mystic and ascetic, she established 17 convents of Reformed Carmelites. Even imprisonment did not deter her.

Despite the demands of her administrative and missionary work, Teresa found time to write the numerous letters that give us rare insights into her personality and concerns. She shows us a practical organizer, a writer of native genius, a warm devoted friend, and, above all, a lover of and the beloved of God.

Her death in 1582, following two years of illness, was peaceful. Her last sight was of the Sacrament brought for her comfort; her last words, "O my Lord! Now is the time that we may see each other."

Rite I   O God, who by the Holy Spirit didst move Teresa of Avila to manifest to thy Church the way of perfection: Grant us, we beseech thee, to be nourished by her excellent teaching, and enkindle within us a lively and unquenchable longing for true holiness; through Jesus Christ, the joy of loving hearts, who with thee and the same Spirit liveth and reigneth, one God, for ever and ever. Amen.

Rite II   O God, by your Holy Spirit you moved Teresa of Avila to manifest to your Church the way of perfection: Grant us, we pray, to be nourished by her excellent teaching, and enkindle within us a keen and unquenchable longing for true holiness; through Jesus Christ, the joy of loving hearts, who with you and the Holy Spirit lives and reigns, one God, for ever and ever. Amen.

For Liturgical Celebration: [Common of a Theologian and Teacher, A17] [Common of a Monastic or Professed Religious, A20] [Of the Incarnation, A39]

October 16

Hugh Latimer and Nicholas Ridley
Bishops and Martyrs, 1555

Hugh Latimer was the outstanding English preacher of the Reformation. His sermons against ecclesiastical abuses led to several trials for heresy, but no proof could be established against his orthodoxy. Latimer was little interested in the refinements of doctrine; his zeal was concentrated on the moral life of Christian clergy and people.

Born of yeoman stock about 1490 in Leicestershire, Latimer graduated from Clare College, Cambridge, and became a Fellow in 1510. Though a conservative, he was attracted to the new currents of reform stemming from the Continental Reformation of the 1520's. King Henry VIII made him a royal chaplain in 1530, and five years later appointed him to the See of Worcester, a position he relinquished in 1539 in opposition to the king's reactionary policies against the progress of the Reformation.

In the reign of Edward VI, Latimer became prominent again as a preacher, but he refused to resume his see. With the accession of Queen Mary in 1553 he was imprisoned, and, on October 16, 1555, he was burned at the stake in Oxford alongside Bishop Nicholas Ridley.

Nicholas Ridley was born in Northumberland and was educated at Pembroke College, Cambridge. While there, he belonged to a circle of young men deeply attracted to the currents of reform inspired by the Continental Reformation.

A supporter of Archbishop Cranmer's reforming agenda, Ridley became the Archbishop's Chaplain in 1537, and vicar of Herne, Kent, in 1538. He was chosen Master of Pembroke in 1540 and chaplain to Henry VIII and Canon of Canterbury in 1541. Two years later he was acquitted of a charge of heresy.

Early in the reign of Edward VI, Ridley was made Bishop of Rochester and participated with Cranmer in the preparation of the first Book of Common Prayer. He was translated to the See of London in 1550, where he was a strong advocate for and administrator of the principles of the Reformation. His unwillingness to recant of his Protestant theology and his opposition to the accession of Queen Mary led to his condemnation and his execution at the side of Bishop Latimer.

Rite I Keep us, O Lord, constant in faith and zealous in witness, that, like thy servants Hugh Latimer and Nicholas Ridley, we may live in thy fear, die in thy favor, and rest in thy peace; for the sake of Jesus Christ, thy Son our Lord, who liveth and reigneth with thee and the Holy Spirit, one God, now and for ever. Amen.

Rite II Keep us, O Lord, constant in faith and zealous in witness, that, like your servants Hugh Latimer and Nicholas Ridley, we may live in your fear, die in your favor, and rest in your peace; for the sake of Jesus Christ, your Son our Lord, who lives and reigns with you and the Holy Spirit, one God, now and for ever. Amen.

For Liturgical Celebration: [Common of a Martyr, A7] [Common of a Pastor, A14] [Of the Holy Cross, A41] [For the Ministry II, A50]

October 17

Ignatius
Bishop of Antioch, and Martyr, c. 115

Ignatius of Antioch, martyred in 115, had a profound sense of two ends—his own, and the consummation of history in Jesus Christ. In ecstasy, he saw his impending martyrdom as the fitting conclusion to a long episcopate. He was accounted the second Bishop of Antioch in Syria.

Seven authentic letters, which Ignatius wrote to Churches while he journeyed across Asia Minor in the custody of ten soldiers ("my leopards," he called them), give valuable insights into the life of the early Church. Of certain Gnostic teachings that exalted the divinity of Jesus at the expense of his humanity, Ignatius wrote: "Be deaf. . . . to any talk that ignores Jesus Christ, of David's lineage, of Mary; who was really born, ate, and drank; was really persecuted under Pontius Pilate; was really crucified and died in the sight of heaven and earth and the underworld. He was really raised from the dead."

In another, he condemned a form of biblicism espoused by some as the method of historical interpretation and the only rule of Church practice. He wrote: "When I heard some people saying, 'If I don't find it in the ancient documents, I don't believe it in the Gospel,' I answered them, 'But it is written there.' They retorted, 'That has got to be proved.' But to my mind it is Jesus Christ who is the ancient documents."

Ignatius maintained that the Church's unity would always spring from that liturgy by which all are initiated into Christ through baptism. He exhorted: "Try to gather more frequently to celebrate God's Eucharist and to praise him . . . At these meetings you should heed the bishop and presbytery attentively and break one loaf, which is the medicine of immortality . . . "

Ignatius regarded the Church as God's holy order in the world. He was, therefore, concerned for the proper ordering of the Church's teaching and worship. He wrote: "Flee from schism as the source of mischief. You should all follow the bishop as Jesus Christ did the Father. Follow, too, the presbytery as you would the apostles; and respect the deacons as you would God's law . . . Where the bishop is present, there let the congregation gather, just as where Jesus Christ is, there is the Catholic Church."

Rite I Almighty God, we praise thy Name for thy bishop and martyr Ignatius of Antioch, who offered himself as grain to be ground by the teeth of wild beasts that he might present to thee the pure bread of sacrifice. Accept, we pray, the willing tribute of our lives and give us a share in the pure and spotless offering of thy Son Jesus Christ; who liveth and reigneth with thee and the Holy Spirit, one God, for ever and ever. Amen.

Rite II Almighty God, we praise your Name for your bishop and martyr Ignatius of Antioch, who offered himself as grain to be ground by the teeth of wild beasts that he might present to you the pure bread of sacrifice. Accept, we pray, the willing tribute of our lives and give us a share in the pure and spotless offering of your Son Jesus Christ; who lives and reigns with you and the Holy Spirit, one God, for ever and ever. Amen.

For Liturgical Celebration: [Common of a Martyr, A7] [Common of a Pastor, A14] [Of the Holy Cross, A41] [For the Ministry II, A50]

October 19

Henry Martyn
Priest, and Missionary to India and Persia, 1812

Translator of the Scriptures and Prayer Book into Hindi and Persian, Henry Martyn, an English missionary in India, died in Armenia when he was thirty-one years old. Though his life was brief, it was a remarkable one.

Martyn was educated at Cambridge. He had intended to become a lawyer, but Charles Simeon (November 12), the notable Evangelical rector of Holy Trinity, Cambridge, inspired him to go to India as a missionary. After serving as Simeon's curate for a short time, Martyn traveled to Calcutta in 1806 as chaplain of the East India Company.

During his five years in India, Martyn preached the gospel, organized private schools, and founded churches. In addition to his work as a missionary, Martyn translated the New Testament and the Book of Common Prayer into Hindi, a valuable missionary aid to the young Anglican Church in India. He also began the study of Farsi, the language of Persia (modern Iran), and translated the New Testament into that language.

Martyn longed to go to Persia; in 1811, his persistence brought him to Shirmas, to become the first English clergyman in that city. He engaged in theological discussions with learned Muslims and corrected his Farsi translations. Obviously gifted with a remarkable facility for languages, Martyn hoped eventually to visit Arabia, and to translate the New Testament into Arabic.

While on his way to Constantinople in 1812, however, he died in the Turkish city of Tokat. The Christian Armenians of the city recognized his greatness and buried him with the honors usually accorded to one of their own bishops. Very soon afterwards, his life of energetic devotion and remarkable accomplishment became widely known. He is remembered as one of the founders of the modern Christian Church in India and Iran.

Rite I   O God of the nations, who didst give to thy faithful servant Henry Martyn a brilliant mind, a loving heart, and a gift for languages, that he might translate the Scriptures and other holy writings for the peoples of India and Persia; Inspire in us, we beseech thee, a love like his, eager to commit both life and talents to thee who gavest them; through Jesus Christ our Lord, who liveth and reigneth with thee and the Holy Spirit, one God, for ever and ever. Amen.

Rite II   O God of the nations, you gave your faithful servant Henry Martyn a brilliant mind, a loving heart, and a gift for languages, that he might translate the Scriptures and other holy writings for the peoples of India and Persia; Inspire in us a love like his, eager to commit both life and talents to you who gave them; through Jesus Christ our Lord, who lives and reigns with you and the Holy Spirit, one God, for ever and ever. Amen.

For Liturgical Celebration: [Common of a Missionary, A11] [For the Mission of the Church, A52]

October 19

William Carey
Missionary to India, 1834

William Carey was an English Baptist missionary who was a major figure in developing the Protestant missionary movement of the nineteenth century.

Born a son of the Church of England on August 17, 1761, near Northampton, Carey took an early interest in his studies and excelled at languages, a gift that would serve him in his ministry. After his village schooling, Carey apprenticed as a cobbler, where he came into contact with a fellow worker who was a Nonconformist. Carey was challenged by this relationship, and he eventually left the Church of England and became a Congregationalist.

Carey developed into a master cobbler, married, and with his wife, Dorothy, had six children, only three of whom survived childhood. During his years as a master cobbler, Carey's interest in languages became a passionate avocation; he learned Italian, French, Dutch, and Hebrew, while increasing his mastery of Latin, a language he had taught himself as a youngster.

Carey's spiritual quest continued. He was re-baptized in 1783 and was a Baptist for the remainder of his life. He became a schoolmaster and served as a Baptist pastor while struggling with his responsibility to foreign missions. He was among the founders, in 1792, of what would become the Baptist Missionary Society. Finally, in 1793, Carey and his companions set out for India.

After transitional periods in Calcutta and nearby Midnapore, in 1800 Carey and his fellow missionaries settled in Serampore, where Carey would spend the rest of his life. He was appointed a professor at Fort Williams College, which had been founded to educate the children of civil servants. While teaching, Carey translated the Bible into Bengali and Sanskrit and the New Testament into other Indian languages and dialects, in addition to providing translations of other Christian literature. Carey also completed a Bengali-English dictionary and other linguistic tools to support missionary work.

In 1818, Carey's mission established Serampore College for the dual purpose of training indigenous ministers and providing a classical education to anyone regardless of caste or national origin.

Rite I   Merciful God, who didst call William Carey to missionary work in India and didst endue him with a zeal for thy Word that led him to translate Scripture into many local languages and dialects: Give us a heart for the spreading of thy Gospel and a thirst for justice among all the peoples of the world; through Jesus Christ our Savior, who sheds thy light and peace throughout humanity, and who liveth and reigneth with thee and the Holy Spirit, one God, now and for ever. Amen.

Rite II   Merciful God, you called William Carey to missionary work in India and gave him a zeal for your Word that led him to translate Scripture into many local languages and dialects: Give us a heart for the spreading of your Gospel and a thirst for justice among all the peoples of the world; through Jesus Christ our Savior, who sheds your light and peace throughout humanity, and who lives and reigns with you and the Holy Spirit, one God, now and for ever. Amen.

For Liturgical Celebration: [Common of a Missionary, A11] [For the Mission of the Church, A52]

October 24

Hiram Hisanori Kano
1986

The Rev. Hiram Hisanori Kano, an Episcopal priest known by some as the "Saint of Nebraska and Colorado," was an agricultural missionary among Japanese Americans in western Nebraska and, while himself a prisoner during the internment of Japanese Americans during World War II, a pastor to American soldiers imprisoned for having been AWOL.

Fr. Kano, born into a Japanese noble family in Tokyo on January 30, 1889, suffered a ruptured appendix while studying agricultural economics at the Imperial Univeristy of Tokyo. During the medical procedure, he received a vision of God and "surrendered" himself. When he began reading the Bible as a result of the experience, he became convinced that his vision had been of the risen Christ. In 1910, he was baptized by Dutch Reformed missionaries.

In 1916, he felt God calling him to America to assist the Japanese settlers making a home in the Midwest to farm. In the early 1920's, Bishop George Allen Beecher of the Missionary District of Western Nebraska discerned, in farmer and educator Kano, the evangelist he was seeking to call Nebraska's Japanese to be God's people. A lay missionary first, Kano was ordained deacon in 1928 and priest in 1936. By the spring of 1934, 250 people had been baptized and 50 confirmed through his ministry.

After arrest on the morning of the Pearl Harbor attack despite his own defense and pleas from his bishop, he spent the next two years in internment camps. He spent time in four different states, always working to help the other internees and imprisoned AWOL soldiers. He served as dean of a school for the internees and taught many courses in agricultural study and English, and he preached the gospel.

After Fr. Kano's release in 1944, he was sent to study at Nashotah House, the Episcopal seminary in Wisconsin, where he earned a master's degree in 1946. He then returned to his ministry in Nebraska.

When the U.S. government finally offered reparations for the internments, Fr. Kano told his bishop, "I don't want the money. God just used that as another opportunity for me to preach the gospel."

Fr. Kano retired in 1957 and moved with his wife to a small farm in Fort Collins, Colorado. He died on October 24, 1988

Rite I   Almighty God, who hast reconciled the world unto thyself through Christ: Entrust to thy Church the ministry of reconciliation, as thou didst to thy servant Hiram Hisanori Kano, and raise up ambassadors for Christ to proclaim thy love and peace wherever conflict and hatred divide; through Jesus Christ our Lord, who liveth and reigneth with thee and the Holy Spirit, one God, now and for ever. Amen.

Rite II   Almighty God, who has reconciled the world to yourself through Christ: Entrust to your Church the ministry of reconciliation, as you did to your servant Hiram Hisanori Kano, and raise up ambassadors for Christ to proclaim your love and peace wherever conflict and hatred divide; through Jesus Christ our Lord, who lives and reigns with you and the Holy Spirit, one God, now and for ever. Amen.

For Liturgical Celebration: [Common of a Pastor, A14] [Of the Holy Spirit, A38] [For Reconciliation and Forgiveness, A68] [For Peace, A55]

October 26

Alfred the Great
King of the West Saxons, 899

Alfred, alone of all English rulers, has been called "the Great," because of his courage and Christian virtues. Born in 849 at Wantage, Berkshire, the youngest of five sons of King Aethelwulf, Alfred spent his life in a time of "battle, murder, and sudden death" during the Viking invasions and settlement in Britain. He was deeply impressed when, on a visit to Rome at the age of four, he was blessed by Pope Leo IV, and two years later, when he witnessed the marriage of Aethelwulf to a young princess of the Frankish court. Following his father's death and the short reigns of his brothers, Alfred became King in 871.

In heroic battles and by stratagems against the Danes, Alfred halted the tide of their invasion and secured control of the southern, and part of the midland, regions of England for the English. After a decisive victory in 878 at Edington over the Danish leader Guthrum, he persuaded his foe to accept baptism. Alfred died on October 26, 899, and was buried in the old Minster at Winchester.

A man of deep piety, Alfred's leadership in battle and administration was grounded by his faith. His biographer Asser wrote of his commitment to a monastic influenced life of prayer, "He learned the daily course, that is, the celebrations of the Hours, and after that certain psalms and many prayers, gathered together in one book for the sake of prayer, which he carried around with him everywhere on his person by day and night, just as we have seen, inseparable from himself, in all of the doings of this present life."

In his later years, Alfred sought to repair the damage that the Viking invasions had inflicted on culture and learning, especially among the parish clergy. With the help of scholars from Wales and the Continent, he supervised translations into English of important classics of theology and history, including works of Pope Gregory the Great, Augustine of Hippo, and the Venerable Bede. In one of them he commented: "He seemed to me a very foolish man, and very wretched, who will not increase his understanding while he is in the world, and ever wish and long to reach that endless life where all shall be made clear."

Rite I   O God, who didst call thy servant Alfred to an earthly throne that he might advance thy heavenly kingdom and didst give him zeal for thy Church and love for thy people: Grant that we, inspired by his example and prayers, may remain steadfast in the work thou hast given us to do for the building up of thy reign of love; through Jesus Christ our Lord, who liveth and reigneth with thee and the Holy Spirit, one God, for ever and ever. Amen.

Rite II   O God, who called your servant Alfred to an earthly throne that he might advance your heavenly kingdom and gave him zeal for your Church and love for your people: Grant that we, inspired by his example and prayers, may remain steadfast in the work you have given us to do for the building up of your reign of love; through Jesus Christ our Lord, who lives and reigns with you and the Holy Spirit, one God, for ever and ever. Amen.

For Liturgical Celebration: [Common of a Saint, A23] [For Vocation in Daily Work, A61]

October 29

James Hannington, Bishop of Eastern Equatorial Africa, and his Companions
Martyrs, 1885

James Hannington was born at Hurstpierpoint, Sussex, September 3, 1847, and was educated at Temple School, Brighton. For six years, he assisted his father in the warehouse business. The family became members of the Church of England in 1867, and the following year, Hannington entered St. Mary Hall, Oxford, where he obtained his BA and MA degrees.

Following his ordination at Exeter, Hannington served as a curate in his native town until, in 1882, he offered himself to the Church Missionary Society for its mission in Victoria, Nyanza, Africa. Serious illness soon required his return to England, but he went out again to Africa in 1884, as Bishop of Eastern Equatorial Africa.

Hannington's mission field was the shores of Lake Victoria. On a difficult venture towards Uganda, he and his party were apprehended by emissaries of King Mwanga, who feared this foreign penetration into his territory. After a week of cruel privations and suffering, he and the remaining members of his company were martyred on October 29, 1885.

Hannington's last words were: "Go, tell Mwanga I have purchased the road to Uganda with my blood." Other martyrs of Uganda (see June 3) shared his fate before the gospel was firmly planted in this heartland of Africa, where today the Church has a vigorous life under an indigenous ministry. Mwanga was eventually exiled to the Seychelles in 1899, where he was received into the Anglican Church and baptized; he died there in 1903.

Rite I   Precious in thy sight, O Lord, is the death of thy saints, whose faithful witness, by thy providence, has its great reward: We give thee thanks for thy martyrs James Hannington and his companions, who purchased with their blood a road into Uganda for the proclamation of the Gospel; and we pray that, with them, we also may obtain the crown of righteousness which is laid up for all who love the appearing of our Savior Jesus Christ; who liveth and reigneth with thee and the Holy Spirit, one God, for ever and ever. Amen.

Rite II Precious in your sight, O Lord, is the death of your saints, whose faithful witness, by your providence, has its great reward: We give you thanks for your martyrs James Hannington and his companions, who purchased with their blood a road into Uganda for the proclamation of the Gospel; and we pray that, with them, we also may obtain the crown of righteousness which is laid up for all who love the appearing of our Savior Jesus Christ; who lives and reigns with you and the Holy Spirit, one God, for ever and ever. Amen.

For Liturgical Celebration: [Common of a Martyr, A7] [Common of a Missionary, A11] [Common of a Pastor, A14] [Of the Holy Cross, A41] [For the Ministry II, A50] [For the Mission of the Church, A52]

October 30

John Wyclif
Priest and Prophetic Witness, 1384

John Wyclif is remembered as a forerunner of the Protestant Reformation.

Born in Yorkshire, England, around 1330, Wyclif was educated at Oxford. Although he served as a parish priest, he spent most of his vocation teaching theology and philosophy at Oxford and was celebrated for his academic achievements.

In 1374, Wyclif defended the position of the Crown during a dispute with the papacy over finances. Because of this newfound notoriety, Wyclif gathered around him a group of powerful patrons who were able to provide a reasonable level of safe haven and security for him. This meant that Wyclif could begin to test some of his theological views that were at odds with and critical of the positions of the medieval church. Without the support of such powerful allies, Wyclif, a priest and university professor, could never have withstood the discipline that would have come his way.

A number of Wyclif's radical ideas got worked out in the centuries that followed, as the movement toward reformation gained momentum. Wyclif believed that believers could have a direct, unmediated relationship with God, not requiring the intervention of the Church or its priesthood. He held that a national Church could be fully and completely the Church and not have to tolerate the interference and abuse of international, i.e., papal, authority. Believing that the Scriptures should be available to all who could read them, and not mediated through the instruction of the Church, Wyclif translated the Vulgate—the Latin edition of the Bible—into English.

The tables turned dramatically when Wyclif questioned the eucharistic doctrine of transubstantiation. He believed that the underlying philosophy was problematic and that the popular piety flowing from it led inevitably to superstitious behaviors. He was condemned for his eucharistic views in 1381. Although Wyclif had nothing to do with inciting the Peasants' Revolt of the same year, he was an easy target for blame. He retired, left Oxford, and died three years later in Leicestershire.

Later reformers John Hus (July 6) and Martin Luther (February 18) acknowledged their debt to Wyclif.

Rite I O God, whose justice continually challenges thy Church to live according to its calling: Grant us, who now remember the work of John Wyclif, contrition for the wounds which our sins inflict on thy Church and such love for Christ that we may seek to heal the divisions which afflict his Body; through the same Jesus Christ, who liveth and reigneth with thee in the unity of the Holy Spirit, one God, now and for ever. Amen.

Rite II O God, your justice continually challenges your Church to live according to its calling: Grant us, who now remember the work of John Wyclif, contrition for the wounds which our sins inflict on your Church and such love for Christ that we may seek to heal the divisions which afflict his Body; through the same Jesus Christ, who lives and reigns with you in the unity of the Holy Spirit, one God, now and for ever. Amen.

For Liturgical Celebration: [Common of a Theologian and Teacher, A17] [Common of a Prophetic Witness, A31]

October 31

Paul Shinji Sasaki,
Bishop of Mid-Japan and of Tokyo, 1946,
and Philip Lindel Tsen,
Bishop of Honan, China, 1954

Paul Sasaki was a bishop of Nippon Sei Ko Kei (a member church of the Anglican Communion), who was persecuted and imprisoned for his support of the independence of his church during the Second World War. Lindel Tsen was the principal leader of Chinese Anglicanism in the middle of the 20th century.

Nippon Sei Ko Kei had been established by missionaries from The Episcopal Church in 1859, with support from the Church of England and the Anglican Church of Canada. During the approach to World War II, the Japanese government ordered all Christians into a "united church," regardless of differences in doctrine or polity. Roughly one third of the dioceses of Nippon Sei Ko Kei joined the new church, but Bishop Paul Sasaki, Bishop of Tokyo and later Primate, refused and inspired most of the church to stay together and faithful to their Anglican heritage. Sasaki was tortured and imprisoned for his resistence, but, after the war, his witness was an inspiring rallying point for the rebuilding of the church. As a result of torture during his imprisonment, Sasaki died on December 21, 1946, in Tokyo.

Lindel Tsen was born in poverty in the Anhui province of China in 1885. As a homeless teenager, he was taken in by Episcopal Church missionaries. Ordained a priest in 1912 by Bishop Huntingdon after studying at Boone Divinty School in Wuchang, he also travelled to America in 1923 for a year of study at Virginia Theological Seminary and another at the Divinity School in Philadelphia. He worked closely with the Canadian Anglican missionaries in China. Tsen became the first Chinese bishop of Honan when he was consecrated assistant bishop of the diocese in 1929 and was the first Chinese bishop to attend a Lambeth Conference.

Bishop Sasaki and Bishop Tsen travelled together to Canada's 1937 General Synod to testify to the unity of Chinese and Japanese Christians, despite the war raging between the two countries.

During World War II, he served his diocese faithfully through harrowing conditions. At the end of the war, Tsen emerged as the leader of the Chinese Anglican Church, becoming the first and only Presiding Bishop of the Chung Hua Sheng Kung Hui, before its formal dissolution by the Communist government. Upon his return from the 1948 Lambeth Conference, Tsen was put under house arrest by the Communist authorities.

He died in Shanghai in 1954.

Rite I   Almighty God, we offer thanks for the faith and witness of Paul Sasaki, bishop in the Nippon Sei Ko Kai, tortured and imprisoned by his government, and Philip Tsen, leader of the Chinese Anglican Church, arrested for his faith. We pray that all Church leaders oppressed by hostile governments may be delivered by thy mercy, and that by the power of the Holy Spirit we may be faithful to the Gospel of our Savior Jesus Christ; who liveth and reigneth with thee and the Holy Spirit, one God, for ever and ever. Amen.

Rite II Almighty God, we thank you for the faith and witness of Paul Sasaki, bishop in the Nippon Sei Ko Kai, tortured and imprisoned by his government, and Philip Tsen, leader of the Chinese Anglican Church, arrested for his faith. We pray that all Church leaders oppressed by hostile governments may be delivered by your mercy, and that by the power of the Holy Spirit we may be faithful to the Gospel of our Savior Jesus Christ; who lives and reigns with you and the Holy Spirit, one God, for ever and ever. Amen.

For Liturgical Celebration: [Common of a Missionary, A11] [Common of a Pastor, A14] [For the Ministry II, A50] [For the Mission of the Church, A52] [For Peace, A55]

OCTOBER 31

NOVEMBER

1
2 Commemoration of All Faithful Departed
3 Richard Hooker, Priest, 1600
4
5
6 William Temple, Archbishop of Canterbury, 1944
7 Willibrord, Archbishop of Utrecht, Missionary to Frisia, 739
8 (alternative date for James Theodore Holly; see March 13)
9
10 Leo the Great, Bishop of Rome, 461
11 Martin, Bishop of Tours, 397
12 Charles Simeon, Priest, 1836
13
14 Samuel Seabury, First American Bishop, 1796
15 Francis Asbury, 1816, and George Whitefield, 1770, Evangelists
16 Margaret, Queen of Scotland, 1093
17 Hugh, 1200, and Robert Grosseteste, 1253, Bishops of Lincoln
18 Hilda, Abbess of Whitby, 680
19 Elizabeth, Princess of Hungary, 1231
20 Edmund, King of East Anglia, 870
21 William Byrd, 1623, John Merbecke, 1585, and Thomas Tallis, 1585, Musicians
22 Cecilia, Martyr at Rome, c. 230
22 Clive Staples Lewis, Apologist and Spiritual Writer, 1963
23 Clement, Bishop of Rome, c. 100
24
25 James Otis Sargent Huntington, Priest and Monk, 1935

26 Isaac Watts, Hymnwriter, 1748
27
28 Kamehameha and Emma, King and Queen of Hawaii, 1864, 1885
29
30

November 2

Commemoration of All Faithful Departed

In the New Testament, the word "saints" is used to describe the entire membership of the Christian community, and, in the Collect for All Saints' Day, the word "elect" is used in a similar sense. From very early times, however, the word "saint" came to be applied primarily to persons of heroic sanctity, whose deeds were recalled with gratitude by later generations.

Beginning in the tenth century, it became customary to set aside another day—as a sort of extension of All Saints—on which the Church remembered that vast body of the faithful who, though no less members of the company of the redeemed, are unknown in the wider fellowship of the Church. It was also a day for particular remembrance of family members and friends.

Though the observance of the day was abolished at the Reformation because of abuses connected with Masses for the dead, a renewed understanding of its meaning has led to a widespread acceptance of this commemoration among Anglicans, and to its inclusion as an optional observance in the calendar of The Episcopal Church.

Rite I O God, the Maker and Redeemer of all believers; Grant to the faithful departed the unsearchable benefits of the passion of thy Son; that, on the day of his appearing they may be manifested as thy children; through Jesus Christ our Lord, who liveth and reigneth with thee and the Holy Spirit, one God, now and for ever. Amen.

Rite II O God, the Maker and Redeemer of all believers; Grant to the faithful departed the unsearchable benefits of the passion of your Son; that, on the day of his appearing, they may be manifested as your children; through Jesus Christ our Lord, who lives and reigns with you and the Holy Spirit, one God, now and for ever. Amen.

For Liturgical Celebration: [For the Departed, A43]

November 3

Richard Hooker
Priest, 1600

In any list of Anglican theologians, Richard Hooker's name would stand high, if not first. He was born in 1553 at Heavitree, near Exeter, and was admitted in 1567 to Corpus Christi College, Oxford, of which he became a Fellow ten years later. After ordination and marriage in 1581, he held a living in Buckinghamshire. In 1586, he became Master of the Temple, in London. Later, he served country parishes in Boscombe, Salisbury, and Bishopsbourne near Canterbury.

A controversy with a noted Puritan led Hooker to prepare a comprehensive defense of the Reformation settlement under Queen Elizabeth I. This work, his masterpiece, was entitled *Laws of Ecclesiastical Polity*. Its philosophical base is Aristotelian, with a strong emphasis upon natural law eternally planted by God in creation. On this foundation, all positive laws of Church and State are grounded—from Scriptural revelation, ancient tradition, reason, and experience.

Book Five of the *Laws* is a massive defense of the Book of Common Prayer, directed primarily against Puritan detractors. Hooker's arguments are buttressed by enormous patristic learning, but the needs of the contemporary worshiper are paramount, and he draws effectively on his twenty-year experience of using the Book. Hooker's vast learning and the quality of his style reveal him to be a man of moderate, patient, and serene character.

Concerning the nature of the Church, Hooker wrote: "The Church is always a visible society of men; not an assembly, but a Society. For although the name of the Church be given unto Christian assemblies, although any multitude of Christian men congregated may be termed by the name of a Church, yet assemblies properly are rather things that belong to a Church. Men are assembled for performance of public actions; which actions being ended, the assembly dissolveth itself and is no longer in being, whereas the Church which was assembled doth no less continue afterwards than before."

Pope Clement VIII is reported to have said that Hooker's work "had in it such seeds of eternity that it would abide until the last fire shall consume all learning."

Rite I O God of truth and peace, who didst raise up thy servant Richard Hooker in a day of bitter controversy to defend with sound reasoning and great charity the catholic and reformed religion: Grant that we may maintain that middle way, not as a compromise for the sake of peace, but as a comprehension for the sake of truth; through Jesus Christ our Lord, who liveth and reigneth with thee and the Holy Spirit, one God, for ever and ever. Amen.

Rite II O God of truth and peace, you raised up your servant Richard Hooker in a day of bitter controversy to defend with sound reasoning and great charity the catholic and reformed religion: Grant that we may maintain that middle way, not as a compromise for the sake of peace, but as a comprehension for the sake of truth; through Jesus Christ our Lord, who lives and reigns with you and the Holy Spirit, one God, for ever and ever. Amen.

For Liturgical Celebration: [Common of a Theologian and Teacher, A17] [Of the Holy Trinity, A37]

November 6

William Temple
Archbishop of Canterbury, 1944

William Temple was a reknowned teacher and preacher, regarded as one of the most exemplary Archbishops of Canterbury of the 20th century. His writings reflect a robust social theology that engages the challenges of modern industrialized society.

Temple was born October 15, 1881, and baptized three weeks later, on November 6, in Exeter Cathedral. His father, Dr. Frederick Temple, Bishop of Exeter and then of London, became Archbishop of Canterbury when William was fifteen. Growing up at the heart of the Church of England, William's love for it was deep and lifelong.

Endowed with a brilliant mind, Temple took a first-class honors degree in classics and philosophy at Oxford, where he was then elected Fellow of Queen's College. At the age of twenty-nine he became headmaster of Repton School, and then, in quick succession, rector of St. James's Church, Piccadilly, Bishop of Manchester, and Archbishop of York.

Though he was never subject to poverty himself, he developed a passion for social justice which shaped his words and his actions. He owed this passion to a profound belief in the Incarnation. He wrote that in Jesus Christ God took flesh and dwelt among us, and, as a consequence, "the personality of every man and woman is sacred."

In 1917, Temple resigned from St. James's, Piccadilly, to devote his energies to the "Life and Liberty" movement for reform within the Church of England. Two years later, an Act of Parliament led to the setting up of the Church Assembly, which for the first time gave the laity a voice in Church matters.

As bishop, and later as archbishop, Temple committed himself to seeking "the things which pertain to the Kingdom of God." He understood the Incarnation as giving worth and meaning not only to individuals but to all of life. He therefore took the lead in establishing the Conference on Christian Politics, Economics, and Citizenship (COPEC), held 1924. In 1940, he convened the great Malvern

Conference to reflect on the social reconstruction that would be needed in Britain once the Second World War was over.

At the same time, he was a prolific writer on theological, ecumenical, and social topics, and his two-volume *Readings in St. John's Gospel*, written in the early days of the war, rapidly became a spiritual classic.

In 1942, Temple was appointed Archbishop of Canterbury and reached an even wider audience through his wartime radio addresses and newspaper articles. However, the scope of his responsibilities and the pace he set himself took their toll. On October 26, 1944, he died at Westgate-on-Sea, Kent, after only two and a half years at Canterbury.

Rite I O God of light and love, who illumined thy Church through the witness of thy servant William Temple: Inspire us, we pray, by his teaching and example, that we may rejoice with courage, confidence, and faith in the Word made flesh, and may be led to establish that city which has justice for its foundation and love for its law; through Jesus Christ, the light of the world, who liveth and reigneth with thee and the Holy Spirit, one God, now and for ever. Amen.

Rite II O God of light and love, you illumined your Church through the witness of your servant William Temple: Inspire us, we pray, by his teaching and example, that we may rejoice with courage, confidence, and faith in the Word made flesh, and may be led to establish that city which has justice for its foundation and love for its law; through Jesus Christ, the light of the world, who lives and reigns with you and the Holy Spirit, one God, now and for ever. Amen.

For Liturgical Celebration: [Common of a Pastor, A14] [For the Ministry II, A50]

NOVEMBER 6

November 7

Willibrord
Archbishop of Utrecht, Missionary to Frisia, 739

We know about Willibrord's life and missionary labors through a notice in the Venerable Bede's *Ecclesiastical History* and a biography by his younger kinsman, Alcuin. He was born in Northumbria about 658, and, from the age of seven, was brought up and educated at Bishop Wilfrid's monastery at Ripon. For twelve years, 678–690, he studied in Ireland, where he acquired his thirst for missionary work.

In 690, with twelve companions, he set out for Frisia (Netherlands), a pagan area that was increasingly coming under the domination of the Christian Franks. There, Bishop Wilfrid and a few other Englishmen had made short missionary visits, but with little success. With the aid of the Frankish rulers, Willibrord established his base at Utrecht, and in 695 Pope Sergius ordained him a bishop and gave him the name of Clement.

In 698, he founded the monastery of Echternach, near Trier. His work was frequently disturbed by the conflict of the pagan Frisians with the Franks, and for a time he left the area to work among the Danes. For three years, 719–722, he was assisted by Boniface, who at a later time came back to Frisia to strengthen the mission. In a very real sense, Willibrord prepared the way for Boniface's more successful achievements by his relations with the Frankish rulers and the papacy, who thus became joint sponsors of missionary work. He died at Echternach, November 7, 739.

Rite I   Almighty and everlasting God, who didst call thy servant Willibrord to proclaim thy Gospel to the people of the Low Countries: Raise up in this and every land evangelists and heralds of thy kingdom, that thy Church may proclaim the unsearchable riches of our Savior Jesus Christ; who liveth and reigneth with thee and the Holy Spirit, one God, now and for ever. Amen.

Rite II   Almighty and everlasting God, who called your servant Willibrord to proclaim your Gospel to the people of the Low Countries: Raise up in this and every land evangelists and heralds of your kingdom, that your Church may proclaim the unsearchable riches of our Savior Jesus Christ; who lives and reigns with you and the Holy Spirit, one God, now and for ever. Amen.

For Liturgical Celebration: [Common of a Missionary, A11] [Common of a Pastor, A14] [For the Ministry II, A50] [For the Mission of the Church, A52]

November 8

(alternative date for James Theodore Holly – see March 13)

November 10

Leo the Great
Bishop of Rome, 461

When Leo was born, about the year 400, the Western Roman Empire was almost in shambles. Weakened by barbarian invasions and by a totally inefficient economic and political system, the structure that had been carefully built by Augustus had become a chaos of internal warfare, subversion, and corruption.

The social and political situation notwithstanding, Leo received a good education, and was ordained deacon, with the responsibility of looking after Church possessions, managing the grain dole, and generally administering finances. He won considerable respect for his abilities, and a contemporary of his, Cassian, described him as "the ornament of the Roman Church and the divine ministry."

In 440, Leo was unanimously elected Pope, despite the fact that he was absent at the time on a mission in Gaul. His ability as a preacher shows clearly in the 96 sermons still extant, in which he expounds doctrine, encourages almsgiving, and deals with various heresies, including the Pelagian and the Manichean systems.

In Gaul, Africa, and Spain, Leo's strong hand was felt, as he issued orders to limit the powers of one over-presumptuous bishop, confirmed the rights of another bishop over his vicars, and selected candidates for holy orders. Leo's letter to the Council of Chalcedon in 451 dealt so effectively with the doctrine of the human and divine natures of the One Person of Christ that the assembled bishops declared, "Peter has spoken by Leo," and affirmed his definition as orthodox teaching. (See page 864 of the Prayer Book.)

With similar strength of spirit and wisdom, Leo negotiated with Attila when the Huns were about to sack Rome. He persuaded them to withdraw from Italy and to accept an annual tribute. Three years later, Genseric led the Vandals against Rome. Again Leo negotiated. Unable to prevent pillaging by the barbarians, he did dissuade them from burning the city and slaughtering its inhabitants. He worked, thereafter, to repair the damage, to replace the holy vessels in the desecrated churches, and to restore the morale of the Roman people.

Leo died in Rome in 461.

Rite I   O Lord our God, grant that thy Church, following the teaching of thy servant Leo of Rome, may hold fast the great mystery of our redemption and adore the one Christ, true God and true Man, neither divided from our human nature nor separate from thy divine Being; through Jesus Christ our Lord, who liveth and reigneth with thee and the Holy Spirit, one God, now and for ever. Amen.

Rite II   O Lord our God, grant that your Church, following the teaching of your servant Leo of Rome, may hold fast the great mystery of our redemption and adore the one Christ, true God and true Man, neither divided from our human nature nor separate from your divine Being; through Jesus Christ our Lord, who lives and reigns with you and the Holy Spirit, one God, now and for ever. Amen.

For Liturgical Celebration: [Common of a Theologian and Teacher, A17] [Common of a Pastor, A14] [Of the Holy Trinity, A37] [For the Ministry II, A50]

November 11

Martin
Bishop of Tours, 397

Martin, one of the patron saints of France, was born about 330 at Sabaria, the modern Szombathely in Hungary. His early years were spent in Pavia in Italy. After a term of service in the Roman army, he traveled about Europe, and finally settled in Poitiers, whose bishop, Hilary, he had come to admire.

According to an old legend, while Martin was still a catechumen, he was approached by a poor man, who asked for alms in the name of Christ. Martin, drawing his sword, cut off part of his military cloak and gave it to the beggar. On the following night, Jesus appeared to Martin, clothed in half a cloak, and said to the saints and angels surrounding him, "Martin, a simple catechumen, covered me with this garment."

Hilary ordained Martin to the presbyterate sometime between 350 and 353, and Martin, inspired by the new monastic movement stemming from Egypt, established a hermitage at nearby Ligugé. To his dismay, he was elected Bishop of Tours in 372. He agreed to serve only if he were allowed to continue his strict, ascetic habit of life. His monastery of Marmoutier, near Tours, had a great influence on the development of Celtic monasticism in Britain, where Ninian, among others, promoted Martin's ascetic and missionary ideals. The oldest church in Canterbury, which antedates the Anglo-Saxon invasions, is dedicated to St. Martin.

Martin was unpopular with many of his episcopal colleagues, both because of his manner of life and because of his strong opposition to their violent repression of heresy. He was a diligent missionary to the pagan folk of the countryside near his hermitage and was always a staunch defender of the poor and the helpless.

Martin died on November 11, 397. His shrine at Tours became a popular site for pilgrimages and a secure sanctuary for those seeking protection and justice.

Rite I   Lord God of hosts, who didst clothe thy servant Martin the soldier with the spirit of sacrifice and set him as a bishop in thy Church to be a defender of the catholic faith: Give us grace to follow in his holy steps, that, at the last, we may be found clothed with righteousness in the dwellings of peace; through Jesus Christ our Lord, who liveth and reigneth with thee and the Holy Spirit, one God, for ever and ever. Amen.

Rite II   Lord God of hosts, you clothed your servant Martin the soldier with the spirit of sacrifice and set him as a bishop in your Church to be a defender of the catholic faith: Give us grace to follow in his holy steps, that, at the last, we may be found clothed with righteousness in the dwellings of peace; through Jesus Christ our Lord, who lives and reigns with you and the Holy Spirit, one God, for ever and ever. Amen.

For Liturgical Celebration: [Common of a Monastic or Professed Religious, A20] [Common of a Pastor, A14] [Of the Incarnation, A39] [For the Ministry II, A50]

November 12

Charles Simeon
Priest, 1836

The historian Thomas Macaulay said about Charles Simeon, "If you knew what his authority and influence were, and how they extended from Cambridge to the most remote corners of England, you would allow that his real sway in the Church was far greater than that of any primate."

Simeon's conversion, in 1779, while still a student, occurred as he was preparing himself to receive Holy Communion, an act required of undergraduates at the University. His first Communion had been a deeply depressing and discouraging experience because of his use of the popular devotional tract, *The Whole Duty of Man*, which emphasized law and obedience as the means of receiving the Sacrament worthily. When he was again preparing for Communion before Easter, he was given a copy of Bishop Thomas Wilson's *Instructions for the Lord's Supper*. Here was a quite different approach, which recognized that the law could not make one righteous and that only the sacrifice of Christ, perceived by faith, could enable one to communicate worthily. This time, the experience of Holy Communion was one of peace and exhilaration, a new beginning of a Christian life whose influence is difficult to exaggerate.

In 1782, the year of his graduation from King's College, Cambridge, he was placed in charge of Trinity Church in that city, while still a deacon. He remained Rector there for 54 years, despite intense early opposition from the churchwardens and congregation over his evangelical preaching.

Simeon's influence and authority developed slowly, but he eventually became the recognized leader of the evangelical movement in the Church of England. He helped to found the Church Missionary Society and was active in recruiting and supporting missionaries, including Henry Martyn (October 19). As a preacher, he ranks high in the history of Anglicanism. His sermons were unfailingly biblical, simple, and passionate.

The influence of Simeon and his friends was thus described by the historian William Edward Hartpole Lecky: "They gradually changed the whole spirit of the English Church. They infused into it a new fire and passion of devotion, kindled a spirit of fervent philanthropy, raised the standard of clerical duty, and completely altered the whole tone and tendency of the preaching of its ministers."

Simeon died on November 13, 1836, in Cambridge, and was buried at King's College.

Rite I   O loving God, we know that all things are ordered by thine unerring wisdom and unbounded love: Grant us in all things to see thy hand; that, following the example and teaching of thy servant Charles Simeon, we may walk with Christ in all simplicity and serve thee with a quiet and contented mind; through Jesus Christ our Lord, who liveth and reigneth with thee and the Holy Spirit, one God, for ever and ever. Amen.

Rite II   O loving God, we know that all things are ordered by your unerring wisdom and unbounded love: Grant us in all things to see your hand; that, following the example and teaching of your servant Charles Simeon, we may walk with Christ in all simplicity and serve you with a quiet and contented mind; through Jesus Christ our Lord, who lives and reigns with you and the Holy Spirit, one God, for ever and ever. Amen.

For Liturgical Celebration: [Common of a Missionary, A11] [For the Mission of the Church, A52]

November 14

Samuel Seabury
First American Bishop, 1796

Samuel Seabury, the first Bishop of The Episcopal Church, was born in Groton, Connecticut, November 30, 1729. After ordination in England in 1753, he was assigned, as a missionary of the Society for the Propagation of the Gospel, to Christ Church, New Brunswick, New Jersey. In 1757, he became rector of Grace Church, Jamaica, Long Island, and in 1766, rector of St. Peter's, Westchester County. During the American Revolution, he remained loyal to the British crown and served as a chaplain in the British army.

After the Revolution, a secret meeting of Connecticut clergymen in Woodbury, held on March 25, 1783, named Seabury or the Rev. Jeremiah Leaming, whichever would be able or willing, to seek episcopal consecration in England. Leaming declined; Seabury accepted, and sailed for England.

After a year of negotiation, Seabury found it impossible to obtain episcopal orders from the Church of England because, as an American citizen, he could not swear allegiance to the crown. He then turned to the Non-juring bishops of The Episcopal Church in Scotland. On November 14, 1784, in Aberdeen, he was consecrated by the Bishop and the Bishop Coadjutor of Aberdeen and the Bishop of Ross and Caithness, in the presence of a number of the clergy and laity.

On his return home, Seabury was recognized as Bishop of Connecticut in Convocation on August 3, 1785, at Middletown. With Bishop William White, he was active in the organization of The Episcopal Church at the General Convention of 1789. With the support of William Smith of Maryland, William Smith of Rhode Island, William White of Pennsylvania, and Samuel Parker of Boston, Seabury kept his promise, made in a concordat with the Scottish bishops, to persuade the American Church to adopt the Scottish form for the celebration of the Holy Eucharist.

In 1790, Seabury became responsible for episcopal oversight of the churches in Rhode Island; and, at the General Convention of 1792, he participated in the first consecration of a bishop on American soil, that of John Claggett of Maryland. Seabury died on February 25, 1796, and is buried beneath St. James' Church, New London.

Rite I   We give thanks to thee, O Lord our God, for thy goodness in bestowing upon this Church the gift of the episcopate, which we celebrate in this remembrance of the consecration of Samuel Seabury; and we pray that, joined together in unity with our bishops and nourished by thy holy Sacraments, we may proclaim the Gospel of redemption with apostolic zeal; through Jesus Christ our Lord, who liveth and reigneth with thee and the Holy Spirit, one God, now and for ever. Amen.

Rite II We give you thanks, O Lord our God, for your goodness in bestowing upon this Church the gift of the episcopate, which we celebrate in this remembrance of the consecration of Samuel Seabury; and we pray that, joined together in unity with our bishops and nourished by your holy Sacraments, we may proclaim the Gospel of redemption with apostolic zeal; through Jesus Christ our Lord, who lives and reigns with you and the Holy Spirit, one God, now and for ever. Amen.

For Liturgical Celebration: [**Common** of a Pastor, A14] [For the Ministry II, A50]

November 15

Francis Asbury, *1816,*
and George Whitefield, *1770*
Evangelists

Two of the great figures to emerge from out of the religious fervor of colonial and post-revolutionary America, George Whitefield and Francis Asbury, shared a common tie to the Methodist movement of John Wesley.

George Whitefield entered Pembroke College, Oxford, as a servitor, one unable to pay tuition and who thus served higher ranked students in exchange for free tuition. There he came under the influence of John and Charles Wesley and was a member of the "Holy Club." In 1736, he was ordained a deacon, and in 1738, he followed John Wesley to Georgia, where Whitefield served a parish in Savannah, Georgia. He returned to England in 1739 to obtain priest's orders to raise funds for his Bethesda orphanage in Georgia. His preaching attracted a wide following in England, Wales, and Scotland. Whitefield, who subscribed to the Calvinist position then prevalent in the Church of England, broke with the Wesleys, the latter being theologically drawn to Arminianism. Whitefield formed and was president of the first Methodist conference, but left that position after a short time to focus on evangelistic efforts.

Whitefield returned to America several times, and his preaching sparked the Great Awakening of 1740. Whitefield preached to thousands throughout the colonies, riding from New York to Charleston on horseback.

Like Whitefield, Francis Asbury was also renowned for his preaching, and also like Whitefield, he rode many miles on horseback each year and preached throughout the colonies. Asbury was sent to America by John Wesley in 1771 and was the only Methodist minister to remain in America when the War for Independence broke out. When the newly independent Methodist Episcopal Church was formed, he and Thomas Coke served as its first two bishops.

Like his mentor John Wesley, Asbury preached in courthouses, public houses, tobacco fields, or wherever a large crowd could be gathered to hear him. Among those he ordained was Richard Allen (March 26), the former slave and founder of the African Methodist Episcopal Church.

Rite I   Holy God, who didst inspire Francis Asbury and George Whitefield with evangelical zeal through their faithful proclamation of the Gospel: Inspire us, we pray, by thy Holy Spirit, that we, like them, may be eager to share thy Good News and lead many to Jesus Christ; who liveth and reigneth with thee and the Holy Spirit, one God, now and for ever. Amen.

Rite II Holy God, you inspired Francis Asbury and George Whitefield with evangelical zeal through their faithful proclamation of the Gospel: Inspire us, we pray, by your Holy Spirit, that we, like them, may be eager to share your Good News and lead many to Jesus Christ; who lives and reigns with you and the Holy Spirit, one God, now and for ever. Amen.

For Liturgical Celebration: [Common of a Missionary, A11] [For the Mission of the Church, A52]

November 16

Margaret
Queen of Scotland, 1093

Shakespeare made familiar the names of Macbeth and Macduff, Duncan, and Malcolm; but it is not always remembered that Malcolm married an English princess, Margaret, about 1070.

With considerable zeal, Margaret sought to change what she considered to be old-fashioned and careless practices among the Scottish clergy. She insisted that the observance of Lent, for example, was to begin on Ash Wednesday, rather than on the following Monday, and that the Mass should be celebrated according to the accepted Roman rite of the Church, and not in barbarous form and language. The Lord's Day was to be a day when, she said, "we apply ourselves only to prayers." She argued vigorously, though not always with success, against the exaggerated sense of unworthiness that made many of the pious Scots unwilling to receive Communion regularly.

Margaret's energies were not limited to reformation of formal Church practices. She encouraged the founding of schools, hospitals, and orphanages, and used her influence with King Malcolm to help her improve the quality of life among the isolated Scottish clans. Together, Margaret and her husband rebuilt the monastery of Iona and founded Dunfermline Abbey, under the direction of Benedictine monks.

In addition to her zeal for Church and people, Margaret was a conscientious wife and the mother of eight children. Malcolm, a strong-willed man, came to trust her judgment even in matters of State. She saw also to the spiritual welfare of her large household, providing servants with opportunity for regular worship and prayer.

Margaret was not as successful as she wished to be in creating greater unity in faith and works between her own native England and the Scots. She was unable, for example, to bring an end to the bloody warfare among the highland clans, and, after her death in 1093, there was a brief return to the earlier isolation of Scotland from

England. Nevertheless, her work among the people and her reforms in the Church made her Scotland's most beloved saint. She died on November 16, 1093, and was buried at Dunfermline Abbey.

Rite I   O God, who didst call thy servant Margaret to an earthly throne that she might advance thy heavenly kingdom, and gave her zeal for thy Church and love for thy people: Mercifully grant that we, who commemorate her this day, may be fruitful in good works and attain to the glorious crown of thy saints; through Jesus Christ our Lord, who liveth and reigneth with thee and the Holy Spirit, one God, for ever and ever. Amen.

Rite II O God, you called your servant Margaret to an earthly throne that she might advance your heavenly kingdom, and gave her zeal for your Church and love for your people: Mercifully grant that we, who commemorate her this day, may be fruitful in good works, and attain to the glorious crown of your saints; through Jesus Christ our Lord, who lives and reigns with you and the Holy Spirit, one God, for ever and ever. Amen.

For Liturgical Celebration: [Common of a Saint, A23] [For Vocation in Daily Work, A61] [For Social Service, A59]

November 17

Hugh, *1200,*
and Robert Grosseteste, *1253*
Bishops of Lincoln

Hugh was born into a noble family at Avalon in Burgundy (France). He became a canon regular at Villard-Benoit near Grenoble. About 1160, he joined the Carthusians, the strictest contemplative religious order, becoming the procurator of their major house, the Grande Chartreuse. With reluctance, he accepted the invitation of King Henry II to become prior of a new foundation of Carthusians in England at Witham, Somerset. With even greater hesitation, Hugh accepted the King's appointment to the See of Lincoln in 1186. He died in London, November 16, 1200, and is buried in Lincoln Cathedral, of which he laid the foundation.

As a bishop, Hugh continued to live as much as possible under the strict discipline of his order. His humility and tact, his total lack of self-regard, and his cheerful disposition made it difficult to oppose him. His people loved him for his unrelenting care of the poor and oppressed. Steadfastly independent of secular influences, he was never afraid to reprove his king for unjust treatment of the people. Hugh refused to raise money for King Richard's foreign wars. Yet Richard said of him, "If all bishops were like my Lord of Lincoln, not a prince among us could lift his head against them."

Robert Grosseteste was a distinguished scholar of law, medicine, languages, sciences, and theology, having risen to prominence from humble beginnings. He was a commentator and translator of Aristotle but sought to refute many of Aristotle's ideas in favor of those of Augustine. Because of Grosseteste's influence, Oxford began to give greater weight to the study of science, particularly geometry, physics, and mathematics.

Roger Bacon, an important progenitor of scientific method, was a pupil of Grosseteste, and John Wyclif was strongly influenced by him as well.

He became Bishop of Lincoln in 1235. He is remembered for the diligence with which he visited the clergy and people of his diocese, teaching, preaching, and celebrating the sacraments, thus refusing to be isolated from the lives of those under his care. He was a steadfast defender of diocesan prerogatives whether against the papacy or the state.

Rite I   Holy God, our greatest treasure, who didst bless Hugh and Robert, Bishops of Lincoln, with wise and cheerful boldness for the proclamation of thy Word to rich and poor alike: Grant that all who minister in thy Name may serve with diligence, discipline and humility, fearing nothing but the loss of thee and drawing all to thee through Jesus Christ our Savior; who liveth and reigneth with thee in the communion of the Holy Spirit, one God, for ever and ever. Amen.

Rite II   Holy God, our greatest treasure, you blessed Hugh and Robert, Bishops of Lincoln, with wise and cheerful boldness for the proclamation of your Word to rich and poor alike: Grant that all who minister in your Name may serve with diligence, discipline and humility, fearing nothing but the loss of you and drawing all to you through Jesus Christ our Savior; who lives and reigns with you in the communion of the Holy Spirit, one God, now and for ever. Amen.

For Liturgical Celebration: [Common of a Pastor, A14] [For the Ministry II, A50]

November 18

Hilda
Abbess of Whitby, 680

"Hilda's career falls into two equal parts," says the Venerable Bede, "for she spent thirty-three years nobly in secular habit, while she dedicated an equal number of years still more nobly to the Lord, in the monastic life."

Hilda, born in 614, was the grandniece of King Edwin. She was instructed by Paulinus (one of the companions of Augustine of Canterbury) in the doctrines of Christianity in preparation for her baptism at the age of thirteen. She lived, chaste and respected, at the King's court for twenty years and then decided to enter the monastic life. She had hoped to join the convent of Chelles in Gaul, but Bishop Aidan was so impressed by her holiness of life that he recalled her to her home country, in East Anglia, to live in a small monastic settlement.

One year after her return, Aidan appointed her Abbess of Hartlepool. There, Hilda established the rule of life that she had been taught by Paulinus and Aidan. She became renowned for her wisdom, eagerness for learning, and devotion to God's service.

Some years later, she founded the abbey at Whitby, where both nuns and monks lived in strict obedience to Hilda's rule of justice, devotion, chastity, peace, and charity. Known for her prudence and good sense, Hilda was sought out by kings and other public men for advice and counsel. Those living under her rule devoted so much time to the study of Scripture and to works of righteousness that many were found qualified for ordination. Several of her monks became bishops; at least one pursued further studies in Rome. She encouraged the poet Caedmon, a servant at Whitby, to become a monk and to continue his inspired writing. All who were her subjects or knew her, Bede remarks, called her "mother."

In 663, Whitby was the site of the famous synod convened to decide divisive questions involved in the differing traditions of Celtic Christians and the followers of Roman order. Hilda favored the Celtic position, but, when the Roman position prevailed, she was obedient to the synod's decision. Hilda died on November 17, 680, surrounded by her monastics, whom, in her last hour, she urged to preserve the gospel of peace.

Rite I   O God of peace, by whose grace the abbess Hilda was endowed with gifts of justice, prudence, and strength to rule as a wise mother over the nuns and monks of her household and to become a trusted and reconciling friend to leaders of the Church: Raise up these gifts in us, that we, following her example and prayers, might build up one another in love to the benefit of thy Church; through Jesus Christ our Lord, who liveth and reigneth with thee and the Holy Spirit, one God, now and for ever. Amen.

Rite II   O God of peace, by whose grace the abbess Hilda was endowed with gifts of justice, prudence, and strength to rule as a wise mother over the nuns and monks of her household and to become a trusted and reconciling friend to leaders of the Church: Raise up these gifts in us, that we, following her example and prayers, may build up one another in love to the benefit of your Church; through Jesus Christ our Lord, who lives and reigns with you and the Holy Spirit, one God, now and for ever. Amen.

For Liturgical Celebration: [Common of a Monastic or Professed Religious, A20] [Common of a Theologian and Teacher, A17] [Of the Incarnation, A39]

November 19

Elizabeth
Princess of Hungary, 1231

Elizabeth's charity is remembered in numerous hospitals that bear her name throughout the world. She was born in 1207 at Pressburg (now Bratislava), daughter of King Andrew II of Hungary, and was married in 1221 to Louis IV, Landgrave of Thuringia, to whom she bore three children. At an early age she showed concern for the poor and the sick, and was thus attracted to the Franciscans who came to the Wartburg in 1223. From them she received spiritual direction. Her husband was sympathetic to her almsgiving and allowed her to use her dowry for this purpose. During a famine and epidemic in 1226, when her husband was in Italy, she sold her jewels and established a hospital, where she cared for the sick and the poor. To supply their needs, she opened the royal granaries. After her husband's death in 1227, the opposition of the court to her "extravagances" compelled her to leave the Wartburg with her children.

For some time, Elizabeth lived in great distress. She then courageously took the habit of the Franciscans—the first of the Franciscan Tertiaries, or Third Order, in Germany. Finally, arrangements with her family gave her a subsistence, and she spent her remaining years in Marburg, living in self-denial, caring for the sick and needy. She died from exhaustion, November 16, 1231, and was canonized by Pope Gregory IX four years later. With Louis of France she shares the title of patron of the Third Order of St. Francis.

Rite I   Almighty God, by whose grace thy servant Elizabeth of Hungary recognized and honored Jesus in the poor of this world: Grant that we, following her example, may with love and gladness serve those in any need or trouble, in the name and for the sake of Jesus Christ; who liveth and reigneth with thee and the Holy Spirit, one God, for ever and ever. Amen.

Rite II   Almighty God, by your grace your servant Elizabeth of Hungary recognized and honored Jesus in the poor of this world: Grant that we, following her example, may with love and gladness serve those in any need or trouble, in the name and for the sake of Jesus Christ; who lives and reigns with you and the Holy Spirit, one God, for ever and ever. Amen.

For Liturgical Celebration: [Common of a Saint, A23] [For Vocation in Daily Work, A61] [For Social Service, A59]

November 20

Edmund
King of East Anglia, 870

Edmund ascended the throne of East Anglia at the age of fifteen, one of several monarchs who ruled various parts of England at that period in her history. The principal source of information about the martyrdom of the young king is an account by Dunstan, who became Archbishop of Canterbury ninety years after Edmund's death. Dunstan had heard the story many years before from a man who claimed to have been Edmund's armor bearer.

Edmund had reigned as a Christian king for nearly fifteen years when Danish armies invaded England in 870. Led by two brothers, Hinguar and Hubba, the Danes moved south, burning monasteries and churches, plundering and destroying entire villages, and killing hundreds. Upon reaching East Anglia, the brothers confronted Edmund and offered to share their treasure with him if he would acknowledge their supremacy, forbid all practice of the Christian faith, and become a figurehead ruler. Edmund's bishops advised him to accept the terms and avoid further bloodshed, but the king refused. He declared that he would not forsake Christ by surrendering to pagan rule, nor would he betray his people by consorting with the enemy.

Edmund's small army fought bravely against the Danes, but the king was eventually captured. According to Dunstan's account, Edmund was tortured, beaten, shot through with arrows, and finally beheaded. By tradition, the date of his death is November 20, 870.

The cult of the twenty-nine-year-old martyr grew very rapidly, and his remains were eventually enshrined in a Benedictine monastery in Bedericesworth—now called Bury St. Edmunds. Through the centuries, Edmund's shrine became a traditional place of pilgrimage for England's kings, who came to pray at the grave of a man who remained steadfast in the Christian faith and loyal to the integrity of the English people.

Rite I   O God of ineffable mercy, thou didst give grace and fortitude to blessed Edmund the king to triumph over the enemy of his people by nobly dying for thy Name: Bestow on us thy servants, we beseech thee, the shield of faith, wherewith we may withstand the assaults of our ancient enemy; through Jesus Christ our Redeemer, who liveth and reigneth with thee and the Holy Spirit, one God, now and for ever. Amen.

Rite II   O God of ineffable mercy, you gave grace and fortitude to blessed Edmund the king to triumph over the enemy of his people by nobly dying for your Name: Bestow on us your servants the shield of faith with which we can withstand the assaults of our ancient enemy; through Jesus Christ our Redeemer, who lives and reigns with you and the Holy Spirit, one God, now and for ever. Amen.

For Liturgical Celebration: [Common of a Martyr, A7] [Of the Holy Cross, A41]

November 21

William Byrd, *1623,* John Merbecke, *1585,* and Thomas Tallis, *1585*
Musicians

John Merbecke was born in 1505, and nothing is known of his childhood. As a young man, he was a chorister at St. George's Chapel, Windsor, and from 1541 until near the time of his death in 1585, he served as chapel organist.

Only a small handful of works by Merbecke have survived, most notably the *Booke of Common Praier Noted*, 1550, composed to accompany the 1549 Book. The appearance of the 1552 Prayer Book made it obsolete, but more recently, Merbecke's musical setting has been widely used.

Thomas Tallis was born near the beginning of the fifteenth century, and very little is known of his early life. After a succession of appointments as a church musician, he spent most of his vocation in service to the Crown as musician to the Chapels Royal under four successive monarchs, both Catholic and Protestant. Although always a Roman Catholic, Tallis had the political savvy to survive the shifts in ecclesial loyalties and the musical acumen to respond to the changing needs of the Church of England. He is regarded as the father of English Church music since the Reformation.

William Byrd was a student, colleague, business partner, and successor of Thomas Tallis. Most likely born in Lincolnshire in 1543, he was appointed organist and choirmaster of Lincoln Cathedral in 1563 and served until he joined Tallis as a gentleman of the Chapels Royal in 1572. Like Tallis, he was a lifelong Roman Catholic but was successful in winning the support for his music among Anglicans of Puritan tendencies, though not without occasional difficulties. His liturgical compositions cover a variety of musical forms: Mass settings, motets, graduals, psalm settings, English anthems, and occasional music for the great feasts of the church. Byrd composed for the keyboard and wrote works perhaps best described as consort music for the more popular enjoyment of the court.

Tallis and Byrd collaborated on a number of projects and together held the Crown Patent for the printing of music and lined music paper for twenty-one years.

Rite I O God most glorious, whose praises art sung night and day by thy saints and angels in heaven: We offer thanks for William Byrd, John Merbecke, and Thomas Tallis, whose music hath enriched the praise that thy Church offers thee here on earth. Grant, we pray thee, to all who are touched by the power of music such glimpses of eternity that we may be made ready to join thy saints in heaven and behold thy glory unveiled for evermore; through Jesus Christ our Lord, who liveth and reigneth with thee and the Holy Spirit, one God, for ever and ever. Amen.

Rite II O God most glorious, whose praises are sung night and day by your saints and angels in heaven: We give you thanks for William Byrd, John Merbecke, and Thomas Tallis, whose music has enriched the praise that your Church offers you here on earth. Grant, we pray, to all who are touched by the power of music such glimpses of eternity that we may be made ready to join your saints in heaven and behold your glory unveiled for evermore; through Jesus Christ our Lord, who lives and reigns with you and the Holy Spirit, one God, for ever and ever. Amen.

For Liturgical Celebration: [Common of an Artist, Writer, or Composer, A27]

November 22

Cecilia
Martyr at Rome, c. 230

Cecilia is the patron saint of singers, organ builders, musicians, and poets. She is venerated as a martyr. Many of the details of her life are unknown, and much of what we do know comes from later periods. She is among the women named in the Roman Canon of the Mass.

According to fifth century sources, Cecilia was of noble birth and was betrothed to a pagan who bore the name Valerian. Cecilia's witness resulted in the conversion of Valerian and his brother, Tiburtius. Because of their conversion, the brothers were martyred and, while Cecilia was burying them, she too was arrested. After several failed attempts to put her to death, she died from injuries sustained by the ordeal. The date of her martyrdom is generally believed to be 230, during the Roman persecution of Christians under Alexander Severus, although some scholars have dated it earlier.

Remembered for the passion with which she sang the praises of God, Cecilia is first depicted in Christian art as a martyr, but, since the fourteenth century, she is often shown playing the organ, a theme picked up by Raphael in his famous altarpiece for San Giovanni-in-Monte, Bologna, painted around 1516. Her story has inspired centuries of artistic representations in paintings, sculptures, mosaics, and stained glass. Composers such as Handel, Purcell, Howells, and Britten have written choral works and mass settings in her honor. Many music schools, choral societies, and concert series bear her name.

In the ninth century, during the pontificate of Pope Paschal I, the remains of Cecilia were uncovered in the catacombs of Callixtus. On orders from the pope, the sarcophagus containing her remains was transferred to the new basilica in the Trastevere region of Rome. Built on what was believed to be the site of Cecilia's home, a church named in her honor had existed on the site since at least the fifth century, and perhaps as early as the late third century, one of the original churches of the City of Rome.

Rite I   Gracious God, whose servant Cecilia didst serve thee in song: Grant us to join her hymn of praise to thee in the face of all adversity and to suffer gladly for the sake of our Lord Jesus Christ; who liveth and reigneth with thee and the Holy Spirit, one God, for ever and ever. Amen.

Rite II Gracious God, whose servant Cecilia served you in song: Grant us to join her hymn of praise to you in the face of all adversity and to suffer gladly for the sake of our Lord Jesus Christ; who lives and reigns with you and the Holy Spirit, one God, for ever and ever. Amen.

For Liturgical Celebration: [Common of a Martyr, A7] [Of the Holy Cross, A41] [Common of an Artist, Writer, or Composer, A27]

November 22

Clive Staples Lewis
Apologist and Spiritual Writer, 1963

"You must make your choice," C. S. Lewis wrote in *Mere Christianity*. "Either this man was, and is, the Son of God, or else a madman or something worse. You can shut Him up as a fool, you can spit at Him and kill Him as a demon, or you can fall at His feet and call Him Lord and God."

Lewis did not always believe this. Born in Belfast on November 29, 1898, Lewis was raised as an Anglican but rejected Christianity during his adolescent years. After serving in World War I, he started a long academic career as a scholar in medieval and renaissance literature at both Oxford and Cambridge. He also began an inner journey that led him from atheism to agnosticism to theism and finally to faith in Jesus Christ.

"Really, a young Atheist cannot guard his faith too carefully," he later wrote of his conversion to theism in *Surprised by Joy*. "Dangers lie in wait for him on every side . . . Amiable agnostics will talk cheerfully about 'man's search for God.' To me, as I then was, they might as well have talked about the mouse's search for the cat. You must picture me all alone in that room at Magdalen, night after night, feeling, whenever my mind lifted even for a second from my work, the steady, unrelenting approach of Him whom I so earnestly desired not to meet. That which I greatly feared had at last come upon me. In the Trinity Term of 1929 I gave in, and admitted that God was God, and knelt and prayed: perhaps, that night, the most dejected and reluctant convert in all England." Two years later, his conversion was completed: "I know very well when, but hardly how, the final step was taken. I was driven to Whipsnade one sunny morning. When we set out, I did not believe that Jesus Christ is the Son of God, and when we reached the zoo, I did."

Lewis's conversion inaugurated a wonderful outpouring of Christian apologetics in media as varied as popular theology, children's literature, fantasy and science fiction, and correspondence on spiritual matters with friends and strangers alike.

In 1956 Lewis married Joy Davidman, a recent convert to Christianity. Her death four years later led him to a transforming encounter with the Mystery of which he had written so eloquently before. Lewis died at his home in Oxford on November 22, 1963. The inscription on his grave reads: "Men must endure their going hence."

Rite I O God of searing truth and surpassing beauty, we give thee thanks for Clive Staples Lewis, whose sanctified imagination lighteth fires of faith in young and old alike: Surprise us also with thy joy and draw us into that new and abundant life which is ours in Christ Jesus, who liveth and reigneth with thee and the Holy Spirit, one God, now and for ever. Amen.

Rite II O God of searing truth and surpassing beauty, we give you thanks for Clive Staples Lewis, whose sanctified imagination lights fires of faith in young and old alike: Surprise us also with your joy and draw us into that new and abundant life which is ours in Christ Jesus, who lives and reigns with you and the Holy Spirit, one God, now and for ever. Amen.

For Liturgical Celebration: [Common of a Theologian and Teacher, A17] [Common of an Artist, Writer, or Composer, A27]

November 23

Clement
Bishop of Rome, c. 100

According to early traditions, Clement was a disciple of the Apostles and the third Bishop of Rome. He is generally regarded as the author of a letter written about the year 96 from the Church in Rome to the Church in Corinth, and known as "First Clement" in the collection of early documents called "The Apostolic Fathers."

The occasion of the letter was the action of a younger group at Corinth, who had deposed the elder clergy because of dissatisfaction with their ministrations. The unity of the Church was being jeopardized by a dispute over its ministry. Clement's letter sets forth a hierarchical view of Church authority. It insists that God requires due order in all things, that the deposed clergy must be reinstated, and that the legitimate superiors must be obeyed.

The letter used the terms "bishop" and "presbyter" interchangeably to describe the higher ranks of clergy, but refers to some of them as "rulers" of the Church. It is they who lead its worship and "offer the gifts" of the Eucharist, just as the duly appointed priests of the Old Testament performed the various sacrifices and liturgies in their time.

Many congregations of the early Church read this letter in their worship, and several ancient manuscripts include it in the canonical books of the New Testament, along with a second letter, which is actually an early homily of unknown authorship. The text of First Clement was lost to the western Church in the Middle Ages, and was not rediscovered until 1628.

Clement writes: "The apostles received the Gospel for us from the Lord Jesus Christ; Jesus the Christ was sent from God. Thus Christ is from God and the apostles from Christ. In both instances, the orderly procedure depends on God's will. So thereafter, when the apostles had been given their instructions, and all their doubts had been set at rest by the resurrection of our Lord Jesus Christ, they went forth in the confidence of the Holy Spirit to preach the Good News of the coming of God's kingdom. They preached in country and city, and appointed their first converts, after testing them by the Spirit, to be the bishops and deacons of future believers."

Rite I   Almighty God, who didst choose thy servant Clement of Rome to recall the Church in Corinth to obedience and stability: Grant that thy Church may be grounded and settled in thy truth by the indwelling of the Holy Spirit; reveal to it what is not yet known; fill up what is lacking; confirm what has already been revealed; and keep it blameless in thy service; through Jesus Christ our Lord, who liveth and reigneth with thee and the Holy Spirit, one God, for ever and ever. Amen.

Rite II Almighty God, you chose your servant Clement of Rome to recall the Church in Corinth to obedience and stability: Grant that your Church may be grounded and settled in your truth by the indwelling of the Holy Spirit; reveal to it what is not yet known; fill up what is lacking; confirm what has already been revealed; and keep it blameless in your service; through Jesus Christ our Lord, who lives and reigns with you and the Holy Spirit, one God, for ever and ever. Amen.

For Liturgical Celebration: [Common of a Martyr, A7] [Of the Holy Cross, A41] [For the Ministry II, A50]

November 25

James Otis Sargent Huntington
Priest and Monk, 1935

In the Rule for the Order of the Holy Cross, James Huntington wrote: "Holiness is the brightness of divine love, and love is never idle; it must accomplish great things." Commitment to active ministry rooted in the spiritual life was the guiding principle for the founder of the first permanent Episcopal monastic community for men in the United States.

James Otis Sargent Huntington was born in Boston in 1854. After graduation from Harvard, he studied theology at St. Andrew's Divinity School in Syracuse, New York, and was ordained deacon and priest by his father, the first Bishop of Central New York. In 1880 and 1881, he ministered in a working-class congregation at Calvary Mission, Syracuse.

While attending a retreat at St. Clement's Church, Philadelphia, Huntington received a call to the religious life. He considered joining the Society of St. John the Evangelist, which had by that time established a province in the United States, but he resolved to found an indigenous American community.

Huntington and two other priests began their common life at Holy Cross Mission on New York's Lower East Side, ministering with the Sisters of St. John Baptist among poor immigrants. The taxing daily regimen of Eucharist, prayer, and long hours of pastoral work soon forced one priest to leave for reason of health. The other dropped out for lack of a vocation. Huntington went on alone; and on November 25, 1884, his life vow was received by Bishop Potter of New York.

As Huntington continued his work among the immigrants, with emphasis on helping young people, he became increasingly committed to the social witness of the Church. His early involvements in the single-tax movement and the labor union movement were instrumental in the eventual commitment of The Episcopal Church to social ministries.

The Order attracted vocations, and, as it grew in the ensuing years, the community moved, first to Maryland, and, in 1902, to West Park, New York, where it established the monastery which is its mother house. Huntington served as Superior on several occasions, continuing his energetic round of preaching, teaching, and spiritual counsel until his death on June 28, 1935.

Rite I O loving God, by thy grace thy servant James Huntington gathered a community dedicated to love and discipline and devotion to the holy Cross of our Savior Jesus Christ: Send thy blessing upon all who proclaim Christ crucified and move the hearts of many to look unto him and be saved; who with thee and the Holy Spirit liveth and reigneth, one God, for ever and ever. Amen.

Rite II O loving God, by your grace your servant James Huntington gathered a community dedicated to love and discipline and devotion to the holy Cross of our Savior Jesus Christ: Send your blessing upon all who proclaim Christ crucified and move the hearts of many to look upon him and be saved; who with you and the Holy Spirit lives and reigns, one God, for ever and ever. Amen.

For Liturgical Celebration: [Common of a Monastic or Professed Religious, A20] [Of the Incarnation, A39] [For the Ministry III, A51]

November 26

Isaac Watts
Hymnwriter, 1748

Isaac Watts is remembered as the father of English hymnody. He was born in Southampton, England, in 1674, the eldest child of a devout Nonconformist family. His academic capabilities, and particularly his ability with the English language, were recognized at an early age. He was offered the resources to enroll at Oxford or Cambridge and pursue ordination in the Church of England, but Watts remained faithful to his background and, in 1690, enrolled in a Nonconformist academy at Stoke Newington. In 1702, Watts was ordained and served the Mark Lane independent congregation in London for a decade before his health made it impossible to continue.

As a hymn writer, Watts wrote more than six hundred hymns, about a quarter of which continue in popular use. Among his works was his *Psalms of David*, a metrical psalter that versified the psalms in English for hymnic use. Perhaps his most enduring contribution in this genre is "O God, our help in ages past" (*The Hymnal 1982*, #680) based upon the opening verses of Psalm 90.

Watts also wrote a wide variety of other hymns and spiritual songs that are well beloved. The attractiveness of his texts is often said to be reflective of Watts' own personal faith: gentle, quiet, sturdy, and deeply devout. This can easily be seen in the final stanza of "When I survey the wondrous cross" (#474):

> Were the whole realm of nature mine,
> That were an offering far too small;
> Love so amazing, so divine,
> Demands my soul, my life, my all!

Among his more enduring hymns are "Jesus shall reign" (#544), "Joy to the world" (#100), and "I sing the almighty power of God" (#398).

Due to ill health, Watts spent the last decades of his life in semi-seclusion, rarely preaching, but devoted his time to writing, as he was able. During this period, his writings took a new turn, and he completed books on logic, human nature, and the English language, in addition to sermons, devotional literature, works for children, and more poetry and hymns.

Watts died in 1748. He is honored with a memorial in Westminster Abbey.

Rite I   God of truth and grace, who didst give Isaac Watts singular gifts to present thy praise in verse, that he might write psalms, hymns, and spiritual songs for thy Church: Give us grace joyfully to sing thy praises now and in the life to come; through Jesus Christ our Savior, who liveth and reigneth with thee and the Holy Spirit, one God, for ever and ever. Amen.

Rite II   God of truth and grace, you gave Isaac Watts singular gifts to present your praise in verse, that he might write psalms, hymns, and spiritual songs for your Church: Give us grace joyfully to sing your praises now and in the life to come; through Jesus Christ our Savior, who lives and reigns with you and the Holy Spirit, one God, for ever and ever. Amen.

For Liturgical Celebration: [Common of an Artist, Writer, or Composer, A27]

November 28

Kamehameha and Emma
King and Queen of Hawaii, 1864, 1885

Within a year of ascending the throne in 1855, the twenty-year-old King Kamehameha IV and his bride, Emma Rooke, embarked on the path of altruism and unassuming humility for which they have been revered by their people. The year before, Honolulu, and especially its native Hawaiians, had been horribly afflicted by smallpox. The people, accustomed to a royalty which ruled with pomp and power, were confronted instead by a king and queen who went about, "with notebook in hand," soliciting from rich and poor the funds to build a hospital. Queen's Hospital, named for Emma, is now the largest civilian hospital in Hawaii.

In 1860, the king and queen petitioned the Bishop of Oxford to send missionaries to establish the Anglican Church in Hawaii. The king's interest came through a boyhood tour of England where he had seen, in the stately beauty of Anglican liturgy, a quality that seemed attuned to the gentle beauty of the Hawaiian spirit. England responded by sending the Rt. Rev. Thomas N. Staley and two priests. They arrived on October 11, 1862, and the king and queen were confirmed a month later, on November 28, 1862. They then began preparations for a cathedral and school, and the king set about to translate the Book of Common Prayer and much of the hymnal.

Kamehameha's life was marred by the tragic death of his four-year-old son and only child, in 1863. He seemed unable to survive his sadness, although a sermon he preached after his son's death expresses a hope and faith that is eloquent and profound. His own death took place only a year after his son's, in 1864. Emma declined to rule; instead, she committed her life to good works. She was responsible for schools, churches, and efforts on behalf of the poor and sick. She traveled several times to England and the Continent to raise funds and became a favorite of Queen Victoria's. Archbishop Longley of Canterbury remarked upon her visit to Lambeth: "I was much struck by the cultivation of her mind . . . But what excited my interest most was her almost saintly piety."

The Cathedral was completed after Emma died. It was named St. Andrew's in memory of the king, who died on that saint's day. Among the Hawaiian people, Emma is still referred to as "our beloved Queen."

Rite I   O Sovereign God, who didst raise up (King) Kamehameha (IV) and (Queen) Emma to be rulers in Hawaii, and didst inspire and enable them to be diligent in good works for the welfare of their people and the good of thy Church: Receive our thanks for their witness to the gospel; and grant that we, with them, may attain to the crown of glory that fadeth not away; through Jesus Christ our Savior and Redeemer, who with thee and the Holy Spirit liveth and reigneth, one God, for ever and ever. Amen.

Rite II   O Sovereign God, who raised up (King) Kamehameha (IV) and (Queen) Emma to be rulers in Hawaii, and inspired and enabled them to be diligent in good works for the welfare of their people and the good of your Church: Receive our thanks for their witness to the gospel; and grant that we, with them, may attain to the crown of glory that never fades away; through Jesus Christ our Savior and Redeemer, who with you and the Holy Spirit lives and reigns, one God, for ever and ever. Amen.

For Liturgical Celebration: [Common of a Saint, A23] [For all Baptized Christians, A42] [For Vocation in Daily Work, A61]

DECEMBER

1 Nicholas Ferrar, Deacon, 1637
1 Charles de Foucauld, Hermit and Martyr in the Sahara, 1916
2 Channing Moore Williams, Missionary Bishop in China and Japan, 1910
3 Francis Xavier, Missionary to the Far East, 1552
4 John of Damascus, Priest, c. 760
5 Clement of Alexandria, Priest, c. 210
6 Nicholas, Bishop of Myra, c. 342
7 Ambrose, Bishop of Milan, 397
8 Richard Baxter, Pastor and Writer, 1691
9
10 Karl Barth, Pastor and Theologian, 1968
10 Thomas Merton, Contemplative and Writer, 1968
11
12
13 Lucy (Lucia), Martyr at Syracuse, 304
14 Juan de la Cruz (John of the Cross), Mystic, 1591
15 John Horden, Bishop and Missionary in Canada, 1893
15 Robert McDonald, Priest, 1913
16 Ralph Adams Cram, 1942, and Richard Upjohn, 1878, Architects, and John LaFarge, Artist, 1910
17 William Lloyd Garrison, 1879, and Maria Stewart, 1879, Prophetic Witnesses
18
19 Lillian Trasher, Missionary in Egypt, 1961
20
21
22 Henry Budd, Priest, 1875

22   Charlotte Diggs (Lottie) Moon, Missionary in China, 1912
23
24
25
26
27
28
29   Thomas Becket, 1170
30   Frances Joseph Gaudet, Educator and Prison Reformer, 1934
31   Samuel Ajayi Crowther, Bishop in the Niger Territories, 1891

December 1
Nicholas Ferrar
Deacon, 1637

Nicholas Ferrar was the founder of a religious community at Little Gidding, Huntingdonshire, England, which existed from 1626 to 1646. His family had been prominent in the affairs of the Virginia Company, but when that company was dissolved, he took deacon's orders and retired to the country.

At Little Gidding, his immediate family and a few friends and servants gave themselves wholly to religious observance. They restored the derelict church near the manor house, became responsible for services there, taught many of the local children, and looked after the health and well-being of the people of the neighborhood. A regular round of prayer according to the Book of Common Prayer was observed, along with the daily recital of the whole of the Psalter. The members of the community became widely known for fasting, private prayer and meditation, and for writing stories and books illustrating themes of Christian faith and morality.

One of the most interesting of the activities of the Little Gidding community was the preparation of "harmonies" of the gospels, one of which was presented to King Charles I by the Ferrar family.

The community did not long survive the death of Nicholas Ferrar. However, the memory of the religious life at Little Gidding was kept alive, principally through Izaak Walton's description in his *Life of George Herbert*: "He (Ferrar) and his family . . . did most of them keep Lent and all Ember-weeks strictly, both in fasting and using all those mortifications and prayers that the Church hath appointed . . . and he and they did the like constantly on Fridays, and on the vigils or eves appointed to be fasted before the Saints' days; and this frugality and abstinence turned to the relief of the poor . . . "

The community became an important symbol for many Anglicans when religious orders began to revive. Its life inspired T.S. Eliot, and he gave the title, "Little Gidding," to the last of his *Four Quartets*, one of the great religious poems of the twentieth century.

Rite I   Lord God, make us worthy of thy perfect love; that, with thy deacon Nicholas Ferrar and his household, we may rule ourselves according to thy Word, and serve thee with our whole heart; through Jesus Christ our Lord, who liveth and reigneth with thee and the Holy Spirit, one God, for ever and ever. Amen.

Rite II   Lord God, make us worthy of your perfect love; that, with your deacon Nicholas Ferrar and his household, we may rule ourselves according to your Word, and serve you with our whole heart; through Jesus Christ our Lord, who lives and reigns with you and the Holy Spirit, one God, for ever and ever. Amen.

For Liturgical Celebration: [Common of a Monastic or Professed Religious, A20] [Of the Holy Trinity, A37]

December 1

Charles de Foucauld
Hermit and Martyr in the Sahara, 1916

Charles de Foucauld, sometimes referred to as Brother Charles of Jesus, was the inspiration behind the founding of new religious communities for both men and women and is often credited with the revival of desert spirituality in the early twentieth century.

Born in Strasbourg, France, in 1858, Charles was orphaned at age six and raised by his grandparents. As a young man, he lost his faith, and, in spite of the discipline of his grandfather, whom he deeply respected, Charles lived a life that was a curious mix of laxity and stubbornness. After training as a career Army officer, Charles served in Algeria and Tunisia, until he resigned his commission in 1882. He then became an explorer in Morocco. There he encountered devout Muslims, whose practice of their faith inspired Charles to begin a search for the faith that was his own. Upon returning to France, he continued his quest, and, in 1886, at age 28, re-discovered God and made a new commitment that would guide the rest of his life. A pilgrimage to the Holy Land deepened his commitment still further.

Charles entered the Cistercian Order of Strict Observance, the Trappists, first in France and then in Syria, for a commitment of seven years. He then returned to the Holy Land and lived as a servant to the convent of the Poor Clares in Nazareth. It was there that he began to develop a life of solitude, prayer, and adoration. The Poor Clares saw in him a vocation to the priesthood, encouraged him in spite of his reluctance, and Charles was ordained a priest in 1901.

Charles then moved to the Sahara, where his desire was to live a "ministry of presence" among "the furthest removed, the most abandoned." He believed his call was to live among those whose faith and culture differed from his own. To witness to Christ among them was not to be eloquent preaching or missionary demands, but "to shout the Gospel with his life." Charles sought to live so that those who saw his life would ask, "If such is the servant, what must the Master be like?"

Charles lived among the Tuareg people, learning their language and culture as he ministered to them. He was shot to death outside his refuge by bandits on December 1, 1916. He is considered a martyr by the Roman Catholic Church.

Rite I   Loving God, who didst restore the Christian faith of Charles de Foucauld through an encounter with Islam in North Africa and didst sustain him in the desert, where he converted many with his witness of presence: Help us to know thee wherever we find thee, that with him, we may be faithful unto death; through Jesus Christ, who liveth and reigneth with thee and the Holy Spirit, one God, now and for ever. Amen.

Rite II   Loving God, who restored the Christian faith of Charles de Foucauld through an encounter with Islam in North Africa and sustained him in the desert, where he converted many with his witness of presence: Help us to know you wherever we find you, that with him, we may be faithful unto death; through Jesus Christ, who lives and reigns with you and the Holy Spirit, one God, now and for ever. Amen.

For Liturgical Celebration: [Common of a Martyr, A7] [Common of a Monastic or Professed Religious, A20] [Of the Holy Cross, A41] [Of the Incarnation, A39]

December 2

Channing Moore Williams
Missionary Bishop in China and Japan, 1910

Bishop Williams, a farmer's son, was born in Richmond, Virginia, on July 18, 1829, and brought up in straitened circumstances by his widowed mother. He attended the College of William and Mary and the Virginia Theological Seminary.

Ordained deacon in 1855, he offered himself for work in China, where he was ordained priest in 1857. Two years later, he was sent to Japan and opened work in Nagasaki. His first convert was baptized in 1866, the year he was chosen bishop for both China and Japan.

After 1868, he decided to concentrate all his work in Japan, following the revolution that opened the country to renewed contact with the western world. Relieved of his responsibility for China in 1874, Williams made his base at Yedo (now Tokyo), where he founded a divinity school, later to become St. Paul's University. At a synod in 1887, he helped bring together the English and American missions to form the Nippon Sei Ko Kai, the Holy Catholic Church of Japan, when the Church there numbered fewer than a thousand communicants.

Williams translated parts of the Prayer Book into Japanese; and he was a close friend and warm supporter of Bishop Schereschewsky, his successor in China, in the latter's arduous work of translating the Bible into Chinese.

After resigning his jurisdiction in 1889, Bishop Williams stayed in Japan to help his successor there, Bishop John McKim, who was consecrated in 1893. Williams lived in Kyoto and continued to work in the opening of new mission stations until his return to America in 1908. He died in Richmond, Virginia, on December 2, 1910.

Rite I   Almighty and everlasting God, we thank thee for thy servant Channing Moore Williams, whom thou didst call to preach the Gospel to the people of China and Japan. Raise up in this and every land evangelists and heralds of thy kingdom, that thy Church may proclaim the unsearchable riches of our Savior Jesus Christ; who liveth and reigneth with thee and the Holy Spirit, one God, for ever and ever. Amen.

Rite II Almighty and everlasting God, we thank you for your servant Channing Moore Williams, whom you called to preach the Gospel to the people of China and Japan. Raise up in this and every land evangelists and heralds of your kingdom, that your Church may proclaim the unsearchable riches of our Savior Jesus Christ; who lives and reigns with you and the Holy Spirit, one God, for ever and ever. Amen.

For Liturgical Celebration: [Common of a Missionary, A11] [Common of a Pastor, A14] [For the Ministry II, A50] [For the Mission of the Church, A52]

December 3

Francis Xavier
Missionary to the Far East, 1552

Francis Xavier was one of the great missionaries of the Church. Born in Spain in 1506, he studied locally before taking up university studies in Paris in 1526, receiving a master's degree in 1530. While in Paris he met Ignatius Loyola and, with a small group of companions, they bound themselves together for the service of God on August 15, 1534, the beginning of what would later become the Society of Jesus, or the Jesuits. After further theological study, Francis and Ignatius were ordained together in 1537.

As the nuncio to the east for the King of Portugal, John III, Francis went to India, arriving at Goa on the western coast in 1542. He later moved south and traveled as well to Sri Lanka (Ceylon) and the Molucca Islands, now Indonesia. For seven years, he labored among the people there, winning many converts to the faith, baptizing, teaching, and trying to ease the suffering of the people. His efforts were not always well received. New Christians were often abused and enslaved and sometimes killed.

In 1549, Francis moved on to the southern region of Japan and immediately set about learning the language and preparing a catechism to support his missionary efforts. In time, he moved north to the imperial capital, Kyoto, and made an effort to see the Mikado, the Japanese emperor. Civil strife and localized resistance made Francis' Japanese efforts difficult, but he came away from the experience with a deep sense of respect for the people and their culture.

After returning to India in 1551, Francis was appointed the Jesuit Provincial for India, but he was not satisfied only to maintain the work already begun. He immediately set out for China, at the time closed to foreigners, in hopes of launching new missionary efforts there. He set up camp near the mouth of the Canton River in August 1552, hoping to secure passage into the country. Later that year he took ill and died, at age forty-six, on December 3, 1552. His remains were later transferred back to Goa, India.

Rite I   Loving God, who didst call Francis Xavier to lead many in India and Japan to know Jesus Christ as their Redeemer: Bring us to the new life of glory promised to all who follow in the Way; through the same Jesus Christ, who with thee and the Holy Spirit liveth and reigneth, one God, for ever and ever. Amen.

Rite II Loving God, you called Francis Xavier to lead many in India and Japan to know Jesus Christ as their Redeemer: Bring us to the new life of glory promised to all who follow in the Way; through the same Jesus Christ, who with you and the Holy Spirit lives and reigns, one God, for ever and ever. Amen.

For Liturgical Celebration: [Common of a Missionary, A11] [Common of a Monastic or Professed Religious, A20] [For the Mission of the Church, A52]

December 4

John of Damascus
Priest, c. 760

John of Damascus was the son of a Christian tax collector for the Muslim Caliph of Damascus. At an early age, he succeeded his father in this office. In about 715, he entered the monastery of St. Sabas near Jerusalem. There he devoted himself to an ascetic life and to the study of the Fathers.

In the same year that John was ordained priest, 726, the Byzantine Emperor Leo the Isaurian published his first edict against the Holy Images, which signaled the formal outbreak of the iconoclastic controversy. The edict forbade the veneration of sacred images, or icons, and ordered their destruction. In 729-730, John wrote three "Apologies (or Treatises) against the Iconoclasts and in Defense of the Holy Images." He argued that such pictures were not idols, for they represented neither false gods nor even the true God in his divine nature; but only saints, or our Lord as man. He further distinguished between the respect, or veneration (*proskynesis*), that is properly paid to created beings, and the worship (*latreia*), that is properly given only to God.

The iconoclast case rested, in part, upon the Monophysite heresy, which held that Christ had only one nature, and since that nature was divine, it would be improper to represent him by material substances such as wood and paint. The Monophysite heresy was condemned by the Council of Chalcedon in 451.

At issue also was the heresy of Manichaeism, which held that matter itself was essentially evil. In both of these heresies, John maintained, the Lord's incarnation was rejected. The Seventh Ecumenical Council, in 787, decreed that crosses, icons, the book of the gospels, and other sacred objects were to receive reverence or veneration, expressed by salutations, incense, and lights, because the honor paid to them passed on to that which they represented. True worship (*latreia*), however, was due to God alone.

John also wrote a great synthesis of theology, *The Fount of Knowledge*, of which the last part, "On the Orthodox Faith," is best known.

To Anglicans, John is best known as the author of the Easter hymns, "Thou hallowed chosen morn of praise" (*The Hymnal 1982*, #198) "Come, ye faithful, raise the strain" (#199; #200), and "The day of resurrection" (#210).

Rite I Confirm our minds, O Lord, in the mysteries of the true faith, set forth with power by thy servant John of Damascus; that we, with him, confessing Jesus to be true God and true Man and singing the praises of the risen Lord, may, by the power of the resurrection, attain to eternal joy; through Jesus Christ our Lord, who liveth and reigneth with thee and the Holy Spirit, one God, now and for ever. Amen.

Rite II Confirm our minds, O Lord, in the mysteries of the true faith, set forth with power by your servant John of Damascus; that we, with him, confessing Jesus to be true God and true Man and singing the praises of the risen Lord, may, by the power of the resurrection, attain to eternal joy; through Jesus Christ our Lord, who lives and reigns with you and the Holy Spirit, one God, now and for ever. Amen.

For Liturgical Celebration: [Common of a Theologian and Teacher, A17] [Of the Holy Trinity, A37]

December 5

Clement of Alexandria
Priest, c. 210

Clement was born in the middle of the second century. He was a cultured Greek philosopher who sought truth in many schools until he met Pantaneaus, founder of the Christian Catechetical School at Alexandria in Egypt. Clement succeeded Pantaneaus as head of that school in about 190, and was for many years an apologist for the Christian faith to both pagans and Christians. His learning and allegorical exegesis of the Bible helped to commend Christianity to the intellectual circles of Alexandria. His work prepared the way for his pupil Origen, the most eminent theologian of early Greek Christianity, and his liberal approach to secular knowledge laid the foundations of Christian humanism. During the persecution under the Emperor Severus in 202, he fled Alexandria. The exact time and place of his death are unknown.

Clement lived in the age of "Gnosticism," a comprehensive term for many theories or ways of salvation current in the second and third centuries, all emphasizing "Gnosis" or "knowledge." Salvation, for Gnostics, was to be had through a secret and rather esoteric knowledge accessible only to a few. It was salvation from the world, rather than salvation of the world. Clement asserted that there was a true Christian Gnosis, to be found in the Scriptures, available to all. Although his understanding of this Christian knowledge—ultimately knowledge of Christ—incorporated several notions of Greek philosophy which the Gnostics also held, Clement dissented from the negative Gnostic view of the world and its denial of the role of free will.

What Rich Man Will Be Saved? was the title of a treatise by Clement on Mark 10:17–31, and the Lord's words, "Go, sell what you have, and give to the poor, and you will have treasure in heaven." His interpretation sanctioned the "right use" of material goods and wealth. It has been contrasted to the interpretation of Athanasius in his *Life of Antony*, which emphasized strict renunciation. Both interpretations can be found in early Christian spirituality: Clement's, called "liberal," and that of Athanasius, "literal."

Among Clement's writings are the hymns, "Sunset to sunrise changes now" (*The Hymnal 1982*, #163) and "Jesus our mighty Lord" (#478).

Rite I O God of unsearchable wisdom, who didst give thy servant Clement grace to understand and teach the truth as it is in Jesus Christ, the source of all truth: Grant to thy Church the same grace to discern thy Word wherever truth is found; through Jesus Christ our unfailing light, who liveth and reigneth with thee and the Holy Spirit, one God, for ever and ever. Amen.

Rite II O God of unsearchable wisdom, you gave your servant Clement grace to understand and teach the truth as it is in Jesus Christ, the source of all truth: Grant to your Church the same grace to discern your Word wherever truth is found; through Jesus Christ our unfailing light, who lives and reigns with you and the Holy Spirit, one God, for ever and ever. Amen.

For Liturgical Celebration: [Common of a Theologian and Teacher, A17] [Of the Holy Spirit, A38] [Of the Incarnation, A39] [For all Baptized Christians, A42]

December 6

Nicholas
Bishop of Myra, c. 342

Very little is known about the life of Nicholas, except that he suffered torture and imprisonment during the persecution under the Emperor Diocletian. It is possible that he was one of the bishops attending the First Ecumenical Council of Nicaea in 325. He was honored as a saint in Constantinople in the sixth century by the Emperor Justinian. His veneration became immensely popular in the West after the supposed removal of his body to Bari, Italy, in the late eleventh century. In England, almost 400 churches were dedicated to him.

Nicholas is famed as the traditional patron of seafarers and sailors, and, more especially, of children. As a bearer of gifts to children, his name was brought to America by the Dutch colonists in New York, from whom he is popularly known as Santa Claus.

Rite I   Almighty God, who in thy love didst give to thy servant Nicholas of Myra a perpetual name for deeds of kindness both on land and sea: Grant, we pray thee, that thy Church may never cease to work for the happiness of children, the safety of sailors, the relief of the poor, and the help of those tossed by tempests of doubt or grief; through Jesus Christ our Lord, who liveth and reigneth with thee and the Holy Spirit, one God, for ever and ever. Amen.

Rite II Almighty God, in your love you gave your servant Nicholas of Myra a perpetual name for deeds of kindness both on land and sea: Grant, we pray, that your Church may never cease to work for the happiness of children, the safety of sailors, the relief of the poor, and the help of those tossed by tempests of doubt or grief; through Jesus Christ our Lord, who lives and reigns with you and the Holy Spirit, one God, for ever and ever. Amen.

For Liturgical Celebration: [Common of a Pastor, A14] [For the Ministry II, A50] [For Social Service, A59]

December 7

Ambrose
Bishop of Milan, 397

Ambrose was the son of a Roman governor in Gaul, and in 373, he himself was governor in Upper Italy. Though brought up in a Christian family, Ambrose had not been baptized. He became involved in the election of a Bishop of Milan only as mediator between the battling factions of Arians and orthodox Christians. The election was important, because the victorious party would control the powerful see of Milan.

Ambrose exhorted the nearly riotous mob to keep the peace and to obey the law. Suddenly both sides raised the cry, "Ambrose shall be our bishop!" He protested, but the people persisted. Hastily baptized, he was ordained bishop on December 7, 373.

Ambrose rapidly won renown as a defender of orthodoxy against Arianism and as a statesman of the Church. He was also a skillful hymnodist. He introduced antiphonal chanting to enrich the liturgy and wrote straightforward, practical discourses to educate his people in such matters of doctrine as Baptism, the Trinity, the Eucharist, and the Person of Christ. His persuasive preaching was an important factor in the conversion of Augustine of Hippo.

Ambrose did not fear to rebuke emperors, including the hot-headed Theodosius, whom he forced to do public penance for the slaughter of several thousand citizens of Salonika.

About Baptism, Ambrose wrote: "After the font (of baptism), the Holy Spirit is poured on you, 'the spirit of wisdom and understanding, the spirit of counsel and strength, the spirit of knowledge and godliness, and the spirit of holy fear'" (*De Sacramentis* 3.8).

A meditation attributed to him includes these words: "Lord Jesus Christ, you are for me medicine when I am sick; you are my strength when I need help; you are life itself when I fear death; you are the way when I long for heaven; you are light when all is dark; you are my food when I need nourishment."

Among hymns attributed to Ambrose are "The eternal gifts of Christ the King" (*The Hymnal 1982*, #233; #234), "O Splendor of God's glory bright" (#5), and a series of hymns for the Hours.

Rite I   O God, who didst give thy servant Ambrose grace eloquently to proclaim thy righteousness in the great congregation and fearlessly to bear reproach for the honor of thy Name: Mercifully grant to all bishops and pastors such excellence in preaching and faithfulness in ministering thy Word, that thy people may be partakers with them of the glory that shall be revealed; through Jesus Christ our Lord, who liveth and reigneth with thee and the Holy Spirit, one God, now and for ever. Amen.

Rite II   O God, you gave your servant Ambrose grace eloquently to proclaim your righteousness in the great congregation and fearlessly to bear reproach for the honor of your Name: Mercifully grant to all bishops and pastors such excellence in preaching and faithfulness in ministering your Word, that your people may be partakers with them of the glory that shall be revealed; through Jesus Christ our Lord, who lives and reigns with you and the Holy Spirit, one God, now and for ever. Amen.

For Liturgical Celebration: [Common of a Theologian and Teacher, A17] [Common of a Pastor, A14] [Common of an Arist, Writer, or Composer, A25] [For the Ministry II, A50]

December 8

Richard Baxter
Pastor and Writer, 1691

Richard Baxter was born in Shropshire in 1615 and educated in the local schools. He was ordained in 1638 and spent the early years of his ministry as a schoolmaster and curate, becoming a chaplain to the parliamentary army at the outbreak of the English Civil War in 1642. Although aligned with the Puritan cause, Baxter was a moderate and stood against the excessive destructiveness of Cromwell's legions.

In 1647, Baxter became the Vicar of Kidderminster. It was there that his pastoral ministry thrived. He set up new patterns for parish catechesis, increased the size of parish buildings to welcome the larger numbers coming to hear him preach, and pioneered a style of pastoral ministry that has enriched the Anglican tradition to this day. Baxter provides his own narrative of his pastoral work in his book, *The Reformed Pastor*, of 1656.

When episcopacy was re-established in England after the Civil War, Charles II offered Baxter an appointment to the see of Hereford. Although more moderate than many, Baxter's Puritan convictions kept him from accepting the post, a decision that made it impossible for him to continue as a priest of the Church of England.

Baxter is remembered in the history of the Book of Common Prayer for the role he played at the Savoy Conference of 1661. There, he argued for the changes that needed to be made in the next prayer book from the vantage point of the Puritans, the so-called "Exceptions." The resulting 1662 Prayer Book shows few of the marks of Baxter's agenda, but his strong advocacy of the Puritan position certainly influenced the shape of the revision.

From 1662 until his death in 1691, Baxter resided in the environs of London. The re-establishment of the monarchy in the state and episcopacy in the church unfortunately made Baxter, remembered for his moderate Puritan posture, a target of unkindness and petty revenge.

A profound example of Baxter's deep joy and piety can be found in the words of the hymn "Ye holy angels bright" (*The Hymnal 1982*, #625).

Rite I We offer thanks, most gracious God, for the devoted witness of Richard Baxter, who, out of love for thee, followed his conscience at cost to himself and at all times rejoiced to sing thy praises in word and deed; and we pray that our lives, like his, may be well-tuned to sing the songs of love, and all our days be filled with praise of Jesus Christ our Lord; who with thee and the Holy Spirit liveth and reigneth, one God, now and for ever. Amen.

Rite II We give you thanks, most gracious God, for the devoted witness of Richard Baxter, who, out of love for you, followed his conscience at cost to himself and at all times rejoiced to sing your praises in word and deed; and we pray that our lives, like his, may be well-tuned to sing the songs of love, and all our days be filled with praise of Jesus Christ our Lord; who with you and the Holy Spirit lives and reigns, one God, now and for ever. Amen.

For Liturgical Celebration: [Common of an Artist, Writer, or Composer, A27]

December 10

Karl Barth
Pastor and Theologian, 1968

Born at Basel, Switzerland, on May 10, 1886, Barth studied at several prestigious universities including Tübingen, Germany. After completing his studies, he served as pastor in two Swiss centers, Geneva and Safenwil. The events of the First World War led Barth to critically question the dominant theology of the day, which, in Barth's view, held a too easy peace between theology and culture. In his *Commentary on Romans*, published in 1918, Barth reasserted doctrines such as God's sovereignty and human sin, central ideas which he believed were excluded and overshadowed in theological discourse at that time.

With Hitler's rise to power, Barth joined the Confessing Church and was chiefly responsible for the writing of the *Barmen Declaration* (1934), one of its foundational documents. In it, Barth claimed that the Church's allegiance to God in Christ gave it the moral imperative to challenge the rule and violence of Hitler. Barth was himself ultimately forced to resign his professorship at Bonn due to his refusal to swear an oath to Hitler.

In 1932, Barth published the first volume of his thirteen-volume opus, the *Church Dogmatics*. Barth would work on the *Dogmatics* until his death in 1968. An exhaustive account of his theological themes and a daring reassessment of the entire Christian theological tradition, the *Dogmatics* gave new thought to some of the central themes first articulated in the *Commentary on Romans*. In the first volume, "The Doctrine of the Word of God," Barth laid out many of the theological notions which would comprise the heart of the entire work, including his understanding of God's Word as the definitive source of revelation, the Incarnation as the bridge between God's revelation and human sin, and the election of the creation as God's great end.

Karl Barth was one of the great thinkers of the twentieth century. Pope Pius XII regarded him as the most important theologian since Thomas Aquinas. This assessment speaks to the respect Barth received from both Protestant and Catholic theologians and to his influence within both theological communities.

Rite I   Almighty God, source of justice beyond human knowledge: We offer thanks that thou didst inspire Karl Barth to resist tyranny and exalt thy saving grace, without which we cannot apprehend thy will. Teach us, like him, to live by faith, and even in chaotic and perilous times to perceive the light of thine eternal glory, Jesus Christ our Redeemer; who liveth and reigneth with thee and the Holy Spirit, ever one God, throughout all ages. Amen.

Rite II Almighty God, source of justice beyond human knowledge: We thank you for inspiring Karl Barth to resist tyranny and exalt your saving grace, without which we cannot apprehend your will. Teach us, like him, to live by faith, and even in chaotic and perilous times to perceive the light of your eternal glory, Jesus Christ our Redeemer; who lives and reigns with you and the Holy Spirit, ever one God, throughout all ages. Amen.

For Liturgical Celebration: [Common of a Theologian and Teacher, A17] [Of the Holy Trinity, A37]

December 10

Thomas Merton
Contemplative and Writer, 1968

Thomas Merton was among the most influential Catholic writers of the twentieth century. His writings cover a broad range of subject matter: spirituality and the contemplative life, prayer, and religious biography. He was also deeply interested in issues of social justice and Christian responsibility. He did not shy away from controversy and addressed race relations, economic injustice, war, violence, and the nuclear arms race.

Merton was born in Prades, France, on January 15, 1915. His father was from New Zealand and his Quaker mother from the United States. After a brief sojourn in England, where Merton was baptized in the Church of England, the family settled in New York. The birth of his brother, the death of his mother, and the romance of his father with the American novelist Evelyn Scott created an unsettling life for Merton for some years. After a brief enrollment at Clare College, Cambridge, Merton settled into life as a student at Columbia University in New York. Merton developed relationships at Columbia that would nurture him for the rest of his life.

Though nominally an Anglican, Merton underwent a dramatic conversion experience in 1938 and became a Roman Catholic. Merton recounts the story of his conversion in *The Seven Storey Mountain*, an autobiography published in 1948, immediately a classic.

Merton entered the Order of Cistercians of the Strict Observance, the Trappists, at the Abbey of Gethsemani, near Bardstown, Kentucky, in 1941. Merton was known in the community as Brother Louis; his gifts as a writer were encouraged by the abbot. In addition to his translations of Cistercian sources and his original works, Merton carried on a prolific correspondence with people around the world on a wide range of subjects. Some of his correspondence takes the form of spiritual direction, some shows his deep affections for friends outside the community, and much of it demonstrates Merton's ability to be fully engaged in the world even though he lived a cloistered life.

Merton died in Bangkok, Thailand, on December 10, 1968, by accidental electrocution, while attending a meeting of religious leaders during a pilgrimage to the Far East.

Rite I Gracious God, who didst call thy monk Thomas Merton to proclaim thy justice out of silence and moved him in his contemplative writings to perceive and value Christ at work in the faiths of others: Keep us, like him, steadfast in the knowledge and love of Jesus Christ; who with thee and the Holy Spirit liveth and reigneth, one God, for ever and ever. Amen.

Rite II Gracious God, you called your monk Thomas Merton to proclaim your justice out of silence and moved him in his contemplative writings to perceive and value Christ at work in the faiths of others: Keep us, like him, steadfast in the knowledge and love of Jesus Christ; who with you and the Holy Spirit lives and reigns, one God, for ever and ever. Amen.

For Liturgical Celebration: [Common of a Monastic or Professed Religious, A20] [Of the Incarnation, A39] [For the Ministry III, A51]

December 13

Lucy (Lucia)
Martyr at Syracuse, 304

Lucy, or Lucia, was martyred at Syracuse, in Sicily, during Diocletian's reign of terror of 303-304, among the most dramatic of the persecutions of early Christians. Her tomb can still be found in the catacombs at Syracuse. She was venerated soon after her death and her cult spread quickly throughout the Church. She is among the saints and martyrs named in the Roman Canon of the Mass.

Most of the details of Lucy's life are obscure. In the tradition, she is remembered for the purity of her life and the gentleness of her spirit. Because her name means "light," she is sometimes thought of as the patron saint of those who suffer from diseases of the eyes.

In popular piety, Lucy is perhaps most revered because her feast day, December 11, was for many centuries the shortest day of the year. (The reform of the calendar by Pope Gregory VIII [1582] would shift the shortest day to December 21/22, depending upon the year.) It was on Lucy's day that the light began gradually to return and the days to lengthen. This was particularly powerful in northern Europe, where the days of winter were quite short. In Scandinavian countries, particularly Sweden, Lucy's day has long been a festival of light that is kept as both an ecclesiastical commemoration and a domestic observance.

In the domestic celebration of Lucia-fest, a young girl in the family dresses in pure white (a symbol of Lucy's faith, purity, and martyrdom) and wears a crown of lighted candles upon her head (a sign that on Lucy's day the light is returning) and serves her family special foods prepared especially for the day. In praise of her service, the young girl is called Lucy for the day.

Rite I Loving God, who for the salvation of all didst give Jesus Christ as light to a world in darkness: Illumine us, with thy daughter Lucy, with the light of Christ, that, by the merits of his passion, we may be led to eternal life; through the same Jesus Christ, who with thee and the Holy Spirit liveth and reigneth, one God, for ever and ever. Amen.

Rite II Loving God, for the salvation of all you gave Jesus Christ as light to a world in darkness: Illumine us, with your daughter Lucy, with the light of Christ, that, by the merits of his passion, we may be led to eternal life; through the same Jesus Christ, who with you and the Holy Spirit lives and reigns, one God, for ever and ever. Amen.

For Liturgical Celebration: [Common of a Martyr, A7] [Of the Holy Cross, A41]

December 14

Juan de la Cruz (John of the Cross)
Mystic, 1591

John of the Cross was unknown outside the Discalced Carmelites for nearly three hundred years after his death. More recently, scholars of Christian spirituality have found in him a hidden treasure. Once described by Thomas Merton as "the church's safest mystical theologian," John has been called the "the poet's poet," "spirit of flame," "celestial and divine."

John was born in 1542 at Fontiveros, near Avila, Spain. After his third birthday, his father died, leaving his mother and her children reduced to poverty. John received elementary education in an orphanage in Medina del Campo. By the age of seventeen, he had learned carpentry, tailoring, sculpturing, and painting through apprenticeships to local craftsmen.

After university studies with the Jesuits, John entered the Carmelite Order in Medina del Campo and completed his theological studies in Salamanca. In 1567, he was ordained to the priesthood and recruited by Teresa of Avila for the reformation of the Carmelite Order.

By the age of thirty-five, he had studied extensively, had been spiritual director to many, and yet devoted himself to the search for God so fully that he reached the peak of the mystical experience: a complete transformation in God.

John became disillusioned with what he considered the laxity of the Carmelites and, in 1568, he opened a monastery of "Discalced" (strict observance) Carmelites, an act that met with sharp resistance from the General Chapter of the Calced Carmelites. John was seized, taken to Toledo, and imprisoned in the monastery. During nine months of great hardship, he comforted himself by writing poetry. It was while he was imprisoned that he composed the greater part of his luminous masterpiece, *The Spiritual Canticle*, as well as a number of shorter poems. Other major works are, *The Ascent of Mount Carmel*, *The*

Living Flame of Love, and *The Dark Night*. It is this latter work, *Noche obscura del alma*, that gave the English language the phrase "dark night of the soul."

After a severe illness, John died on December 14, 1591, in Ubeda, in southern Spain.

Rite I Judge eternal, throned in splendor, who gavest Juan de la Cruz strength of purpose and mystical faith that sustained him even through the dark night of the soul: Shed thy light on all who love thee, in unity with Jesus Christ our Savior; who with thee and the Holy Spirit liveth and reigneth, one God, for ever and ever. Amen.

Rite II Judge eternal, throned in splendor, you gave Juan de la Cruz strength of purpose and mystical faith that sustained him even through the dark night of the soul: Shed your light on all who love you, in unity with Jesus Christ our Savior; who with you and the Holy Spirit lives and reigns, one God, for ever and ever. Amen.

For Liturgical Celebration: [Common of a Theologian and Teacher, A17] [Common of a Monastic or Professed Religious, A20] [Of the Holy Spirit, A38] [Of the Incarnation, A39]

December 15

John Horden
Bishop and Missionary in Canada, 1893

Born in Exeter, England, in 1828, John Horden was apprenticed to the blacksmith's trade as a young boy, and devoted his spare hours to self-education. He eventually qualified as a schoolteacher and attended the Vicar's Bible Class at St. Thomas, Exeter, where he was educated in the Bible and in missionary work. Horden, along with some friends, volunteered his services to the Church Missionary Society, but was told to wait due to his young age.

Finally, in 1851, he received a letter informing him that he was being appointed mission schoolmaster in Moose Factory, James Bay, on the southern end of Hudson Bay, in Canada. He immediately devoted himself to learning Cree, the native language of those whom he served. Over time, Horden's ability as a linguist was evident in his ability to function in no less than five First Nations' languages, plus Norwegian, English, Greek and Latin.

In addition to working with the Native peoples of the region, Horden regarded it as part of his work to serve the employees of the Hudson's Bay Company. With their help, he built a schoolhouse and church, and developed a variety of ministries to serve the people in this remote territory. He ministered to his people through several epidemics, often in the face of rugged, unforgiving conditions.

In 1872, he was recalled to England to receive episcopal orders, and following his ordination in Westminster Abbey, he was appointed the first bishop of the Diocese of Moosonee. He returned to James Bay, traveling to the outer regions of his vast diocese, often by dog-team in harsh weather. Many congregations in the small towns and cities of the area trace their formation back to the inspiring work of Bishop Horden.

Horden died in Moose Factory on January 12, 1893.

Rite I   Creator God, whose hands holdeth the storehouses of the snow and the gates of the sea, and from whose Word springeth forth all that is: We bless thy holy Name for the intrepid witness of thy missionary John Horden, who followed thy call to serve the Cree and Inuit nations of the North. In all the places we travel, may we, like him, proclaim thy Good News and draw all into communion with thee through thy Christ; who with thee and the Holy Spirit liveth and reigneth, one God, in glory everlasting. Amen.

Rite II   Creator God, whose hands hold the storehouses of the snow and the gates of the sea, and from whose Word springs forth all that is: We bless your holy Name for the intrepid witness of your missionary John Horden, who followed your call to serve the Cree and Inuit nations of the North. In all the places we travel, may we, like him, proclaim your Good News and draw all into communion with you through your Christ; who with you and the Holy Spirit lives and reigns, one God, in glory everlasting. Amen.

For Liturgical Celebration: [Common of a Missionary, A11] [Common of a Pastor, A14] [For the Ministry II, A50] [For the Mission of the Church, A52]

December 15

Robert McDonald
Priest, 1913

Robert McDonald was a priest, missionary, and archdeacon, who served among the First Nations peoples of Canada.

McDonald was born in 1829 in Point Douglas, Manitoba. He attended local schools, worked alongside his father on the family farm, and married Julia Kuttag, with whom he had nine children.

Although McDonald showed initial reluctance, he responded to the church's call to mission service among the native peoples of Canada. He was ordained a priest in 1853 and took charge of the Islington Mission on the Winnipeg River. It was there that he discovered his gift for languages, and it was there that he became fluent in the language of the Ojibway Tribe and began to translate the Bible.

In 1862, the Church Missionary Society persuaded McDonald to establish a new mission at Fort Yukon. It was here, as later at Fort McPherson, where McDonald made his enduring contribution to the tribes of the Tinjiyzoo Nation. He developed a written alphabet for the Tukudh language so that the people could read the texts of the Christian tradition. He also published a grammar and dictionary in Tukudh, both of which remain standard reference works. Over the next forty years, working together with his wife, Julia, and other translators, he accomplished the translation of the whole of the Bible, the Book of Common Prayer, a hymnal, and other texts. Possessing these common texts was critical not only to the Christian mission, but also had a unifying impact on the common life of the various tribes in the region.

McDonald retired from the Church Missionary Society in 1904 and lived in Winnipeg, Manitoba, until his death on August 29, 1913. He is buried in the cemetery of St. John's Anglican Cathedral.

Rite I God of ice, sea, and sky, who didst call thy servant Robert McDonald, making him strong to endure all hardships for the sake of serving thee in the Arctic: Send us forth as laborers into thy harvest, that by patience in our duties and compassion in our dealings, many may be gathered to thy kingdom; through Jesus Christ our Lord, who is alive and reignest with thee and the Holy Spirit, one God, now and for ever. Amen.

Rite II God of ice, sea, and sky, you called your servant Robert McDonald and made him strong to endure all hardships for the sake of serving you in the Arctic: Send us forth as laborers into your harvest, that by patience in our duties and compassion in our dealings, many may be gathered to your kingdom; through Jesus Christ our Lord, who is alive and reigns with you and the Holy Spirit, one God, now and for ever. Amen.

For Liturgical Celebration: [Common of a Missionary, A11] [Common of a Pastor, A14] [For the Mission of the Church, A52]

December 16

Ralph Adams Cram, *1942, and*
Richard Upjohn, *1878, Architects,*
and # John LaFarge, *Artist, 1910*

Ralph Adams Cram and Richard Upjohn were major architects whose influence on the design and decoration of Episcopal churches in the late 19th and early 20th centuries is without equal.

Cram was born on this day in 1863 at Hampton Falls, New Hampshire. After an apprenticeship in Boston, Cram established his own firm in 1890, specializing in designing churches. Heavily influenced by Anglo-Catholic principles, Cram was a leading proponent for an "American gothic revival"—buildings that were reminiscent of the ritual and structural dominance of the medieval period. Because of his many commissions for chapels and other buildings on college and university campuses, Cram is also remembered as the originator of the "collegiate gothic" style. Among his works is the great gothic nave of the Cathedral of St. John the Divine, New York City.

Richard Upjohn was born in 1802 in England, where he trained as a cabinetmaker. He immigrated to the United States in 1829 and eventually took up residence in Boston, where he worked as a draftsman, art teacher, and eventually an architect. His first major commission was for a gothic-style building for St. John's Episcopal Church in Bangor, Maine, a building that was later destroyed by fire. He was commissioned in 1839 to design and supervise the construction of a new building for the Parish of Trinity Church, Wall Street, New York City. It was completed in 1846 and continues as Upjohn's most well known accomplishment.

Upjohn is also remembered for his sketchbooks of small wood-frame designs for churches in rural towns and villages. These designs were widely copied and adapted. As a result, Upjohn was among the early progenitors of "carpenter gothic."

John Lafarge was born in 1835 in New York City and was a devout Roman Catholic. As an artist, LaFarge worked in a variety of media but is most often remembered for the murals that decorate Trinity Church, Boston, and the Church of the Ascension, New York City, among others. He also made significant contributions to ecclesiastical decoration in stained glass.

Rite I Gracious God, we offer thanks for the vision of Ralph Adams Cram, John LaFarge, and Richard Upjohn, whose harmonious revival of the Gothic enriched our churches with a sacramental understanding of reality in the face of secular materialism; and we pray that we may honor thy gifts of the beauty of holiness given through them, for the glory of Jesus Christ; who liveth and reigneth with thee and the Holy Spirit, one God, in glory everlasting. Amen.

Rite II Gracious God, we thank you for the vision of Ralph Adams Cram, John LaFarge, and Richard Upjohn, whose harmonious revival of the Gothic enriched our churches with a sacramental understanding of reality in the face of secular materialism; and we pray that we may honor your gifts of the beauty of holiness given through them, for the glory of Jesus Christ; who lives and reigns with you and the Holy Spirit, one God, in glory everlasting. Amen.

For Liturgical Celebration: [Common of an Artist, Writer, or Composer, A27] [On the Anniversary of the Dedication of a Church, A47]

December 17

William Lloyd Garrison, *1879,*
and Maria Stewart, *1879*
Prophetic Witnesses

William Lloyd Garrison was born in Newburyport, Massachusetts, in 1805. His father, a sailor, had abandoned the family when he was five years old. His experience of poverty at a young age awakened in him a religious zeal for justice and a hatred for slavery. After working on a Quaker periodical in Baltimore, Garrison returned to Boston and, with the help of the black community, started his own antislavery paper, *The Liberator.*

His proclamation of purpose in the first issue became famous around the country: "On [the subject of slavery] I do not wish to think, or speak, or write, with moderation. No! No! Tell a man whose house is on fire to give a moderate alarm . . . but urge me not to use moderation in a cause like the present."

The *Liberator* came to be the dominant voice in the abolitionist movement, demanding immediate emancipation without compensation to slave owners. Garrison invoked the ire and rage of people all over the country, particularly in slaveholding states. In 1835, an angry mob attacked Garrison, who was jailed for his own safety.

In what was a radical policy for the time, Garrison opened up his columns to black and female writers. Among those to respond to his call was Maria W. Stewart, a freeborn African American woman who showed up at his office in 1831 with several essays that were published in *The Liberator.*

Born in Hartford, Connecticut, Stewart was orphaned at the age of five and grew up in the home of a white minister. She married James W. Stewart, a successful shipping outfitter, but was widowed just three years later. Soon after, she experienced a religious conversion and responded with her vigorous antislavery advocacy. Her efforts called upon African Americans in the south to rise up against slavery and for northern blacks to resist racial restrictions. In addition, Stewart was an early advocate for women's rights.

When her speaking career ended after three years, she became a schoolteacher and then Head Matron of Freedom's Hospital in Washington D.C., which was later to become Howard University. Stewart also spent the years after the Civil War organizing an Episcopal Sunday School, which taught basic literacy to more than 100 at a time in the District of Columbia.

Rite I   God, in whose service alone is perfect freedom: We give thanks to thee for William Lloyd Garrison and Maria Stewart, who witnessed that all are made in thine image and likeness. Fill us, like them, with the perseverance to break every chain of enslavement, that, by thy Holy Spirit, thy people may overcome bondage and ignorance; through the merits of Jesus Christ our Redeemer, who with thee and the Holy Spirit liveth and reigneth, one God, now and for ever. Amen.

Rite II   God, in whose service alone is perfect freedom: We thank you for for William Lloyd Garrison and Maria Stewart, who witnessed that all are made in your image and likeness. Fill us, like them, with the perseverance to break every chain of enslavement, that, by your Holy Spirit, your people may overcome bondage and ignorance; through the merits of Jesus Christ our Redeemer, who with you and the Holy Spirit lives and reigns, one God, now and for ever. Amen.

For Liturgical Celebration: [Common of a Prophetic Witness, A31]

December 19

Lillian Trasher
Missionary in Egypt, 1961

Lillian Hunt Trasher was born in 1887 in Brunswick, Georgia. Raised by her mother (originally a Quaker) as a Roman Catholic, Trasher joined the Church of God in 1912, in which she was ordained, and later became a member of the (Pentecostal) Assemblies of God. As a young woman, she worked at an orphanage in North Carolina, not knowing at the time that her life's work would be devoted to caring for abandoned children.

In 1909, while engaged to a man she loved deeply, she heard the testimony of a missionary from India, and she was aware at that moment that she could not be married. God had called her to service as a missionary. Not knowing where she would go, she opened her Bible and read Acts 7:34: "I have seen, I have seen the affliction of my people which is in Egypt, and I have heard their groaning and am come down to deliver them. And now come, I will send thee to Egypt."

In 1910, she arrived in Alexandria, Egypt, with her sister Jennie, and they found their way to the town of Asyut in Upper Egypt near the Nile. Shortly after arriving, Lillian was called to the bedside of a dying mother whose malnourished daughter was also near death. Though ordered by the mission directors to return the child to the village, Trasher refused to abandon her to poverty and certain death. In 1911, she rented a small house and some furniture and nursed the child back to health.

As she took in additional children, she had to rely on charity, though she eventually received aid from the newly-formed Assemblies of God in the United States. In 1916, she was able to purchase additional land, the buildings for which were built from bricks which Lillian and the older children made themselves. In 1919, she was ordered out of the country by the British government in the midst of political turmoil, and, when she returned, she took in widows and the blind in addition to children. Despite the Nazi invasion of Egypt and the subsequent violence during World War II, she kept her orphanage running. When she died in 1961, she had become known as the "Mother of the Nile" and had cared for nearly 25,000 Egyptian children. Her orphanage remains open today.

Trasher died in Egypt on December 17, 1961.

Rite I   God, whose everlasting arms support the universe: We offer thanks for moving the heart of Lillian Trasher to heroic hospitality on behalf of orphaned children in great need, and we pray that we also may find our hearts awakened and our compassion stirred to care for thy little ones, through the example of our Savior Jesus Christ and by the energy of thy Holy Spirit, who broodest over the world as a mother over her children; for they live and reign with thee, one God, for ever and ever. Amen.

Rite II   God, whose everlasting arms support the universe: We thank you for moving the heart of Lillian Trasher to heroic hospitality on behalf of orphaned children in great need, and we pray that we also may find our hearts awakened and our compassion stirred to care for your little ones, through the example of our Savior Jesus Christ and by the energy of your Holy Spirit, who broods over the world like a mother over her children; for they live and reign with you, one God, for ever and ever. Amen.

For Liturgical Celebration: [Common of a Missionary, A11] [Common of a Pastor, A14] [For the Mission of the Church, A52]

December 22

Henry Budd
Priest, 1875

Henry Budd was the first person of First Nations ancestry to be ordained in the Anglican tradition in North America. He is remembered for his service among the Cree in Western Canada.

Budd was an orphan, and the date of his birth is unknown. He entered a mission school that was a joint venture with the Hudson's Bay Company to provide a Christian education to the First Nations people in the area of Rupert's Land, the vast expanse of land that encircled Hudson Bay before its division into Canadian provinces. Before embarking on a vocation as a priest and teacher, he worked as a clerk for the Hudson's Bay Company.

Henry Budd's ministry began as a lay teacher in the Red River region of Manitoba, where he taught at St. John's Anglican Parish School. He and his wife, Betsy, remained in the area for the next thirteen years, where Budd taught school and served as a lay minister in the Anglican Church.

Ordained to the priesthood on December 22, 1850, having been trained largely by personal mentoring and tutoring from other clergy, Budd was assigned to the Mission at Nipawim where he worked as a pastor until 1867. Thereafter, Budd returned to The Pas, where he was put in charge of a vast area encompassing several communities, and where he continued his vocation as both priest and teacher. Records of the Church Missionary Society indicate that Budd was paid half of what the white missionaries were paid on account of his race.

Henry Budd is remembered as an eloquent speaker and writer in both Cree and English. He endeared himself to those he served by exhibiting clearly in the living of his life the Christian principles he preached and the values he taught. Enduring among his many contributions are his translations of the Scriptures and the Book of Common Prayer into the Cree language.

Budd died on April 2, 1875, just a few days after he had conducted Easter services. He is buried in The Pas, Manitoba.

Rite I   Creator of light, we offer thanks for thy priest Henry Budd, who carried the great treasure of Scripture to his people the Cree nation, earning their trust and love. Grant that his example may call us to reverence, orderliness, and love, that we may give thee glory in word and action; through Jesus Christ our Savior, who with thee and the Holy Spirit liveth and reigneth, one God, for ever and ever. Amen.

Rite II Creator of light, we thank you for your priest Henry Budd, who carried the great treasure of Scripture to his people the Cree nation, earning their trust and love. Grant that his example may call us to reverence, orderliness, and love, that we may give you glory in word and action; through Jesus Christ our Savior, who with you and the Holy Spirit lives and reigns, one God, for ever and ever. Amen.

For Liturgical Celebration: [Common of a Missionary, A11] [Common of a Pastor, A14] [For the Mission of the Church, A52]

December 22

Charlotte Diggs (Lottie) Moon
Missionary in China, 1912

Born in Virginia in 1840, Charlotte Diggs (Lottie) Moon was the child of pious and affluent Baptist parents. Precocious in schooling, she received an MA in Classics, thereby earning one of the first graduate degrees awarded a woman in the South. She had a gift for languages, learning first the biblical and Romance languages—and then later, and famously, Mandarin.

Lottie Moon's piety lagged behind her learning, and through her teens she remained indifferent to her Baptist heritage. During a revival at age eighteen, she experienced a powerful conversion and devoted the rest of her life to Christ.

After college, Moon taught school in Alabama, Kentucky, and Georgia, one of the few occupations open to educated women in the South. Another vocation became available to her when Southern Baptists began to appoint women as foreign missionaries in 1872, and the following year, at age 33, Moon accepted an appointment in China.

Moon settled in Northern China and continued her work of education for girls. She soon became restless in teaching, and she began evangelizing among adults, particularly women. Her supervisors disapproved of her initiative, but Moon quickly gained credibility because of her ease in relating, woman-to-woman.

Lottie Moon's ceaseless correspondence with Baptist women in the United States, seeking their support and encouraging would-be missionaries, was instrumental in the denomination's burgeoning missionary movement. She appealed to women for a special offering for missionaries at Christmastime in 1887. Her influence led to the formation of the Women's Missionary Union in 1888, which continues the Lottie Moon Christmas Offering as a hallmark of Southern Baptist practice.

On arriving in China, Moon remained aloof from the Chinese, thinking them her cultural inferiors. Over time, however, she found a deep respect for Chinese culture, adopting not only their language but their dress and customs. As she wrote, "It is comparatively easy to give oneself to mission work, but it is not easy to give oneself to an alien people. Yet the latter is much better and truer work than the former."

Lottie Moon died on Christmas Eve, 1912.

Rite I O God, who in Christ Jesus hast brought Good News to those who are far off and to those who are near: We praise thee for awakening in thy servant Lottie Moon a zeal for thy mission and for her faithful witness among the peoples of China. Stir up in us the same desire for thy work throughout the world, and give us the grace and means to accomplish it; through the same Jesus Christ our Savior, who liveth and reigneth with thee and the Holy Spirit, one God, for ever and ever. Amen.

Rite II O God, in Christ Jesus you have brought Good News to those who are far off and to those who are near: We praise you for awakening in your servant Lottie Moon a zeal for your mission and for her faithful witness among the peoples of China. Stir up in us the same desire for your work throughout the world, and give us the grace and means to accomplish it; through the same Jesus Christ our Savior, who lives and reigns with you and the Holy Spirit, one God, for ever and ever. Amen.

For Liturgical Celebration: [Common of a Missionary, A11] [Common of a Pastor, A14] [For the Mission of the Church, A52]

December 29

Thomas Becket
1170

Thomas Becket was born in London in 1118, of a wealthy Norman family, and educated in England and in France. He then became an administrator for Theobald, Archbishop of Canterbury. Later, he was sent to study law in Italy and France and, after being ordained deacon, he was appointed Archdeacon of Canterbury. His administrative skills eventually brought him to the notice of King Henry II, who, to Thomas's surprise, appointed him Chancellor of England. He and the King became intimate friends, and because of Becket's unquestioning loyalty and support of the King's interests in both Church and State, Henry secured Thomas's election as Archbishop of Canterbury in 1162. Becket, foreseeing a break with his Royal Master, was reluctant to accept. As Archbishop he changed, as he tells us, "from a patron of play actors and a follower of hounds, to being a shepherd of souls." He also defended the interests of the Church against those of his former friend and patron, the King. The struggle between the two became so bitter that Thomas sought exile at an abbey in France.

When he returned to England six years later, the fragile reconciliation between Henry and the Archbishop broke down. In a fit of rage the King is alleged to have asked his courtiers, "Who will rid me of this turbulent priest?" Four barons, taking Henry's words as an order, made their way to Canterbury, and, upon finding the Archbishop in the cathedral on December 29, 1170, struck him down with their swords. Later, when the monks of Canterbury undressed Thomas's body to wash it and prepare it for burial, they discovered that under his episcopal robes their worldly and determined Archbishop was wearing a hair shirt. While such a garment hardly proves that a person is a saint, it clearly indicates that Thomas was motivated in the exercise of his office by far more than political considerations. His final words to the four barons before receiving the fatal blow were, "Willingly I die for the name of Jesus and in the defense of the Church."

Rite I O God, our strength and our salvation, who didst call thy servant Thomas Becket to be a shepherd of thy people and a defender of thy Church: Keep thy household from all evil and raise up among us faithful pastors and leaders who are wise in the ways of the gospel; through Jesus Christ, the shepherd of our souls, who liveth and reigneth with thee and the Holy Spirit, one God, for ever and ever. Amen.

Rite II O God, our strength and our salvation, you called your servant Thomas Becket to be a shepherd of your people and a defender of your Church: Keep your household from all evil and raise up among us faithful pastors and leaders who are wise in the ways of the gospel; through Jesus Christ, the shepherd of our souls, who lives and reigns with you and the Holy Spirit, one God, for ever and ever. Amen.

For Liturgical Celebration: [Common of a Martyr, A7] [Common of a Pastor, A14] [For the Ministry II, A50] [Of the Holy Cross, A41]

December 30

Frances Joseph Gaudet
Educator and Prison Reformer, 1934

Frances was born in a log cabin in Holmesville, Mississippi, in 1861, of African American and Native American descent. Raised by her grandparents, she later went to live with a brother in New Orleans, where she attended school and Straight College.

While still a young woman, Gaudet dedicated her life to prison reform. In 1894, she began holding prayer meetings for black prisoners. She wrote letters for them, delivered messages, and found them clothing. Later, she extended this ministry to white prisoners as well. Her dedication to the imprisoned and to penal reform won her the respect of prison officials, city authorities, the governor of Louisiana, and the Prison Reform Association.

In 1900, she was a delegate to the international convention of the Women's Christian Temperance Union in Edinburgh, Scotland. Gaudet worked to rehabilitate young blacks arrested for misdemeanors or vagrancy, becoming the first woman to support young offenders in Louisiana. Her efforts helped to found the Juvenile Court.

Deeply committed to the provision of good education, she eventually purchased a farm and founded the Gaudet Normal and Industrial School. In time, it expanded to more than 105 acres, with numerous buildings, and also served as a boarding school for children with working mothers. Gaudet served as its principal until 1921, when she donated the institution to The Episcopal Church in Louisiana. Though it closed in 1950, the Gaudet Episcopal Home opened in the same location four years later to serve African American children aged four to sixteen.

Frances Joseph Gaudet died on December 30, 1934.

Rite I   Merciful God, who didst raise up thy servant Frances Joseph Gaudet to work for prison reform and the education of the forgotten and oppressed: Encourage us by her example and prayers to work for those denied the fullness of life, that all may experience thy perfect freedom; through Jesus Christ, who liveth and reigneth with thee and the Holy Spirit, one God, for ever and ever. Amen.

Rite II   Merciful God, who raised up your servant Frances Joseph Gaudet to work for prison reform and the education of the forgotten and oppressed: Encourage us by her example and prayers to work for those denied the fullness of life, that all may experience your perfect freedom; through Jesus Christ, who lives and reigns with you and the Holy Spirit, one God, for ever and ever. Amen.

For Liturgical Celebration: [Common of a Prophetic Witness, A31] [For Social Service, A59] [For Education, A60]

December 31

Samuel Ajayi Crowther
Bishop in the Niger Territories, 1891

In Canterbury Cathedral, on St. Peter's Day, June 29, 1864, Samuel Ajayi Crowther (c. 1807 – 1891) was ordained the first African bishop in Nigeria for "the countries of Western Africa beyond the limits of the Queen's domains."

Crowther's gifts to the Church were many. A skilled linguist, he helped translate the Bible and Book of Common Prayer into Yoruba and other West African languages. He founded schools and training colleges, where he encouraged the study of the gospel, traditional subjects, and farming methods that allowed students to raise basic crops and cotton as sources of income.

As a child, Crowther had been captured in 1822, during a Nigerian civil war, and sold to Portuguese slave traders. Intercepted by a British anti-slavery patrol, the ship and its human cargo were taken to Freetown, Sierra Leone, a haven for freed captives after the British Parliament abolished the slave trade in 1807. There, Crowther was educated at a Church Missionary Society (CMS) school, was baptized in 1825, and became a teacher in Sierra Leone, an active center of African Christian ministry that sent indigenous lay and ordained ministers throughout West Africa.

Crowther's leadership skills were soon evident, and, in 1842, the CMS sent him to their Islington, England, training college. He was ordained a year later, returned to Sierra Leone, and then moved on to Yoruba territory. He also made extended mission journeys to the interior of Nigeria, where, in encounters with Muslims, he was known as a humble, patient listener and a thoughtful, non-polemical partner in dialogue.

At the time of his ordination as bishop, the British tried to keep missionary activity solely under the control of white British clerics, some of whom set about subverting Crowther's authority, something he patiently endured, while actively continuing his expansive work among Africans. Despite the difficulties, Crowther's achievement was considerable, and he has been called the most widely known African Christian of the nineteenth century. He created a solid base from which a much later generation of indigenous African leadership emerged to chart their own political and ecclesial futures.

Crowther died in 1891.

In 2015, Archbishop of Canterbury Justin Welby officially apologized on behalf of the Church of England for its treatment of Crowther.

Rite I   O God, who dost lead those whom thou lovest from captivity into the grace of the gospel, we give thanks to thee for Samuel Crowther, whom thou didst call to become a bishop in thy Church: Grant that thy Holy Word may be heard, loved, and lived in all corners of the world, that we and all thy people may proclaim, by word and example, the Good News of God in Jesus Christ; who liveth and reigneth with thee and the Holy Spirit, one God, for ever and ever. Amen.

Rite II   O God, who leads those whom you love from captivity into the grace of the gospel, we thank you for Samuel Crowther, whom you called to become a bishop in your Church: Grant that your Holy Word may be heard, loved, and lived in all corners of the world, that we and all your people may proclaim, by word and example, the Good News of God in Jesus Christ; who lives and reigns with you and the Holy Spirit, one God, for ever and ever. Amen.

For Liturgical Celebration: [Common of a Missionary, A11] [Common of a Pastor, A14] [For the Ministry II, A50] [For the Mission of the Church, A52]

Appendix

Appendix

There are people worthy of commemoration who do not qualify under the "reasonable passage of time" guideline. The method of appointing General Convention Legislative Committees and Interim Bodies tends to encourage short-term corporate memory. We believe that these people should remain in the Church's memory, even though they do not currently meet all of the criteria for additions. We hope that they will be given serious consideration in the future, and we encourage local and regional commemorations to continue (it has been the Church's custom, since the second century, to commemorate Christians on the anniversary of their death). The following list is intended to be representative rather than exhaustive.

Date of Death	Commemoration
January 23, 1993	Thomas A. Dorsey, composer/musician
January 25, 1999 and September 25, 1995	Sadie Louise Delaney and Annie Elizabeth "Bessie" Delaney, lay women, lives of service
March 2, 1985	William Stringfellow, lawyer
March 8, 2000	Carmen St. John Hunter, educator, missionary, executive
April 23, 1993	Cesar Chavez, labor leader
May 29, 1992	Ruby Middleton Forsythe, educator and founder, Faith Memorial School, Pawley's Island, South Carolina
May 30, 2002	Suzanne Radley Hiatt, priest

June 27, 1985	Marion Kelleran, seminary faculty
July 13, 1975	Laurence Clifton Jones, educator
July 19, 1997	John Hines, Presiding Bishop
August 16, 2005	Frère Roger Schütz, founder of Taizé
August 21, 1994	Tan Sri John Savarimuthu, Bishop of Western Malaysia
August 22, 1996	Alicia "Cristina" Rivera, OSH, monastic
August 24, 1986	Cynthia Clark Wedel, ecumenist (NCCC and WCC)
September 6, 2007	Allen Crite, artist
September 10, 1976	Mordecai Johnson, educator
September 15, 1990	Dora P. Chaplin, theologian
October 3, 2006	Alberto Ramento, Obispo Maximo, Philippine Independent Church
October 10, 1971	Isabelo de los Reyes, Jr., Obispo Maximo, Philippine Independent Church
October 23, 1983	Cyril Lakshman Wickremesinghe, Bishop of Kuranagala, Sri Lanka
October 29, 1969	Clarence Jordan, evangelist
November 4, 1997	Marianne H. Micks, theologian
November 22, 1990	Benito Cabanban, first Prime Bishop, Episcopal Church in the Philippines
December 29, 1968	Austin Farrer, theologian

Commons of Saints and Propers for Various Occasions

The festival of a saint is observed in accordance with the rules of precedence set forth in the Calendar of the Church Year (BCP, 15–18).

At the discretion of the Celebrant, and as appropriate, any of the following Collects and any of the following Scripture lessons may be used

a. At the commemoration of a saint recognized by the worshipping community for which no Proper is provided in the Book of Common Prayer;

b. At the patronal festival or commemoration of a saint not listed in the Calendar.

For the commemoration of individuals drawn from *A Great Cloud of Witnesses,* the tags offer guidance as to which propers may be most appropriate. Material may be chosen across categories to fit the individual and circumstances being celebrated.

Only the Propers for Various Occasions referred to in this resource are contained below. The complete set of Propers for Various Occasions are contained in both the Book of Common Prayer (BCP, 927–31) and *Weekday Eucharistic Propers 2015.*

Commons of Saints

Common of a Martyr

Of a Martyr I

I O Almighty God, who didst give to thy servant *N.* boldness to confess the Name of our Savior Jesus Christ before the rulers of this world and courage to die for this faith: Grant that we may always be ready to give a reason for the hope that is in us and to suffer gladly for the sake of the same our Lord Jesus Christ; who liveth and reigneth with thee and the Holy Spirit, one God, for ever and ever. *Amen.*

II Almighty God, who gave to your servant *N.* boldness to confess the Name of our Savior Jesus Christ before the rulers of this world and courage to die for this faith: Grant that we may always be ready to give a reason for the hope that is in us and to suffer gladly for the sake of our Lord Jesus Christ; who lives and reigns with you and the Holy Spirit, one God, for ever and ever. *Amen.*

Of a Martyr II

I O Almighty God, by whose grace and power thy holy martyr N. triumphed over suffering and was faithful even unto death: Grant us, who now remember *him* with thanksgiving, to be so faithful in our witness to thee in this world, that we may receive with *him* the crown of life; through Jesus Christ our Lord, who liveth and reigneth with thee and the Holy Spirit, one God, for ever and ever. *Amen.*

II Almighty God, by whose grace and power your holy martyr N. triumphed over suffering and was faithful even to death: Grant us, who now remember *him* in thanksgiving, to be so faithful in our witness to you in this world, that we may receive with *him* the crown of life; through Jesus Christ our Lord, who lives and reigns with you and the Holy Spirit, one God, for ever and ever. *Amen.*

Of a Martyr III

I Almighty and everlasting God, who didst enkindle the flame of thy love in the heart of thy holy martyr N.: Grant to us, thy humble servants, a like faith and power of love, that we who rejoice in *her* triumph may profit by *her* example; through Jesus Christ our Lord, who liveth and reigneth with thee and the Holy Spirit, one God, for ever and ever. *Amen.*

II Almighty and everlasting God, who kindled the flame of your love in the heart of your holy martyr N.: Grant to us, your humble servants, a like faith and power of love, that we who rejoice in *her* triumph may profit by *her* example; through Jesus Christ our Lord, who lives and reigns with you and the Holy Spirit, one God, for ever and ever. *Amen.*

Old Testament
Job 16:6–10
Isaiah 44:21–26a
Isaiah 53:8–12
Jeremiah 12:1–3a
Jeremiah 15:15–21
Daniel 3:13–25
Daniel 6:10–16
Habakkuk 2:9–14
Sirach (Ecclesiasticus) 51:1–12
2 Esdras 2:42–48

Psalm
31:1–5
44:20–26
116 or 116:1–8
121
124
126

New Testament
Romans 12:14–21
2 Corinthians 6:2b–10
2 Timothy 2:8–13; 3:10–12
Hebrews 10:32–36
James 1:2–12
1 Peter 3:14–18,22
1 Peter 4:12–19
Revelation 6:9–11
Revelation 7:13–17
Revelation 12:7–12

Gospel
Matthew 5:1–12
Matthew 10:16–22
Matthew 24:9–14
Mark 8:34–38
Luke 6:17–23
Luke 12:2–12
Luke 14:26–33
Luke 21:9–19
John 12:20–26
John 15:1–7

Preface of a Saint

Preface of Holy Week

Common of a Missionary

Of a Missionary I

I   Almighty and everlasting God, we thank thee for thy servant N., whom thou didst call to preach the gospel to the people of_____ (*or* to the_____ people). Raise up, we beseech thee, in this and every land, evangelists and heralds of thy kingdom, that thy Church may proclaim the unsearchable riches of our Savior Jesus Christ; who liveth and reigneth with thee and the Holy Spirit, one God, now and for ever. *Amen.*

II Almighty and everlasting God, we thank you for your servant N., whom you called to preach the gospel to the people of_____ (*or* to the_____ people). Raise up in this and every land evangelists and heralds of your kingdom, that your Church may proclaim the unsearchable riches of our Savior Jesus Christ; who lives and reigns with you and the Holy Spirit, one God, now and for ever. *Amen.*

Of a Missionary II

I Almighty God, who willest to be glorified in thy saints, and didst raise up thy servant *N.* to be a light in the world: Shine, we pray thee, in our hearts, that we also in our generation may show forth thy praise, who hast called us out of darkness into thy marvelous light; through Jesus Christ our Lord, who liveth and reigneth with thee and the Holy Spirit, one God, now and for ever. *Amen.*

II Almighty God, whose will it is to be glorified in your saints, and who raised up your servant *N.* to be a light in the world: Shine, we pray, in our hearts, that we also in our generation may show forth your praise, who called us out of darkness into your marvelous light; through Jesus Christ our Lord, who lives and reigns with you and the Holy Spirit, one God, now and for ever. *Amen.*

Old Testament
Exodus 3:7–12
Isaiah 2:2–5
Isaiah 49:1–6
Isaiah 49:22–23
Isaiah 52:7–10
Isaiah 60:1–7
Jeremiah 1:4–8
Ezekiel 36:22–27
Micah 4:1–5
Wisdom 13:1–5

Psalm
67
98 or 98:1–4
96 or 96:1–7
97 or 97:1–9
100
102:12–22

New Testament
Acts 1:1–9
Acts 17:22–31
Romans 10:12–17
1 Corinthians 9:19–23
1 Corinthians 12:1–11
Ephesians 2:13–18
1 Thessalonians 2:2b–12
2 Timothy 1:8–14
1 John 1:1–4
Revelation 22:1–6

Gospel
Matthew 5:13–16
Matthew 9:35–38
Matthew 28:16–20
Mark 1:14–20
Mark 4:1–9
Luke 8:11–15
Luke 10:1–9
John 1:29–34
John 4:34–38
John 17:5–13

Preface of Pentecost

Preface of Apostles

Common of a Pastor

Of a Pastor I

I O heavenly Father, Shepherd of thy people, we give thee thanks for thy servant N., who was faithful in the care and nurture of thy flock; and we pray that, following *his* example and the teaching of *his* holy life, we may by thy grace grow into the stature of the fullness of our Lord and Savior Jesus Christ; who liveth and reigneth with thee and the Holy Spirit, one God, for ever and ever. *Amen.*

II Heavenly Father, Shepherd of your people, we thank you for your servant N., who was faithful in the care and nurture of your flock; and we pray that, following *his* example and the teaching of *his* holy life, we may by your grace grow into the stature of the fullness of our Lord and Savior Jesus Christ; who lives and reigns with you and the Holy Spirit, one God, for ever and ever. *Amen.*

Of a Pastor II

I O God, our heavenly Father, who didst raise up thy faithful servant N. to be a [bishop and] pastor in thy Church and to feed thy flock: Give abundantly to all pastors the gifts of thy Holy Spirit, that they may minister in thy household as true servants of Christ and stewards of thy divine mysteries; through Jesus Christ our Lord, who liveth and reigneth with thee and the same Spirit, one God, for ever and ever. *Amen.*

II O God, our heavenly Father, who raised up your faithful servant N., to be a [bishop and] pastor in your Church and to feed your flock: Give abundantly to all pastors the gifts of your Holy Spirit, that they may minister in your household as true servants of Christ and stewards of your divine mysteries; through Jesus Christ our Lord, who lives and reigns with you and the Holy Spirit, one God, for ever and ever. *Amen.*

Old Testament
Exodus 28:15,21,29–30
Deuteronomy 15:7–11
Deuteronomy 26:16–19
1 Kings 8:54–62
Proverbs 3:1–2, 5–8
Ecclesiastes 3:1–11
Isaiah 49:8–13
Ezekiel 34:11–16
Amos 5:14–15
Malachi 2:4–7

Psalm
23
42 or 42:1–5
84 or 84:7–11
110 or 110:1–4
112
115 or 115:1–2, 9–13

New Testament
Acts 20:17–35
Romans 12:4–13
1 Corinthians 12:27–31
Galatians 5:22–6:2
Ephesians 2:19–22
Ephesians 3:14–21
1 Thessalonians 5:13b–24
2 Timothy 1:3–7
1 Peter 5:1–4
1 John 4:13–21

Gospel
Matthew 11:1–6
Matthew 24:42–47
Matthew 25:14–21
Mark 9:33–37
Mark 10:13–16
Luke 5:27–31
Luke 12:35–44
Luke 14:1,7–14
John 15:12–17
John 21:15–17

Preface of a Saint

Preface of the Dedication of a Church

Common of a Theologian and Teacher

Of a Theologian and Teacher I

I O God, who by thy Holy Spirit dost give to some the word of wisdom, to others the word of knowledge, and to others the word of faith: We praise thy Name for the gifts of grace manifested in thy servant N., and we pray that thy Church may never be destitute of such gifts; through Jesus Christ our Lord, who with thee and the same Spirit liveth and reigneth, one God, for ever and ever. *Amen.*

II O God, by your Holy Spirit you give to some the word of wisdom, to others the word of knowledge, and to others the word of faith: We praise your Name for the gifts of grace manifested in your servant N., and we pray that your Church may never be destitute of such gifts; through Jesus Christ our Lord, who with you and the Holy Spirit lives and reigns, one God, for ever and ever. *Amen.*

Of a Theologian and Teacher II

I O Almighty God, who didst give to thy servant N. special gifts of grace to understand and teach the truth as it is in Christ Jesus: Grant, we beseech thee, that by this teaching we may know thee, the one true God, and Jesus Christ whom thou hast sent; who liveth and reigneth with thee and the Holy Spirit, one God, for ever and ever. *Amen.*

II Almighty God, you gave to your servant N. special gifts of grace to understand and teach the truth as it is in Christ Jesus: Grant that by this teaching we may know you, the one true God, and Jesus Christ whom you have sent; who lives and reigns with you and the Holy Spirit, one God, for ever and ever. *Amen.*

Old Testament
Exodus 33:14–23
Nehemiah 8:1–3,5–8
Proverbs 3:1–7
Proverbs 9:1–10
Proverbs 23:15–19
Song of Solomon 3:1–4
Isaiah 42:5–9
Wisdom 7:7–14
Wisdom 10:9–14
Sirach (Ecclesiasticus) 14:20–27

Psalm
34:11–18
66:16–20
86:8–13
119:1–8
119:89–96
119:97–104

New Testament
Acts 8:26–31
Romans 9:18–26
1 Corinthians 2:6–10,13–16
1 Corinthians 3:5–11
Ephesians 1:3–10
Colossians 1:11–20
Colossians 2:2–12
2 Timothy 4:1–5
1 Peter 1:10–16
1 John 1:5–2:2

Gospel
Matthew 5:17–20
Matthew 11:25–30
Matthew 13:47–52
Matthew 18:10–14
Matthew 19:13–15
Luke 7:31–35
John 6:60–69
John 12:44–50
John 16:7–15
John 17:18–23

Preface of a Saint

Preface of Trinity Sunday

Preface of the Incarnation

Common of a Monastic or Professed Religious

Of a Monastic I

I O God, whose blessed Son became poor that we, through his poverty, might be rich: Deliver us, we pray thee, from an inordinate love of this world, that, inspired by the devotion of thy servant N., we may serve thee with singleness of heart and attain to the riches of the age to come; through the same thy Son Jesus Christ our Lord, who liveth and reigneth with thee, in the unity of the Holy Spirit, one God, now and for ever. *Amen.*

II O God, whose blessed Son became poor that we, through his poverty, might be rich: Deliver us from an inordinate love of this world, that we, inspired by the devotion of your servant N., may serve you with singleness of heart and attain to the riches of the age to come; through Jesus Christ our Lord, who lives and reigns with you, in the unity of the Holy Spirit, one God, now and for ever. *Amen.*

Of a Monastic II

I O God, by whose grace thy servant N., enkindled with the fire of thy love, became a burning and a shining light in thy Church: Grant that we also may be aflame with the spirit of love and discipline, and may ever walk before thee as children of light; through Jesus Christ our Lord, who with thee, in the unity of the Holy Spirit, liveth and reigneth, one God, now and for ever. *Amen.*

II O God, by whose grace your servant N., kindled with the flame of your love, became a burning and a shining light in your Church: Grant that we also may be aflame with the spirit of love and discipline, and walk before you as children of light; through Jesus Christ our Lord, who lives and reigns with you, in the unity of the Holy Spirit, one God, now and for ever. *Amen.*

Old Testament
2 Samuel 22:22–29
1 Kings 19:9–12
Job 22:21–28
Proverbs 2:1–11
Proverbs 4:1–9
Proverbs 7:1–4
Song of Solomon 4:12–16
Song of Solomon 8:6–7
Sirach (Ecclesiasticus) 39:1–10
Sirach (Ecclesiasticus) 51:13–22

Psalm
34 or 34:1–8
45
119:161–168
122
133
134

New Testament
Acts 2:42–47a
Romans 5:1–5
Romans 12:1–2
1 Corinthians 9:24–27
2 Corinthians 6:1–10
Philippians 3:7–15
Colossians 4:2–6
2 Peter 1:3–11
1 John 2:15–17
1 John 5:1–5

Gospel
Matthew 6:24–33
Matthew 11:7–11
Matthew 12:46–50
Mark 10:17–21
Mark 12:28–34a
Luke 9:57–62
Luke 12:33–37
John 6:34–38
John 12:27–36
John 16:25–33

Preface of a Saint

Preface of Lent 2

Preface of the Epiphany

Common of a Saint

Of a Saint I

I O Almighty God, who hast compassed us about with so great a cloud of witnesses: Grant that we, encouraged by the good example of thy servant N., may persevere in running the race that is set before us, until at length, through thy mercy, we may with *him* attain to thine eternal joy; through Jesus Christ, the author and perfecter of our faith, who liveth and reigneth with thee and the Holy Spirit, one God, for ever and ever. *Amen.*

II Almighty God, you have surrounded us with a great cloud of witnesses: Grant that we, encouraged by the good example of your servant N., may persevere in running the race that is set before us, until at last we may with *him* attain to your eternal joy; through Jesus Christ, the pioneer and perfecter of our faith, who lives and reigns with you and the Holy Spirit, one God, for ever and ever. *Amen.*

Of a Saint II

I O God, who hast brought us near to an innumerable company of angels and to the spirits of just men made perfect: Grant us, during our earthly pilgrimage, to abide in their fellowship, and in our heavenly country to become partakers of their joy; through Jesus Christ our Lord, who liveth and reigneth with thee and the Holy Spirit, one God, now and for ever. *Amen.*

II O God, you have brought us near to an innumerable company of angels, and to the spirits of just men made perfect: Grant us, during our earthly pilgrimage, to abide in their fellowship, and in our heavenly country to become partakers of their joy; through Jesus Christ our Lord, who lives and reigns with you and the Holy Spirit, one God, now and for ever. *Amen.*

Of a Saint III

I   O Almighty God, who by thy Holy Spirit hast made us one with thy saints in heaven and on earth: Grant that in our earthly pilgrimage we may ever be supported by this fellowship of love and prayer and may know ourselves to be surrounded by their witness to thy power and mercy. We ask this for the sake of Jesus Christ, in whom all our intercessions are acceptable through the Spirit, and who liveth and reigneth for ever and ever. *Amen.*

II Almighty God, by your Holy Spirit you have made us one with your saints in heaven and on earth: Grant that in our earthly pilgrimage we may always be supported by this fellowship of love and prayer and know ourselves to be surrounded by their witness to your power and mercy. We ask this for the sake of Jesus Christ, in whom all our intercessions are acceptable through the Spirit, and who lives and reigns for ever and ever. *Amen.*

Old Testament
Deuteronomy 6:3–9
2 Samuel 23:2–5
Proverbs 31:13–22, 24–26
Isaiah 40:27–31
Isaiah 43:16–21
Lamentations 3:25–36
Micah 6:6–8
Wisdom 3:1–9
Wisdom 9:7–12
Sirach (Ecclesiasticus) 2:7–11

New Testament
Romans 8:26–30
1 Corinthians 1:26–31
2 Corinthians 1:3–7
Galatians 3:23–29
Philippians 3:17–21
Philippians 4:4–9
Hebrews 12:1–2
1 Peter 1:3–9
Revelation 7:9–12
Revelation 19:4–9

Psalm
1
15
34 or 34:15–22
111
130
131

Gospel
Matthew 7:21–27
Matthew 13:44–46
Matthew 25:1–13
Matthew 25:31–40
Mark 3:31–35
Luke 6:17–23
Luke 6:27–36
John 10:25–30
John 13:31–35
John 14:8–14

Preface of a Saint

Preface of All Saints

Preface of Baptism

Common of an Artist, Writer, or Composer

Of an Artist, Writer, or Composer

I   Eternal God, light of the world and Creator of all that is good and lovely: We bless thy name for inspiring [N. and] all those who, with images and music and words, hath filled us with desire and love for thee; through Jesus Christ our Savior, who with thee and the Holy Spirit liveth and reigneth, one God, for ever and ever. *Amen.*

II Eternal God, light of the world and Creator of all that is good and lovely: We bless your name for inspiring [N. and] all those who with images and music and words have filled us with desire and love for you; through Jesus Christ our Savior, who with you and the Holy Spirit lives and reigns, one God, for ever and ever. *Amen.*

Old Testament
Exodus 35:1–5a,24–29
1 Kings 7:13–14, 40b–45
1 Chronicles 15:16,19–25,28
1 Chronicles 25:1a, 6–8
1 Chronicles 29:14b–19
2 Chronicles 7:1–6

Psalm
45:1–7
47
90 or 90:14–17
96 or 96:1–7
118:19–29
150

New Testament
2 Corinthians 3:1–3
Ephesians 2:17–22
Colossians 2:1–7

Revelation 15:1–4
Gospel
Matthew 7:24–29
Luke 2:8–14
John 21:15–17,24–25

Preface of an Artist, Writer, or Composer

I   Because in the beauty of holiness thou hast called us to worship thee; and hast given faithful artists, writers, and composers to illumine our prayer from age to age.

II   Because in the beauty of holiness you call us to worship you, and you have given faithful artists, writers, and composers to illumine our prayer from age to age.

Common of the Blessed Virgin Mary, Godbearer

Of the Blessed Virgin Mary I

I   Almighty God, by thy saving grace thou didst call Mary of Nazareth to be the mother of thine only Son: inspire us by the same grace to follow her example of bearing God to the world. We pray through Jesus Christ her Son our Savior. *Amen.*

II   Almighty God, of your saving grace you called Mary of Nazareth to be the mother of your only begotten Son: Inspire us by the same grace to follow her example of bearing God to the world. We pray through Jesus Christ her Son our Savior. *Amen.*

Of the Blessed Virgin Mary II

I Holy God, we magnify thy Name for calling the blessed Virgin Mary to bear thy Word of hope to the poor, the hungry, and those who have no voice: Give unto us thy grace and strength, that we might proclaim thy Good News in every age, with every tongue; through Jesus Christ our Savior, in the power of thy Holy Spirit. *Amen.*

II Holy God, we magnify your Name for calling the blessed Virgin Mary to bear your Word of hope to the poor, the hungry, and those who have no voice: Give us grace and strength to proclaim your Good News in every age, with every tongue; through Jesus Christ our Savior, in the power of your Holy Spirit. *Amen.*

Old Testament
Isaiah 43:9-13,19a

Psalm
34:1-8

New Testament
1 Corinthians 1:26-31

Gospel
Luke 1:42-55

Preface of the Blessed Virgin Mary

I Because even as blessed Mary didst consent to become Godbearer for the world, thou hast called us to bear thy Word to all whom our lives touch.

II Because as blessed Mary consented to become Godbearer for the world you call us to bear your Word to all whom our lives touch.

Common of a Prophetic Witness

Of a Prophetic Witness in the Church

I Gracious Father, we pray for thy holy Catholic Church. Fill it with all truth, in all truth, with all peace. Where it is corrupt, purify it; where it is in error, direct it; where in anything it is amiss, reform it. Where it is right, strengthen it; where it is in want, provide for it; where it is divided, reunite it; for the sake of Jesus Christ thy Son our Savior, who with thee and the Holy Spirit liveth and reigneth, one God, now and for ever. *Amen.*

II Gracious Father, we pray for your holy Catholic Church. Fill it with all truth, in all truth, with all peace. Where it is corrupt, purify it; where it is in error, direct it; where in anything it is amiss, reform it. Where it is right, strengthen it; where it is in want, provide for it; where it is divided, reunite it; for the sake of Jesus Christ your Son our Savior, who with you and the Holy Spirit lives and reigns, one God, now and for ever. *Amen.*

Of a Prophetic Witness in Society

I Almighty God, whose prophets hath taught us righteousness in the care of thy poor: By the guidance of thy Holy Spirit, grant that we may do justice, love mercy, and walk humbly in thy sight; through Jesus Christ, our Judge and Redeemer, who liveth and reigneth with thee and the same Spirit, ever one God. *Amen.*

II Almighty God, whose prophets taught us righteousness in the care of your poor: By the guidance of your Holy Spirit, grant that we may do justice, love mercy, and walk humbly in your sight; through Jesus Christ, our Judge and Redeemer, who lives and reigns with you and the same Spirit, one God, now and for ever. *Amen.*

Old Testament
Exodus 22:21–27
Numbers 11:26–29
2 Chronicles 28:8–15
Isaiah 55:11–56:1
Jeremiah 22:1–4
Jeremiah 26:12–15
Ezekiel 22:23–30
Ezekiel 34:1–6,20–22
Amos 7:10–15
Wisdom 5:15–20

Psalm
2:1–2,10–12
12:1–7
72:1–4, 12–14
103:6–14
113
126

New Testament
Acts 14:14–17,21–23
Acts 22:30–23:10
1 Corinthians 13:1–13
Galatians 4:3–7
Ephesians 6:10–20
James 2:1–8
James 2:14–17
2 Peter 1:16–21
1 John 3:11–17
1 John 4:16b–21

Gospel
Matthew 10:40–42
Matthew 11:2–6
Matthew 21:12–16
Mark 4:21–29
Luke 4:14–21
Luke 11:5–10
Luke 13:10–17
Luke 18:1–8
John 8:30–32
John 17:1–5

Preface of a Prophetic Witness in the Church

I   For thou dost cleanse and renew thy Church by the witness of thy saints, calling people in every age to holiness of life through the indwelling of thy Holy Spirit.

II   For you cleanse and renew your Church by the witness of your saints, calling people in every age to holiness of life through the indwelling of your Holy Spirit.

Preface of a Prophetic Witness in Society

I   Because in every age thou hast called brave souls to proclaim righteousness for the transformation of the world, that all may welcome the coming of thy holy reign.

II   Because in every age you have called brave souls to proclaim righteousness for the transformation of the world, that all may welcome the coming of your holy reign.

Preface of God the Holy Spirit

Common of a Scientist or Environmentalist

Of a Scientist or Environmentalist

I God of grace and glory, thou didst create and sustain the universe in majesty and beauty: We thank you for [N. and] all in whom thou hast planted the desire to know thy creation and to explore thy work and wisdom. Lead us, like them, to understand better the wonder and mystery of creation; through Christ thy eternal Word, through whom all things were made. *Amen.*

II God of grace and glory, you create and sustain the universe in majesty and beauty: We thank you for [N. and] all in whom you have planted the desire to know your creation and to explore your work and wisdom. Lead us, like them, to understand better the wonder and mystery of creation; through Christ your eternal Word, through whom all things were made. *Amen.*

Old Testament
Genesis 2:9–20
Exodus 15:22–26
1 Kings 4:29–34
2 Kings 2:19–22
Job 26:1–14
Job 28:1–12
Job 38:1–11
Ezekiel 36:33–38
Wisdom 7:15–22
Sirach (Ecclesiasticus) 1:1–10

Psalm
8
19:1–6
34:8–14
50:1–15
104 or 104:1–25

New Testament
2 Corinthians 13:1–6
Ephesians 1:17–23
Revelation 1:7–8,12–16

Gospel
John 15:1–8
John 20:24–27

Preface of a Scientist or Environmentalist

I Because thou dost inspire us to seek thy face in the wonders of thy creation and revealest thy work, that thy people may rejoice in thy many gifts.

II Because you inspire us to seek your face in the wonders of your creation, and you reveal your work, so that your people may rejoice in your many gifts.

Preface of God the Father

Preface of the Epiphany

Various Occasions from *The Book of Common Prayer*

Of the Holy Trinity

    Of the Holy Trinity

I   Almighty God, who hast revealed to thy Church thine eternal Being of glorious majesty and perfect love as one God in Trinity of Persons: Give us grace to continue steadfast in the confession of this faith and constant in our worship of thee, Father, Son, and Holy Spirit; who livest and reignest, one God, now and for ever. *Amen.*

II   Almighty God, you have revealed to your Church your eternal Being of glorious majesty and perfect love as one God in Trinity of Persons: Give us grace to continue steadfast in the confession of this faith and constant in our worship of you, Father, Son, and Holy Spirit; for you live and reign, one God, now and for ever. *Amen.*

Old Testament
Exodus 3:11-15

New Testament
Romans 11:33-36

Psalm
29

Gospel
Matthew 28:18-20

    Preface of Trinity Sunday

Of the Holy Spirit

Of the Holy Spirit

I Almighty and most merciful God, grant, we beseech thee, that, by the indwelling of thy Holy Spirit, we may be enlightened and strengthened for thy service; through Jesus Christ our Lord, who liveth and reigneth with thee, in the unity of the same Spirit, ever one God, world without end. *Amen.*

II Almighty and most merciful God, grant that, by the indwelling of your Holy Spirit, we may be enlightened and strengthened for your service; through Jesus Christ our Lord, who lives and reigns with you, in the unity of the Holy Spirit, one God, now and for ever. *Amen.*

Old Testament
Isaiah 61:1-3

New Testament
1 Corinthians 12:4-14

Psalm
139:1-17
139:1-9

Gospel
Luke 11:9-13

Preface of Pentecost

Of the Incarnation

Of the Incarnation

I O God, who didst wonderfully create, and yet more wonderfully restore, the dignity of human nature: Grant that we may share the divine life of him who humbled himself to share our humanity, thy Son Jesus Christ; who liveth and reigneth with thee, in the unity of the Holy Spirit, one God, for ever and ever. *Amen.*

II O God, who wonderfully created, and yet more wonderfully restored, the dignity of human nature: Grant that we may share the divine life of him who humbled himself to share our humanity, your Son Jesus Christ; who lives and reigns with you, in the unity of the Holy Spirit, one God, for ever and ever. *Amen.*

Old Testament
Isaiah 11:1-10
Genesis 17:1-8

New Testament
1 John 4:1-11
1 Timothy 3:14-16

Psalm
111
132:11-19

Gospel
Luke 1:26-33(34-38)
Luke 11:27-28

Preface of the Epiphany

Of the Holy Eucharist

Especially suitable for Thursdays

Of the Holy Eucharist

I God our Father, whose Son our Lord Jesus Christ in a wonderful Sacrament hath left unto us a memorial of his passion: Grant us so to venerate the sacred mysteries of his Body and Blood, that we may ever perceive within ourselves the fruit of his redemption; who liveth and reigneth with thee and the Holy Spirit, one God, for ever and ever. *Amen.*

II God our Father, whose Son our Lord Jesus Christ in a wonderful Sacrament has left us a memorial of his passion: Grant us so to venerate the sacred mysteries of his Body and Blood, that we may ever perceive within ourselves the fruit of his redemption; who lives and reigns with you and the Holy Spirit, one God, for ever and ever. *Amen.*

Old Testament
Deuteronomy 8:2-3

Psalm
34
116:10-17

New Testament
Revelation 19:1-2a,4-9
1 Corinthians 10:1-4,16-17
1 Corinthians 11:23-29

Gospel
John 6:47-58

Preface of the Epiphany

Of the Holy Cross

Especially suitable for Fridays

Of the Holy Cross

I Almighty God, whose beloved Son willingly endured the agony and shame of the cross for our redemption: Give us courage, we beseech thee, to take up our cross and follow him; who liveth and reigneth with thee and the Holy Spirit, one God, now and for ever. *Amen.*

II Almighty God, whose beloved Son willingly endured the agony and shame of the cross for our redemption: Give us courage to take up our cross and follow him; who lives and reigns with you and the Holy Spirit, one God, now and for ever. *Amen.*

Old Testament
Isaiah 52:13-15; 53:10-12

New Testament
1 Corinthians 1:18-24

Psalm
40:1-11
40:5-11

Gospel
John 12:23-33

Preface of Holy Week

For all Baptized Christians

Especially suitable for Saturdays

For all Baptized Christians

I   Grant, O Lord God, to all who have been baptized into the death and resurrection of thy Son Jesus Christ, that, as we have put away the old life of sin, so we may be renewed in the spirit of our minds and live in righteousness and true holiness; through the same Jesus Christ our Lord, who liveth and reigneth with thee, in the unity of the Holy Spirit, one God, now and for ever. *Amen.*

II   Grant, Lord God, to all who have been baptized into the death and resurrection of your Son Jesus Christ, that, as we have put away the old life of sin, so we may be renewed in the spirit of our minds and live in righteousness and true holiness; through Jesus Christ our Lord, who lives and reigns with you, in the unity of the Holy Spirit, one God, now and for ever. *Amen.*

Old Testament
Jeremiah 17:7-8
Ezekiel 36:24-28

Psalm
16:5-11

New Testament
Romans 6:3-11

Gospel
Mark 10:35-45

Preface of Baptism

For the Departed

For the Departed

I O eternal Lord God, who holdest all souls in life: Give, we beseech thee, to thy whole Church in paradise and on earth thy light and thy peace; and grant that we, following the good examples of those who have served thee here and are now at rest, may at the last enter with them into thine unending joy; through Jesus Christ our Lord, who liveth and reigneth with thee, in the unity of the Holy Spirit, one God, now and for ever. *Amen.*

II Eternal Lord God, you hold all souls in life: Give to your whole Church in paradise and on earth your light and your peace; and grant that we, following the good examples of those who have served you here and are now at rest, may at the last enter with them into your unending joy; through Jesus Christ our Lord, who lives and reigns with you, in the unity of the Holy Spirit, one God, now and for ever. *Amen.*

For the Departed

I Almighty God, we remember this day before thee thy faithful servant N.; and we pray that, having opened to *him* the gates of larger life, thou wilt receive *him* more and more into thy joyful service, that, with all who have faithfully served thee in the past, *he* may share in the eternal victory of Jesus Christ our Lord; who liveth and reigneth with thee, in the unity of the Holy Spirit, one God, for ever and ever. *Amen.*

II Almighty God, we remember before you today your faithful servant N.; and we pray that, having opened to *him* the gates of larger life, you will receive *him* more and more into your joyful service, that, with all who have faithfully served you in the past, *he* may share in the eternal victory of Jesus Christ our Lord; who lives and reigns with you, in the unity of the Holy Spirit, one God, for ever and ever. *Amen.*

Any of the Collects appointed for use at the Burial of the Dead may be used instead.

Old Testament
Isaiah 25: 6-9
Isaiah 61:1-3
Wisdom 3:1-5,9
Lamentations 3:22-26,31-33
Job 19:21-27a

Psalm
116
103:13-22
130
23
42
46
90:1-12
106:1-5
121
139:1-11

New Testament
1 Corinthians 15:50-58
Romans 8:14-19,34-35,37-39
1 Corinthians 15:20-26,35-38,
   43-44,53-58
2 Corinthians 4:16-5:9
1 John 3:1-2
Revelation 7:9-17
Revelation 21:2-7

Gospel
John 5:24-27
John 6:37-40
John 11:21-27
John 10:11-16
John 14:1-6

Preface of the Commemoration of the Dead

Of the Reign of Christ

Of the Reign of Christ

I Almighty and everlasting God, whose will it is to restore all things in thy well-beloved Son, the King of kings and Lord of lords: Mercifully grant that the peoples of the earth, divided and enslaved by sin, may be freed and brought together under his most gracious rule; who liveth and reigneth with thee and the Holy Spirit, one God, now and for ever. *Amen.*

II Almighty and everlasting God, whose will it is to restore all things in your well-beloved Son, the King of kings and Lord of lords: Mercifully grant that the peoples of the earth, divided and enslaved by sin, may be freed and brought together under his most gracious rule; who lives and reigns with you and the Holy Spirit, one God, now and for ever. *Amen.*

Old Testament
Daniel 7:9-14
Jeremiah 23:1-6
Ezekiel 34:11-17

New Testament
Colossians 1:11-20
1 Corinthians 15:20-28
Revelation 1:4b-8

Psalm
93
Canticle 18
46
95:1-7

Gospel
John 18:33-37
Matthew 25:31-46
Luke 23:35-43
Mark 11:1-11
Luke 19:29-38

Preface of the Ascension

Preface of Baptism

On the Anniversary of the Dedication of a Church

On the Anniversary of the Dedication of a Church

I O Almighty God, to whose glory we celebrate the dedication of this house of prayer: We give thee thanks for the fellowship of those who have worshiped in this place; and we pray that all who seek thee here may find thee and be filled with thy joy and peace; through Jesus Christ our Lord, who liveth and reigneth with thee, in the unity of the Holy Spirit, one God, now and for ever. *Amen.*

II Almighty God, to whose glory we celebrate the dedication of this house of prayer: We give you thanks for the fellowship of those who have worshiped in this place, and we pray that all who seek you here may find you and be filled with your joy and peace; through Jesus Christ our Lord, who lives and reigns with you, in the unity of the Holy Spirit, one God, now and for ever. *Amen.*

Old Testament
1 Kings 8:22-30
Genesis 28:10-17

Psalm
84
84:1-6

New Testament
1 Peter 2:1-5,9-10

Gospel
Matthew 21:12-16

Preface of the Dedication of a Church

For the Unity of the Church

For the Unity of the Church

I   Almighty Father, whose blessed Son before his passion prayed for his disciples that they might be one, even as thou and he are one: Grant that thy Church, being bound together in love and obedience to thee, may be united in one body by the one Spirit, that the world may believe in him whom thou didst send, the same thy Son Jesus Christ our Lord; who liveth and reigneth with thee, in the unity of the same Spirit, one God, now and for ever. *Amen.*

II   Almighty Father, whose blessed Son before his passion prayed for his disciples that they might be one, as you and he are one: Grant that your Church, being bound together in love and obedience to you, may be united in one body by the one Spirit, that the world may believe in him whom you have sent, your Son Jesus Christ our Lord; who lives and reigns with you, in the unity of the Holy Spirit, one God, now and for ever. *Amen.*

Old Testament
Isaiah 35:1-10

New Testament
Ephesians 4:1-6

Psalm
122

Gospel
John 17:6a,15-23

Preface of Baptism
Preface of Trinity Sunday

For the Ministry

For the Ministry I

I Almighty God, the giver of all good gifts, who of thy divine providence hast appointed various orders in thy Church: Give thy grace, we humbly beseech thee, to all who are [now] called to any office and ministry for thy people; and so fill them with the truth of thy doctrine and clothe them with holiness of life, that they may faithfully serve before thee, to the glory of thy great name and for the benefit of thy holy Church; through Jesus Christ our Lord, who liveth and reigneth with thee, in the unity of the Holy Spirit, one God, now and for ever. *Amen.*

II Almighty God, the giver of all good gifts, in your divine providence you have appointed various orders in your Church: Give your grace, we humbly pray, to all who are [now] called to any office and ministry for your people; and so fill them with the truth of your doctrine and clothe them with holiness of life, that they may faithfully serve before you, to the glory of your great Name and for the benefit of your holy Church; through Jesus Christ our Lord, who lives and reigns with you, in the unity of the Holy Spirit, one God, now and for ever. *Amen.*

Old Testament
Numbers 11:16-17, 24-29

New Testament
1 Corinthians 3:5-11

Psalm
99
27:1-9

Gospel
John 4:31-38

Preface of the Apostles

For the Ministry II

I O God, who didst lead thy holy apostles to ordain ministers in every place: Grant that thy Church, under the guidance of the Holy Spirit, may choose suitable persons for the ministry of Word and Sacrament and may uphold them in their work for the extension of thy kingdom; through him who is the Shepherd and Bishop of our souls, Jesus Christ our Lord, who liveth and reigneth with thee and the same Spirit, one God, for ever and ever. *Amen.*

II O God, you led your holy apostles to ordain ministers in every place: Grant that your Church, under the guidance of the Holy Spirit, may choose suitable persons for the ministry of Word and Sacrament and may uphold them in their work for the extension of your kingdom; through him who is the Shepherd and Bishop of our souls, Jesus Christ our Lord, who lives and reigns with you and the Holy Spirit, one God, for ever and ever. *Amen.*

Old Testament
1 Samuel 3:1-10

New Testament
Ephesians 4:11-16

Psalm
63:1-8

Gospel
Matthew 9:35-38

Preface of the Season

For the Ministry III

I Almighty and everlasting God, by whose Spirit the whole body of thy faithful people is governed and sanctified: Receive our supplications and prayers, which we offer before thee for all members of thy holy Church, that in their vocation and ministry they may truly and godly serve thee; through our Lord and Savior Jesus Christ, who liveth and reigneth with thee, in the unity of the same Spirit, one God, now and for ever. *Amen.*

II Almighty and everlasting God, by whose Spirit the whole body of your faithful people is governed and sanctified: Receive our supplications and prayers, which we offer before you for all members of your holy Church, that in their vocation and ministry they may truly and devoutly serve you; through our Lord and Savior Jesus Christ, who lives and reigns with you, in the unity of the Holy Spirit, one God, now and for ever. *Amen.*

Old Testament
Exodus 19:3-8

New Testament
1 Peter 4:7-11

Psalm
15

Gospel
Matthew 16:24-27

Preface of Baptism

Preface of the Season

For the Mission of the Church

For the Mission of the Church I

I O God, who hast made of one blood all the peoples of the earth, and didst send thy blessed Son to preach peace to those who are far off and to those who are near: Grant that people everywhere may seek after thee and find thee, bring the nations into thy fold, pour out thy Spirit upon all flesh, and hasten the coming of thy kingdom; through the same thy Son Jesus Christ our Lord, who liveth and reigneth with thee and the same Spirit, one God, now and for ever. *Amen.*

II O God, you have made of one blood all the peoples of the earth, and sent your blessed Son to preach peace to those who are far off and to those who are near: Grant that people everywhere may seek after you and find you, bring the nations into your fold, pour out your Spirit upon all flesh, and hasten the coming of your kingdom; through Jesus Christ our Lord, who lives and reigns with you and the Holy Spirit, one God, now and for ever. *Amen.*

Old Testament
Isaiah 2:2-4

New Testament
Ephesians 2:13-22

Psalm
96:1-7

Gospel
Luke 10:1-9

Preface of the Season

Preface of Pentecost

For the Mission of the Church II

I   O God of all the nations of the earth: Remember the multitudes who have been created in thine image but have not known the redeeming work of our Savior Jesus Christ and grant that, by the prayers and labors of thy holy Church, they may be brought to know and worship thee as thou hast been revealed in thy Son; who liveth and reigneth with thee and the Holy Spirit, one God, for ever and ever. *Amen.*

II   O God of all the nations of the earth: Remember the multitudes who have been created in your image but have not known the redeeming work of our Savior Jesus Christ; and grant that, by the prayers and labors of your holy Church, they may be brought to know and worship you as you have been revealed in your Son; who lives and reigns with you and the Holy Spirit, one God, for ever and ever. *Amen.*

Old Testament
Isaiah 49:5-13

New Testament
Ephesians 3:1-12

Psalm
67

Gospel
Matthew 28:16-20

Preface of the Season

Preface of Pentecost

For the Nation

For the Nation

I   Lord God Almighty, who hast made all peoples of the earth for thy glory, to serve the in freedom and peace: Grant to the people of our country a zeal for justice and the strength of forbearance, that we may use our liberty in accordance with thy gracious will; through Jesus Christ our Lord, who liveth and reigneth with thee and the Holy Spirit, one God, for ever and ever. *Amen.*

II Lord God Almighty, you have made all the peoples of the earth for your glory, to serve you in freedom and on peace: Give to the people of our country a zeal for justice and the strength of forbearance, that we may use our liberty in accordance with your gracious will; through Jesus Christ our Lord, who lives and reigns with you and the Holy Spirit, one God, for ever and ever. *Amen.*

The Collect for Independence Day may be used instead.

Old Testament
Isaiah 26:1-8

New Testament
Romans 13:1-10

Psalm
47

Gospel
Mark 12:13-17

Preface of Trinity Sunday

For Peace

For Peace

I   O Almighty God, kindle, we beseech thee, in every heart the true love of peace, and guide with thy wisdom those who take counsel for the nations of the earth, that in tranquility thy dominion may increase till the earth is filled with the knowledge of thy love; through Jesus Christ our Lord, who liveth and reigneth with thee, in the unity of the Holy Spirit, one God, now and for ever. *Amen.*

II   Almighty God, kindle, we pray, in every heart the true love of peace, and guide with your wisdom those who take counsel for the nations of the earth, that in tranquility your dominion may increase until the earth is filled with the knowledge of your love; through Jesus Christ our Lord, who lives and reigns with you, in the unity of the Holy Spirit, one God, now and for ever. *Amen.*

Old Testament
Micah 4:1-5

Psalm
85:7-13

New Testament
Ephesians 2:13-18
Colossians 3:12-15

Gospel
John 16:23-33
Matthew 5:43-48

Preface of the Season

For Rogation Days II

For Commerce and Industry

I Almighty God, whose Son Jesus Christ in his earthly life shared our toil and hallowed our labor: Be present with thy people where they work; make those who carry on the industries and commerce of this land responsive to thy will; and give to us all a pride in what we do, and a just return for our labor; through Jesus Christ our Lord, who liveth and reigneth with thee, in the unity of the Holy Spirit, one God, now and for ever. *Amen.*

II Almighty God, whose Son Jesus Christ in his earthly life shared our toil and hallowed our labor: Be present with your people where they work; make those who carry on the industries and commerce of this land responsive to your will; and give to us all a pride in what we do, and a just return for our labor; through Jesus Christ our Lord, who lives and reigns with you, in the unity of the Holy Spirit, one God, now and for ever. *Amen.*

Old Testament
Sirach (Ecclesiasticus) 38:27-32

New Testament
1 Corinthians 3:10-14

Psalm
107:1-9

Gospel
Matthew 6:19-24

Preface of the Season

For the Sick

For the Sick

I   Heavenly Father, giver of life and health: Comfort and relieve thy sick servants, and give thy power of healing to those who minister to their needs, that those *(or N., or NN.)* for whom our prayers are offered may be strengthened in their weakness and have confidence in thy loving care; through Jesus Christ our Lord, who liveth and reigneth with thee and the Holy Spirit, one God, now and for ever. *Amen.*

II Heavenly Father, giver of life and health: Comfort and relieve your sick servants, and give your power of healing to those who minister to their needs, that those *(or N., or NN.)* for whom our prayers are offered may be strengthened in their weakness and have confidence in your loving care; through Jesus Christ our Lord, who lives and reigns with you and the Holy Spirit, one God, now and for ever. *Amen.*

Old Testament
2 Kings 20:1-5

Psalm
13
86:1-7
23
91
103
145:14-22

New Testament
James 5:13-16
2 Corinthians 1:3-5
Hebrews 12:1-2
1 John 5:13-15

Gospel
Mark 2:1-12
Matthew 9:2-8
Mark 6:7, 12-13
Luke 17:11-19
John 6:47-51

Preface of the Season

For Social Justice

For Social Justice

I Almighty God, who hast created us in thine own image: Grant us grace fearlessly to contend against evil and to make no peace with oppression; and, that we may reverently use our freedom, help us to employ it in the maintenance of justice in our communities and among the nations, to the glory of thy holy Name; through Jesus Christ our Lord, who liveth and reigneth with thee and the Holy Spirit, one God, now and for ever. *Amen.*

II Almighty God, who created us in your own image: Grant us grace fearlessly to contend against evil and to make no peace with oppression; and, that we may reverently use our freedom, help us to employ it in the maintenance of justice in our communities and among the nations, to the glory of your holy Name; through Jesus Christ our Lord, who lives and reigns with you and the Holy Spirit, one God, now and for ever. *Amen.*

Old Testament
Isaiah 42:1-7

New Testament
James 2:5-9,12-17

Psalm
72
72:1-4,12-14

Gospel
Matthew 10:32-42

Preface of the Season

For Social Service

For Social Service

I O Lord our heavenly Father, whose blessed Son came not to be ministered unto but to minister: Bless, we beseech thee, all who, following in his steps, give themselves to the service of others; that with wisdom, patience, and courage, they may minister in his name to the suffering, the friendless, and the needy; for the love of him who laid down his life for us, the same thy Son our Savior Jesus Christ, who liveth and reigneth with thee and the Holy Spirit, one God, for ever and ever. *Amen.*

II Heavenly Father, whose blessed Son came not to be served but to serve: Bless all who, following in his steps, give themselves to the service of others; that with wisdom, patience, and courage, they may minister in his Name to the suffering, the friendless, and the needy; for the love of him who laid down his life for us, your Son our Savior Jesus Christ, who lives and reigns with you and the Holy Spirit, one God, for ever and ever. *Amen.*

Old Testament
Zechariah 8:3-12,16-17

New Testament
1 Peter 4:7-11

Psalm
146
22:22-27

Gospel
Mark 10:42-52

Preface of the Season

For Education

For Education

I Almighty God, the fountain of all wisdom: Enlighten by thy Holy Spirit those who teach and those who learn, that, rejoicing in the knowledge of thy truth, they may worship thee and serve thee from generation to generation; through Jesus Christ our Lord, who liveth and reigneth with thee and the same Spirit, one God, for ever and ever. *Amen.*

II Almighty God, the fountain of all wisdom: Enlighten by your Holy Spirit those who teach and those who learn, that, rejoicing in the knowledge of your truth, they may worship you and serve you from generation to generation; through Jesus Christ our Lord, who lives and reigns with you and the Holy Spirit, one God, for ever and ever. *Amen.*

Old Testament
Deuteronomy 6:4-9,20-25

New Testament
2 Timothy 3:14–4:5

Psalm
78:1-7

Gospel
Matthew 11:25-30

Preface of the Season

For Vocation in Daily Work

For Vocation in Daily Work

I Almighty God our heavenly Father, who declarest thy glory and showest forth thy handiwork in the heavens and in the earth: Deliver us, we beseech thee, in our several occupations from the service of self alone, that we may do the work which thou givest us to do, in truth and beauty and for the common good; for the sake of him who came among us as one that serveth, thy Son Jesus Christ our Lord, who liveth and reigneth with thee and the Holy Spirit, one God, for ever and ever. *Amen.*

II Almighty God our heavenly Father, you declare your glory and show forth your handiwork in the heavens and in the earth: Deliver us in our various occupations from the service of self alone, that we may do the work you give us to do in truth and beauty and for the common good; for the sake of him who came among us as one who serves, your Son Jesus Christ our Lord, who lives and reigns with you and the Holy Spirit, one God, for ever and ever. *Amen.*

Old Testament
Ecclesiastes 3:1,9-13

New Testament
1 Peter 2:11-17

Psalm
8

Gospel
Matthew 6:19-24

Preface of the Season

For Labor Day

For Labor Day

I Almighty God, who hast so linked our lives one with another that all we do affects, for good or ill, all other lives: So guide us in the work we do, that we may do it not for self alone, but for the common good; and, as we seek a proper return for our own labor, make us mindful of the rightful aspirations of other workers, and arouse our concern for those who are out of work; through Jesus Christ our Lord, who liveth and reigneth with thee and the Holy Spirit, one God, for ever and ever. *Amen.*

II Almighty God, you have so linked our lives one with another that all we do affects, for good or ill, all other lives: So guide us in the work we do, that we may do it not for self alone, but for the common good; and, as we seek a proper return for our own labor, make us mindful of the rightful aspirations of other workers, and arouse our concern for those who are out of work; through Jesus Christ our Lord, who lives and reigns with you and the Holy Spirit, one God, for ever and ever. *Amen.*

Old Testament
Sirach (Ecclesiasticus) 38:27-32

New Testament
1 Corinthians 3:10-14

Psalm
107:1-9
90:1-2,16-17

Gospel
Matthew 6:19-24

Preface of the Season

New Propers for Various Occasions

For the Care of God's Creation

Care of God's Creation

I   Bountiful Creator, thou openest thy hand to satisfy the needs of every living creature: Make us continually thankful for thy loving providence, and grant that we, remembering the account we must one day give, may be faithful stewards of thine abundance, for the benefit of the whole creation; through Jesus Christ our Lord, through whom all things are made, who liveth and reigneth with thee and the Holy Spirit, one God, for ever and ever. *Amen.*

II   Bountiful Creator, you open your hand to satisfy the needs of every living creature: Make us always thankful for your loving providence, and grant that we, remembering the account we must one day give, may be faithful stewards of your abundance, for the benefit of the whole creation; through Jesus Christ our Lord, through whom all things were made, and who lives and reigns with you and the Holy Spirit, one God, for ever and ever. *Amen.*

Old Testament
1 Kings 4:29-30,33-34

New Testament
Acts 17:24-31

Psalm
145:1-7,22

Gospel
John 1:1-5,9-14

Preface for the Care of God's Creation

I   For thou hast brought us into being and called us to care for the earth.

II Because you have brought us into being and called us to care for the earth.

For the Goodness of God's Creation

Goodness of God's Creation

I God of creation, we thank thee for all that thou hast made and called good: Grant that we may rightly serve and conserve the earth and live at peace with all thy creatures; through Jesus Christ, the firstborn of all creation, in whom thou art reconciling the whole world unto thyself. *Amen.*

II God of creation, we thank you for all that you have made and called good: Grant that we may rightly serve and conserve the earth and live at peace with all your creatures; through Jesus Christ, the firstborn of all creation, in whom you are reconciling the whole world to yourself. *Amen.*

Old Testament
Job 14:7-9

New Testament
Romans 1:20-23

Psalm
104:24-31

Gospel
Mark 16:14-15

Preface for the Goodness of God's Creation

I Because in thy loving kindness, thou hast brought the whole creation into being and blessed its goodness.

II Instead of a Preface, Prayer D is recommended for use with this Proper.

On the Occasion of a Disaster

On the Occasion of a Disaster

I Compassionate God, whose Son Jesus wept at the grave of his friend Lazarus: Draw near to us in this time of sorrow and anguish, comfort those who mourn, strengthen those who are weary, encourage those in despair, and lead us all to fullness of life; through the same Jesus Christ, our Savior and Redeemer, who liveth and reigneth with thee, in the unity of the Holy Spirit, God for ever and ever. *Amen.*

II Compassionate God, whose Son Jesus wept at the grave of his friend Lazarus: Draw near to us in this time of sorrow and anguish, comfort those who mourn, strengthen those who are weary, encourage those in despair, and lead us all to fullness of life; through the same Jesus Christ, our Savior and Redeemer, who lives and reigns with you, in the unity of the Holy Spirit, God for ever and ever. *Amen.*

Old Testament
Job 14:7-13
Jeremiah 31:15-20

Psalm
60:1-5
130
80:1-7
23

New Testament
Romans 8:35-38
Revelation 21:1-7
Romans 8:18-25

Gospel
Luke 6:20-26
Mark 13:14-27

Preface of God the Son

Preface of the Commemoration of the Dead

A66   NEW PROPERS FOR VARIOUS OCCASIONS

On the Anniversary of a Disaster

On the Anniversary of a Disaster

I   God of steadfast love, who didst lead thy people through the wilderness: Be with us as we remember [and grieve]. By thy grace, lead us, we pray, in the path of new life, in the company of thy saints and angels; through Jesus Christ, the Savior and Redeemer of the world. *Amen.*

II God of steadfast love, who led your people through the wilderness: Be with us as we remember [and grieve]. By your grace, lead us in the path of new life, in the company of your saints and angels; through Jesus Christ, the Savior and Redeemer of the world. *Amen.*

Old Testament
Job 14:7-13
Jeremiah 31:15-20

Psalm
60:1-5
130
80:1-7
23

New Testament
Romans 8:35-38
Revelation 21:1-7
Romans 8:18-25

Gospel
Luke 6:20-26
Mark 13:14-27

Preface of God the Son

Preface for Commemoration of the Dead

For Reconciliation and Forgiveness

Reconciliation and Forgiveness

I God of compassion, thou hast reconciled us in Jesus Christ, who is our peace: Enable us to live as Jesus lived, breaking down walls of hostility and healing enmity. Give us grace to make peace with those from whom we are divided, that, forgiven and forgiving, we may ever be one in Christ; who with thee and the Holy Spirit reigneth for ever, one holy and undivided Trinity. *Amen.*

II God of compassion, you have reconciled us in Jesus Christ, who is our peace: Enable us to live as Jesus lived, breaking down walls of hostility and healing enmity. Give us grace to make peace with those from whom we are divided, that, forgiven and forgiving, we may ever be one in Christ; who with you and the Holy Spirit reigns for ever, one holy and undivided Trinity. *Amen.*

Old Testament
Genesis 8:12-17,20-22

Psalm
51:1-17

New Testament
Hebrews 4:12-16

Gospel
Luke 23:32-43

Preface of Reconciliation and Forgiveness

I Because by the cross of our Lord Jesus Christ thou hast reconciled all things to thyself, not counting our sins against us and renewing our hearts to forgive as we have been forgiven.

II Because by the cross of our Lord Jesus Christ you have reconciled all things to yourself, not counting our sins against us and renewing our hearts to forgive as we have been forgiven.

For Space Exploration

Space Exploration

I Creator of the universe, whose dominion extends through the immensity of space: guide and guard those who seek to fathom its mysteries [especially N.N.]. Save us from arrogance, lest we forget that our achievements are grounded in thee, and, by the grace of thy Holy Spirit, protect our travels beyond the reaches of earth, that we may glory ever more in the wonder of thy creation: through Jesus Christ, thy Word, by whom all things came to be, who with thee and the Holy Spirit liveth and reigneth, one God, for ever and ever. *Amen.*

II Creator of the universe, your dominion extends through the immensity of space: guide and guard those who seek to fathom its mysteries [especially N.N.]. Save us from arrogance, lest we forget that our achievements are grounded in you, and, by the grace of your Holy Spirit, protect our travels beyond the reaches of earth, that we may glory ever more in the wonder of your creation: through Jesus Christ, your Word, by whom all things came to be, who with you and the Holy Spirit lives and reigns, one God, for ever and ever. *Amen.*

Old Testament
Job 38: 4-12,16-18

New Testament
Revelation 1:7-8,12-16

Psalm
19:1-6
Canticle 12

Gospel
John 15:5-9

Preface of God the Father
Preface of the Epiphany

Guidelines for Continuing Alteration of the Calendar

Criteria for Additions to *A Great Cloud of Witnesses*

As indicated above, *A Great Cloud of Witnesses* offers a wide and diverse collection of people from across Christian history and the Episcopal story. As our common life continues to unfold, new names will need to be added. These criteria provide guidelines for how these additions will be considered.

Criterion 1: Historicity

Christianity is a radically historical religion, so in almost every instance it is not theological realities or spiritual movements but exemplary witness to the gospel of Christ in lives actually lived that is remembered in our family story. Like all families, however, our family includes important matriarchs and patriarchs about whom little verifiable information is known, yet whose names and stories still exert influence on how we understand ourselves in relation to them.

Criterion 2: Christian Discipleship

The family story captured here is uniquely and identifiably a Christian story. This set of stories commemorates the ways particular Christians live out the promises of baptism. A worthy summary of these promises is captured in our BBaptismal Covenant (BCP, 304-305), including a commitment to the Triune God as captured in the Apostles' Creed; continuing in the apostles' teaching and fellowship, the breaking of bread and the prayers; resisting evil and repenting when necessary; proclaiming by word and example the Good News of God in Christ; seeking and serving Christ in all persons; and striving for justice and peace among all people. Rather than being an anachronistic checklist, these should be considered general guidelines for considering holistic Christian life and practice. There may be occasional exceptions where not all of these promises are successfully kept, or when the person in question is not a Christian, yet the person's life and work exemplify Christ, significantly impacting the ongoing life of the Church and contributing to our fuller understanding of the gospel.

Criterion 3: Significance

Those remembered should have been in their lifetime extraordinary, even heroic servants of God and God's people for the sake, and after the example, of Jesus Christ. They may also be people whose creative work or whose manner of life has glorified God, enriched the life of the Church, or led others to a deeper understanding of God. In their varied ways, those remembered have revealed Christ's presence in, and Lordship over, all of history; and continue to inspire us as we carry forward God's mission in the world.

Criterion 4: Range of Inclusion

Particular attention should be paid to Episcopalians and other members of the Anglican Communion. Attention should also be paid to the inclusion of people of different genders and races, of lay people (witnessing in this way to our baptismal understanding of the Church), and of ecumenical partners and people who have had their own distinctive influence upon us. In addition to the better-known, it is important also to include those "whose memory may have faded in the shifting fashions of public concern, but whose witness is deemed important to the life and mission of the Church" (Thomas Talley).

Criterion 5: Local Observance

Normally, significant remembrance of a particular person already exists within the Church at the local and regional levels before that person is included in the Church's larger story.

Criterion 6: Perspective

The introduction of new names should be done with a certain economy lest the balance of the whole be overwhelmed. In the cases of those departed less than forty years ago—particularly in the case of controversial names—care should be given to seeing them from the perspective of history. Names added should show a broad influence upon the Church and should result from a widespread desire expressed across the Church over a reasonable period of time.

Criterion 7: Combined Remembrances

Not all those included need to be remembered "in isolation." Where there are close and natural links between persons to be remembered, a joint commemoration would make excellent sense (for example, the Reformation martyrs, Latimer and Ridley; and two bishops of Lincoln, Robert Grosseteste and Hugh).

Procedures for Local Calendars and Memorials

Local and regional commemoration normally occurs for many years prior to churchwide recognition.

The Book of Common Prayer (pp. 13, 18, 195, and 246) permits memorials not listed in the Calendar, provides collects and readings for them (the Common of Saints), and recognizes the bishop's authority to set forth devotions for occasions for which no prayer or service has been provided by the Prayer Book. Although the Prayer Book does not require the bishop's permission to use the Common of Saints for memorials not included in the Calendar, it would seem appropriate that the bishop's consent be requested.

While these guidelines cannot provide procedures for initiating local, diocesan, or regional memorials that would govern all such commemorations, this process is suggested:

A. A congregation, diocese, or other community or organization establishes a memorial for a specific day, using the above criteria to guide the decision.

B. A collect is appointed from the Common of Saints or composed, perhaps in consultation with the Standing Commission on Liturgy and Music or the diocesan or parish liturgical commission. Suitable tags indicating relevant virtues, charisms, and Commons may also be indicated if desired. A brief description of the person or group is written, in accord with these Guidelines and Procedures.

C. The congregation, diocese, province, or organization proceeds to keep the memorial.

D. Those interested in promoting a wider commemoration begin to share these materials with others, suggesting that they also adopt the memorial. If at some time it is desired to propose a local commemoration for churchwide recognition, documented evidence of the spread and duration of local commemoration is essential to include in the proposal to the Standing Commission on Liturgy and Music.

Some commemorations, perhaps many, will remain local, diocesan, or regional in character. This in no way reduces their importance to those who revere and seek to keep alive the memory of beloved and faithful witnesses to Christ.

Procedures for Churchwide Recognition

All requests for consideration of individuals or groups to be included in *A Great Cloud of Witnesses* shall be submitted to the Standing Commission on Liturgy and Music for evaluation and subsequent recommendation to the next General Convention for acceptance or rejection (cf. Resolution A119s of the 1991 General Convention).

Each proposal must include:

a) detailed rationale for commemoration based on the "Criteria for Additions to *A Great Cloud of Witnesses*" (above) and demonstrating how this person manifests Christ and would enhance the devotional life of the Church;

b) An inspirational 350-word biographical sketch of the person to be commemorated, preferably including some of the person's own words;

c) Information concerning the spread and duration of local or international commemoration of this individual or group;

d) Suggested collect and readings.

A. Proposals must be received by the Chair of the Standing Commission on Liturgy and Music no less than eighteen months prior to the next General Convention.

B. The chair of the Calendar Committee of the Standing Commission on Liturgy and Music will communicate with:

1. Organizations submitting proposed commemorations;

2. The Secretary of the General Convention regarding names and addresses of any groups applying for exhibit space in order to present to Convention delegates a potential addition to *A Great Cloud of Witnesses*;

3. The chairs of the Cognate Committees on Prayer Book, Liturgy, and Music, in order to facilitate the review of submissions.

C. The Calendar Committee of the Standing Commission on Liturgy and Music will arrange for:
1. Submission of appropriate resolutions to General Convention;
2. Publication of same in the Blue Book;
3. Distribution of pertinent materials to members of the Cognate Committees on Prayer Book, Liturgy, and Music, as may be needed;
4. Preparation of materials for *A Great Cloud of Witnesses*.

Dioceses, bishops, and deputies are always able to submit a proposal for a new commemoration directly to the General Convention. Such proposals are commonly referred to the Standing Commission on Liturgy and Music for evaluation during the following triennium; only on very rare occasions has the General Convention approved a new commemoration that has not first been reviewed by the Standing Commission on Liturgy and Music.

Procedures to Remove Commemorations from *A Great Cloud of Witnesses*

A commemoration may be removed from *A Great Cloud of Witnesses* by the same procedure by which one is added, namely, by proposal to the Standing Commission on Liturgy and Music or directly to the General Convention. Proposed deletions of commemorations must be forwarded to the Chair of the Standing Commission on Liturgy and Music no less than 18 months prior to the next General Convention.